"This timely and well-researched volume brings together an amazing group of scholars who provide the first comprehensive evidence-based analysis of the post-2016 social and economic transformation that is taking place in Uzbekistan. A must read for any reader interested in what the new Uzbekistan is."

Sergei Guriev, *Provost and Professor of Economics, Sciences Po, Paris*

"This book is a seminal work in the field of development economics, particularly in the context of transition countries … an essential read for those interested in Uzbekistan's economic transformation."

Masato Hiwatari, *Associate Professor, Graduate School of Arts and Sciences, University of Tokyo*

"This book is critical for understanding the political economy of reforms in Uzbekistan, drawing on perspectives of top experts in the field. It sheds light on the country's reform trajectory, focusing on economic liberalization, healthcare, education, and governance. The analysis is invaluable for grasping the nuances of Uzbekistan's development and the broader implications for transitional economies worldwide. It is essential reading for anyone seeking to understand reform dynamics in Central Eurasia."

Jennifer Brick Murtazashvili, *Founding Director, Center for Governance and Markets and Professor of International Affairs, University of Pittsburgh*

New Uzbekistan

This book reviews and analyses the comprehensive socio-economic reforms undertaken in Uzbekistan since 2016 by the government led by President Shavkat Mirziyoyev. The volume takes the reader through the different sectors of the economy and the effects of reforms on the country's citizens. The various developments are detailed, examining the gains and the gaps in terms of policy and implementation. Using the broad tools of economics and, in particular, of development economics, the authors present evidence to drive their conclusions and recommendations, and also draw on comparative cases from policy and practice to illustrate alternative approaches and results from measures in other transition countries.

Implementing Uzbekistan's ambitious economic transformation into a market economy is a challenging process that takes time. This book provides the first systematic and comprehensive discussion of the government's reform areas, including the macroeconomic fundamentals, business and investment climate, the energy, transport, health, education, social protection, financial, banking and agriculture sectors, regional trade, tourism and transport connectivity, reform of state-owned enterprises, as well as public services, citizen engagement and gender equality.

The editors have, where appropriate, matched external specialists in the field with co-authors based in Uzbekistan itself. Other chapters, for example, those on macroeconomic stability and the financial system, have drawn on the expertise of economists from the IMF and the World Bank, who have had experience working on Uzbekistan. Thus, each chapter, independent of the others, offers information and analysis for use by researchers examining the economics of present-day Uzbekistan, development economics and Central Asia.

Bakhrom Mirkasimov is Rector at Westminster International University in Tashkent (WIUT) and President of Association of Sociologists of Uzbekistan (ASU).

Richard Pomfret is Professor of Economics Emeritus at the University of Adelaide, Australia, and Senior Adjunct Professor in International Economics at The Johns Hopkins University School of Advanced International Studies (SAIS Europe), Bologna, Italy.

Europa Perspectives: Emerging Economies

The Europa Emerging Economies series from Routledge, edited by Robert E. Looney, examines a wide range of contemporary economic, political, developmental and social issues as they affect emerging economies throughout the world. Complementing the *Europa Regional Surveys of the World* series and the *Handbook of Emerging Economies*, which was also edited by Professor Looney, the volumes in the *Europa Emerging Economies* series will be a valuable resource for academics, students, researchers, policy-makers, professionals, and anyone with an interest in issues regarding emerging economies in the wider context of current world affairs.

There will be individual volumes in the series which provide in-depth country studies, and others which examine issues and concepts; all are written or edited by specialists in their field. Volumes in the series are not constrained by any particular template, but may explore economic, political, governance, international relations, defence, or other issues in order to increase the understanding of emerging economies and their importance to the world economy.

Robert E. Looney is a Distinguished Professor at the Naval Postgraduate School, Monterey, California, who specializes in issues relating to economic development in the Middle East, East Asia, South Asia and Latin America. He has published over 20 books and 250 journal articles, and has worked widely as a consultant to national governments and international agencies.

Pakistan at Seventy
A handbook on developments in economics, politics and society
Edited by Shahid Javed Burki with Iftekhar Ahmed Chowdhury and Asad Ejaz Butt

Mauritius: A Successful Small Island Developing State
Edited by Boopen Seetanah, Raja Vinesh Sannasee and Robin Nunkoo

Development and Stabilization in Small Open Economies
Theories and Evidence from Caribbean Experience
DeLisle Worrell

New Uzbekistan
The Third Renaissance
Edited by Bakhrom Mirkasimov and Richard Pomfret

For further information, see https://www.routledge.com/Europa-Perspectives-Emerging-Economies/book-series/EPEE.

New Uzbekistan

The Third Renaissance

Edited by
Bakhrom Mirkasimov and Richard Pomfret

Routledge
Taylor & Francis Group
LONDON AND NEW YORK

Designed cover image: © Shutterstock

First published 2024
by Routledge
4 Park Square, Milton Park, Abingdon, Oxon OX14 4RN

and by Routledge
605 Third Avenue, New York, NY 10158

Routledge is an imprint of the Taylor & Francis Group, an informa business

British Library Cataloguing in Publication Data
A catalogue record for this book is available from the British Library

Library of Congress Cataloging-in-Publication Data
A catalog record has been requested for this book

ISBN: 9781032753355 (hbk)
ISBN: 9781032753386 (pbk)
ISBN: 9781003473497 (ebk)

DOI: 10.4324/9781003473497

Typeset in Times New Roman
by Taylor & Francis Books

Contents

Figures

Tables

Boxes

Editors and Contributors

Bakhrom Mirkasimov. Rector, Westminster International University in Tashkent (WIUT).

Richard Pomfret. Professor of Economics Emeritus, University of Adelaide, Australia, and Senior Adjunct Professor in International Economics, The Johns Hopkins University School of Advanced International Studies (SAIS Europe), Bologna, Italy.

Iroda Akhmedova.Research Assistant, Westminster International University in Tashkent (WIUT).

Kamiljon Akramov. Senior Research Fellow, International Food Policy Research Institute (IFPRI).

Nargiza Alimukhamedova. Associate Professor, Westminster International University in Tashkent (WIUT) and Associate Researcher, CERGE-EI and Prague University of Economics and Business, Czech Republic.

Kathryn Anderson.Professor Emerita of Economics, Vanderbilt University, USA.

Etenesh Asfaw. Senior Research Fellow, Center for Policy Research and Outreach, Westminster International University in Tashkent (WIUT).

Zohid Askarov. Associate Professor and Dean of the School of Business and Economics, Westminster International University in Tashkent (WIUT).

Davit Babasyan. Senior Financial Sector Specialist, World Bank.

Charles Becker. Research Professor, Duke University, USA.

Nodir Djanibekov. Research Associate, Department of Agricultural Policy, Leibniz Institute of Agricultural Development in Transition Economies (IAMO), Halle (Saale), Germany.

Lawrence Dwight. Senior Economist, International Monetary Fund.

Shenggen Fan. Chair Professor, College of Economics and Management, China Agricultural University, Beijing, China and CGIAR System Board Member.

Randall K. Filer. Professor of Economics, Hunter College and the Graduate Center of the City University of New York, USA, Senior Scholar of Economics at CERGE-EI, Prague, Czech Republic and ISET, Tbilisi, Georgia.

Thomas Herzfeld. Head of the Department of Agricultural Policy, Leibniz Institute of Agricultural Development in Transition Economies (IAMO), Halle (Saale), Germany and Professor at Martin-Luther-Universität Halle-Wittenberg, Halle (Saale), Germany.

Obid Khakimov. Director, Center for Economic Research and Reforms under the Administration of the President of the Republic of Uzbekistan.

Justin Yifu Lin. Dean, Institute of New Structural Economics, Dean, Institute of South-South Cooperation and Development and Honorary Dean, School of National Development, Peking University, People's Republic of China.

Ahliddin Malikov. Course Leader (MSc Applied Economics), Senior Lecturer, Westminster International University in Tashkent (WIUT); PhD candidate, University of Westminster, London.

Cindy Malvicini. Deputy Director General, South Asia Department, Asian Development Bank (ADB).

Martin Melecky. Lead Economist, World Bank.

Lijie Ni. Junior Researcher, Academy of Global Food Economics and Policy, China Agricultural University, Beijing, China.

Shakhzod Nomozov. Lecturer, Westminster International University in Tashkent (WIUT).

Jamshid Normatov. Head of Economics Department, Westminster International University in Tashkent (WIUT).

Martin Petrick. Professor of Agricultural, Food and Environmental Policy and Visiting Research Fellow at IAMO, Institute of Agricultural Policy and Market Research and Center for International Development and Environmental Research (ZEU), Justus Liebig University Giessen, Germany.

Jeffrey Sachs. University Professor and Director of the Center for Sustainable Development, Columbia University, USA, and President of the UN Sustainable Development Solutions Network.

Sodyq Safoev. First Deputy Chairman of the Senate of the Oliy Majlis of the Republic of Uzbekistan and Rector, University of World Economy and Diplomacy.

Michelle Schultze. Research Assistant, Duke University, USA.

Akhtem Useinov. Senior Research and Development Officer, Westminster International University in Tashkent (WIUT).

Jia Yu. Director of International Development Cooperation Department, Senior Operations Officer, Institute of New Structural Economics, Peking University, People's Republic of China.

Foreword

Bakhrom Mirkasimov and Richard Pomfret

This book aims to capture and assess the dramatic economic changes in Uzbekistan since the death of the first President in 2016. The scene is set in the Introduction by views from an insider and an outsider: Sodyq Safoev, First Deputy Chairperson of the Uzbekistan Senate, and Cindy Malvicini, head of the Tashkent office of the Asian Development Bank from 2017 to 2022.

The early chapters of this book aim to assess the overall impact from a development and a macroeconomic perspective. The subsequent chapters assess the reforms in sectors such as health, finance, agriculture, and foreign trade, and their impact on living standards and institutions. Implementation and outcomes have been affected by major external disruptions including the COVID-19 pandemic in 2020 and 2021 and the Russia–Ukraine war since February 2022; the former is addressed in the final chapter, while the war is still ongoing as we write.

Although there is discussion of institutions and of reform implementation, the treatment of politics in New Uzbekistan, of the political economy of reform or of the 2023 constitutional changes, is more limited. The model of transition from central planning and the type of market-based economy established in the quarter century after independence created vested interests that might be opposed to reform, but a detailed analysis of these forces is beyond this book's scope. Similarly, although foreign economic relations are covered, especially in Chapter 7, foreign policy is not addressed from political, security, or other angles.

The reform package has been extensive and while chapter authors have covered a number of issues, some aspects have not been covered in this book. Irrigation is discussed in the agriculture chapters: broader issues of water, energy, and climate change will surely assume increasing importance in years to come. While education is not covered systematically, in the Introduction, Sodyq Safoev highlights the youth of the country's population, which is potentially a major asset for the Uzbek economy, but could easily be squandered.

The approach behind most of the chapters was to match an external specialist in the field with a co-author based in Uzbekistan itself. Exceptions are the chapters on macroeconomic stability and on the financial system, where we drew on the expertise of economists from the IMF and the World Bank, who have had experience working on the New Uzbekistan.

Each chapter is the sole responsibility of the authors, and each chapter can be read independently. No attempt was made to impose common interpretations. Consequently, there is some repetition across the chapters and also some disagreement about the desirability or practical significance of specific measures. The former highlights the interconnectedness of the various reform areas, while the latter reflects the ferment of ideas inevitably accompanying rapid economic change, as well as the perspectives of different experts and authors.

The mythical bird Semurg, or Humo, with its outstretched wings, dominates the New Uzbekistan National Park in Tashkent and is a central symbol of the national Renaissance. With its huge wings, the bird will protect the country and its people from everything bad; it will also lead people to happiness and enlightenment. In Alisher Navoi's poem "The Language of Birds", Semurg warned that the way would be long and difficult. The reforms analyzed in this book will face unpredicted challenges and have unintended consequences; the road to New Uzbekistan may be long, but it promises to be exciting.

Foreword to the Sustainable Development Goals Forum

Jeffrey Sachs

On September 24, 2021, Westminster International University in Tashkent hosted an international conference on *New Uzbekistan's National Sustainable Development Goals (SDGs): Milestones and Perspectives* that was conducted in a hybrid mode. The conference was a joint initiative between the Senate of the Oliy Majlis of the Republic of Uzbekistan, the Youth Affairs Agency of the Republic of Uzbekistan, UNDP in Uzbekistan, the World Bank in Uzbekistan, Westminster International University in Tashkent (WIUT), and the University of World Economy and Diplomacy (UWED). The welcome message from Jeffrey Sachs, professor at Columbia University and President of the UN Sustainable Development Solutions Network, and introduction by Sodyq Safoev, were presented at the conference, as were several of the papers collected in this volume. The second part of the Introduction to this volume is by Cindy Malvicini who, as country officer for the Asian Development Bank during the entire period from President Karimov's death until after the 2021 conference, is uniquely placed to provide an outsider's perspective of the process of building the New Uzbekistan.

We reproduce below Jeffrey Sachs' video message to the SDG forum:

A special thanks to Westminster International University in Tashkent for your leadership of today's SDG Forum for Uzbekistan and for your very kind invitation to make a few remarks. I want to thank the government of Uzbekistan and the universities: Westminster International University and other partners for working so diligently and creatively on Uzbekistan's sustainable development.

I know that the government and its university partners are searching for pathways to address the climate stresses that Uzbekistan faces as a country where at least 80% of the land is dry land and desert, and where water stress is increasing because of global climate change, also, where the vast potential for renewable energy is going to be tapped in the future. Uzbekistan will need and will make a transformation from a fossil fuel-based economy to one that can effectively tap Uzbekistan's vast solar potential but also significant wind potential, geothermal potential, and hydropower potential. So, Uzbekistan is a country that has vast renewable energy potential and vast potential to become an exporter of not a fossil fuel but of a zero-carbon power.

One of the keys to successful transformation for Uzbekistan, indeed, will be close cooperation with neighboring countries and active participation in regional programs such as the Belt and Road Initiative of China that will help to ensure that Uzbekistan can play its role as a transport hub and as a commercial and a financial hub for Central Asia and a bridge between East Asia and the European Union, indeed. So, I think that there are very exciting and positive pathways to the sustainable development of the energy transformation, the transformation to precision agriculture with highly efficient water use, and the transformation to a digital society, in which fiber connects Uzbekistan with all of the world and enables Uzbekistan to play in increasing role in the global economy online and an economy that will be an important hub for transport and for services, and of course I may add a great destination as one of the most beautiful places in the world with the some of the most important cultural heritage, and architectural genius in the world.

The Sustainable Development Solutions Network is working with universities around the world on these pathways of change, and Uzbekistan's pathways involve many fascinating and complex challenges of how to design a zero-carbon energy system, and how to transform the agriculture system to one of the resiliencies in the face of water stress, and how to integrate Uzbekistan into a regional, Euro-Asian wide economic activity. It would be a great honor and pleasure for the global Sustainable Development Solutions Network to intensify our work together, and our partnerships to support your wonderful country in its transformation to sustainable development.

Introduction

Sodyq Safoev

(First Deputy Chairperson of the Senate of Uzbekistan's Parliament)

Our main goal is to build a social state for people

Over the past five years, Uzbekistan has greatly achieved development in such important areas as increasing employment and real incomes, social protection, ensuring active participation of women in society, affordable housing policy, science, and youth policy. In short, under the leadership of President of Uzbekistan Shavkat Mirziyoyev, a "great leap" has been made in Uzbekistan.

Uzbek miracle

This "Uzbek miracle" did not happen accidentally. All of this was attained on the basis of a well-planned, long-term Action Strategy from the very beginning. This path was not easy either. It was carried out at the cost of a number of sleepless nights, in extremely difficult socio-economic and politically complex conditions, through continuous dialogue with the community on their issues, in some cases to solve centuries-old problems.

As the President of Uzbekistan, Shavkat Mirziyoyev, emphasized in his speech at the inauguration ceremony, the priority principle "In the name of human honour and dignity" will now be the main criterion in the activities of all levels of authority in the country. As the head of state emphasized, "From now on, we will organize our activities on the basis of the new principle of 'human – society – state'".

The head of state considers good social policy as one of the main goals of the country's development. The people of Uzbekistan did not experience the benefits of social policy for many years. For the past five years, people have started experiencing a social policy in practice and expressing their feelings with a "turns out it's possible" mood.

In fact, *the social sphere is one of the concepts of national security.* Among the main *threats* to the stability of society in this regard are income stratification, demographic changes, the growth of the number of unemployed and labor migration, the decline of literacy, the outflow of talented youth, premature death, morbidity, the worsening of the level of disability, the occurrence of epidemics and pandemics.

One of the great achievements we have made over the past five years is that we have eliminated these threats. This is explained by the development of new policy in the country, as we have noted above.

It should be noted that the reforms have become irreversible. Over the past five years, not only our people, but the whole world is starting to believe in and admire the large-scale reforms in Uzbekistan.

After the 2021 Presidential election, I read an article published in the Malaysian *Oic Today* business and investment magazine. It was emphasized that President Shavkat Mirziyoyev's success in the election is associated with the major reforms implemented based on the Strategy of Actions on the five priority directions of the development of the Republic of Uzbekistan in 2017–2021. It is recognized that the most important administrative, legal, and economic reforms have been carried out in the country during this period.

Uzbekistan has become a country of intense reforms. Problems that have been pending for many years have been resolved. An atmosphere of religious tolerance and friendly cooperation with neighboring countries has been formed in the country. A policy of gender equality was pursued and forced labor was abolished. Social protection of the population was provided. All this has been achieved through hard work based on the Action Strategy.

Today, the international community recognizes these changes in the country as an "Uzbek Miracle". This is a wide recognition. In history, there have been few countries like ours that have been able to perform result-based reforms in just five years. Undoubtedly, President Shavkat Mirziyoyev deserves recognition for his hard work on reform initiatives. The reputable Turkish publication "Ankasam" recently recognized the leader of Uzbekistan as one of the leading statesmen of the Turkic world.

Social policy in the lives of people

If we analyze the state programs related to the implementation of the Action Strategy, we will see that the social sphere is receiving more and more attention every year. This fact clearly shows that the New Uzbekistan is being built as a social state.

In 2021 alone, the volume of loans aimed at further supporting the entrepreneurial initiatives, start-ups and ideas of young people amounted to 600 billion soums.

Commercial banks will provide loans to young entrepreneurs in the amount of not more than 100,000 US dollars in the national currency at 14% per annum, and loans in foreign currency at 3% per annum for up to seven years.

The "Iron Book", "Women's Book", and "Youth Book" systems have been developed for families affected by unemployment, and opportunities such as providing soft loans and allocating land for farming have been expanded to ensure their employment. The practice of allocating subsidies of up to 7 million soums for the purchase of equipment and tools needed by citizens to start their activities has been established.

Thousands of new jobs have been created to provide employment.

For years, housing has been an open question for many people. Reforms that began in 2017 have also supported housing provision, to eliminate this problem. Two years ago, the mortgage system was radically reformed. Now, people have an opportunity to buy property. On average 35,000 apartments are being built annually under mortgage programs.

One of the most important reforms – the Constitution – came into force. The constitutional rights of citizens were restored. This can be seen in the example of reforms in the "propiska" system.

The national currency reforms provided solutions to cash and bank card related issues, which eliminated many social problems.

Consistent work on improving healthcare, including maternal and child health, and ensuring gender equality is now producing results. Morbidity rates have been decreasing and life expectancy has increased among the population.

Youth State policy has been revised. Forced labor was banned. In general, we can discuss many important aspects of the Action Strategy relating to social policy. Many social policy results are now being experienced in our daily lives.

Youth policy has structurally changed in content and format

As Louis Aragon said, "*Young people dream. Old people remember*", we, as representatives of the middle generation, also remember our youth and admire the current youth of our country. In the last century, the boundaries of youth were different. Today's Uzbek youth are not the same as before. Their worldviews and aspirations are unique, and the conditions and opportunities created by the government are worth admiring. After all, the new generation is the youth of the New Uzbekistan.

Today, 60% of the population of Uzbekistan is represented by the youth. Therefore, the youth policy has become a priority of public policy. It is no coincidence that the first law signed by the President in 2016 was the Law on State Youth Policy.

Over the past five years, the government has adopted more than 50 laws and other normative legal acts aimed at supporting the rights and interests of young people, which is clear proof of the country's youth-oriented policy.

The Agency for Youth Affairs, which is responsible for working with young people in Uzbekistan, has been launched within the government. Youth parliaments have been established in the chambers of the Oliy Majlis. There are more than 260 young deputies in local councils of community deputies.

While the share of deputies under the age of 30 worldwide is 2.6%, in Uzbekistan this figure is more than 6%. Measures are being taken to further increase this number.

Based on a resolution of the Senate Council, regional community boys and girls have been assigned to the members of the Senate; the school of youth parliamentarians was established in local councils of community deputies; and a new generation of reserve personnel of active and enterprising young people was formed. By the decision of the Senate, a rating system was introduced for the implementation of the state policy on youth in the regions.

There are children in some parts of the world who do not have access to food and schooling. Staying alive, eating bread in the morning, and staying with their parents would be dreams for these children.

Today, the children of Uzbekistan dream of competing globally to show their knowledge and skills, to take up winning positions. There are all grounds for this. For example, primary and secondary education coverage level is 100% in Uzbekistan. We are planning to increase pre-school education coverage levels to 80% and increase the level of access to tertiary education to 60% in the coming years. In the 21st century, no country can achieve progress without developing the education system. Therefore, fundamental reforms in New Uzbekistan have been focused on the education system.

In order to support young people, improve the system of protection of students in need and ensure the principle of social justice, starting from the 2021–2022 academic year, a grant from the President of the Republic of Uzbekistan was introduced for 200 students who scored the highest points in entrance exams to higher education institutions.

The practice of issuing educational loans to families with two or more children studying on a contract basis at a higher education institution and the student repaying this at the end of the study period has been established. The number of state grants for higher education has increased by 25%, and the number of state grants for women from families in need has doubled.

The number of higher education institutions in the country has exceeded 140, and branches of 26 foreign higher education institutions have been opened. In comparison to 2016, the number of universities in the country was 77.

Over the next five years, the quota for higher education will triple, creating opportunities for 182,000 young men and women to become students. This means that the application of school graduates to higher education will reach 28% of their total number. Four years ago, the figure was only 9%.

The number of state grants has increased from 21,000 to 47,000, and special grants to enter universities have been provided to 2,000 girls from families in need this year. The monthly salary of professors and teachers has been increased 3.5 times. The number of applicants has also doubled.

In order to support children in need of social protection in education and further employment, and to treat children with serious illnesses, the Public

Fund for Child Support was established allocating 100 billion soums from the state budget to finance the implementation of these goals.

One of the government resolutions regulates the reimbursement (partial) of renting expenses by students studying in public higher education institutions on a lease basis from the state budget.

It is no secret that some of our young people are going abroad to work. These young people do not do that for fun. Before the new policy began in Uzbekistan, no one was interested in asking about the reasons behind this work migration. Moreover, returning migrants were facing employment barriers in the public sector.

Shavkat Mirziyoyev has radically changed this situation. In order to protect the rights of citizens of Uzbekistan temporarily working abroad, the activities of the Foreign Labour Migration Agency have been revised and developed.

The Action Strategy pays special attention to supporting the intellectual potential of the young generation. In particular, to support the scientific and innovative projects of youth, 50 billion soums has been allocated. Starting from 2021, "Academic Mobility" and "Future Scientist" competitions were organized for the youth. Moreover, the increased quotas for the graduate education programs, including PhDs and DScs, are expected to provide high returns.

For decades, schoolchildren were "studying" in the cotton fields during cotton harvesting periods. Generations of young men and women experienced this before and during the first decades of independence.

As a result of the determined efforts of President Shavkat Mirziyoyev, all forms of forced labor in Uzbekistan, in particular child labor, were abolished. The report published by the US State Department in 2020 confirms this. It was noted that "Uzbekistan's great efforts to address this issue set a new standard for the countries of the region", and praised the work carried out in the country under the leadership of the President.

Another noteworthy aspect is that just a few amendments made to the *Law on Guarantees of the Rights of the Child* in 2020–2021, have yielded concrete practical results. There is an article in this law on "Guarantees and rights of children from illegal displacement protection". With the initiative of the Head of the State, five support operations called "Mehr" were organized. More than 550 women and children in difficult situations in Syria, Iraq, and Afghanistan have been returned to Uzbekistan and were provided with housing and employment for women.

The above law also includes a provision that "Guarantees the right of children in need of social protection to housing". In 2021 alone, more than 120 billion soums were allocated from the state budget to provide housing to 757 orphans and children deprived of parental care. This process will be also included in the state budgets in the coming years.

In addition, work has started with UNICEF to deinstitutionalize orphanages and place orphans and children deprived of parental care in shelters close to family and family environments.

In order to provide young families with affordable housing and introduce a transparent setting of the system, the government adopted a resolution "On measures to build apartment for youth in 2021–2023".

All these youth-oriented reforms support the conceptual framework of the youth policy in the country to continue sustainable development and social welfare of the country.

Social reforms establish strong people-oriented policy

Ensuring maternal and child health and women's active participation in society is a phenomenon of development. Any state that ignores these two important issues will inevitably face a crisis.

Therefore, the Action Strategy, which was launched five years ago, focused on strengthening public health and ensuring gender equality.

In recent years, a number of measures have been taken to improve the health of the population. In particular, the Presidential Decree of July 26, 2021 "On measures to further improve the quality of medical care provided to the population" defines the establishment of **35** inter-district centers of joint injuries and acute vascular diseases in district (city) medical associations.

In addition, the "Guaranteed Package" was approved in order to gradually introduce the system of medical services to the population within the package of free medical services and medicines provided by the state.

The practice of determining permanent disability without further examination of persons with obvious signs of disability and anatomical defects when they are found to be disabled has been established.

In order to create more favorable conditions for citizens in the accrual of pensions and benefits, a system of calculation of the length of service without the need for supporting documents on the basis of existing records in the employment record book was created.

Over the past five years, among other areas the country has implemented a number of positive reforms in the area of supporting women, providing them with state socio-economic aid and protection of their rights.

In particular, the law "On guarantees of equal rights and opportunities for women and men" was adopted. The Senate of the Oliy Majlis adopted a resolution approving the strategy for achieving gender equality in the Republic of Uzbekistan by 2030.

The documents set out the main directions of state policy in the field of equal rights and opportunities for women and men. In order to identify and eliminate the norms of gender discrimination in the legislation, it is planned to conduct a gender-legal examination of these documents and their drafts.

The Commission on Gender Equality of the Republic of Uzbekistan and the Committee on Women and Gender Equality in the Senate of the Oliy Majlis have been established. The activities of the Research Institute "Mahalla va Oila", the State Targeted Fund for Women's Support, the

Republican Rehabilitation and Adaptation of Women and 28 regional, inter-district centers, republican and regional Women's Public Councils, the republican commission for systematic resolving the women's issues, providing them with social support have been set up.

The Ministry of Mahalla and Family Support of the Republic of Karakalpakstan, regional and Tashkent city administrations, and the first deputy heads of district (city) departments were equated to the status of deputy khokims as advisers on women's issues to regional, district (city) khokims.

The State Targeted Fund for the Support of Women has been established and 512 billion soums have been allocated from the state budget.

Until the election of President Mirziyoyev, there has been a need for support in the eyes of women who were in difficult social situations. There was no interest in improving the conditions for women who were raising their children alone, renting a house, or had a disability. Their issues were not able to be spoken; some committed suicide and others felt left behind. Such cases are the result of difficult living conditions and desperation.

The President's social policy changed that. Today, a procedure has been introduced to build and provide affordable housing for mothers with disabilities, low-income, single-parent families, and those in need of improved housing conditions. The housing conditions of about 5,500 women in difficult social situations have been improved at a cost of 124.6 billion soums. In addition, 17,740 people have received soft loans worth 393.4 billion soums.

Targeted assistance was also provided and more than 1 trillion 950 million soums were directed to 883,000 women over the age of 30 in need of socio-economic protection.

Financial assistance was provided to 5,140 women with disabilities, the group in most need of home repairs. Rental compensation was paid to 11,000 women living in non-residential areas, who did not have housing in their own name or in the name of other family members, of whom 4,769 were provided with reduced-price affordable housing.

Medical services were provided to 161,578 women in need of medical protection; 3,037 of them were treated free of charge in regional centers and specialized clinics in the capital. Women with serious illnesses were admitted to republican level clinical hospitals and operated from state budget funds.

In recent years, the activity of women in socio-political life has increased significantly. In particular, the share of women in the Legislative Chamber of the Oliy Majlis was 32%. About 25% of deputies in the Senate and the Jogorku Kenesh of the Republic of Karakalpakstan are women. The share of women in management positions increased to 26% and in entrepreneurship to 25%. In 2016, there were 3,000 reserve leadership positions, and in 2021, their number increased to over 15,000.

For the first time, the symbolic badge "Respectable Woman" was established for women, including housewives, who have shown activism and initiative not only in public and state life, but also in bringing up children. At that, 855 women (290 in 2019, 287 in 2020, 278 in 2021) were awarded with this symbolic badge.

Currently, the number of women studying in higher education institutions is 365,000, which is 47% of the total number of students; 144 of them are from orphanages, 1,598 are those included in the "Iron Book", and 993 in the "Youth Book".

Women constitute 41% of the staff in the Ministry of Higher and Secondary Special Education system. In particular, there are currently 879 women DSc degree holders, 2,208 PhD degree holders, 833 professors, and 2,024 associate professors in the Higher and Secondary Special Education system. Moreover, four rectors, 56 deputy rectors, 199 deans of faculties and deputy deans are women.

According to the analysis of three years of country data provided by the industry, the share of female students is growing from year to year. The number of students continuing their studies at the master's level was 4,488 in 2019, 12,855 in 2020, and 13,600 in 2021.

The Council of Ministers of the Republic of Karakalpakstan, khckimiyats of the regions, and the city of Tashkent provided payments to study on a contract basis for 1,431 girls, who lost one or both parents, as well as single women in need.

Of course, maternal and child health will continue to be a constant focus, remaining one of the key areas of our reforms.

In this regard, I would like to recall the policy of our great ancestor Amir Temur – the great commander and statesman, in the administration of the powerful empire. In his guide on building a social country for people, our great ancestor writes:

> Let a merchant who has lost their capital be given enough gold from the treasury to restore their capital. If any of the peasants and citizens are unable to cultivate, let them be provided with the necessary seeds and tools for planting. If a citizen's house is damaged and they cannot repair it, they should be provided with the necessary equipment and support.

The Strategy of Actions, initiated by President Shavkat Mirziyoyev five years ago was a major policy toward achieving the country's development goals.

As a result of reforms based on the Action Strategy, Uzbekistan's domestic and foreign policies have changed. The countries of the world have started recognizing Uzbekistan as the country which pursues a pragmatic and open policy and continues its new initiatives.

Society-oriented reforms in the country have raised great hopes in our people. This policy is supported by our citizens and is highly valued internationally.

In addition, our citizens held a historic election in October of 2021 – re-electing with full confidence President Shavkat Mirziyoyev for a second term. Today we are entering a new stage of development. This will be done on the basis of the New Uzbekistan strategy initiated by the President.

We have big goals. In this way, the principle of "In the name of human honour and dignity" is taken as the main goal. The principle "From the strategy of action – to the strategy of development" has been put on the agenda as the main criterion that will bring a greater level of quality to all our reforms. The development strategy, as a program of practical action, defines the renewed domestic and foreign policy of Uzbekistan and plays a crucial role in laying the foundation stone of the Third Renaissance.

At the same time, one aspect needs to be understood: genuine reforms will never be easy. Human history teaches that structural reforms, especially in the early stages, always strengthen emerging issues and contradictions. Time for reforms is always limited, they are always associated with threats. Being able to make changes without compromising sustainability is the biggest challenge and the great art.

We can say with confidence that the great results of today's far-sighted endeavors will not keep us waiting long. In a few years, the development strategy will undoubtedly yield even brighter results than it does today.

An outsider's view of reforms

Cindy Malvicini

(Formerly the Asian Development Bank Country Director for Uzbekistan December 2018–2022, after being Deputy Country Director and Officer-in-Charge for Uzbekistan since 2017. In 2022 she moved to ADB's head office in Manila.)

Reforms pave the way for deepened development cooperation

Significant reforms and changes moved forward when President Mirziyoyev reached out to the rural population, asking international finance institutions to help address social and economic disparities prevalent across the country. Tashkent city as Uzbekistan's capital was growing economically, but other regions were not. The President's visits to the regions raised awareness within the government of the plight of the people. Prior to 2017, Uzbekistan pursued a different path that focused on self-reliance, a closed economy with significant government interference in every aspect of social and economic life. The reform agenda was limited, resulting in small or incremental changes. This also limited cooperation with development partners. The focus was mostly on high-level investment projects. Before reforms the government mostly sought infrastructure development on the ground to improve the well-being of people. So, we did many investment projects in transport, road and railway. We also worked on upgrading power plants, irrigation systems, water supply, and sanitation systems.

The government did not leverage the potential of development partners and private sector support to significantly improve the livelihoods of the population and promote inclusive economic growth. The changes initiated post-2016 created the environment for more intense reforms. Uzbekistan became open to cooperation with a greater number of development partners. The leadership announced that Uzbekistan was opening its doors to good international practice. Many early-stage reforms, such as foreign exchange liberalization, making the central bank more independent, and reforming state-owned enterprises are complete or well underway. These early successes built trust among development partners and assured that the government is serious in its path to reforms. Further reforms in restructuring governance in key areas like power (energy), road transport, water, PPPs, banking sector allowed the reform momentum to continue and allowed for the private sector to play a greater role while the government focused on creating an enabling environment.

The government now needs to stay on course, and become even more transparent and reliable. The people need to hold government leaders and employees, and development agencies, accountable for their work in a fair and transparent way, building on this early progress. Since more development agencies started work in this new era, the government may even better coordinate development partners to ensure development assistance is efficient and without duplication. Strong monitoring helps ensure external assistance is used effectively.

Every year the government assesses the status of their economic reforms. They held two conferences, October 2021 and November 2022, and plan to do so each year. This helped them assess their accomplishments and define future steps and possible corrections.

Asian development bank's engagement

The way ADB engaged with the government changed in 2017 with the new administration. The administration increasingly involved international partners and valued their advice. The government wanted to open and transition to a market-based economy and knew they would face challenging unfamiliar reforms. They sought international finance institutions like ADB's advice. Though we were actively and consistently engaged as the largest development partner before 2017, our work broadened. We still did core infrastructure development projects, but ADB and other development partners started doing more advisory work, and policy-based support to realize the government's reform agenda.

Debt management

Before the reforms, Uzbekistan was conservative in borrowing and kept its public debt-to-GDP ratio at 10.5 as of year-end 2016. While it may be considered conservative, the effect resulted in significant underinvestment in key infrastructure and curtailed economic activities of the private sector, and underutilization of a growing workforce. Before the 2017 reforms, economic data was not accurate. The new administration went back and re-examined the data, then adjusted it. The government frankly admitted growth statistics were exaggerated. Then they adjusted the previous three years of data downward. For example, they published 8% growth in 2016 and then went back and changed the rate to 5.9%. This bold step gained the new government international respect. Further, the government committed itself to greater transparency and improved quality of data by working with the IMF and ADB.

For debt management many countries consider a general threshold of no more than 60% of GDP for their public borrowing. Then the more you grow, the more you can afford to borrow and service debt. In 2018, the government began work with ADB on a proper debt management strategy and developed a debt management plan. The plan assessed what it would borrow from less expensive lenders such as development banks and other sources of finance.

The purpose of the plan was also to provide discipline and accountability to the Ministry of Finance. Under a new law, the Ministry of Finance would report to parliament saying, this is how much we're planning on borrowing this year; we will not breach that level unless we explain why and ask for your permission. That gave the Ministry of Finance more restraint and backing. When many requests came for more borrowing, they could say, no, we have a law in place, we can't breach it. There were exceptions to this, like crises. So during the height of the COVID-19 pandemic, the government borrowed more than originally expected to support the economy and help people through health and social assistance programs. The Russian invasion of Ukraine caused another great economic disruption. With international capital markets at stress, the government required more support to sustain the reform momentum by helping small and medium enterprises, and needy people in general to keep access to services and subsidies.

Now, the government has become far more transparent in its external borrowing. The Ministry of Finance regularly publishes information on what it finances. However, the government could further improve the transparency of the agencies that borrow from development partners. They can report to the people more regularly about how they are spending funds and how projects are performing. Civil society could hold the government more accountable for slow-moving projects and seek more information from the government and donors. These achievements make sure people are doing their jobs in a timely way.

National development planning and governance

Development planning was done poorly before the reforms. The government focused on the use of state funds without the involvement of the private sector, resulting in less than optimal allocation of resources and underfunding, which led to the deterioration of existing infrastructure. Lack of proper assessment and lack of feedback from the public resulted in significant underinvestment. Sectoral agencies lacked guiding documents to plan and set priorities for their work. In January 2018, the administration directed every sector agency to quickly create a sector strategy and plan. This was healthy. Later they created a second five-year national plan, more robust than the first. They increased their capacity in development planning. An inadequate governance structure with government agencies combining regulatory and commercial functions (e.g., power sector) resulted in vested interests and inefficiencies as the government intended to build all infrastructure using its own or loan resources.

For example, ADB helped the government develop a water resources strategy. It was consultative, bringing together irrigation, basin management, river basin specialists, and water supply managers. Water is insufficient and crucial for agriculture, industry, and household consumption. We gathered people to form a common strategy and plan for implementation. We provided international consultants and partnered with the International Water Management Institute to prepare the strategy.

Transformation and privatization of state-owned enterprises

Since the fall of the Soviet Union, the mentality of a big government, that controlled and provided for every need of the people, largely persisted. Many state-owned enterprises (SOEs) were an unsustainable legacy of that era. They were not functioning like companies; not considering either their financial sustainability or quality of service delivery to their clients.

The Ministry of Finance propped up SOEs with funding from the national budget. SOEs were not run by proper boards but by bureaucrats without interest in the company's profitability. SOEs were not accountable. Subsidizing SOEs, including state-owned banks, was an endless drain on the economy.

The general mindset of SOE leadership was that they do not need to be fully accountable. However, recognizing that the government is not always the most efficient owner and manager, it quickly made a list of companies that could be reformed and assets that could be offloaded. Many SOEs had peripheral services that were not part of their core business. For example, the railway company was not just doing railways, they had schools, farms, etc. So, one first step was to divest these noncore assets by focusing on core functions. Second, look at reforming the SOEs and then identifying certain ones to privatize and sell altogether.

Under the reforms, the government accepted advice from international finance institutions; not only to reduce duplication and improve efficiency, but to better manage funds allocated from the budget to the state apparatus. By reducing SOEs and unnecessary agencies, the government had more to spend on social issues and development priorities.

The government appointed supervisory boards over many companies. They recruited internationals to serve on those boards, advise them and decide with them. This process is time-consuming. The example of other states in the region, which have gone through SOE privatization, demonstrates you want to do so systematically and well, rather than piecemeal or impulsively.

Each multilateral development bank received a list of companies to focus on according to their expertise. Then each MDB supported and advised those SOEs. We would get into the specifics of what was happening in their organization, and then together we would develop transformation plans, and the reform steps the SOE should follow. To measure SOE performance and areas for transformation, development partners used scorecards as part of their support.

One reason utilities, such as the electric company, were not cost-effective is they did not charge a recovery rate to ensure the sustainable replacement of existing assets. For example, in 2016, before the initial rate adjustment, people were paying UZS191/kWh. In 2018 the rate increased to UZS295/kWh. Many people did not earn enough to immediately afford the increase. To ensure the transition was smooth and provide proper safety nets to vulnerable groups, the government asked ADB to help the government develop a tariff recovery methodology. They gauged what it would take to meet their operation and maintenance expenses and the costs to develop their services. Then they knew how much to charge and gradually increase tariffs. The electric company adjusted its tariffs in several increments but was put on hold because of the crises of COVID-19 and Russia's invasion of Ukraine.

A key aspect of tariff reform was separating tariffs from subsidies. Prereforms, the state-subsidized everyone. However, under reforms, many people could afford to pay the cost recovery tariff. The government realized the tariff should be charged correctly and target people who need relief through other ways. The World Bank, UNICEF, and others helped the government refine its social assistance methodology and put in place a more accurate social assistance registry of the needy. So instead of subsidizing all customers, subsidized electricity targeted people in need. This change in approach also removed distortions in the market and opened new avenues to attach private sector investment in the power sector.

The government strongly supported the privatization agenda. But it takes a long time and must be done right. You do not want to privatize all SOEs, but you want to focus on transforming them. SOE transformation needs to continue in earnest with time-bound plans. The steps many companies must go through to transform may take years. Underlying documents may need to change, such as their bylaws, and they must change their ways of working.

Public–private partnerships

Before the reforms, public–private partnerships (PPPs) did not exist. As a legacy of the Soviet model, the government had little interest in attracting foreign direct investment and privatizing companies. Reforms opened the door to private sector development.

The government shifted its mindset – whatever the private sector could do better they should do. PPP is a step toward foreign direct investment, toward a company investing in the country. The costs of doing business were high. Many investors shied away from investing. Uzbekistan had a history of challenges with commercial law not being followed. This gives a country a negative reputation. Investors were not ready to do business and set up their companies. They needed incentives, some backing, and guarantees in case things go badly.

The PPP approach enabled projects to be done through a partnership where both the government and the company put their interests at stake. So the government established a PPP law. When government partners noticed deficiencies, the government quickly amended the law.

This is an area where the ADB, EBRD, and the World Bank all supported the government. We trained government staff and continued to work with them to develop proper competitively tendered PPP projects. It is a different way of procuring a service, to have different companies bid on projects as potential partners with the government. The ADB and IFC are providing significant advisory support to the government that brought the best practices and expertise in structuring PPP transactions that consider the interest of the government and private sector in a balanced way.

Take solar power, for example. The government set aside land to build a 500-megawatt solar field that would connect to the grid through transmission lines. We helped them create a tender document, a procurement document that would invite bids on that solar field. The bidders would be screened for capacity then the bidder with the lowest tariff and cost to develop the project would be selected. We demonstrated the savings in the cost per kilowatt hour. Earlier, to attract FDI, there were many what I call "handshake deals". Representatives of foreign governments or companies would market their country's businesses. They would deal with the government directly. This practice has been significantly reduced.

Before, there were solar projects done without inviting competition. We worked with the government, and based on national interest and increased competence of the country, there was a rapid need to transition to competitive bidding. A competitive process resulted in a much lower rate per kWh. Competitive tendering is much more cost-effective for the government. Energy including solar and wind projects was only the first sector to apply competitive bidding. PPPs were broadened to other sectors like water supply and sanitation. ADB facilitated the first PPP tender for a wastewater treatment plant in 2020. An old poorly functioning wastewater treatment plant was dumping effluence into a river. Through a competitive tender, a company is coming in to build a new treatment plant on the same property

What the government was doing with our support was demonstrating and piloting the effective use of PPPs. As companies can take a PPP approach in any sector. We identified potential PPP projects for health and education, building and maintaining schools and hospitals through private companies. This allows school and hospital administrators to focus less on their buildings and more on education and healthcare.

With PPPs in particular, you need to make sure you're doing it right. You need good lawyers behind it, good legal documents, and good regulatory environments, to make it fair and transparent. Because you do not want these to fail, or create a negative reputation for the country.

The government was learning how to facilitate PPPs. In the first stage, there were only a handful of people that knew what a PPP was. This is where international advisors came in. ADB supported two international advisors with long-term experience in other countries to come to Uzbekistan. Then the PPP development agency recruited nationals who became experts in PPP. So every sector is getting new experience. Energy, relying on its own capacity, used PPP for several solar tenders. They built up their own group of internal experts. Every time you work in a sector, you have to build expertise at the agency level.

Conclusion

For the last six years, I have witnessed how Uzbekistan has become determined to change livelihood and economic governance with a clear reform agenda. It set long-term development goals to join upper-middle-income countries by doubling income per capita to $4,000 by 2030. This entails a firm commitment to and more persistent pursuit of reforms. I witnessed how budgeting public spending became more transparent, responsive to people's needs for public services and infrastructure, and consistent with medium-term development objectives. In 2023, Uzbekistan reformed public investment planning with a clear timeline and criteria for prioritizing development projects for the next three years. This demonstrates the government's willingness to adopt best practices from development partners such as ADB. In the same vein, I anticipate that the reform momentum will continue to be driven by key champions in the central government who ensure the reforms are on track with time-bound plans. The reforms demand transparency and greater accountability of the executive branch to the people, a strong independent judiciary and clear communication and understanding of the benefits of reforms to the people and government workers. I call on these champions to ensure that the quality of reform is consistent with international best practices and changes to improve the livelihood of 36 million people in Uzbekistan.

I see how Asian countries feel the impact of climate change on their economies. I foresee an opportunity for Uzbekistan's economy to become more competitive in the region through a timely transition to a green economy. Fulfilling the country's commitments to the Paris Agreement goals entails transforming all production and services from fossil fuels to a green and circular economy within the next decade. Uzbekistan's Strategy of Transitioning to a Green Economy by 2030 with time-bound actions, specific ownership, and accountability is a good start. The government set ambitious goals, generating 30% of electricity from renewable sources, and reducing greenhouse gas emissions by 35%. To do this, I urge the government to support changes in consumer behavior more assertively. Part of this requires raising awareness of the overall benefits of a green economy to people and the private sector. Subsidizing electric vehicle manufacturing and sales, and household use of solar panels and water heaters, would be incentives to change consumer behavior. External markets for food, textiles, petrochemicals, and machinery impose new and stricter standards on carbon emissions during production. The incentives are high to transform into a green low-carbon economy. I call on the government to speed up green development as a means and foundation for long-term economic growth.

I recognized how the results of reforms and economic development depended on skilled and competent labor during my work in Uzbekistan. I was glad reforming education and healthcare were the government's priorities. However, modernizing both pillars of human capital required substantial investments. Public resources for education and healthcare are limited. Private sector engagement in upgrading schools and healthcare through, for example, public–private partnerships is critical. Skills in the broader areas of science, technology, engineering, and math (STEM) will determine Uzbekistan's labor competitiveness in the next decade. In healthcare, I recommend allocating public and private resources to develop the capacity of healthcare staff while digitizing the sector. Competent staff and fully digitized data will play a crucial role in providing compulsory health insurance, and most importantly increasing quality and access to healthcare.

Uzbekistan faced many challenges when it started socio-economic reforms in 2017. After significant gains, it faces even greater challenges. Sticking to reforms, accelerating green growth, and prioritizing capacity in education are core elements of Uzbekistan's future growth and development.

Abbreviations and Acronyms

ABWU	The Association of Business Women of Uzbekistan
ADB	Asian Development Bank
AIIB	Asian Infrastructure Investment Bank
AY	academic year
BCP	border crossing point
BOP	balance of payments
BRI	Belt and Road Initiative (of China)
BTI	Bertelsmann Transformation Index
CAD	comparative advantage defying
CAF	comparative advantage following
CAR	capital adequacy ratio
CAREC	Central Asia Regional Economic Cooperation
CBU	Central Band of Uzbekistan
CERR	Center of the Research and Reforms
CIS	Commonwealth of Independent States
CMDA	Capital Market Development Agency
CO_2	carbon dioxide
COVID-19	coronavirus disease 2019
CPMM	Corridor Performance Monitoring and Management Programme (CAREC)
CSTO	Collective Security Treaty Organization
DB	Doing Business (report by the World Bank)
EAEU	Eurasian Economic Union
EBRD	European Bank for Reconstruction and Development
ECE	UN Economic Commission for Europe
ECI	Economic Complexity Index
ECHR	European Convention on Human Rights
e-GDDS	Enhanced General Data Dissemination Standard (IMF)
EPCA	Enhanced Partnership and Cooperation Agreement (with the EU)
ESCAP	UN Economic and Social Commission for Asia and the Pacific
EU	European Union

FCP	financial consumer protection
FDI	foreign direct investment
FRD	Fund for Reconstruction and Development
FX	foreign exchange
GoU	Government of Uzbekistan
GDP	gross domestic product
GIZ	German Agency for International Cooperation
GNI	gross national income
GSP	Generalized System of Preferences
GUAM	Georgia, Ukraine, Azerbaijan, and Moldova
ha	hectare
HDI	Human Development Index (of the UNDP)
HKSAR	Hong Kong Special Administrative Region
ICWC	Interstate Commission for Water Coordination in Central Asia
IEA	International Energy Agency
IFC	International Finance Corporation
IFI	International Financial Institutions
IFPRI	International Food Policy Research Institute
IFRS	International Financial Reporting Standards
ILO	International Labor Organization
IMDA	Insurance Market Development Agency
IMF	International Monetary Fund
ISCAD	International Strategic Center for Agri-Food Development
IsDB	Islamic Development Bank
kg	kilogram
Kph	Kilometers per hour
KWh	kilowatt hour
L2CU	Listening to Citizens of Uzbekistan
MAR	Macau Special Administrative Region
MFN	most favored nation
MMR	maternal mortality rate
MO	microcredit organization
MoF	Ministry of Finance
MSME	Micro, small and medium-sized enterprises
NFIS	National Financial Inclusion Strategy
NIE	new institutional economics
NPL	non-performing loan
NSE	New Structural Economics
OEC	Observatory of Economic Complexity
OECD	Organization for Economic Cooperation and Development
OIE	old institutional economics
OSCE	Organization for Security and Cooperation in Europe
PCA	Partnership and Cooperation Agreement (with the EU)
PPP	public-private partnership

QR	Quick Response code – 2D barcodes consisting of pixels
R&D	research and development
SACA	State Anti-corruption Agency
SCO	Shanghai Cooperation Organization
SCS	State Committee on Statistics
SDGs	Sustainable Development Goals
SEZ	Special economic zone
SIC ICWC	Scientific Information Center of the Interstate Commission for Water Coordination in Central Asia
SMEs	Small and medium-sized enterprises
SOCB	state-owned commercial banks
SOE	State-owned enterprise
SSC	State Statistics Committee
STC	State Tax Committee
STEM	science, technology, engineering and math
UFRD	Uzbekistan Fund for Reconstruction and Development
UNDP	United Nations Development Programme
UNFPA	United Nations Population Fund
UNICEF	United Nations Children's Fund
UNODOC	the Office of the United Nations High Commissioner for Human Rights, the United Nations Office on Drugs and Crime
USD	US dollars
USDA	US Department of Agriculture
UZS	Uzbekistan Soum
VAT	value-added tax
VNR	Voluntary National Review
WB	World Bank
WDI	World Development Indicators
WGI	World Governance Indicators
WIUT	Westminster International University in Tashkent
WTO	World Trade Organization

Unless otherwise stated, $ refers to US dollars, € euros, ¥ Japanese yen, and £ British pounds.

1 Uzbekistan before and after the 2016 socio-economic reforms

Justin Yifu Lin, Jia Yu and Shakhzod Nomozov

1.1 The social and economic performance of Uzbekistan since independence

1.1.1 Economic recovery and growth

All Central Asian republics, Uzbekistan, Kazakhstan, Kyrgyzstan, Tajikistan and Turkmenistan, saw their GDP drop sharply in 1991 due to the severe trade shock and economic dislocation that accompanied the breakup of the Soviet Union. From 1991 to 1995, the GDP in constant dollars declined by 31.0% in Kazakhstan, 44.8% in Kyrgyzstan, and 59.2% in Turkmenistan, with Uzbekistan being comparatively moderate at 18.8% (Table 1.1).

By 2000, Uzbekistan's GDP (in constant dollar terms) had recovered to 98% of its 1991 level as compared with 82% for Turkmenistan, 78% for Kazakhstan, 72% for Kyrgyzstan and 41% for Tajikistan (Table 1 1). Subsequently, as shown in Table 1.2, all Central Asian republics have shown

Table 1.1 GDP (constant 2015 US$) in Selected Asian Countries 1991–2021

	1991	*1995*	*2000*	*2010*	*2016*	*2020*	*2021*
Central Asia							
Uzbekistan	31.95	26.04	31.47	60.88	91.31	108.16	116.19
Kazakhstan	84.84	58.53	66.18	146.56	186.42	205.83	214.06
Kyrgyzstan	4.86	2.68	3.52	5.26	6.97	7.26	7.52
Tajikistan	6.59	2.69	2.70	5.90	8.84	11.43	12.48
Turkmenistan	12.54	8.31	10.33	21.7	38.02	45.71*	NA
East Asia							
Cambodia		4.14	5.91	12.77	19.30	23.02	23.72
Vietnam	47.75	66.84	95.53	177.34	255.26	322.78	331.13
China	1120	1830	2770	7550	11,802	14,620	15,800

Source: World Bank Data.

Note: *2019 data.

DOI: 10.4324/9781003473497-1

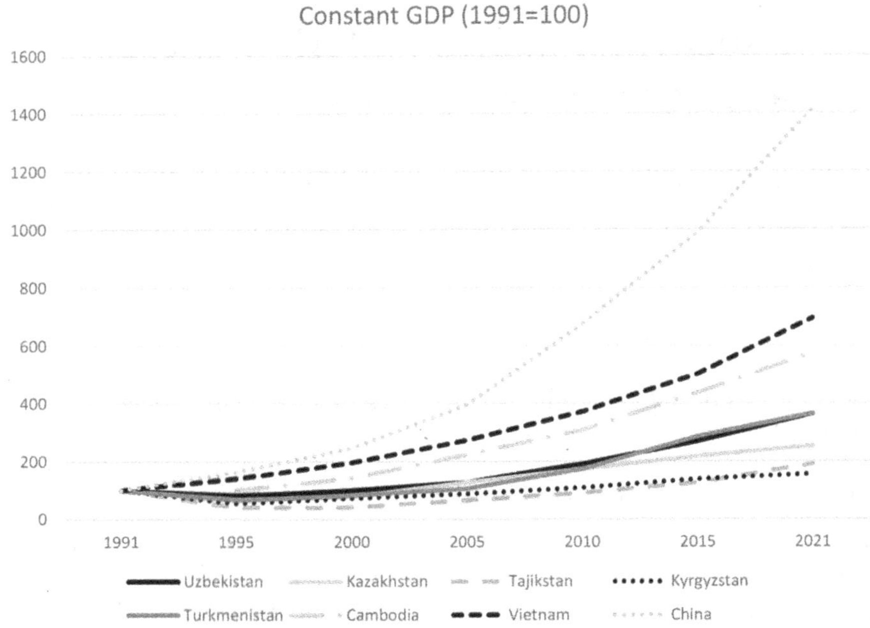

Figure 1.1 GDP growth in real terms in selected Asian countries 1991–2021
Source: Computed based on GDP (constant 2015 US$), World Bank World Development Indicators.

Table 1.2 Average Annual GDP Growth in Central Asian Countries (1991–2021)

Average per year	*1991–2000*	*2000–2010*	*2010–2016*	*2016–2021*	*1991–2021*
		Central Asia			
Uzbekistan	–0.2%	6.8%	7.0%	4.9%	4.4%
Kazakhstan	–2.7%	8.3%	4.1%	2.8%	3.1%
Kyrgyzstan	–3.5%	4.1%	4.8%	7.9%	1.5%
Tajikistan	–9.4%	8.1%	6.9%	7.1%	7.0%
Turkmenistan	–2.1%	7.7%	9.8%	NA	4.7%*
		East Asia			
Cambodia	NA	8.0%	7.1%	4.2%	NA
Vietnam	8.0%	6.4%	6.3%	5.3%	6.7%
China	10.6%	10.5%	7.7%	5.0%	9.2%

Source: computed based on GDP (constant 2015 US$), World Bank World Development Indicators.

Note: *1991–2009.

relatively strong economic performance. Between 2000 and 2010, the average annual growth rate in real terms was 6.8% in Uzbekistan, while Kazakhstan achieved 8.3%, Tajikistan 8.1% and Turkmenistan 7.7%. Only the growth in Kyrgyzstan was significantly slower at 4.1%. In particular, over the six years from 2010 to 2016, Uzbekistan maintained a high level of growth at an average annual growth rate of 7.0%, but slowed down to 4.9% from 2016 to 2021.

Compared to East Asia, Uzbekistan's growth was generally slower at 4.4% from 1991 to 2021, while Vietnam experienced 6.7% and China 9.2% during 1991–2021 (Figure 1.1).

1.1.2 Economic diversification

Since 2000, Uzbekistan has also experienced significant changes in its economic structure. In 2000, agriculture represented 34.4% of GDP. As the economy grew, the share of agriculture in GDP declined to 30.6% in 2010 and went down further to 26.9% in 2021. The share of industry went up from 23.1 in 2000 to 29.1% in 2005, then declined to 24.8% in 2015, but increased to 34.5% in 2021. Uzbekistan was the only country from the former Soviet republics that succeeded in increasing the share of industry in GDP.

Growing exports has supported GDP growth in Uzbekistan. The export of merchandise increased from $2.4 billion in 2000 to $11.6 billion in 2010 and $14.0 billion in 2021. As shown in Table 1.4, the composition of exports underwent some changes. In 2000, 77.2% of exports were primary commodities, of which agricultural raw materials (mainly cotton) represented 40.2% of total exports. By 2016, the share of agricultural raw materials represented 16% of the total exports, and this dropped to less than 3% in 2021. In contrast, among the primary commodities, the share of ores and metals increased from 6.3% in 2000 to 12.2% in 2016, and went up to 16.6% in 2021;

Table 1.3 Uzbekistan's Output Structure (Percentage of GDP at Basic Prices), 2000–2021

Year	*Agriculture*	*Industry*	*Service*
2000	34.4%	23.1%	42.5%
2005	29.5%	29.1%	41.4%
2010	30.6%	24.1%	45.3%
2015	32.1%	24.8%	43.1%
2016	32.1%	25.1%	42.8%
2020	27.1%	34.2%	38.7%
2021	26.9%	34.5%	38.5%

Source: ADB, Uzbekistan Key Indicators.

Table 1.4 Uzbekistan's Merchandise Exports 2000–2021 ($ Million)

	2000	2005	2010	2015	2016	2019	2020	2021
Total exports	2382	3955	11,627	9438	8969	14,885	13,259	14,002
Primary commodities	1839	2792	8146	6717	6448	11,150	9697	8780
—agriculture	957	936	2925	1676	1475	532	322	382
—fuel	468	609	1280	1077	947	2700	1077	1195
—ores and metals	151	521	1917	1363	1099	1581	1296	2328
—precious stones and gold	67	222	581	1493	1862	4779	5578	3454
Manufactured goods	543	1163	3481	2721	2521	3735	3562	5222
—labor-intensive	246	374	1149	1221	1130	2158	1992	3011
—low-skill	48	73	173	164	151	148	174	198
—medium-skill	123	382	926	426	361	350	455	526
—high-skill	126	334	1233	910	879	1079	942	1487

Source: UNCTAD Statistics.

while the share of golds and other precious stones increased from 2.8% in 2000 to 20.8% in 2016, and went up to 24.7% in 2021.

More significantly, the share of manufactured goods increased from 22.8% in 2000 to 28.0% in 2016, and this went up to 37.3% in 2021. It is very interesting to note that while the share of labor and resource-intensive goods (such as paper, furniture and textiles) in total exports of manufactured goods was relatively high (up to 57.6% in 2021), the share of high skills and technology-intensive manufactured goods (such as chemicals, measuring equipment) in the total export of manufactured goods has been consistently higher than the share of low-skill (such as iron and steel) and medium-skill manufactured goods (such as vehicle engines and parts). In 2021, the share of high-skill and technology-intensive manufactured goods was 28.5%, compared to 10.1% for medium-skill goods and 3.8% for low-skill goods.

1.1.3 Progress in the Human Development Index

Uzbekistan also made significant progress in terms of the Human Development Index (HDI)[1] (Tables 1.1–1.5). From 2000 to 2020, Uzbekistan's HDI value raised from 0.599 to 0.727, an increase of 21.4%. Uzbekistan's HDI value in 2020 put the country in the high human development category—positioning it at 107 out of 189 countries and territories.

Table 1.5 shows Uzbekistan's progress in each of the HDI indicators. Between 2000 and 2020, Uzbekistan's life expectancy at birth increased by 4.4 years, mean years of schooling increased by 2.8 years and expected years of schooling increased by 1.8 years. Uzbekistan's GNI per capita increased by 173% between 2000 and 2020.

As a comparison, Uzbekistan's 2020 HDI of 0.727 is below Kazakhstan's 0.811 (ranked 56 in the world) and Turkmenistan's 0.745 (ranked 91) but higher than Kyrgyzstan of 0.692 (ranked 118) and Tajikistan of 0.685

Table 1.5 Uzbekistan's Human Development Index

	Life expectancy at birth	*Expected years of schooling*	*Mean years of schooling*	*GNI per capita (2017 PPP$)*	*HDI value*
2000	67.2	10.7	9.1	2614	0.599
2005	68.4	11.5	9.8	3281	0.633
2010	69.7	11.4	10.7	4715	0.669
2015	70.9	11.7	11.4	6186	0.701
2016	71.2	11.8	11.4	6415	0.705
2017	71.4	12.0	11.7	6652	0.713
2018	71.6	12.0	11.8	6894	0.717
2019	71.7	12.1	11.8	7142	0.720
2020	70.9*	12.5	11.9	7917	0.727

Source: UNDP.

Note: *Uzbekistan's life expectancy at birth was reduced by 0.8 years in 2020 due to the COVID-19 pandemic.

(ranked 112). Uzbekistan's HDI is lower than Kazakhstan and Turkmenistan mainly because these two resource-rich countries have higher GNI per capita. In 2020, Kazakhstan's GNI per capita (2017 PPP$) was $23,943, and Turkmenistan's GNI per capita was $13,121, compared with $7917 for Uzbekistan.

1.2 Assessment of economic reform policies 1991–2016

1.2.1 "Uzbek model of development" under President Karimov

Since its independence in 1991, Uzbekistan has proceeded more cautiously than other transition economies to build the framework and institutions of a market economy. Mr. Islam Karimov was the first president of independent Uzbekistan; he strongly advocated for a gradual approach rather than "shock therapy" for the economic transition. Moreover, President Karimov believed that the state had to provide the necessary administrative capacity for the balanced growth of public and private sectors during the transition. The growth framework proposed by President Karimov was characterized as the "Uzbek model of development", or "socially-oriented free market economy". In short, the Uzbek model was constructed based on five principles: i) priority of economy over politics, ii) placing the state as the main driving force for reforms, iii) rule of law in all areas of society, iv) strong social policy and protection of vulnerable population, v) phased and evolutionary approach to a market economy.

In contrast to the advice of International Financing Institutions (IFIs) based on the "Washington Consensus" which advocated full-fledged trade liberalization, price liberalization and privatization, Uzbekistan under President Karimov preferred to transform its economy using its own form and pace in policy reforms. The European Bank of Reconstruction and Development (EBRD) defined a series of "transition indicators" to measure the progress made by different countries in meeting the indicators of the Washington Consensus (see Box 1.1).

Box 1.1 Classification system for transition indicators defined by EBRD

Competition policy

1 No competition legislation and institutions.

2 Competition policy legislation and institutions set up; some reduction of entry restrictions or enforcement action on dominant firms.

3 Some enforcement actions to reduce abuse of market power and to promote a competitive environment, including break-ups of dominant conglomerates; substantial reduction of entry restrictions.

4 Significant enforcement actions to reduce abuse of market power and to promote a competitive environment.

4+ Standards and performance typical of advanced industrial economies: effective enforcement of competition policy; unrestricted entry to most markets.

Price liberalization

1 Most prices formally controlled by the government.

2 Price controls for several important product categories, state procurement at non-market prices remains substantial.

3 Substantial progress on price liberalization: state procurement at non-market prices largely phased out.

4 Comprehensive price liberalization; utility pricing which reflects economic costs.

4+ Standards and performance typical of advanced industrial economies: comprehensive price liberalization; efficiency-enhancing regulation of utility pricing.

Trade and foreign exchange system

1 Widespread import and/or export controls or very limited legitimate access to foreign exchange.

2 Some liberalization of import and/or export controls; almost full current account convertibility in principle but with a foreign exchange regime that is not fully transparent (possibly with multiple exchange rates).

3 Removal of almost all quantitative and administrative import and export restrictions; almost full current account convertibility.

4 Removal of all quantitative and administrative import and export restrictions (apart from agriculture) and all significant export tariffs; insignificant direct involvement in exports and imports by ministries and state-

owned trading companies; no major non-uniformity of customs duties for non-agricultural goods and services; full and current account convertibility.

4+ Standards and performance norms of advanced industrial economies: removal of most tariff barriers; membership in WTO.

Governance and enterprise restructuring

1 Soft budget constraints (lax credit and subsidy policies weakening financial discipline at the enterprise level); few other reforms to promote corporate governance.

2 Moderately tight credit and subsidy policy but weak enforcement of bankruptcy legislation and little action taken to strengthen competition and corporate governance.

3 Significant and sustained actions to harden budget constraints and to promote corporate governance effectively (e.g., through privatization combined with tight credit and subsidy policies and/or enforcement of bankruptcy legislation).

4 Substantial improvements in corporate governance, for example, an account of an active corporate control market; significant new investment at the enterprise level.

4+ Standards and performance typical of advanced industrial economies: effective corporate control exercised through domestic.

Large-scale privatization

1 Little private ownership.

2 Comprehensive scheme almost ready for implementation; some sales completed.

3 More than 25 per cent of large-scale enterprise assets in private hands or in the process of being privatized (with the process having reached a stage at which the state has effectively ceded its ownership rights), but possibly with major unresolved issues regarding corporate governance.

4 More than 50 per cent of state-owned enterprise and farm assets in private ownership and significant progress on corporate governance of these enterprises.

4+ Standards and performance typical of advanced industrial economies: more than 75 per cent of enterprise assets in private ownership with effective corporate governance.

Source: EBRD: www.ebrd.com/publications/transition-report-archive

As shown in Table 1.6, ten years after independence, the progress of transition toward a full market economy in Uzbekistan was slow (with an unweighted average score of 2.1), trailing behind Kyrgyzstan (3.0), Kazakhstan (2.9), Tajikistan (2.6), though ahead of Turkmenistan (1.3). If a score of 3 is considered a “passing grade”, Uzbekistan “passed” only in terms of “small-scale privatization”, whereas the competition policy, price

Table 1.6 Progress in Transition in Central Asian Countries by 2001

	Competition Policy	*Price Liberalization*	*Trade and Forex Liberalization*	*Enterprise Restructuring*	*Large-Scale Privatization*	*Small-Scale Privatization*	*Unweighted Average*
Uzbekistan	2	2	–2	–2	–3	3	2.1
Kazakhstan	2	3	+3	2	3	4	2.9
Kyrgyzstan	2	3	4	2	3	4	3
Tajikistan	–2	3	+3	–2	+2	–4	2.6
Turkmenistan	1	2	1	1	1	2	1.3

Source: EBRD, Transition Report 2001.

liberalization, trade and forex liberalization, enterprise restructuring and large-scale privatization were all considered inadequate by EBRD.

While Uzbekistan's score in economic transition, resembling China and Vietnam, was considered by IFIs as relatively "poor" in terms of implementing competitive policy, price and trade liberalization, Uzbekistan's economic performance was comparable with or even better than those countries that had a better score in economic transition.

Building on its social and economic achievements since independence, Uzbekistan issued its Welfare Improvement Strategy (WIS) in 2007, which was the main articulation of the government's development vision and strategy to "form a modern and diversified economy able to compete in world markets". The WIS identified specific sectors and industries for the government to prioritize that would enhance the economy's competitiveness by moving away from raw materials toward manufacturing products of higher value-added. These include the following:

1 Basic industrial sectors such as fuel and energy industries (electricity, oil and gas), chemical industries (petroleum, biochemistry and pharmaceutical) and ferrous and non-ferrous metallurgical industries;
2 Labor-intensive industries (textiles, leather and footwear and construction); and
3 Machinery, transport and electrical equipment industries (automobiles, agricultural machine-building, cable and conductors).

In particular, the development of automotive industry was a typical example of industrial policy in Uzbekistan, based on assembling well-known global brands and facilitating a gradual localization of production (Box 1.2).

Box 1.2 The Automotive Industry in Uzbekistan

The government's industrial strategy for the sector is implemented through Uzavtosanoat (Uzbekistan Automotive Industry), a state-owned umbrella organization that controls all the major projects relating to the automotive industry in the country.

The automotive industry in Uzbekistan started with the construction of a car plant in 1992, followed by production plants for small trucks and buses in 1996 and the assembly of large trucks and buses in 2009. These three automotive producers are: UzAuto Motors specializes in the production of passenger cars, SamAuto specializes in the production of small trucks and buses, and MAN Auto-Uzbekistan for the production of trucks and buses.

UzAuto Motors was originally established as a joint venture with a Korean producer, Daewoo Motors, in Asaka, a small town in the Andijon region. The new plant, with an annual production capacity of 200,000 cars, started production in 1996. In 2001, Daewoo Motors in Korea was acquired by General Motors (GM), which resulted in the rebranding of the joint venture from UzDaewooAuto to GM Uzbekistan in 2008. Uzavtosanoat initially owned 75% and GM the remaining 25% of the company shares. In 2019, Uzavtosanoat became the sole owner of GM Uzbekistan and rebranded it to UzAuto Motors. UzAuto Motors has three plants located in Andijon, Khorazm and Tashkent with a combined annual production capacity of 300,000 passenger cars. The localization of production has been gradual and relatively slow. According to UzAuto Motors, it reached 50% in 2019. The most notable example of the localization program was the establishment of an engine plant in Tashkent in 2008. The plant, GM Powertrain Uzbekistan, has a maximum production capacity of 360,000 engines per annum.

In 1996, the government set up another joint venture with a Turkish company, which specialized in the production of buses and small to medium-sized trucks. The new plant, located in Samarkand and branded SamKochAuto, started production in 1999. In 2006, Uzavtosanoat purchased the Turkish share in the company and rebranded it to SamAuto (Samarkand Automobile Plant).

In 2009, the government set up the third joint venture to produce heavy goods vehicles in Samarkand with MAN Bus and Truck Company, Germany. The plant, named JV MAN Auto-Uzbekistan, started the production of trucks with a gross vehicle weight of 15–50 tons in 2009. It has an annual production capacity of 3,000 trucks. In order to benefit from economies of scale and potential positive externalities, the government intends to expand the sector and make it more competitive in the near future. In March 2020, Uzavtosanoat signed an agreement with Volkswagen Group to produce light commercial vehicles. It is also working with Hyundai to produce buses, trucks and electric cars.

As an infant industry, the automotive industry was highly protected in Uzbekistan. Imported cars, buses and trucks were subject to high customs duties, which can vary depending on the year of manufacturing, country of origin and engine volume. In 2020 Uzbekistan produced 270,000 light vehicles and about 7% were exported, mainly to Russia, Kazakhstan, Ukraine and Belarus.

Source: Kobil Ruziev (2021). Uzbekistan's Development Experiment: An Assessment of Karimov's Economic Legacy, Europe-Asia Studies.

It is noted that Uzbekistan's industry strategy was largely supported by its significant resource rents, calculated as the difference between the price of a commodity and the average cost of producing it, from its natural resources industry. Uzbekistan's average rents were around 28% of GDP in 2000–2009, and around 19% of GDP in 2010–2016 based on World Bank data. These rents enabled the channeling of surplus funds to targeted industrial projects.

In order to manage the resource rents more effectively, the government in 2006 set up a special sovereign wealth fund—the Fund for Reconstruction and Development (FDR). One of the FDR's main objectives was to use these funds to co-finance strategic government-selected projects. The government usually spends a stable proportion of tax revenues from the natural resource sector, equivalent to about 2–3% of GDP, and saves the rest with the FDR.

1.2.2 Issues and challenges of Uzbekistan's economic policy from 1991 to 2016

Uzbekistan's economic development and transformation, compared to other Central Asian transition countries, has largely been a success story since independence. Under President Karimov, Uzbekistan chose its own strategy of a gradual transition to a market economy in accordance with the country's culture, history and socio-economic conditions at the time.

This strategy of gradualism enabled Uzbekistan to achieve stability, relatively high growth rates and also some level of diversification of its economic structure. As a result, by 2016, Uzbekistan was more diversified in its economy than its Central Asian neighbors and was able to produce a wide range of manufactured goods including light vehicles, trucks, buses, chemicals, construction materials, textiles and electronics, etc. Moreover, many modern roads and transport logistic infrastructures have been built in Uzbekistan. In particular, the total route-km of rail lines increased from 3483 km in 1995 to 4304 km in 2016. In 2011, Uzbekistan became the 15th country in the world to launch a high-speed train line (between Tashkent and Samarkand). The fast-speed railway was extended to Bukhara and Karshi in August 2015.

It is noted that Uzbekistan's industrial strategy and growth model under President Karimov focused mainly on state-induced capital accumulation. More than 8000 state-owned enterprises (SOEs) dominated the economy, particularly in energy, metallurgy and mining, telecommunication, agriculture, machinery, and transport. Many SOEs, often combining regulatory and operational functions, dominated key sectors of the economy. However, a side effect of this strategy is that the economic system became increasingly rigid, characterized by extensive state involvement, poor governance and low inflows of foreign direct investment (FDI).

Under such circumstances, the inflow of foreign direct investment had been limited. The cumulative foreign investment (stock), $8.7 billion by 2016, was much below the stock of FDI in Turkmenistan ($31.9 billion) and Kazakhstan ($143.1 billion) in the same year. Even the limited foreign investment in Uzbekistan was largely directed by the government into sectors that the government considered as "strategic" (such as automotive industry) for its vision of an industrialized nation, but not really in line with the country's prevailing comparative advantage of an abundant supply of labor and meeting the needs of generating jobs to avoid high unemployment rate.

Despite the progress made in urban infrastructure, old and deteriorated infrastructure, such as power supply, roads, irrigation and drainage, water supply and sanitation, and solid waste management outside the big cities, especially in small towns and in rural areas, was a constraint to businesses and economic growth. More than 40% of energy sector capacity was in plants aged between 40 to 50 years, which required urgent replacement or major rehabilitation; transmission and distribution losses were high at more than 20%.

Moreover, Uzbekistan's exports were still dominated by raw materials. According to the data compiled by the Observatory of Economic Complexity, from 2000–2016, Uzbekistan's economy became relatively less complex in terms of its Economic Complexity Index (ECI), moving from the 52nd to the 87th position in the world's ECI rank.[2]

1.3 Acceleration of structural reforms since 2016 and early results

1.3.1 Wide-ranging liberalization policies

Building on the sound macroeconomic fundamentals from President Karimov's administration, President Mirziyoyev highlighted his overarching economic development strategy in the Presidential Decree, "On the Strategy for the Further Development of the Republic of Uzbekistan", issued on February 7, 2017. For the new phase of Uzbekistan's economic transition, the government has committed to reducing the poverty rate by half by 2026 and enabling Uzbekistan to become an upper-middle-income country by 2030. There is also an emphasis on reducing the role of the state in economic production and refocusing the state's role as an effective public investor and enabler of the private sector.

President Mirziyoyev has introduced wide-ranging liberalization policies in almost all spheres of economic life, aiming to improve the lives of its citizens, enable business development and further economic open up to the world. Uzbekistan's reforms have proceeded with a breadth and speed that have exceeded the pace of many earlier transition economies at a similar stage of the process. Major macroeconomic reforms that have been implemented since 2017 include:

- Trade and foreign exchange liberalization: In 2017, the government unified the official and parallel market exchange rates, liberalized access to foreign exchange and reduced trade tariffs.
- Price liberalization: Prices of most goods and services have been liberalized, including key food items (flour, bread) and fuel. Utility tariffs have been raised but remain regulated and below cost recovery.
- Tax reforms: The government adopted a considerable reduction in direct taxes on private enterprises and labor in 2019 and widened the tax base, by lowering thresholds and eliminating exemptions and privileges, thus safeguarding revenues.

- Reform and privatization of SOEs: a decree "On measures to accelerate the reform of enterprises with the participation of the state and privatization of state assets" was issued in October 2020, with a list of large state-owned enterprises and economic associations subject to transformation approved. In March 2022, a new Presidential Decree "On additional measures to further reduce state participation in the economy and accelerate privatization" (the Resolution) was adopted.
- Monetary and financial sector reforms: A new central bank law adopted in 2019 enhanced the Central Bank of Uzbekistan's independence, with price and financial stability as its mandate.
- Agricultural reforms: The government reduced the amount of arable land assigned to grow wheat and cotton, allowing more space for higher-earning crops. It also raised farm-gate prices for wheat and cotton to market levels and abolished the system of state orders.

In order to attract more foreign investment, President Mirziyoyev issued the "Presidential Regulation on Fundamental Measures to Improve the Investment Climate" in August 2018, providing a number of incentive measures, including a decrease, from 30% to 15%, of the minimum share of foreign investment in the share capital of a legal entity with foreign investment.

Another important step in improving the investment climate is the expansion of free economic zones. In fact, the first free economic zone in Uzbekistan was established in the Karamin district of the Navoi region in 2008. In May 2019, President Mirziyoyev signed a decree making the entire territory of Navoi region a free economic zone for the period up to January 1, 2030, with the possibility of a further extension of this period. The main goals of this decision are to attract foreign direct investment to create innovative, high-tech, export-oriented and import-substituting enterprises producing high-value-added products. Further, the law "On Special Economic Zones (SEZs)" was adopted in February 2020, which provides for five types of SEZs: free economic zones; special scientific and technological zones; tourist and recreational zones; free trade zones; and special industrial zones.

Since 2017, Uzbekistan has also been undertaking reforms to improve the enabling environment for private sector development, including SMEs. Commencing in January 2019, tax system distortions that unfairly burdened small businesses were removed. Tax rates for small firms were reduced (unified tax rate from 5% to 4%, property tax rate from 5% to 2%, and dividend tax from 10% to 5%). Tax policy and administration reforms have resulted in 30,000 new firms entering the standard tax regime and boosting tax revenue in 2019. To support entrepreneurship, the value-added tax rate was reduced from 20% to 15% in October 2019.

International Financing Institutions welcomed and strongly supported the new wave of reform measures in Uzbekistan. In addition to the ADB, the World Bank, the Japan International Cooperation Agency (JICA), and Islamic Development Bank (IsDB) that have been Uzbekistan's traditional development partners for a long time, the European Bank for Reconstruction and Development, the European Investment Bank and the Asian Infrastructure Investment Bank also started their operations in Uzbekistan. The public and publicly guaranteed loans were $17.01 billion in 2020 compared to $6.6 billion in 2016.

1.3.2 Early results of the reforms under President Mirziyoyev and key challenges

According to the World Bank's Ease of Doing Business (DB) Report,[3] Uzbekistan's DB ranking was 69 among 190 countries and territories in 2020, an improvement of 18 position from 2016. In 2020, among the ten indicators, Uzbekistan was performing very well in "starting a business" (ranking 8), and quite well in "enforcing contracts" (ranking 22), "getting electricity" (ranking 33), "protecting minority investors" (ranking 37); poor in "getting credit" (ranking 67), "paying taxes" (ranking 69), "registering property" (ranking 72); and problematic in "resolving insolvency" (ranking 100), "dealing with construction permits" (ranking 132) and "trading across borders" (ranking 152).

As the investment environment improved, the inflow of FDIs increased to $1.7 billion per annum on average between 2017–2021, compared to $0.9 billion per annum on average between 2012–2016. Moreover, with government policies to develop the private sector, the role of SMEs in the economy has become significant, particularly in terms of providing employment. According to the IMF, about 411,203 SMEs were registered and active at the end of 2020, up 4% year-on-year. SMEs accounted for 54% of GDP in 2019–2020, with sectoral breakdown being 97% in agriculture, 82% in trade, 72% in construction, and 52% in services. SMEs accounted for 27% of exports and 62% of imports. Their share of investment was 40%. SMEs are the largest employers, providing 78% of formal and informal jobs combined in 2018, compared with 50% in 2000.

Despite shocks from the COVID-19 pandemic, Uzbekistan's economy has shown relatively strong resilience. The pandemic caused a sharp slowdown in 2020, but the real growth remained positive at 1.9%. In 2021, helped by government stimulus measures, the growth rate rebounded sharply to 7.4%. Despite the shock caused by the pandemic, the government of Uzbekistan continued to accelerate the pace of structural reforms to ensure strong, sustainable and inclusive longer-term growth, while enhancing resilience.

It is fair to note that the new government after 2016 inherited robust macroeconomic conditions from President Karimov's administration. Indeed, President Karimov left behind a more sophisticated and diversified economy and sound macroeconomic fundamentals including moderate inflation, low government debt and a large stock of international reserves. These factors provided a firm foundation for the successor government's reforms that are likely to facilitate sustainable and dynamic growth in the future.

After a wave of exchange rate, trade and price liberalization reforms, the government's focus is shifting to deeper structural constraints. Going forward, Uzbekistan is facing three key challenges in terms of job creation, SOEs reforms and regional connectivity.

First, the most challenging issue is job creation. The country's high share of young people coupled with largely jobless economic growth is a key area for concern. Despite the progress in advancing the transition to a market economy since 2016, not enough quality jobs have been created in Uzbekistan to keep pace with demographic growth and fulfill the poverty reduction target. In 2020, official statistics estimated unemployment at 10.5% of the active labor force, while another 34.0% of the working-age population was inactive. The government's ultimate objectives of improving the quality of people's lives and enabling the creation of quality jobs can only be achieved by developing labor-intensive industries consistent with the country's comparative advantages. New jobs need to be created through the greater and more dynamic participation of the private sector in the economy, but it is clear that markets alone cannot guarantee the needed job creation. More rapid job creation and more equitable growth require a more capable state that can support inclusive and competitive market-led growth.

Second, SOE reform is another key challenge to Uzbekistan. Up to now, the economy is still dominated by SOEs that operate across most sectors. According to the World Bank, about 2580 tier 1 SOEs account for around 18% of employment and 20% of exports. SOEs are responsible for production in key economic sectors and all high-priority activities identified in government industrial policies. Most state-owned assets are concentrated in 15 large SOEs, with total assets in 2019 equivalent to 57% of GDP.

SOEs have long benefited from public spending that offsets costs, including both financing (often in loans at advantageous interest rates) and administered input prices. A high share of quasi-fiscal subsidies going to SOEs flows via public utilities (electricity, gas, water, district heating) as part of public service obligations, but are also available to SOEs in commercial sectors, such as aviation, automobiles, chemicals and fertilizers. The quasi-fiscal subsidies are not explicitly recorded in the budget and are estimated at about 6% of GDP. Explicit budget subsidies to SOEs represented another 1% of GDP in 2020. However, even these sizable resources have been insufficient to ensure adequate investment. The net financial performance of the largest SOEs in the economy was modestly positive in 2020. Including subsidies, profits of about 1.5% of GDP offset losses of about 1.0% of GDP, with most losses arising from technical losses in natural gas, lower export prices and hot water distribution companies (about two-thirds of the total financial losses generated by the largest SOEs in 2020).

Third, being a double-landlocked country, limited transport connectivity with neighboring countries and other international economic growth poles is a major constraint to job creation and trade growth in key economic sectors. According to the World Bank, Uzbekistan has the highest transportation costs in the Central Asia region, its average shipment costs are about $1.75 (per truck kilometer), about 32% more than in Kazakhstan and 23% more than in the Kyrgyz Republic. The quality of Uzbekistan's road and rail transport network is declining due to a lack of proper maintenance, aging rolling stock and weaknesses in public investment. Roads account for 88% of domestic passenger and short-haul cargo transport and about 10% of the international carriage of goods, but a large backlog of rehabilitation work has accumulated. About half of Uzbekistan's rail network is linked to international rail corridors, but outdated rolling stock creates significant delivery delays and losses in transit, leading to a steady decline in rail freight volumes.

Uzbekistan also lags far behind its peers in digital connectivity. Uzbekistan's external connectivity to neighbors and to global internet peers is weak. Deficiencies in internet speeds, bandwidth, and user costs in Uzbekistan continue to impact residential users negatively and constrain economic growth across many sectors.

1.4 Recommendations to Uzbekistan based on China's experience

In consideration of Uzbekistan's key challenges, we present China's experience in developing labor-intensive jobs, SOE reform as well as support in expanding regional connectivity through the Belt and Road Initiative (BRI).

1.4.1 Development of labor-intensive industries through SEZs

The "flying geese" pattern describes China's own development path. Following market liberalization in 1978, factories from more developed economies, especially in East Asia (including Hong Kong and Taiwan regions), relocated to the east coast of mainland China to exploit its comparative advantage in labor-intensive, export-oriented manufacturing.

Adopting practices from neighboring regions, China followed what is known as the "Three-Plus-One" trade model (Box 1.3) in order to develop labor-intensive industries and integrate quickly into the global production chains, whereby foreign-funded factories provide equipment, management skills and international orders facilitated by local governments' supportive policies.

Box 1.3 "Three-Plus-One" trade model: a successful method that allowed China to host the first batch of labor-intensive manufacturing and kick-start the industrialization process

At the beginning of China's reform and opening-up in 1978, FDI was brought mostly by overseas Chinese entrepreneurs from Hong Kong and Macao regions. These investors financed the purchase of equipment, sent necessary raw materials, and taught local workers how to perform production in relatively simple factory environments. The products were then sold to buyers on the international market connected to the investors. Profits gained were first used to pay the salaries of local workers and then to repay the initial investment in equipment and raw materials. The typical process for the relocation of "flying geese" industries to mainland China was as follows: processing of incoming materials, assembling the imported parts, producing according to prefabricated samples, and benefiting from trade subsidies from the government, a model often described as "borrowing ships to sail the seas".

The "three-plus-one" trading model first appeared in 1978, a successful method of corporate trade initiated during reform and opening-up. In July 1978, the first processing-specialized garment factory was jointly set up by Hong Kong businessmen and by the Taiping Garment Factory of Dongguan County (Guangdong Province). The factory was called Taiping Purse and was the first domestic firm to specialize in processing components from abroad.

This initiative was approved by the central government soon. By issuing the "Trial Regulations on Subsidizing Processing Enterprises and SMEs" in August 1978, the central government well-defined and approved the "Three-Plus-One" trading model, where foreign enterprises provided equipment (including foreign investment in shed construction), raw materials and samples, and were responsible for exporting all products. The local Chinese companies were responsible for providing land, construction of the sheds financed by investors, and labor. The Chinese and foreign parties agreed not to calculate the initial input from the two sides as a condition to enable the formation of a new "three-plus-one" trading model enterprise. In 1978, the central government hosted a meeting between the Guangdong provincial government and Hong Kong businessmen. After the meeting, the nation's first "three-plus-one" format was officially agreed upon. This kind of company was soon to be embraced in various parts of Guangzhou city and other coastal areas. Local party secretaries/mayors actively approached firms in Hong Kong to invest in their towns. With the demonstration effect and knowledge transfer of "Three-Plus-One" firms, township and village-level enterprises soon started flourishing, and since then, labor-intensive industries in mainland China have grown exponentially.

In the early era of reform, the Chinese government began to formulate relevant policies for the "Three-Plus-One" trading model, including regulations for foreign capital investment in mainland enterprises and factory management systems. These policies fundamentally changed the macro-level business environment in China. The central government selected coastal provinces including the southern Guangdong and Fujian provinces as pilot areas, giving them considerable policy freedom to explore potential methods for developing their local economies through trial and error. In 1979, the

State Council issued the "Provisions on the Major Development of Foreign Trade to Increase Foreign Exchange Income", which aims at expanding the autonomy of regions and enterprises practicing foreign trade, encouraging exports, and setting up SEZs.

Following the 1979 central directive conferring increased foreign trade authority to Guangdong and Fujian, the first SEZs were established between 1979 and 1980 in Shenzhen, Zhuhai, Shantou (Guangdong Province) and Xiamen (Fujian Province). Guangdong, led by a group of officials with an "ice-breaking" mentality, began drafting SEZ legislation. In 1980, the central government approved the "Regulations on Special Economic Zones in Guangdong Province", China's first major piece of SEZ legislation. It conferred to the Shenzhen SEZ advantages such as a 15% corporate profit tax compared to 33% in the rest of China and 17% in neighboring Hong Kong. Guangdong and Fujian were also granted customs autonomy.

At the same time, the regulations contained many gray areas left at the discretion of SEZ authorities, including wage levels, land rents, lease duration and conflict resolution. This opacity can be especially off-putting for foreign investors who do not have a good understanding of local culture and networks. By the end of 1981, the four zones accounted for almost 60% of total FDI in China. While they eventually attracted investment from the United States and Europe, the vast majority came from Taiwan Province, Hong Kong (HKSAR today) and Macau (MSAR today).

An important, distinctive feature of China's first SEZs is that they served as laboratories to experiment with economic reform. In the planned economy inherited from the Mao era, SEZs were circumscribed testing grounds for new, liberal policies for China's gradual transition toward a market economy. For instance, contracted labor and flexible wage systems were first introduced in the Shenzhen SEZ and later diffused to the rest of the economy. The transfer of land use rights, although forbidden by the Constitution at that time, was legalized by Guangdong's provincial government for investors in Shenzhen in 1987.

Vital to the SEZs' role as places of experimentation and innovation is a remarkably high level of decentralization. Beyond increased authority for the provincial government hosting SEZs, the zones themselves enjoyed an exceptional level of autonomy. In 1988, Shenzhen, which already enjoyed the same political status as the provincial capital Guangzhou, was upgraded to the administrative level of a province for economic planning purposes. In 1992, the central government went further by directly delegating the law-making power from the People's Congress to the governments of the four cities that are developing SEZs.

Even though many policies once pioneered by SEZs have since then spread to the rest of the economy, Chinese SEZs remain a place of experimentation as they still enjoy a special degree of political and fiscal autonomy. They have the power to develop municipal laws and regulations. They are also allowed to retain a large share of tax customs and foreign exchange revenues generated within the zones. The same is true for many other open economic areas established over the years in China. In fact, China experimented with the concept of SEZ itself and introduced many different types of zones to prepare the country for evolving economic challenges—from international processing trade and WTO ascension in the 2000s to high technology development and financial liberalization today.

Today, China faces the challenge of rising labor costs and industrial upgrading as its industries shift from labor-intensive to more capital-intensive modes. This is leading to a new round of "flying geese" industrialization as many enterprises producing labor-intensive commodities relocate their production outside China to reduce costs, which is a golden opportunity for other developing economies to take over low-skill labor-intensive manufacturing from China.

1.4.2 SOEs reforms through gradual and dual-track approach

Since starting the reform and opening-up at the end of 1978, China has grown at 9.2% annually for 40 years—a miracle in human history. The Chinese government's focal point of reform from the very beginning has been SOEs. Before the reform and opening-up in 1978, China had a centrally planned economy, and SOEs played a key role in the national economy, accounting for more than 70% of the GDP at that time.

When the transition started, almost all firms in China were state-owned. The SOEs had to bear two types of "policy burdens". First, a "strategic policy burden". Many SOEs in China were the legacy of the state's comparative advantage-defying (CAD) heavy industry-oriented development strategy adopted in the 1950s for the purpose of catching up with the United States in 15 years and overtaking the United Kingdom in ten years. Due to defying China's comparative advantages, the SOEs were nonviable in open, competitive markets and bore a strategic policy burden.

Another burden is a "social burden". Before the reform, production and investment were concentrated in the capital-intensive industries, which did not create enough jobs. As the government was responsible for full employment in the urban areas, it overstaffed the SOEs. These redundant workers had not been regarded as a burden from the SOEs' point of view before the reform, because all the investment and expenditures of the SOEs were covered by fiscal appropriations. But after the reform of replacing the fiscal appropriation with bank loans in 1983, the burden of supporting these redundant workers was shifted to the SOEs, thus creating a "social policy burden". In addition to redundant workers, the social policy burdens for the SOEs also include pensions for the retired staff, which used to be covered by fiscal appropriations and after changing to bank loans in 1983 the obligation of providing pensions shifted to SOEs. Both the strategic burden and the social burden are policy burdens, resulting in policy-induced losses in a competitive market. Because the state is accountable for those policy burdens, it grants SOEs policy subsidies (such as access to low interest-rate bank loans, market monopoly, sheltering from import competition and so on).

During the transition process for SOEs, China adopted a pragmatic, gradual, dual-track approach. The government introduced a profit retention system to SOEs, giving workers the right to partially share the productivity improvements. This transition strategy allowed China to maintain stability by avoiding the collapse of old priority industries and to achieve dynamic growth by simultaneously turning its comparative advantages into competitive advantages. The quick accumulation of capital and upgrading of comparative advantages also allowed China to tap into the potential of latecomers' advantages in the industrial upgrading process. In addition, the dynamic growth in the newly liberalized sectors created the conditions for reforming the old priority sectors. The quick accumulation of capital gradually turned those capital-intensive industries from China's comparative disadvantages to comparative advantages. Firms in those sectors became viable in an open, competitive market. As a result, protections and subsidies become unnecessary for their survival. The government can eliminate the remaining protections and subsidies as they become redundant.

Another key approach to reform SOEs was "grasping the large and letting the small go" ("zhuada fangxiao"). i.e., privatizing small SOEs while corporatizing large SOEs. From the new structural economics (NSE) perspective, small enterprises are generally in the comparative advantage following (CAF) labor-intensive industries and have no strategic burden.[4] The social burden of redundancy and pensions can be easily stripped off, as these small enterprises are generally located in cities, where land is valuable. After privatization, with the unity of ownership and management, problems of information asymmetry and incentive incompatibility no longer exist. Moreover, the proceeds from land appreciation are sufficient to support layoffs and pensions. So, the reforms of small SOEs are quite effective.

After implementing the "zhuada fangxiao" reform, the existing SOEs in China are generally large enterprises, which can be classified into three categories: First, strategic capital-intensive CAD industries, including aviation, aerospace, warship, core chip manufacturing, new materials, etc. Second, natural monopoly industries have a major bearing on the national economy, such as power, telecommunication, highways, railways, and ports. Third, competitive industries that are consistent with China's comparative advantages, such as steel, cement and equipment manufacturing industries.

For the first category of industries, many of them are needed for national defense and economic security. Some of them in this category, such as the core computer chips and new materials, if China did not develop them, the key technologies would be controlled and held back by some developed countries, or companies in those countries may charge exorbitant patent royalties. So, in the long run, it is actually cost-effective to develop these industries indigenously. Industries in this category are too capital-intensive to be China's comparative advantage at the current level of development, so without protection and subsidies, these firms are not likely to be viable. In the early days of reform and opening-up, firms in this category of industries accounted for a significant proportion of the national economy, and they received covert subsidies in the form of distorted factor prices, such as concessional loans. Now that the proportion of those firms has significantly dropped, the covert subsidies can be replaced by direct fiscal subsidies in the form of financing their R&D projects and procuring their products as commonly practiced in developed countries for their strategic industries.

For natural monopoly industries in the second category, firms are usually of massive scale and lack competition, and it is challenging to overcome information asymmetries and moral hazards caused by incentive incompatibility. That is why the efficiency of natural monopoly industries, even in advanced countries, be they state-owned or private, is generally lower than that of competitive industries. The likely moral hazard and abuse of the monopoly to raise prices will hurt the interests of consumers, who are vulnerable. Prices of natural monopoly industries should be regulated by the state. This is the practice in developed economies too, regardless the firms are state-owned or private, and state-owned natural monopoly firms are likely easier to regulate than private natural monopoly firms, as many of which become politically powerful oligarchs.

For the competitive industries in the third category, their firms no longer have a strategic burden. As long as their redundant workers and pensions of retired workers are taken care of by the social safety net, their social policy burden will not exist any longer. So, these CAD industries become CAF industries. In this case, when we compare SOEs of the third category with their private counterparts, SOE's efficiency is not necessarily lower. Of course, if the SOEs are performing well, there is no need to privatize.

Considering that privatization is not necessarily the answer to boosting the efficiency of SOEs, China proposes a "mixed-ownership" approach to further reform SOEs. The mixed-ownership approach introduces private firms as strategic investors in SOEs. These private firms have rich managerial expertise and are more responsive to market demand. The key is to establish a reasonable incentive system and to strengthen oversight. First, under mixed ownership, the incentive mechanism adopted by large private firms can be introduced to better motivate managers. Second, private firms may also be more responsive to market demand and technological trends, which is conducive to the operation and long-term development of firms with mixed ownership. However, in the case of SOEs of the first two categories, it is important to prevent private equity owners from seeking more financial subsidies or monopolies.

Overall, through this gradual, dual-track approach, China achieved "reform without losers" and moved gradually but steadily to a well-functioning market economy. Today, China's private sector—which has been revving up since the global financial crisis—is now serving as the main driver of China's economic growth. The combination of numbers 60/70/80/90 are frequently used to describe the private sector's contribution to the Chinese economy: they contribute 60% of China's GDP, and are responsible for 70% of innovation, 80% of urban employment and provide 90% of incremental jobs.

1.4.3 Policy recommendations to Uzbekistan

According to the World Bank's assessment, achieving Uzbekistan's 2030 ambitions to become an upper-middle-income country by 2030 and to halve poverty, will require Uzbekistan's average annual real GDP growth to be close to 10%. Increasing the pace and quality of job creation will critically depend on a different role for the state in the economy and the reallocation of resources within the economy to more productive and sustainable uses. While the government's reforms aim at reducing the role of the state as a producer and competitor to private enterprises, the state should play more the role of an enabler in the market economy.

Such an enabling role by government should be reflected in job creation through the promotion of labor-intensive industries, SOEs reforms and the development of regional connectivity.

First, for job creation. Based on China's experiences, it is recommended that the Uzbekistan government actively promote labor-intensive industries in accordance with its comparative advantages. The government should liberalize the entry of private enterprises, joint ventures and foreign direct investment in labor-intensive sectors, in which Uzbekistan has comparative advantages, and also proactively facilitate the growth of new industries by setting up enclaves such as Special Economic Zones and export processing zones to overcome the bottleneck of hard and soft infrastructure in their growth.

The government's facilitation ability is an important factor in attracting investors. The government leader's direct involvement in investment promotion will enhance the investors' confidence. Specifically, the government should ensure competitive and effective labor costs; ensure competitive prices for transportation and other production factors; and provide one-stop-shop services to lower transaction costs.

In this process, both central and local level governments are essential in implementing successful investment promotion. For investment promotion to be effective, targeting international buyers simultaneously while attracting manufacturers is necessary as buyers' weight largely in the decision-making. Local firms can benefit and play an important role in the cluster by taking sub-orders from the leading foreign companies, as well as providing services. This arrangement will transfer the technology, management and quality requirements for international markets to local firms and help some of them become outsourcing firms for international buyers in the future. To build up a competitive export-oriented cluster quickly, the government may encourage the local firms to better adopt technology transfer, and better engage with leading international firms. On the other hand, the government may also encourage leading firms to link with local firms by purchasing local inputs, providing training, and distributing orders.

Second, for SOE reforms. It is noted that Uzbekistan had already followed an approach that is similar to China, i.e., privatizing the small and medium SOEs first. From the perspective of new structural economics, we recommend a gradual and dual-track approach to SOEs instead of all-round full privatization of all large SOEs in Uzbekistan. If subsidies are eliminated immediately, many SOEs in the priority sectors would collapse, causing a contraction of GDP, a surge in unemployment, and acute social disorders.

It is therefore advisable to identify the strategic burden and social burden of SOEs and classify existing SOEs into three categories: i) strategic capital-intensive CAD industries; ii) natural monopoly industries that have a major bearing on the national economy; iii) competitive industries that are consistent with Uzbekistan's comparative advantages. For the first category of SOEs, continued government support may apply in the form of financing their R&D projects and procuring their products. For the second category of SOEs, price regulation must be applied by the state. As for the third category of SOEs, as their social burden (i.e., redundant workers and pensions of retired workers) are taken care of by the national social security systems, these SOEs should compete in the market. A mixed-ownership approach by introducing a private strategic investor may be considered to improve these SOEs governance and competitiveness.

Third, for regional connectivity. Improved cross-border transport connections and digital connectivity can provide an anchor for increasing growth and job creation. Uzbekistan is well-placed to be one of the biggest beneficiaries of the BRI. With the largest and youngest labor force in the region and considerable agricultural and manufacturing capacity, the potential for a significant BRI dividend is high for increasing Uzbekistan's exports, attracting FDI, and further GDP growth. In particular, cooperation under the Belt and Road Initiative has been fruitful, and major projects are making steady progress. All four lines of the China–Central Asia natural gas pipeline run through Uzbekistan and are interconnected with Uzbekistan's gas pipeline network. The tunnel on the Angren–Pap railway line, the longest tunnel in Central Asia, has been successfully completed. More transport potential is being unleashed from the China–Kyrgyzstan–Uzbekistan highway and the China–Kazakhstan–Uzbekistan railway. And preparations for the China–Kyrgyzstan–Uzbekistan railway project are well underway.

Even though the COVID-19 pandemic and regional conflict are reshaping global supply chains, the regional integration agenda will remain a key ingredient of development strategies for Uzbekistan. In fact, a common transport infrastructure and digital connectivity continue to make sense as the case for international trade remains strong through differences in comparative advantage, specialization and economies of scale.

Overall, BRI improvements in transport infrastructure are estimated to reduce Uzbek shipment time by almost 15%, the largest reduction among BRI countries. As such, Uzbekistan will be transforming from a land-locked country to a land-linked country for sustainable development.

Notes

1 The Human Development Index (HDI) is a statistic developed and compiled by the United Nations since 1990 to measure various countries' levels of social and economic development. It is composed of four principal areas of interest: mean years of schooling, expected years of schooling, life expectancy at birth, and gross national income (GNI) per capita.

2 The Economic Complexity Index (ECI) measures the relative knowledge intensity of an economy.

3 Launched in 2002, the World Bank's Doing Business project provided objective measures of business regulations and their enforcement. The project looked at domestic small and medium-size companies and measured the rules affecting them throughout their lifecycles. The final report was published in 2020, thereafter the World Bank Group management decided to discontinue the Doing Business Report. However, the Doing Business website continues to be publicly available as an archive of knowledge and data.

4 NSE uses the neoclassical approach to study the determinants and impacts of economic structure and its evolution, which are the nature of modern economic growth, in an economy's development. The main idea of NSE is as follows: economic structures, including the structure of technology and industry, which determines labor productivity, and hard and soft infrastructure, which determines transaction costs, are endogenous to the endowment structure, which is given at any specific time and changeable over time, in an economy. The best way to achieve dynamic growth in an economy is to develop the economy's industries by following the comparative advantage determined by its endowment structure. The economy with such industries and appropriate hard and soft infrastructure will be most competitive, produce the largest surplus, have the highest possible returns to capital and thus savings, ensure the fastest upgrading of the endowment structure and achieve the most rapid industrial upgrading and income growth. In this process, the firms will be viable in an open, competitive market and a developing economy can enjoy the latecomer advantage, have a faster technological innovation and industrial upgrading than high-income economies, converge to high-income countries.

Reference

Ruziev, K. (2021). Uzbekistan's Development Experiment: An Assessment of Karimov's Economic Legacy, *Europe-Asia Studies*, 73:7, 1303–1329, doi:10.1080/09668136.2021.1919602.

2 Economic reforms and macroeconomic developments

Lawrence Dwight[1]

2.1 Overview of Uzbekistan's economy

With a per capita gross domestic product (GDP) of about US$ 2,000, Uzbekistan is classified as a lower-middle-income country. Uzbekistan's population was 36 million in 2022, making it the largest country in Central Asia by population. As a result, Uzbekistan has a sizable domestic market and its economy is relatively diverse. In 2022, agriculture and industry each comprise about a quarter of GDP, construction is close to 10 percent and services (transportation, trade, and other services) is about 40 percent.[2] Harvard's *Atlas of Economic Complexity* ranked Uzbekistan as the 78th most complex of 133 countries in 2020 and noted that Uzbekistan's economy is slightly more complex than expected for its income level.[3]

Despite being doubly landlocked, Uzbekistan has significant trade. In 2019, before the COVID-19 pandemic and Russia's invasion of Ukraine reduced trade, total exports of goods and services exports were 28 percent of GDP and goods and services imports were 44 percent of GDP. Exports are dominated by primary products. In 2019, gold made up a quarter of all exports, and petroleum products (primarily natural gas) made up 14 percent (Figure 2.1). Other significant exports included transportation services, food, and tourism. Uzbekistan's exports are also diversified by destination. Neighboring countries (Afghanistan, Kazakhstan, the Kyrgyz Republic, and Tajikistan) accounted for almost 20 percent of exports with China and Russia each accounting for about 15 percent. Gross remittance inflows from workers abroad provided a significant source of income, averaging about 15 percent of GDP.

Uzbekistan's economy has a sizable informal sector. In 2021, of Uzbekistan's 13.5 million workers, 45 percent were employed in the formal sector (about 15 percent in government, 20 percent in small and medium-sized businesses or as entrepreneurs, 5 percent in state enterprises, and 5 percent in large private companies). About 40 percent of workers were employed in the informal sector and another 15 percent (about 1–2 million) worked abroad, primarily in Russia.

Despite being a low-middle-income country, Uzbekistan has a well-educated population and good social indicators. According to the latest

DOI: 10.4324/9781003473497-2

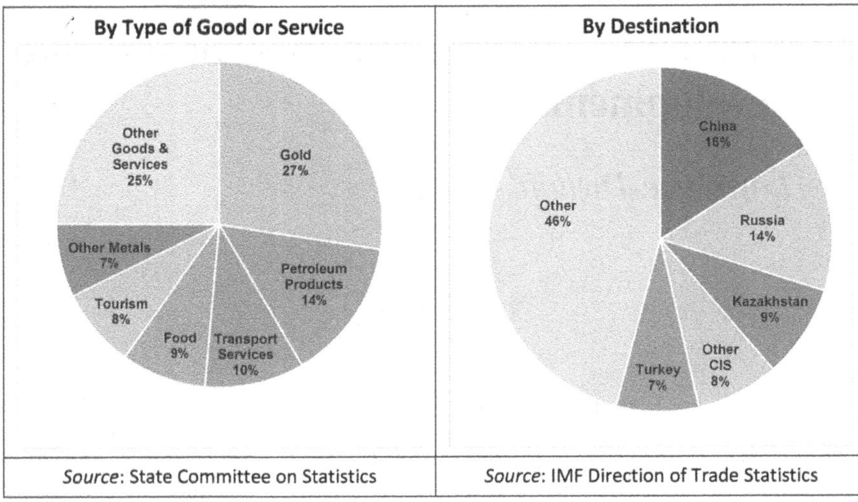

Figure 2.1 Uzbekistan: main exports, 2019
Source: State Committee on Statistics and IMF Direction of Trade Statistics.

World Development Indicators, Uzbekistan has a literacy rate of 100 percent, 95 percent of the population has completed secondary education, and 22 percent of the population has completed some tertiary education.[4] On social indicators, 100 percent of the population has access to electricity and basic sanitation services and 98 percent of the population has access to basic drinking water services. Less than 3 percent of the population was undernourished.

2.2 Economic developments before reforms (2011–2016)

From independence until 2016, government policies emphasized a state-led growth model with heavy intervention in the economy, import substitution, and restrictions on trade and foreign exchange transactions. This model effectively created a dual economy, with preferential access to credit and foreign exchange for state and well-connected businesses. Less connected firms and the informal sector lacked access to these resources.

Nonetheless, prior to reforms Uzbekistan's key economic statistics appeared relatively good (Figure 2.2). From 2011 to 2016, real growth averaged 7 percent per year, while the unemployment rate averaged 5 percent. Consumer inflation, although moderately high at between 10 and 12 percent, was declining. Uzbekistan was running consistent current account surpluses and external debt remained below 25 percent of GDP. Economic policies also appeared to be strong. The government implemented a conservative fiscal policy with the budget in surplus or close to balance. As a result, the government had no need to borrow domestically and no treasury bills or bonds outstanding. Public external debt was also low at less than 10 percent of GDP. Similarly, the Central Bank of Uzbekistan (CBU) implemented a conservative monetary policy. The policy rate was above inflation, resulting in positive real interest rates. Broad money growth was in line with nominal GDP growth in most years, suggesting that monetary policy was not inflationary.

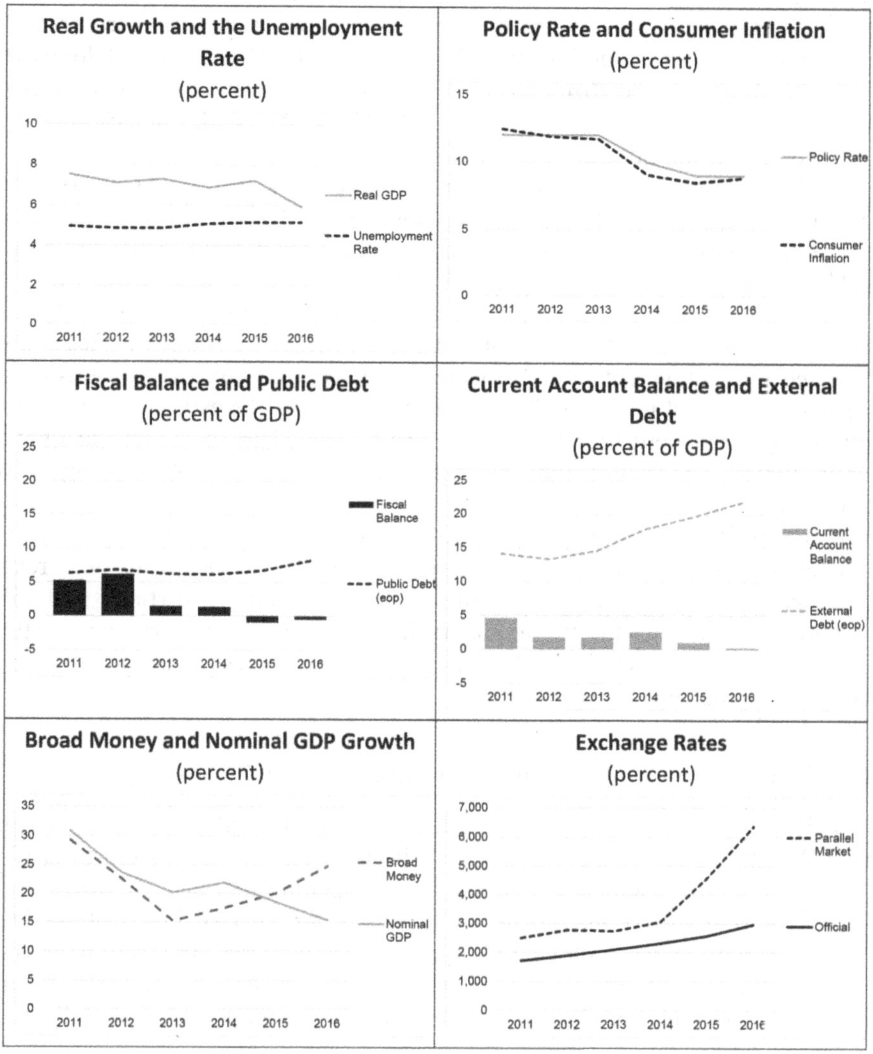

Figure 2.2 Uzbekistan: key economic indicators prior to reforms, 2011–2016
Source: Central Bank of Uzbekistan and Ministry of Finance data and author's calculations.

However, there were indications of imbalances and inefficiencies in the economy. While the current account was in surplus, foreign exchange (FX) was rationed, with the government and state enterprises receiving FX at the more favorable official exchange rate. The premium in the parallel FX market was 45 percent in 2011 but had grown to more than 100 percent by 2016. Similarly, bank credit was rationed. Many loans were being directed to state enterprises for specific purposes at below-market interest rates. For example, state banks made directed loans to the cotton and grain sectors and the Fund for Reconstruction and Development (FRD)[5] made FX loans to finance imports in prioritized industries. In 2016, the growth of broad money accelerated and the exchange rate premium widened, suggesting the development of inflationary pressures.

By 2017, there was consensus that the state-led development model was not efficient and was failing to create enough jobs. Uzbekistan's working-age population had grown by more than 20 percent from 2000–2010, and from 2011 to 2016 growth of employment barely kept pace with the growth of the labor force. Moreover, the reported unemployment rate of 5 percent was likely underestimated. When employment statistics were revised in 2018, the reported unemployment rate rose to over 9 percent (compared with less than 6 percent reported in 2017). The revision also raised the estimate of workers abroad by 60 percent to 2.4 million in 2018 (equivalent to 16 percent of the labor force), suggesting that workers were having trouble finding jobs domestically.

Thus, in 2016 when President Karimov passed away and Shavkat Mirziyoyev became President, Uzbekistan's macroeconomic situation was relatively good, although there were underlying economic distortions and job creation was insufficient. It was dissatisfaction with the performance of the state-led growth model rather than an economic crisis which set the stage for the reforms that began in 2017.

2.3 Economic reforms and developments since 2017

In February 2017, a Presidential Decree announced a "Strategy of Action in Five Priority Areas of Development of the Republic of Uzbekistan in 2017–2021."[6] The five elements included: (i) deepening political reforms and reforming public administration; (ii) ensuring the rule of law and further reforming the judicial and legal systems; (iii) developing and liberalizing the economy; (iv) developing society, including by creating jobs and enhancing social protection; and (v) ensuring security, interethnic and religious harmony, and a mutually beneficial foreign policy.

Regarding development and liberalization of the economy, the Action Strategy laid out an ambitious agenda:

> … aimed at further strengthening macroeconomic stability and maintaining high rates of economic growth, increasing competitiveness,

modernization and intensive development of agriculture, continuing institutional and structural reforms to reduce the presence of the state in the economy, further strengthening the protection of the rights and priority role of private property, stimulating the development of small business and private business entrepreneurship, comprehensive and balanced socio-economic development of regions, districts and cities, active attraction of foreign investment in the sectors of the economy and regions of the country by improving the investment climate.

2.3.1 Exchange rate unification and foreign exchange liberalization (2017)

Prior to 2017, the Central Bank of Uzbekistan described its exchange rate system as a managed float.[7] Given that the som had fluctuated within a 2 percent margin around a trend depreciation against the US dollar, the International Monetary Fund (IMF) classified the *de facto* exchange rate system as crawl-like (Figure 2.3, Panel A). There were also multiple exchange markets and exchange rates. The official rate was available to the government, state enterprises, and entities in priority sectors, while other entities could obtain foreign exchange at the parallel market rate, which was about double the official rate. Uzbekistan also imposed restrictions on access to foreign exchange. Exports were subject to surrender requirements of between 25 and 50 percent, the authorities rationed foreign exchange, and there were significant delays in providing FX for some current account transactions.[8]

In its first major macroeconomic reform, on September 5, 2017, Uzbekistan unified exchange rates and liberalized access to foreign exchange. The official exchange rate rose from 4,210 to 8,100 Uzbekistan som (UZS) per US dollar (USD), close to the parallel market rate, a depreciation of 48 percent (measured as USD obtained per UZS). At the same time, the authorities liberalized firms' and individuals' access to foreign exchange, eliminated surrender requirements, discontinued FX rationing, and reduced delays in access to FX. In June 2018, the government reduced import tariffs, with the average tariff rate falling from 15 to 7.5 percent.

The CBU characterizes the current exchange system as floating, with the exchange rate determined by the supply and demand for foreign exchange on Uzbekistan's currency exchange. However, the CBU also intervenes in the FX market to: (i) smooth exchange rate volatility and (ii) offset injections of domestic currency that arise when it purchases domestically produced gold (the neutrality principle).

Following the September 2017 depreciation, the som appreciated for eight months, likely reflecting prior overshooting of the exchange rate. Since then Uzbekistan's real exchange rate against the US dollar has been relatively stable (Figure 2.3, Panel B) and at the end of 2022 was at the same level as in May 2018. The stable real exchange rate reflected nominal depreciation in line with the inflation differential between Uzbekistan and the United States.

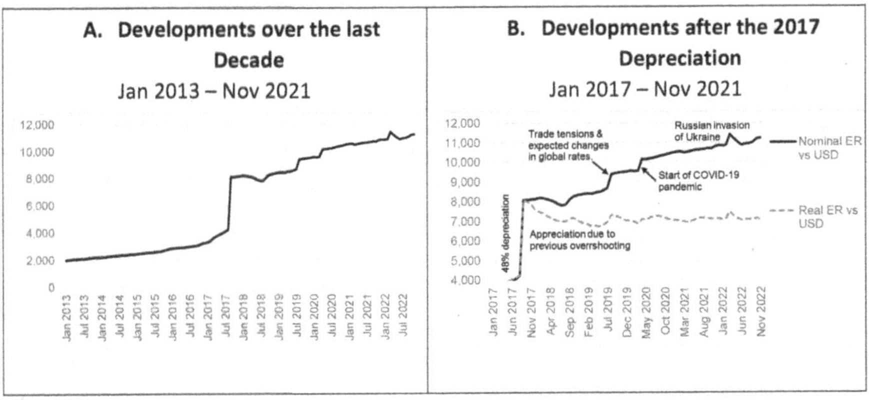

Figure 2.3 Uzbekistan: exchange rate developments (Uzbekistan som per US dollar)
Source: Central Bank of Uzbekistan data and author's calculations.

In particular, the nominal exchange rate depreciated at a rate of about 4 percent per year, with additional step depreciations of 9 percent between July and August 2019 (due to global trade tensions and expected changes in US interest rates) and 6 percent in April 2020 (due to the onset of the COVID-19 pandemic). The currency depreciated 5 percent at the start of Russia's invasion of Ukraine but returned to its pre-invasion trend over subsequent months.

The unification of exchange rates and FX liberalization had a substantial impact on Uzbekistan's external position. Prior to liberalization, Uzbekistan's current account was consistently in surplus ranging from +0.2 to +4.6 percent of GDP (Figure 2.4). The exchange rate depreciation and liberalization of trade and access to foreign exchange dramatically changed the structure of the current account. The value of exports of goods and services had fallen by a quarter in US dollar terms from 2011 to 2016. After the reforms, they increased by 60 percent from 2016 to 2019.[9] Similarly, the value of imports of goods and services rose 80 percent and remittances from Uzbekistan citizens abroad rose 50 percent. The overall result was that the current account balance fell from a slight surplus in 2016 to a deficit of 5.5 percent of GDP in 2019. It is usual for developing and transition economies to run trade deficits as it allows them to import capital goods which generate higher rates of return on domestic investment.

Uzbekistan's experience of imports rising faster than exports is contrary to what one would expect following a large depreciation. The rising cost of imports in som and the falling cost of exports in US dollars would be expected to reduce imports and increase exports over time. While the increase in exports materialized, it was more than offset by the increase in imports. This suggests that the liberalization of access to foreign exchange and the reduction of import tariff rates had a larger impact than the exchange rate depreciation. The surge in remittances after 2017 suggests that

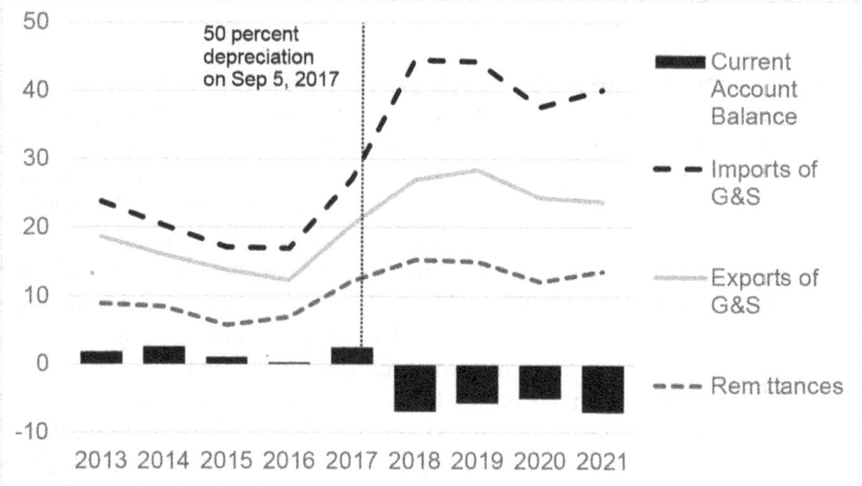

Figure 2.4 Uzbekistan: current account developments, 2013–2021 (percent of GDP)
Source: Central Bank of Uzbekistan data and author's calculations.

the lifting of foreign exchange restrictions reduced disincentives to repatriate foreign exchange and encouraged an increase in remittances.

2.3.2 Fiscal reforms and fiscal policy

Since 2017, Uzbekistan has undertaken fiscal reforms in two principal areas: (i) continuous administrative and institutional reforms focused on the budget, tax administration, and debt management and (ii) a major reform of the tax system in 2019–2020.

i **Administrative and Institutional Reforms**: Since 2017 Uzbekistan has carried out several major institutional reforms with technical assistance from international financial institutions and bilateral partners.

- **Budget**: Since 2017, the coverage of the general government budget has gradually expanded. Initially, the budget only covered the central state budget and extra-budgetary funds (of which the pension fund is the primary component). Later, coverage was expanded to include the Fund for Reconstruction and Development and projects financed by external borrowing. And in 2022, the government started to report off-budget accounts of ministries and agencies.[10] In 2019, annual budgets, which were previously issued by government decree, became subject to parliamentary debate and approval. From 2017–2022, the government also made progress in implementing a public financial management strategy, boosting government transparency, and improving the assessment of fiscal risks.

- **Tax administration**: To improve operations, the State Tax Committee (STC) reorganized along functional lines and strengthened the governance of local offices. It stepped up taxpayer education and overhauled the audit process to reduce abuses. The STC established a large taxpayer office in 2019, introduced comprehensive digitization, and moved to a risk-based approach to tax compliance.
- **Debt management**: In 2018, the Ministry of Finance established a Debt Management Office. The Office has improved debt management with the implementation of the UN's Debt Management and Analysis System, a system for recording and tracking public debt. The government also began to include limits on the contracting of public and publicly guaranteed external debt in the annual budget to ensure public debt sustainability. This limit has recently been expanded to include domestic debt. The government is now classifying requests for public debt guarantees according to risk, with larger guarantees requiring higher levels of approval. In 2022, parliament passed a debt law that limits PPG debt to 60 percent of GDP and aims to limit contingent liabilities from state enterprises.
- In 2018, the government began issuing domestic treasury bills and bonds to provide a new source of financing, develop the local debt market, and provide an interest rate benchmark for domestic borrowing. However, the outstanding treasury stock has remained small (about 0.5 percent of GDP at the end of 2021). The government also began issuing five and ten-year sovereign bonds in US dollars in 2019 and three and five-year sovereign bonds in som in 2020. Outstanding sovereign bonds amounted to about 4 percent of GDP at the end of 2021.

ii **2019–2020 Tax Reform**: The goal of the reform was to simplify the tax system and reduce the tax burden on workers and private businesses while maintaining revenues by broadening the tax base. Key reforms included:

- Increasing the *corporate tax rate* from 14 to 15 percent, while lowering the revenue threshold. This increased the number of firms subject to the tax by about five times.
- Consolidating the *personal income tax* by reducing three tiers to one, resulting in an effective increase in the tax rate from 10 to 12 percent.
- Eliminating the *single social tax* levied on enterprise turnover which was used to fund education, health, and infrastructure projects and reducing workers' contributions to the *pension* fund. After the reforms, general revenues were used to fund these programs.

- Reducing the *value-added tax* (VAT) rate from 20 to 15 percent, while broadening the tax base by reducing the revenue threshold.[11] This increased the number of firms subject to the VAT by three and a half times.

Subsequent tax reforms have focused on leveling the playing field and further broadening the tax base, including by eliminating privileges and exemptions. Uzbekistan has substantial reserves of gold, copper, natural gas, and oil and would like to attract additional investment in the mining and petroleum sectors. In 2021, the government introduced a new tax regime for mining companies. It equalized taxes for private and state enterprises, lowered subsoil tax (royalty) rates, and introduced a special rent tax.

Developments and Impact

Evaluating the impact of fiscal reforms on subsequent outcomes is difficult due to other significant events that occurred during 2017–2022. In addition to the tax reform implemented in 2019–2020, revenues were affected by the FX liberalization in 2017 and the COVID-19 pandemic in 2020–2021.

The *2017 exchange rate depreciation and FX liberalization* boosted revenues by 4 percentage points of GDP in 2018 (Figure 2.5, Panel A). This was largely due to the increase in the domestic currency value of gold exports and goods imports. While the volume of gold exports and the USD price of gold were relatively unchanged, the September 2017 depreciation caused the average exchange rate (UZS/USD) to rise 75 percent in 2017 and 55 percent in 2018 (Figure 2.5, Panel B). As a result, the value of gold exports in som increased by about the same amount. The increased profits of mining companies showed up the following year (2018) in the mining tax and in other revenues, where dividends to the government are reported. The FX liberalization also contributed to a surge in imports, which rose almost 50 percent in dollar terms and 130 percent in som terms. As about 40 percent of VAT revenues are collected from imported goods, this resulted in a surge in VAT

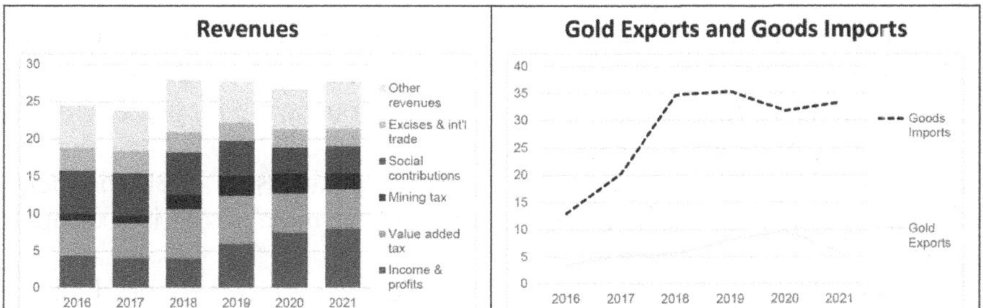

Figure 2.5 Uzbekistan: revenue performance, 2016–2021 (percent of GDP)
Source: Ministry of Finance and data and author's calculations.

revenues in 2018.[12] Excises and international taxes were relatively unchanged as excises were levied per unit rather than per value and the FX reform was accompanied by a reduction in import tariffs.

The *2019–2020 tax reform* was largely revenue neutral. The elimination of the single social tax and reduction in the pension contribution lowered social contributions, while other revenues also dropped. This was largely offset by increases in corporate income taxes, as the lower threshold dramatically expanded the number of firms subject to the tax, and mining taxes as gold exports denominated in som rose 85 percent. Revenues from VAT were largely unchanged as the reduction in the tax rate was offset by the expansion of the tax base. Thus, the 2019 tax reform largely achieved its purpose by reducing tax rates on labor (social contributions) and private enterprises (VAT and profits tax rates) while obtaining more revenues from the expansion of the tax base (profits tax and VAT).

The *COVID-19 pandemic* caused overall revenues to fall by one percent of GDP in 2020 but these losses were reversed in 2021. With slower global growth and trade, Uzbekistan's goods imports fell by 3.5 of GDP in 2020. The decline in imports as well as domestic spending caused VAT revenues to fall. However, the pandemic also led to a 27 percent increase in the USD price of gold, helping to boost corporate income taxes. During the pandemic, the government implemented its previously planned structural increase in social assistance. The number of households receiving assistance more than doubled from 0.6 million in 2019 to more than 2 million in 2022 and social assistance spending increased by almost 2 percent of GDP.

2.3.3 Monetary and financial reforms

Inflation Targeting. Prior to reforms, the Central Bank of Uzbekistan's monetary framework focused on the stability of the exchange rate, with targets for broad money as the main intermediate target. Following the 2017 exchange rate and FX reforms, monetary policy shifted to focus on price stability. The CBU planned for a gradual transition to inflation targeting, taking account of the impact of the real exchange rate and reserve money on consumer inflation.[13]

Central Bank Law. In October 2019, Uzbekistan enacted a new Central Bank Law which formalized Uzbekistan's transition to an inflation targeting regime. It set price stability as the objective of monetary policy, granted the CBU operational independence, and prohibited the CBU from financing the government. The law also required the external audits of CBU financial statements and the appointment of two independent members to its executive board.

Presidential Decree. A November 2019 a Presidential decree elaborated on the new regime by directing the CBU to target a permanent reduction in inflation to 5 percent by 2023.[14] The decree also called for the coordination of monetary, fiscal, and antimonopoly policies; liberalization of regulated prices; and deepening of financial intermediation. Commercial banks could set interest rates themselves and interest rates on directed loans were required to be no lower than the CBU refinancing rate. The latter measure reduced the implicit subsidy on preferential loans and improved the transmission of monetary policy by tying the interest rate on such loans to the CBU policy rate.

Monetary Operations. With these changes, the CBU policy rate became the main instrument of monetary policy. The CBU also established an overnight deposit facility, introduced a new framework for open market operations, and set a band for the interbank interest rate. The CBU has also upgraded its ability to model and forecast inflation.

Structural Factors. While most prices had been liberalized following Uzbekistan's independence in 1992, in 2017 approximately 15 percent of the goods in the consumer price index (CPI) were still subject to *price controls.* From 2017–2022, the government lifted most remaining controls on food prices (about 5 percent of the CPI), including bread and wheat. The government also lifted price controls on gasoline and other petroleum products. In 2019, the government increased prices for natural gas and electricity although some prices, particularly for households, remained below cost recovery levels. While not formalized, government wages were informally linked to past inflation, resulting in some momentum in prices. In addition, trend depreciation of the exchange rate resulted in inertia in imported goods prices that are included in consumer prices.

Financial Reforms. Uzbekistan's financial system is dominated by state banks. As of early 2021, Uzbekistan had more than 30 banks, of which 11 were state banks holding 82 percent of banking system assets. In November 2019, Uzbekistan enacted a new Banking Law.[15] The law sets requirements for the establishment, operation, and governance of banks and gives banks independence in making decisions on financial transactions. The law also gives the CBU the power to regulate and supervise banks. A May 2020 Presidential decree set the strategy for reform of the banking system.[16] It called for improving efficiency, ensuring financial stability, reducing the state's share, and improving the quality of financial services. Of note, the strategy called for improving corporate governance, privatizing several state banks, increasing non-state banks' share of bank assets from 15 to 60 percent, and attracting at least three strategic foreign investors by 2025.

Developments and impact

The transition to inflation targeting along with generally tight monetary policy has coincided with a gradual reduction in inflation. Consumer inflation peaked at 20 percent three months after the 2017 depreciation of the exchange rate and had fallen to 14 percent by the end of 2018. A first round of energy price increases and expansion of the VAT in 2019 raised inflation to 15 percent at year-end despite a tight monetary policy. During the

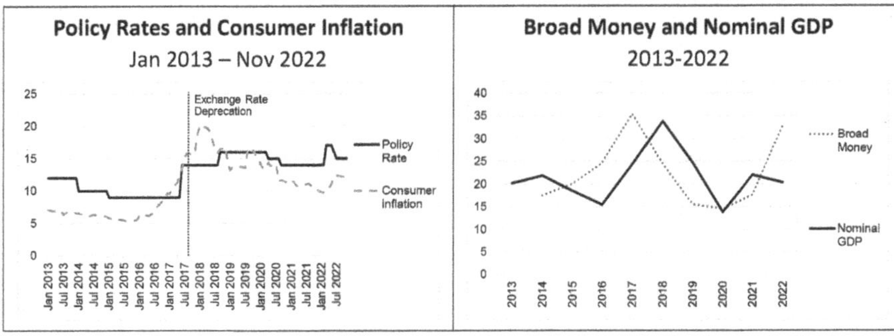

Figure 2.6 Uzbekistan: monetary policy, inflation, and growth (percent change over a year earlier)

Source: Central Bank and State Committee on Statistics data and author's calculations.

COVID-19 crisis, a fall in demand and a +3 percent real policy rate led to a decline in consumer inflation to 11 percent at the end of 2020 and 10 percent at the end of 2021. In 2022, as supply shortages and global inflation spilled into Uzbekistan, inflation rose above 12 percent at year-end.

Regarding financial reforms, the 2019 Bank Law and 2020 Presidential Decree promoted progress in corporate governance, including by appointing independent board members. Ipoteka Bank was privatized in 2022, but financial market disruptions caused the privatization it be put on hold. Overall, the complexity of financial sector reforms has caused them to take longer than initially expected.

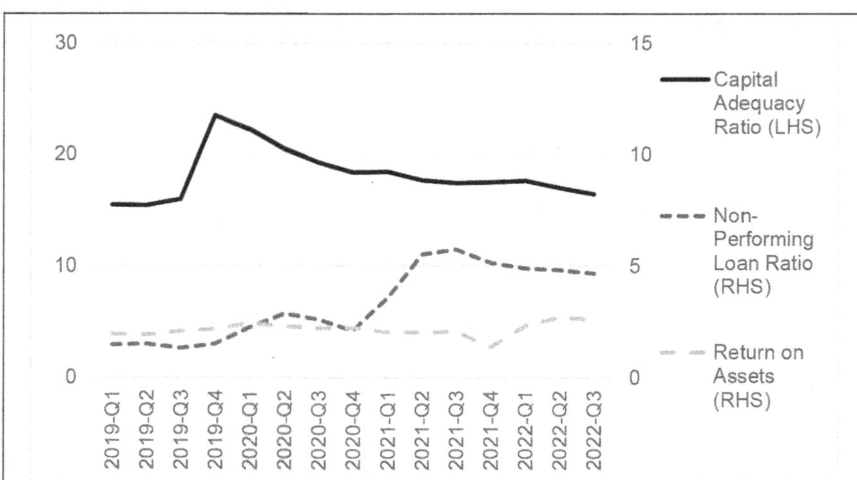

Figure 2.7 Uzbekistan: selected financial soundness indicators, 2019 Q1–2022 Q3 (percent)

Source: Central Bank of Uzbekistan.

Banks' financial soundness indicators suggest that Uzbekistan's banks are relatively healthy (Figure 2.7). The banking system's capital adequacy ratio (CAR) was 16 percent in the third quarter of 2022 above standard benchmarks. The non-performing loan (NPL) ratio was 4.6 percent. However, the CAR has declined and the NPL ratio has increased since late 2019 due to the pandemic.

2.3.4 Accounting and statistics

Perhaps less exciting than other reforms, but no less important, have been improvements to statistics and accounting standards. Accurate information is crucial for good policymaking, to evaluate reforms, and to improve corporate governance. At the beginning of reforms, the State Committee on Statistics (SCS) received a mandate to improve economic statistics and bring them up to international standards.[17] In 2018, Uzbekistan implemented the IMF's Enhanced General Data Dissemination Standard, an international standard for providing information on the coverage, timeliness, quality, access, and integrity of data.[18] It also began providing public access to official statistics through its National Summary Data Page (NSDP).[19] In 2019, the government approved a National Strategy for the Development of Statistics 2020–2025.[20]

Along with these reforms to the framework for statistics, significant improvements have been made in sectoral statistics. For example, the CBU has improved Uzbekistan's *balance of payments* statistics and started reporting Uzbekistan's *international investment position* and *gross external debt*. It has improved *monetary statistics* and is reporting core *financial soundness indicators*. The MOF has greatly improved the coverage of *government finance statistics* and reporting of *public sector debt*. The SCS has improved the compilation of price indices including the *consumer price index, producer price index, residential property price index*, and *export and import price indices*. Finally, the SCS has made significant improvements to national accounts, including a revision which raised estimates of the size of the agriculture sector and raised estimated GDP by approximately 25 percent.

Another important step has been moving Uzbekistan's firms to International Financial Reporting Standards (IFRS). In 2020, the government mandated that all large enterprises, including state enterprises, prepare financial statements based on IFRS starting in 2021.[21] Improved financial accounts allow the government to make better decisions about the management, restructuring, and privatization of state enterprises. They also provide additional information to foreign investors in a familiar format, thereby promoting foreign investment.

2.4 Recent challenges

2.4.1 2020–2021: the COVID-19 pandemic

The COVID-19 pandemic resulted in a large shock to Uzbekistan's economy. The pandemic slowed global growth, disrupted trade, and lowered

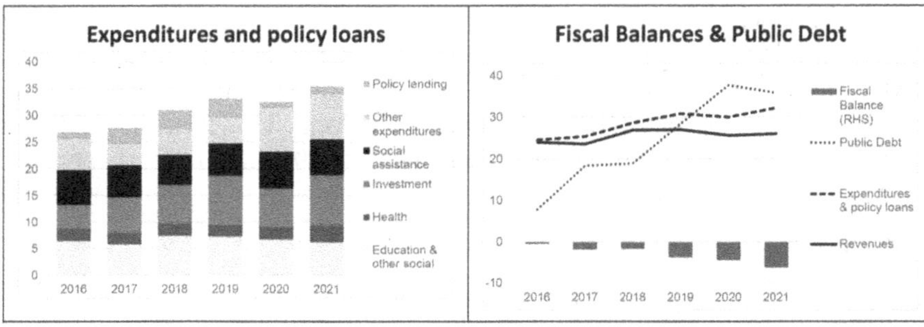

Figure 2.8 Uzbekistan: expenditures, fiscal balances, and debt, 2016–2021 (percent of GDP)
Source: Ministry of Finance data and author's calculations.

commodity prices. In Uzbekistan, the pandemic led to a 15 percent reduction in both exports and imports in 2020 in US dollar terms. Travel restrictions and fewer job opportunities resulted in a 30 percent drop in the number of workers abroad and an 8 percent decline in remittance inflows. Domestically, these external shocks and restrictions to deal with the pandemic reduced economic activity, particularly in mining, travel and accommodation, and transportation.

The authorities responded with a large stimulus package. As monetary policy was focused on achieving the inflation target, the primary tool was fiscal policy. In 2020 and 2021, the government provided a fiscal stimulus of about 5 percent of GDP (Table 2.1). This included an increase in health spending for treatment and public health measures, additional social assistance to support vulnerable families, while tax breaks and additional investment helped support the economy. The additional expenditures were financed

Table 2.1 Uzbekistan: 2020–2021 Fiscal Stimulus in Response to the COVID-19 Crisis (percent of GDP)

Policy Stimulus	5.1
Tax Relief	0.7
Expenditures	4.4
Economy and investment	4.0
Health	1.2
Education	0.7
Social safety net	0.6
Other expenditures and policy lending	–2.0
Non-Policy Effects	**–3.0**
Higher-than-expected revenues	–3.0
Total Fiscal Stimulus	**2.1**

Source: Ministry of Finance data and author's calculations.

in part by higher-than-expected revenues and reductions in other expenditures. As a result, Uzbekistan's overall fiscal deficit increased from 3.8 percent of GDP in 2019 to 6.2 percent of GDP in 2021. The government began fiscal consolidation in 2022 with the aim of reducing the deficit to 3 percent of GDP in the medium term. This should result in public debt stabilizing at a moderate level of about 40 percent of GDP (Figure 2.8).

The stimulus succeeded in supporting the economy. Uzbekistan maintained positive growth of almost 2 percent in 2020 (while many other countries contracted) and growth rebounded to 7.4 percent in 2021. Trade and remittances increased by about 20 percent in 2021. Notwithstanding the increase in the fiscal deficit, public debt stabilized at about 36 percent of GDP.

2.4.2 2022: Invasion of Ukraine and higher global inflation and interest rates

Russia's invasion of Ukraine was expected to have a significant negative impact on Uzbekistan and other Central Asia Countries in 2022. Before the invasion, Russia constituted about 20 percent of imports and 12 percent of exports, 1–2 million Uzbekistan citizens worked in Russia each year, Russian investors provided substantial financing to firms in Uzbekistan, and remittances inflows (primarily from Russia) provided income of about 15 percent of GDP. Previous experience also suggested a substantial negative impact. Following Russia's occupation of Crimea and the implementation of Western sanctions against Russia in 2014, Uzbekistan's overall trade and remittance inflows fell by 10 and 20 percent, respectively, in dollar terms. Similarly, global inflation and supply constraints had the potential to cause spillovers increasing inflation in Uzbekistan. And the increase in global interest rates made foreign borrowing more expensive.

However, as of the end of 2022, the impact of these shocks has been limited. Uzbekistan's exchange rate depreciated 5 percent between February and March 2022 when the invasion began but appreciated to its previous trend between April and June 2022. The number of workers in Russia remained high. And rather than falling, remittances inflows were two and a half times higher in the second and third quarters of 2022 compared with a year earlier. Real GDP growth, at 5.7 percent, was in line with pre-COVID-19 growth rates.[22]

Increases in global food and commodity prices have contributed to higher inflation. At the end of 2022, consumer price inflation had risen to over 12 percent (up from about 10 percent at the end of 2021) and food inflation had accelerated to about 16 percent. However, the CBU raised the policy rate by 3 percentage points to 17 percent in March 2022, then gradually lowered it to 15 percent during 2022. This should help lower future inflation. The increase in global interest rates made external borrowing more expensive. The yield to maturity on Uzbekistan's 2029 USD sovereign bond rose to 8.5 percent by late 2022, compared with 4.5 percent at the end of 2021. Given the significant increase in interest rates, the government did not issue a USD sovereign bond as it had in previous years. Nonetheless, financing from international financial institutions made up for the shortfall.[23]

2.5 Economic outlook and the reform agenda

Since reforms started in 2017, Uzbekistan's economic performance has been strong. Notwithstanding shocks from the COVID-19 pandemic, Russia's invasion of Ukraine, and an increase in global inflation and interest rates, Uzbekistan was able to achieve average real growth of 5.5 percent from 2018 to 2022. The government has been able to reduce fiscal deficits and public debt is stabilizing at moderate levels. Similarly, the CBU has transitioned to inflation targeting and reacted quickly to economic shocks by adjusting its policy rate. As a result, inflation fell from a high of 20 percent following the 2017 depreciation to 12 percent at the end of 2022.

The good macroeconomic performance has been due in part to the major economic reforms implemented during this period. Key reforms have included unifying the exchange rate and liberalizing trade and access to foreign exchange; reforming the tax system to reduce the burden on private enterprises and workers while maintaining revenues; transitioning to inflation targeting and making the CBU more independent; implementing government administrative and institutional reforms; and significantly improving economic statistics.

The authorities should continue sound macroeconomic policies and reform economic institutions and administration. On fiscal policy, this includes further improving the budget process, fiscal risk assessment and reporting (particularly arising from state enterprises and public–private partnerships), management of public investment, tax administration, and adjustments to tax policy. On monetary policy, the CBU can further strengthen governance, communication, and transparency. On financial sector policies, the CBU can boost risk-based supervision and macro-prudential policies. Finally, on statistics additional work can be done to estimate the size of the informal economy and subscribe to the IMF's Special Dissemination Standards.

With good progress on macroeconomic reforms, future efforts can focus on *structural reforms*. The structural agenda remains substantial and is, in some ways, more difficult than macroeconomic reforms as structural reforms are more complex and take longer to implement. This agenda could include:

- Completing *price liberalization*, particularly of energy prices. While energy prices for businesses have been raised substantially, electricity and natural gas prices for households remain low. Higher energy prices would encourage conservation, better use of resources, and help Uzbekistan tackle the challenges of climate change. They would also avoid a drain on budget resources that could be used more productively elsewhere.

- Continuing *reform of state enterprises*, including state banks. Good progress has been made in improving the governance of state enterprises. Further restructuring, including privatization as appropriate, would help to make these enterprises more efficient and create jobs.
- Further *sectoral reforms*. Already, reforms in the agricultural sector, which accounts for a quarter of GDP, are yielding results. For example, Uzbekistan has moved away from labor and water-intensive cotton farming toward higher value-added textile and horticultural production.
- Progress on *accession to the World Trade Organization* (WTO). Accession to the WTO would provide easier access to global markets, allow Uzbekistan to benefit from comparative advantage, boost economic diversification, and promote higher product standards.
- Achieving the *Sustainable Development Goals* (SDGs). In 2018, Uzbekistan adopted 125 SDG-related targets focused on improving job growth, resilience to climate change, governance, and access to education, health, and social services. Prior to the pandemic, the IMF estimated that an additional 8 percent of GDP would be needed to achieve the SDGs by 2030.

Notes

1 Senior Economist, International Monetary Fund. The views expressed in this chapter are those of the author and do not necessarily represent the views of the IMF, its Executive Board, or IMF management.

2 Net taxes on products made up the remaining share of GDP.

3 See Uzbekistan's page on the *Atlas for Economic Complexity* website for more details.

4 See the World Bank's *World Development Indicators.*

5 The FRD functions like a combination of a development bank and a sovereign wealth fund. Its FX assets are deposited in the CBU and have been used to provide capital to state banks and policy loans to state enterprises. In the past, the FRD accumulated FX assets by receiving part of the proceeds from government gold sales. Currently, new FRD loans and investments are financed from returns on previous loans and investments.

6 See Presidential Decree UP-4947, "On the Action Strategy for Further Development of the Republic of Uzbekistan." Presidential Decrees and other legislation are available on LexUZ online.

7 Descriptions of Uzbekistan's exchange system can be found in the IMF's Annual Report on Exchange Arrangements and Exchange Arrangements (AREAER).

8 See IMF, Republic of Uzbekistan: 2018 Article IV Consultation, Informational Annex, p. 3 for details.

9 The year 2019 is used to evaluate impact of reforms on exports and imports as the COVID-19 pandemic struck in 2020 and lowered trade across the world. The impact of the COVID-19 pandemic is discussed in more detail below.

10 In 2017, at the beginning of reforms, expenditures on the state budget amounted to 15.5 percent of GDP and extrabudgetary funds to 6.5 percent of GDP. FRD lending and investments were 3 percent of GDP and projects financed by external borrowing were 0.5 percent of GDP. Off-budget accounts of ministries and agencies were not reported in 2017 but were estimated at 1.5 percent of GDP in 2022.

11 The government further reduced the VAT rate to 12 percent in 2023.
12 Specifically, in 2018 VAT rose by 1.9 percent of GDP, other revenues by 1.6 percent of GDP, and mining taxes by 0.9 percent of GDP.
13 For additional details on the transition see: Moayad Al Rasasi and Ezequiel Cabezon, Uzbekistan: Transition to Inflation Targeting. IMF Working Paper 22/229.
14 See Presidential Decree UP-5877, "Improving Monetary Policy with a Phased Transition to an Inflation Targeting Regime."
15 See ZRU-580, Law on Banks and Banking.
16 See Presidential Decree UP-5992, "Strategy for Reforming the Banking system of the Republic of Uzbekistan for 2020–2025."
17 See Presidential Decree PP-3165, "Measures to Improve the Activities of the State Committee of Statistics" (July 31, 2017).
18 See Uzbekistan Implements the IMF's Enhanced General Data Dissemination System (May 3, 2018).
19 See Uzbekistan's National Summary Data Page. More details can be found in SCS press releases available on its website. The IMF updates recent progress in the statistical annexes of IMF Article IV Staff Reports (see footnote 5).
20 See the National Strategy for the Development of Statistics, 2020–2025 (December 2019) and Presidential Decree PD-4796 "Measures to Further Improve and Develop the National Statistical System of the Republic of Uzbekistan" (August 3, 2020).
21 See Presidential Decree PP-4611, "Additional Measures for the Transition to International Financial Reporting Standards" (February 24, 2020).
22 For further discussion see IMF, Republic of Uzbekistan, Staff Report for the 2022 Article IV Consultation. Other IMF staff reports can be found in the documents section of the IMF country page for Uzbekistan.
23 For example, the World Bank provided a development policy loan of US$950 million in 2022 compared with a loan of US$400 million in 2021. The loans are provided with a mix of market based and concessional interest rates with long maturities (30 years).

3 Healthcare reforms and achievements

Iroda Akhmedova, Charles Becker and Michelle Schultze

3.1 Overview

More than three decades have passed since the USSR dissolved and Uzbekistan became an independent country. The changes have been momentous: in many respects, today's Uzbekistan hardly resembles its Soviet predecessor. A myriad of policies has been introduced and conditions have changed. Many have been successful, and some have been astonishingly successful; others have helped little.

This chapter focuses on healthcare policies and reforms, and their implementation and results. We begin with a discussion of conditions at the time of independence, followed by a presentation of major policy initiatives. We then turn to a discussion of varying patterns within Uzbekistan. To get a sense of relative achievements, we use data from nearby districts in Kazakhstan to create a "synthetic Uzbekistan" – or, more accurately, comparators for the Tashkent, Navoi, Jizzakh, and Karakalpakstan provinces. A concluding section discusses the challenges ahead.

A broad sense of Uzbekistan's health achievements and challenges can be seen by examining crude indicators from 1990 to 2019 – that is, from the late Soviet era through to the last pre-COVID-19 year. The World Bank database (www.data.worldbank.org) makes it possible to compare Uzbekistan with former Soviet countries, including Belarus, Kazakhstan, Kyrgyz Republic, and Russia, as well as successful developers such as China and Turkey. This exercise is not without problems: the quality of statistical agencies varies across countries and over time, as in many countries does the definition of a live birth and hence infant mortality (Anthopolos and Becker, 2010). Nonetheless, it points to several key features that invite more detailed analysis in the pages that follow.

Notably,

- The Uzbekistan 2019 infant mortality rate was only 22% of its 1990 value, a decline comparable to the 80% fall in the six comparator nations listed above.
- Uzbekistan did not experience the precipitous 1990–1995 decline in male life expectancy (by six years in Kazakhstan and Russia; by three years in

DOI: 10.4324/9781003473497-3

Belarus and Kyrgyzstan) accompanying the collapse of the USSR, though male life expectancy did stagnate between 1990 and 2000.

- Male life expectancy in Uzbekistan rose by an astonishing six years between 2000 and 2019, when it reached 70 years (an increase from 63 years in 1990). Only Turkey, where male life expectancy rose from 61 years (1990) to 66 (2000) to 75 (2019) consistently outperformed Uzbekistan on this measure.
- Female life expectancy in Uzbekistan enjoyed a substantial but smaller post-transition jump, rising from 70 (2000) to 74 (2019) years. The five-year increase over the entire period is less than in China (+8 years) or Turkey (+13 years). Put differently, while in 2019 male life expectancy in Uzbekistan equaled the unweighted average of the six comparator countries (and was slightly lower in 1990), life expectancy for women was 4.3 years lower (an increased deficit from 3.5 years in 1990).

In short, it is impossible not to be impressed by Uzbekistan's achievements in reducing infant health risks and in improving life expectancy for men. However, healthcare gains for women have lagged slightly, both relative to Uzbekistani men and to international comparators. In the following pages, we seek possible explanations for these patterns.

It is important to emphasize that relative neglect of women's health is not the likeliest explanation for these patterns. Indeed, given the substantial decline in infant mortality and steady declines in maternal mortality, and completed secondary schooling ratios that are essentially the same for boys and girls, gender neglect is not apparent – though it is worth noting that while maternal mortality declined by one-third in Uzbekistan between 2000 and 2017, it fell by 70% in Russia and by 84% in Kazakhstan. However, we suspect that rapid healthy lifestyle improvements in the male population may be particularly important as a source of gender health improvement differences. Specifically, it is worth noting that alcohol consumption is lower in Uzbekistan than in Russia, China, and in other Central Asian countries.

3.2 Reform measures and health sector investments, 2010–2022

After the installation of a new government led by Shavkat Mirziyoyev, several major economic and social reforms were undertaken to further sustainable development and to improve Uzbekistan's healthcare system. In February 2017, President Mirziyoyev signed a decree "On the Development Strategy of Uzbekistan" approving Action Strategies for five priority areas within the overall national 2017–2022 development strategy. Among the top priorities was the public healthcare system, especially primary healthcare, medical assistance to vulnerable people, and emergency medical services. These objectives are aimed at developing both quality and accessibility, thereby improving healthcare indicators.

This initial directive was followed in December 2018 by Presidential Decree №5590 "On Comprehensive Measures to Radically Improve the Healthcare System of the Republic of Uzbekistan," adopted in accordance with implementation 2017–2022 Development Strategy. This decree also approved an underlying concept paper and program implementation guide, which served as the core legislative base. The following areas were designated as the most critical directions:

- Improving medical service quality by clarifying responsibilities of and protections for medical personnel, as well as protecting patients' rights;
- Improving the medical sector funding system, determining the amount of state-guaranteed free medical care, introducing a per-treatment reimbursement system for clinics, and introducing a new funding mechanism for individuals along with the gradual introduction of mandatory medical insurance;
- Formation of a "cluster" model and modern healthcare management system; introducing best practices for management and quality control of the healthcare system based on global standards; accrediting pharmaceutical and medical institutions; and licensing all medical and pharmaceutical activities;
- Increasing the quality, popularity, and effectiveness of medical care, as well as developing a medical standardization system. Concurrently, moves were made to strengthen preventive care and encourage healthy lifestyles. Disease prevention was also to be addressed by introducing cutting-edge methods of diagnosis and treatment and creating effective models of patronage services and dispensaries;
- Developing the private healthcare system and public-private partnership; improving the competitive environment; encouraging "medical tourism" (in essence, travel abroad for advanced healthcare); and creating favorable conditions to attract more private health sector investment;
- Development of the pharmaceutical industry; improving drug pricing policies; expansion of varieties and volumes of drugs as well as medical equipment and products;
- Developing an effective system of education, training and professional development of medical personnel, including accreditation of medical scientific and educational institutions in accordance with international standards by introducing modern medical educational programs, methods and techniques;
- Developing genetic testing, emergency and specialized medical care for women and children by introducing modern screening programs; improving the maternal and child protection system by creating "Mother and Child" regional multidisciplinary medical complexes and institutions;
- Implementing an electronic healthcare system by creating integrated information systems and databases based on uniform national standards.

Table 3.1 Uzbekistan: Major Health Reforms and Policy Initiatives Since 2017

Major national-level reforms and policy documents	• Presidential Decree №5590 "On Comprehensive Measures to Fundamentally Improve the Healthcare System of the Republic of Uzbekistan," December 2018; • "Concept for the Development of the Healthcare System of the Republic of Uzbekistan" for 2019–2025, December 2018; • Resolution of the President of the Republic of Uzbekistan №4668 "On Additional Measures for the Development of the Folk Medicine in the Republic of Uzbekistan," April 2020; • Resolution of the President of the Republic of Uzbekistan №5124 "On Additional Measures for the Comprehensive Development of the Sphere of Health Care," May 2021.
Maternal and child health reforms and initiatives	• Resolution of the President of the Republic of Uzbekistan №3440 "On the State Program for the Early Detection of Congenital and Hereditary Diseases in Children for the Period 2018–2022," December 2017; • Resolution of the President of the Republic of Uzbekistan №4513 "On Improving the Quality and Further Expanding the Coverage of Medical Care Provided to Women of Reproductive Age, Pregnant Women and Children," November 2019.
Major reform policies on medical personnel training	• Resolution of the President of the Republic of Uzbekistan №4666 "On Measures to Implement a Completely New System of Training and Continuous Professional Development of Staff in the Health Sphere," April 2020; • Decree of the President of the Republic of Uzbekistan №6221 "On the Consistent Continuation of the Reforms Implemented in Health Care System and the Creation of the Necessary Conditions for Increasing the Capacity of the Medical Workers," May 2021.
Major public health reforms and initiatives	• Resolution of the President of the Republic of Uzbekistan №3071 "On Measures for Further Development of Specialized Medical Care to the Population of the Republic of Uzbekistan," June 2017; • Resolution of the President of the Republic of Uzbekistan №3493 "On Measures to Further Improve the System to Counter the Spread of the Disease Caused by the Human Immunodeficiency Virus in the Republic of Uzbekistan," January 2018; • Resolution of the President of the Republic of Uzbekistan №3494 "On Measures for the Accelerated Improvement of the System of Emergency Care," January 2018; • Resolution of the President of the Republic of Uzbekistan №3715 "On Measures to Radically Improve the Prevention, Diagnosis and Treatment of Allergic Diseases," May 2018; • Resolution of the President of the Republic of Uzbekistan №3729 "On Measures for the Further Improvement of the System to Counter the Spread of Influenza and Other Acute Respiratory Infections in the Republic of Uzbekistan," May 2018; • Resolution of the President of the Republic of Uzbekistan №4063 "On Measures for the Prevention of Non-Communicable Diseases, Support of a Healthy Lifestyle and Increasing the Level of Physical Activity of the Population," December 2018; • Resolution of the President of the Republic of Uzbekistan №4190 "On Approval of the Concept of Development of the Mental Health Service of the Population of the Republic of Uzbekistan for 2019–2025," February 2019; • Resolution of the President of the Republic of Uzbekistan №4295 "On the Approval of the National Program to Improve Endocrinological Care to the Population of the Republic of Uzbekistan," April 2019; • Decree of the President of the Republic of Uzbekistan №6099 "On Measures for the Wide Implementation of a Healthy Lifestyle and Further Development of Mass Sports," October 2020; • Resolution of the President of the Republic of Uzbekistan №4887 "On Additional Measures to Provide Healthy Nutrition of the Population," November 2020.

Major private healthcare reforms and initiatives	• Resolution of the President of the Republic of Uzbekistan №2863 "On Measure for the Further Development of the Private Health Sector," April 2017; • Resolution of the President of the Republic of Uzbekistan №4290 "On Measures to Develop Public-Private Partnerships in the Sphere of Health Care," April 2019; • Resolution of the President of the Republic of Uzbekistan №4737 "On the Creation of Additional Conditions for the Provision of Emergency Medical Services by Non-State Medical Organizations," May 2020.
Major policy documents related to the COVID-19 response	• Decree of the President of the Republic of Uzbekistan №5969 "On Priority Measures to Mitigate the Negative Impact of The Coronavirus Pandemic and the Global Crisis on Sectors of Economy," March 2020; • Resolution of the President of the Republic of Uzbekistan №4649 "On Additional Measures to Prevent the Wide Spread of the Coronavirus Infection in the Republic of Uzbekistan," March 2020; • Resolution of the President of the Republic of Uzbekistan №4652 "On Additional Measures to Support Medical Workers and Workers of Sanitary and Epidemiological Service Involved to Counter the Spread of the Coronavirus Infection," March 2020 following Resolution №4737 "On Measures for Further Incentives of Employees of the Sanitary and Epidemiological Service During the Coronavirus Pandemic," April 2020; • Resolution of the President of the Republic of Uzbekistan №4691 "On Measures to Attract External Assistance to Support the Population, Budget, Basic Infrastructure and Business Entities During the Coronavirus Pandemic," April 2020.
Major reforms and policy initiatives in the pharmaceutical industry	• Resolution of the President of the Republic of Uzbekistan №3489 "On Measures for Further Regulation of Production and Import of Medicines and Medical Products," January 2018; • Resolution of the President of the Republic of Uzbekistan №4310 "On Measures for Further Development of the System of Medical and Pharmaceutical Education and Service," May 2019; • Resolution of the President of the Republic of Uzbekistan №4662 "On Additional Measures to Meet the Population's Needs for Medicines, Medical Products, Medical Equipment and Emergency Goods," March 2020.

Source: https://lex.uz/docs/, Authors' analysis.

Table 3.1 outlines major healthcare reforms and policy documents that have been implemented since 2017 to date. The initiative was exceptionally comprehensive and ambitious, inviting assessment as to whether the measures have been effective or have been a case of overreach. As the following pages document, in general the preliminary results have been impressive.

Figure 3.1 documents the more than doubling of real social expenditures during the period between 2010 and 2021, and the rise in healthcare expenditures from roughly one-quarter to one-third of the total. This surge is concentrated from 2018 onward: the Uzbekistan Government backed its ambitious plans with a large real spending increase.

Where does Uzbekistan stand relative to comparator nations? WHO data for 2012 suggest that the 5.9% of GDP that Uzbekistan spent on health expenditures was quite close to the median value for CIS countries (6.3%), Turkey (also 6.3%), the Baltic states, and Balkan countries. Western European values were higher, but they generally have higher elderly population shares. Indeed, while Kazakhstan's population structure is older than Uzbekistan's, its health expenditure/GDP share (4.8%) is noticeably lower. The

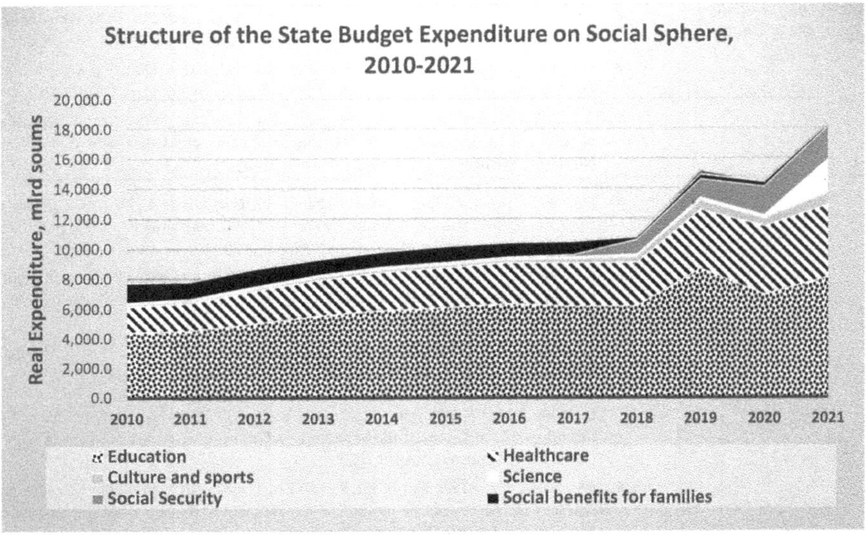

Figure 3.1 Uzbekistan: state budget social sphere expenditures, 2010–2021
Source: www.openbudget.uz/ru/outcomesView#RANGE!C8, Authors' analysis.

same is true for Armenia (4.5%), Azerbaijan (5.4%), and Belarus (5.0%). In short, even before Uzbekistan's concerted effort to improve healthcare, its effort was already impressive by regional standards.

3.2.1 Training of doctors

In Uzbekistan, as of 2019, physicians, surgeons, dentists, pediatricians, and obstetrician-gynecologists account for 21.0%, 12.0%, 9.0%, 6.2%, and 6.6% of the total medical workforce in the economy, respectively (www.stat.uz). As with other Central Asian countries, Uzbekistan has faced a serious shortage of skilled health workers. According to a 2019 Ministry of Health report, there is a shortage of nearly 13,000 skilled medical personnel across the country, or about 2% of the total number (gazeta.uz). Accessibility of doctors is even more difficult in poorer and more remote regions, such as Surkhandarya and Jizzakh with an average of 15 and 16 medical staff per 10,000 population respectively, compared to 80 in Tashkent City and 27 countrywide.

Recent reforms have focused on improving the training of healthcare professionals, increasing accessibility to highly qualified doctors especially outside of major cities, introducing international standards into the training of medical personnel, and taking steps to integrate education, research, and healthcare practice. 2020 Presidential Decree №4666 "On Measures to Implement a Completely New System of Training and Continuous Professional Development of Staff in the Health Sphere" identified several reform initiatives:

- Starting from AY 2020–2021, the establishment of a separate medical higher educational institution for training doctors in sanitary and epidemiological surveillance, and public health;
- Opening new branches and clinics in cooperation with the Russian National Research Medical University (RNRMU) and Bahcesehir University (Turkey). A branch of RNRMU then opened in Tashkent in 2021, with academic activity starting the following year;
- Introduction of two Master's degree programs in Healthcare Administration, at Westminster International University in Tashkent (WIUT) and Akfa University, with 50 government grants for students in the programs starting in AY 2022–2023;
- In AY 2020–2021, transforming 47 medical colleges located in the Republic of Karakalpakstan, 13 regions, and Tashkent City into Public Health Colleges named after Abu Ali ibn Sino. The reformed institutions added training in nutrition, valeology, psychology, pharmacology, kinesiology, occupational pathology, and rehabilitation. Successful graduates of these colleges then have the option to continue their education from their second year at the higher education medical schools, subject to passing entrance tests and interviews;
- From September 1, 2020, organizing scientific councils for awarding PhD and Doctor of Science (DSc) degrees to graduates of medical schools located in the cities of Andijan, Bukhara, Fergana, Nukus, Samarkand and Urgench;
- Establishing a Central Multidisciplinary Clinic based in Republican Clinical Hospital No. 1 in Tashkent to train medical personnel based on international standards and opening regional branches in Jizzakh, Kashkadarya, Navoi, Namangan and Syrdarya, where there are no medical higher educational institutions (www.rkb-center.uz);
- Introducing a mandatory certification procedure for doctors, including re-certification every five years through a new online certification system ensuring transparency, and canceling the certification fee for medical staff of primary healthcare institutions.

3.2.2 Private healthcare

As of 2020, Uzbekistan had 1232 hospitals; of these 593 were private hospitals. However, private hospitals are increasing in importance: 44 of the 49 new hospitals that opened in 2021 were private.

Several initiatives have been undertaken since 2017 with the goal of strengthening and improving the role of private medical organizations. In 2017, Presidential Decree №2863 "On Measures for the Further Development of the Private Health Sector" laid out a comprehensive plan for private health sector reforms. A number of exemptions were given for private medical institutions; other changes included:

- Private medical hospitals and clinics (except clinics providing dental and cosmetic services) were exempted from paying all taxes until January 2022, with an aim of allocating those released funds to purchase modern medical and technical equipment, to construct new buildings, to renovate existing structures and to provide free medical services for socially vulnerable people;
- All private medical entities were exempted until January 2025 from customs duties on imports of new medical equipment, parts, and consumables for medical devices;
- New private medical firms and businesses (excluding dentistry and cosmetology) in rural areas were exempted from all taxes for ten years from the date of registration. In addition, state license fees were reduced from ten to five times the official minimum wage;
- All foreign doctors, managerial personnel, and technical specialists who maintain medical equipment employed in private medical organizations were exempted from personal income taxes. Their incomes also were exempted from private medical organizations' social contribution charges. These exemptions specifically aimed at attracting more foreign doctors and specialists by creating favorable work conditions;
- Commercial banks were encouraged to provide long-term loans to private medical organizations for establishing start-up capital, purchasing, constructing or reconstructing buildings, and purchasing modern medical equipment. Moreover, banks also were "advised" to provide consumer loans to those receiving private medical services.

In addition, private medical organizations have been authorized to expand their range of medical services to include many that were prohibited before. Specifically, from 2019, private medical organizations are allowed to establish birth centers, and to treat diseases and pathological conditions of newborns and infants up to 1 year old.

In order to further develop private healthcare, 2019 Presidential Decree №4290 "On Measures to Develop Public-Private Partnerships in the Sphere of Health Care" set forth a legal framework. According to this framework, state support is given to investors for investing in private healthcare as part of the implementation of public-private partnership projects, with funding of USD 150 million provided through authorized commercial banks. This was followed in 2020 by a resolution "On the Creation of Additional Conditions for the Provision of Emergency Medical Services by Non-State Medical Organizations," which aimed to encourage the private provision of emergency medical services by exempting them from payment of customs duties on import of new ambulances.

Following this resolution, some 2224 new ambulances were purchased and the number of modern ambulances increased from 24 in 2016 to 435 in 2021. In addition, at the beginning of 2023, 110 latest-generation Volkswagen Caddy ambulances were imported and distributed across the regions. As of

January 2023, there are 2938 ambulances operating throughout the country of which 648 are registered as needing to be replaced.

Furthermore, from 2016 to 2021 there were the following developments in the emergency care system: the number of emergency centers increased from 818 to 1666, emergency care service centers increased from 1648 to 2685, the average service radius decreased from 15–20 km to 9–12 km, the average arrival time for a call decreased from 25–30 minutes to 8–12 minutes, and funds allocated for drugs per call increased from 500 UZS to 7700 UZS.

In his speech on May 5, 2022, President Mirziyoyev[1] addressed several healthcare issues, particularly in emergency care at a district level. According to the Presidential Decree №3973 "On Measures to Improve the Ambulance Service in the Republic of Uzbekistan" issued in 2018, the Emergency Care Development Fund was established under the Ministry of Health to provide practical support to the development of the ambulance services and improve its technical base.

3.2.3 Health insurance

In 2019, the Cabinet of Ministers developed a law "On Compulsory Health Insurance" based on 2018 Presidential Decree №5590 "On Comprehensive Measures to Fundamentally Improve the Healthcare System of the Republic of Uzbekistan." This law laid out a legal framework of compulsory health insurance, mechanism, and implementation phases. Compulsory state health insurance began to be gradually introduced in January 2021. The goal is to ensure access to free, high-quality, and essential medical services. A pilot project has been launched in the Syrdarya region with the transfer of healthcare funding to resources generated by universal state insurance revenues. Concurrently, new "electronic polyclinics" were established with WHO support, after WHO and Uzbekistan signed a two-year cooperation agreement in 2020 with the objectives of achieving universal state insurance and health coverage.

Tele-health[2]

In 2020, Uzbekistan opened its first telemedicine clinic in Muynak in Karakalpakstan, the most remote region of the country. It provides both in-person examinations and online consultations and medical check-ups. Utilizing both domestic and international specialists. The following year, the National Chamber of Innovative Healthcare in cooperation with the Republican Specialized Scientific and Practical Medical Center of Cardiology started a broader telemedicine program. Pilot projects using cardiological telemetry equipment were launched in the Tashkent region: Karshi, Jizzakh, and Chilanzar districts.

With the help of Ucard-100 electrocardiographs, patient electrocardiograms (ECGs) will be transferred to the Republican Center of

Cardiology's UNET telemetry complex. This telemetry equipment will make it possible to organize screening, preventive examination and diagnostics of cardiovascular diseases in the regions. This should substantially improve diagnosis and cardiological care for the population outside the capital city; the quality of medical services in primary healthcare centers should significantly increase as well. Presumably, improved diagnostics will be accompanied by local doctors' learning from interaction with specialists in the Republican Cardiology Center.

The joint pilot project is intended as well to demonstrate the possibility of organizing a high level of medical care for all Uzbekistanis, regardless of location. Telemedicine enhances timely diagnosis and enables more immediate; it also saves doctors' time and effort, as they can help patients almost immediately from their workplaces. Utilization of specialists and more accurate diagnosis enables more targeted, aggressive treatments, thereby raising local general doctors' capacities. This is especially important in cardiology, where conditions are often life-threatening.

It is worth noting (and important for the empirical analysis that follows) that Uzbekistan is not the only country in the region to develop telemedicine. Since the inception of a telemedicine network in 2004, Kazakhstan has progressively built a wide-ranging service platform as a key component of the national approach to strengthening healthcare delivery in rural settings and achieving the country's goal of universal health coverage. Within the national *Strategy 2050*, Kazakhstan's government intends to develop the network further and to introduce "smart medical services," online prevention and treatment, and further scaling up of digital health. The network has been gradually extended with advances in communications infrastructure and now comprises 209 healthcare facilities at district, regional, and national levels.

In sum, Uzbekistan has undertaken a vast set of healthcare sector reforms in recent years. It is far too early to fully assess their effectiveness, either individually or as a whole. At the same time, it is important to get a broad sense of relative achievements. Given Uzbekistan's major efforts, how has the country fared relative to nearby comparators? Do health outcome patterns reflect widening or narrowing gaps across regions and demographic groups?

It is only possible to sketch answers to these questions and to provide descriptive statistics. We take two approaches. First, we explore intra-Uzbekistan patterns for health outcomes that might reasonably be expected to respond fairly rapidly to policy changes. Thus, we focus on measures such as infant mortality, cardiovascular disease, and pulmonary disease rather than long-gestation cancers. Second, we contrast parts of Uzbekistan with neighboring regions in Kazakhstan, which has excellent, detailed health data at the raion (district, or county) level. To do this, we match regions that are similar, creating what we term "synthetic Uzbekistan." We also provide direct comparisons of outcomes in Tashkent with nearby Shymkent, the largest city in southern Kazakhstan. These comparisons may prove useful in identifying the relative effectiveness of Uzbekistani government policy –

while acknowledging that greater oil wealth gives Kazakhstan a natural advantage.

3.3 Uzbekistan healthcare and population health achievements, 1991–2022

Uzbekistan's health achievements since independence have been impressive. Life expectancy and infant mortality improvements have been noted above; regional patterns in infant mortality are discussed below. In addition, this section explores (a) structural changes in healthcare provision and (b) average length of hospital stay. We then (c) consider trends in a major infectious disease, tuberculosis, and (d), in contrast, provide patterns for the incidence of cancers, which have long-gestation periods and do not respond rapidly to policy changes.

As Figure 3.2 shows, Uzbekistan experienced a steady decline in the number of physicians per 1000 population between 2001 and 2014. While this partly reflects a growing denominator (population growth), it also reflects the emigration of skilled labor and stagnation in total supply. The downward trend ceased with the emergence of the Mirziyoyev Administration; since then, numbers have grown.

Figure 3.2 also points to the dominance of skilled medical personnel in Tashkent. That is hardly surprising. More important is the considerable and

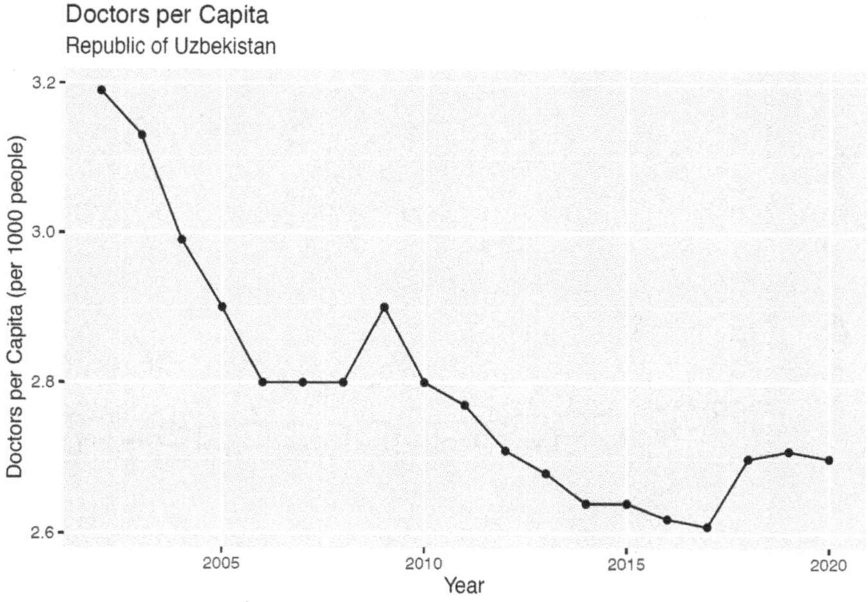

Figure 3.2a Doctors per capita, at the national level, by region, and over time
Source: Authors' calculations based on the State Statistics Committee of the Republic of Uzbekistan data.

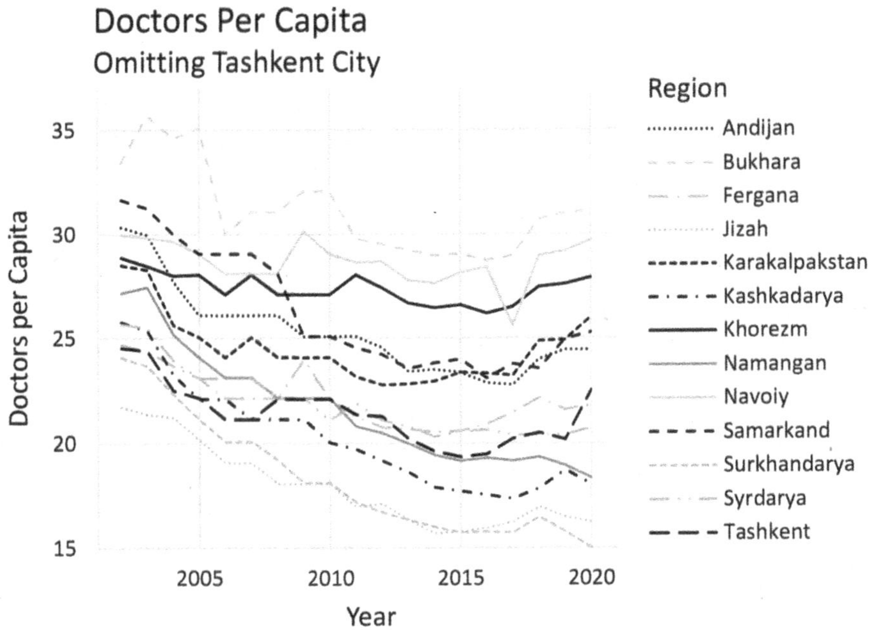

Figure 3.2b Doctors per capita, at the national level, by region, and over time
Source: Authors' calculations based on the State Statistics Committee of the Republic of Uzbekistan data.

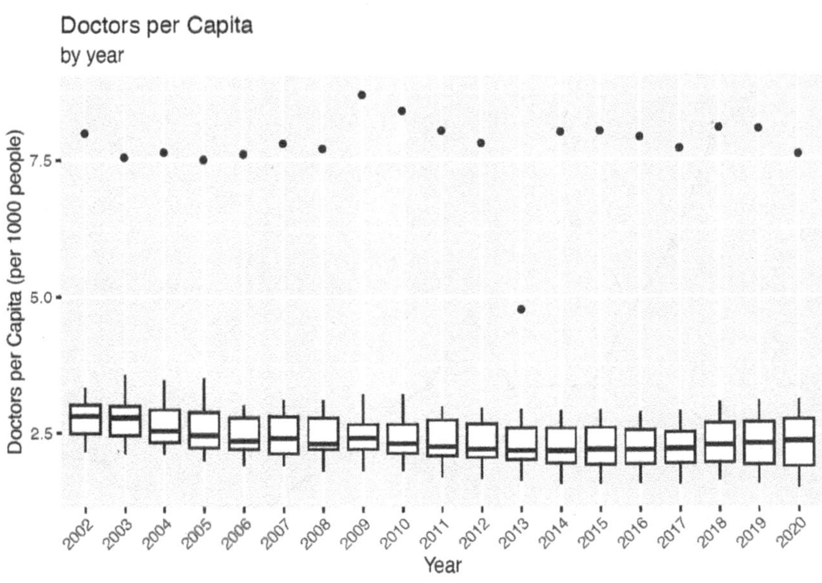

Figure 3.2c Doctors per capita, at the national level, by region, and over time
Source: Authors' calculations based on the State Statistics Committee of the Republic of Uzbekistan data.

sustained disparity among the regions. Moreover, this disparity appears to be growing. Regions including Andijan, Bukhara, and Karakalpakstan are witnessing increased physician density, while declines continue in Namangan, Jizzakh, Kashkadarya, and, above all, Surkhandarya. These patterns do not obviously relate to the overall level of urbanization (Figure 3.3), though it is quite possible that this is disguised by the concentration of medical personnel in towns and cities in predominantly rural regions – and their relative absence in densely populated rural parts of the Ferghana Valley.

While the medical doctor population has stabilized and started increasing, at the same time there has been a secular decline in the average length of hospital stay (Figure 3.4). We regard this as a transformative sign. Soviet health policy involved long, curative rests in hospitals, ignoring the fact that the risk of contracting infections or communicable diseases is far greater in most hospitals than in most private homes. However, high hospital bed occupancy rates served as an easy marker of "productivity," as well as a justification for subsequent funding increases. In the post-Soviet era, Uzbekistan experienced a sharp, ongoing decline (until the COVID-19 pandemic) in average length of stay from roughly 15 days at the end of the USSR to only 3–4 days in 2020. This was a secular decrease that occurred in all regions, signaling a shift to modern medical practices. While we lack confirming data, it seems overwhelmingly likely that the decline was

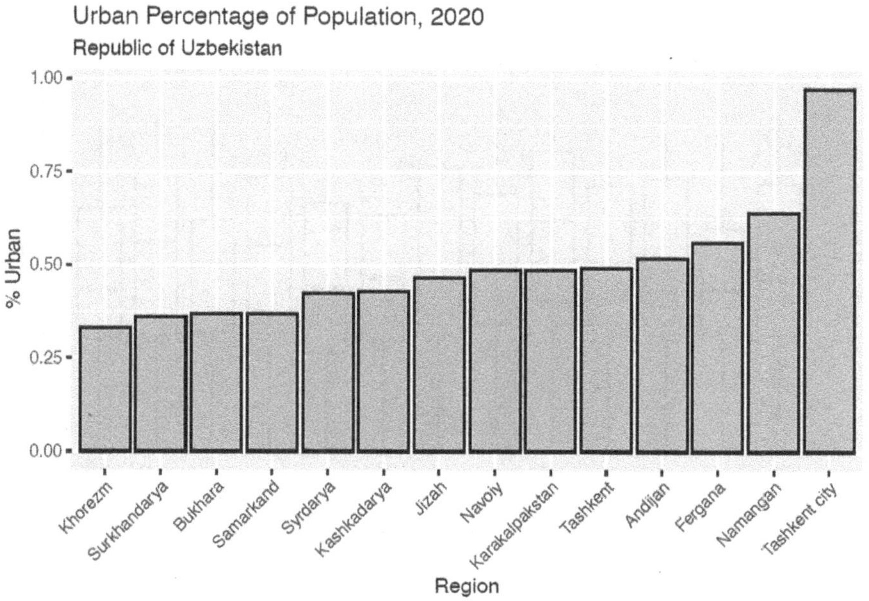

Figure 3.3 Urbanization across Uzbekistan's regions
Source: Authors' calculations based on the State Statistics Committee of the Republic of Uzbekistan data.

associated with a sharp fall in secondary infections and a rise in patient recovery markers.

The bureaucratic motive story also receives visual support from the final part of Figure 3.4, which graphs the length of stay against the number of hospitals in each province over time. Replacing the number of hospitals with the number of available beds yields exactly the same patterns. In 10 of 14 regions, a positive relationship emerges, suggesting in light of improving health metrics that patients are kept in hospitals to justify existing capacity.

The next step is to get a broad sense of the effectiveness of the system's performance over time and, if possible, the recent reforms. We focus on two measures that seem likely to be responsive to the healthcare system improvements: infant mortality rates, and the incidence and prevalence of tuberculosis.

Figure 3.5 provides Uzbekistan's infant mortality rate (IMR; defined as age 0–1 deaths per 1000 live births) since 2000. The reader should be cautioned: figures tend to be underestimates, and there are systematic patterns to underestimates as well. The reason is simple: almost no one will report deaths that did not occur, while both maternity care units and midwives have incentives to report newborn deaths as stillbirths. Thus, Anthopolos and Becker (2010) estimate that infant mortality in neighboring Kyrgyzstan is 25% higher than reported figures – after acknowledging that their correction does not capture all sources of error. Furthermore, underreporting is

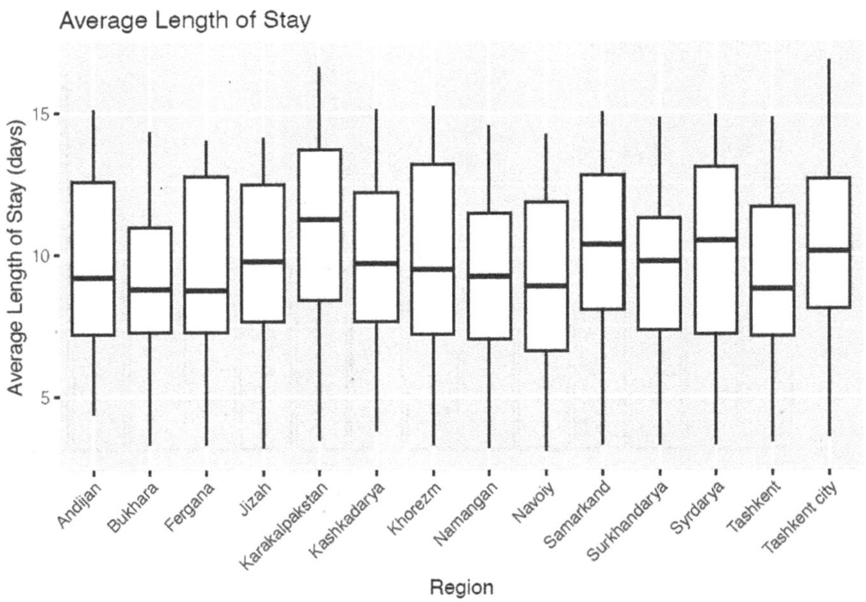

Figure 3.4a Average length of hospital stay, Uzbekistan 1992–2022, by region and year
Source: Authors' calculations based on the State Statistics Committee of the Republic of Uzbekistan data.

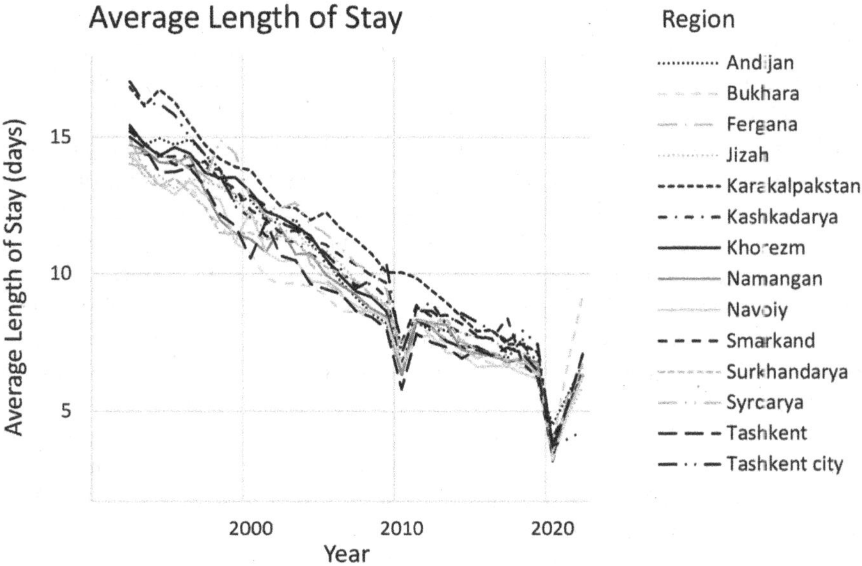

Figure 3.4b Average length of hospital stay, Uzbekistan 1992–2022, by region and year
Source: Authors' calculations based on the State Statistics Committee of the Republic of Uzbekistan data.

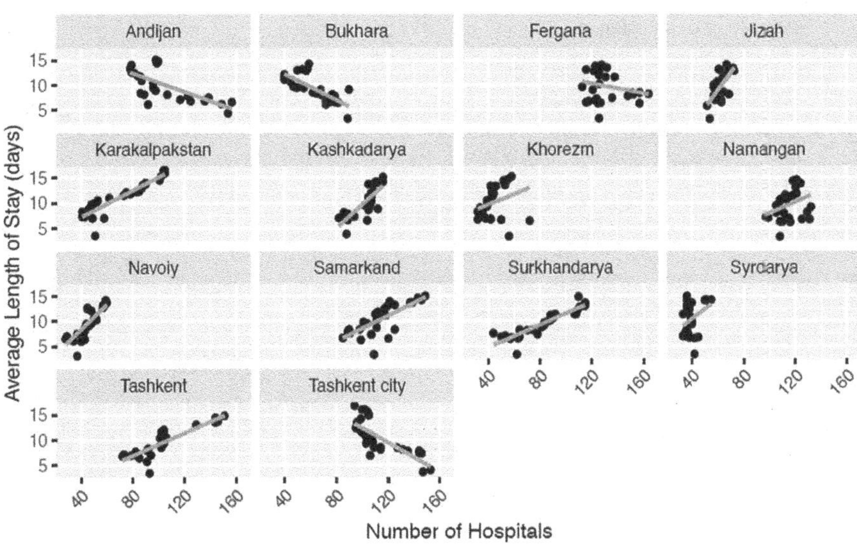

Figure 3.4c Average length of hospital stay, Uzbekistan 1992–2022, by region and year
Source: Authors' calculations based on the State Statistics Committee of the Republic of Uzbekistan data.

especially likely in settings with poor monitoring – namely, outside of major urban areas with regulated *roddom*s (birthing centers) and hospitals. It is also possible that more remote areas still use the Soviet definition of a live birth, which included lower bounds for birthweight and gestation period.

The implication for Uzbekistan is that actual IMR likely declined more rapidly even than the striking declines shown, as data quality and monitoring systematically improved, especially after 2014. For the nation as a whole, reported IMR declined from 19 to 9 (per 1000 live births) during this period, with the latter figure comparable to those in high-income countries. Likely underreporting in rural areas shows up via the relatively high level of infant mortality in Tashkent City, which in reality almost certainly has the lowest risk (though it is also possible that high-risk cases from the provinces are transferred there).

Most important is the decline in IMR across all regions, as consistent regional data trends remove the possibility of an anomalous regional result driving the national aggregate. The increase in infant mortality in 2014–2017 (depending on location) that interrupted the trend may or may not reflect a true regression rather than improved monitoring.

Tuberculosis is a major, chronic communicable disease with disabling and sometimes fatal consequences. It has been identified both by the Uzbekistan government and WHO as a major target. As Figure 3.6 shows, the TB incidence rate has more than halved in the past two decades. The pace of decline

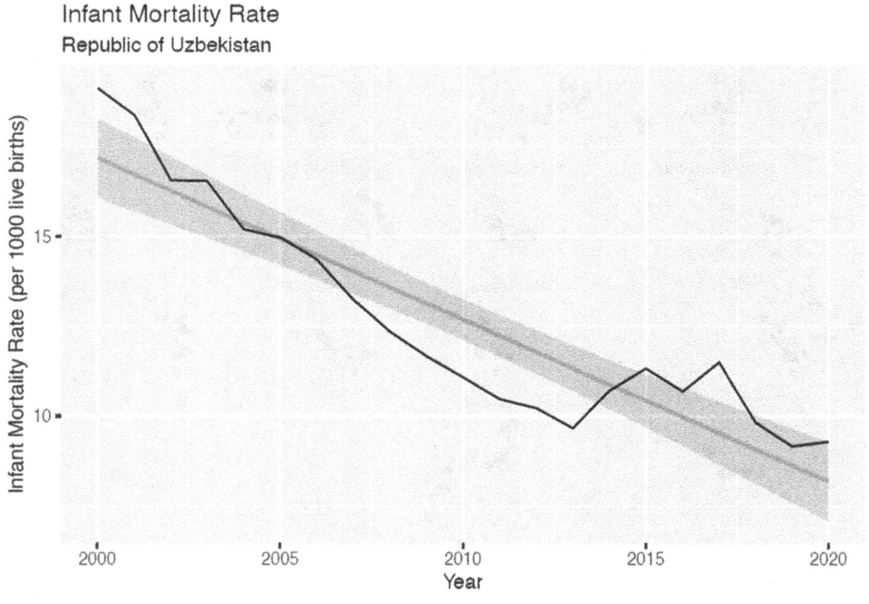

Figure 3.5a Infant mortality rate, Uzbekistan 2000–2020, by region and year
Source: Authors' calculations based on the State Statistics Committee of the Republic of Uzbekistan data.

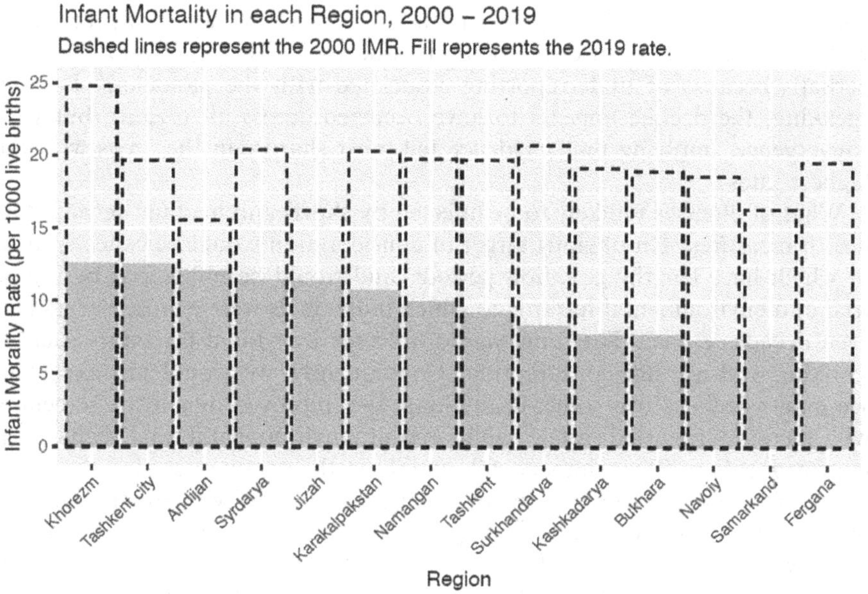

Figure 3.5b Infant mortality rate, Uzbekistan 2000–2020, by region and year
Source: Authors' calculations based on the State Statistics Committee of the Republic of Uzbekistan data.

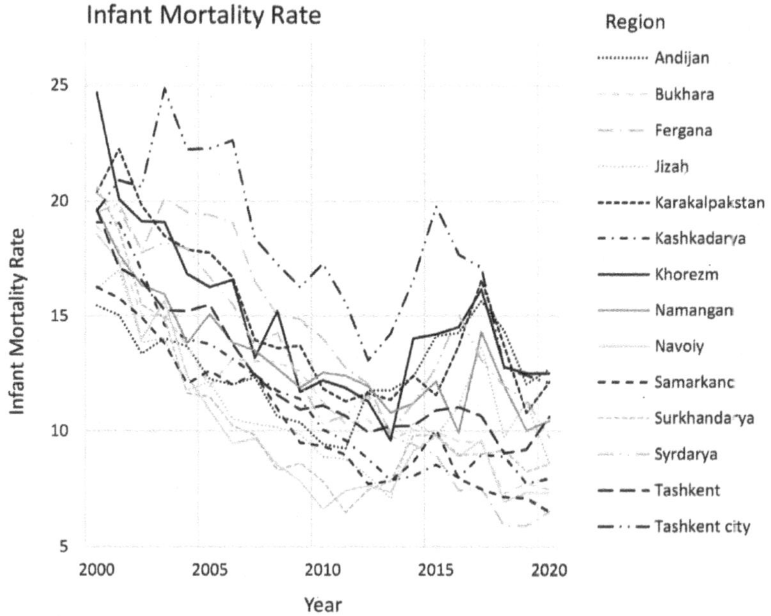

Figure 3.5c Infant mortality rate, Uzbekistan 2000–2020, by region and year
Source: Authors' calculations based on the State Statistics Committee of the Republic of Uzbekistan data.

appears to have been fairly steady until 2020, which witnessed a precipitous decline – perhaps because of isolation associated with COVID-19, but also perhaps because of underreporting associated with the pandemic. Broadly speaking, the decline appears to have occurred across all regions, but with convergence, implying that incidence fell most sharply in the areas with the highest rates.

What of illnesses unlikely to be affected by short- and medium-term public health measures? An obvious target of consideration would be cancers, most of which have lengthy gestation periods, and would be influenced by industrial and environmental hazards to which individuals were exposed years and even decades earlier. The same would hold for individual behaviors such as smoking and alcohol consumption. Consequently, we would not expect to see major declines over time; if anything, the improved diagnostic screening will increase reported rates, while recent environmental and behavioral improvements will have impacts felt mainly in the coming decades.

The picture that emerges is one of remarkable stability over time (Figure 3.7). Substantial regional differences emerge, likely reflecting (a) variation in quality of diagnosis (which is likely greater in Tashkent City), (b) variation in population age structure (Tashkent's residents are also older), (c) variation both in competing hazards (in particular, externally caused mortality) and lifestyle cofactors (in particular, smoking), and (d) variation in

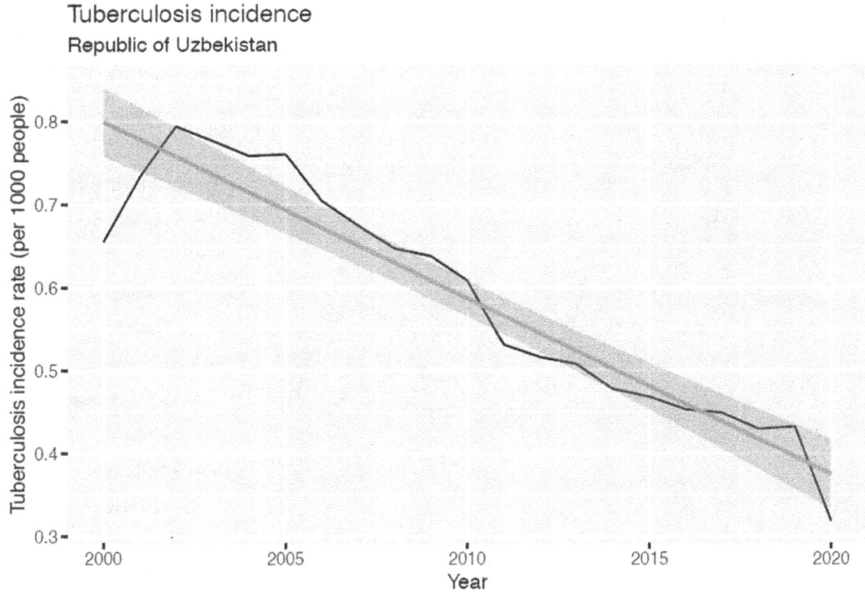

Figure 3.6a Tuberculosis incidence and prevalence (dashed lines), Uzbekistan 2000–2021, by region and year

Source: Authors' calculations based on the State Statistics Committee of the Republic of Uzbekistan data.

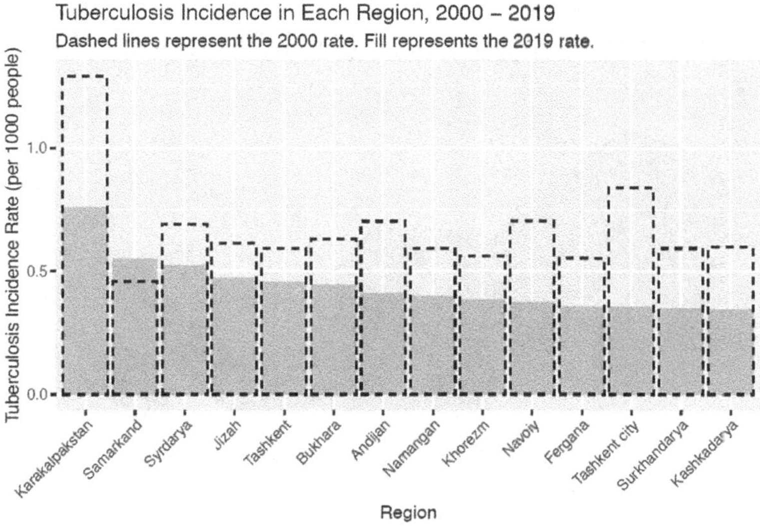

Figure 3.6b Tuberculosis incidence and prevalence (dashed lines), Uzbekistan 2000–2021, by region and year

Source: Authors' calculations based on the State Statistics Committee of the Republic of Uzbekistan data.

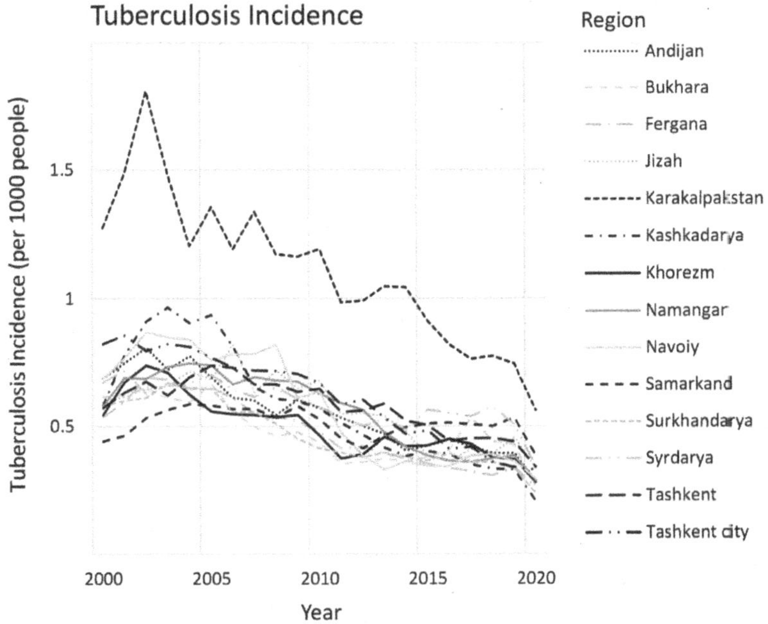

Figure 3.6c Tuberculosis incidence and prevalence (dashed lines), Uzbekistan 2000–2021, by region and year

Source: Authors' calculations based on the State Statistics Committee of the Republic of Uzbekistan data.

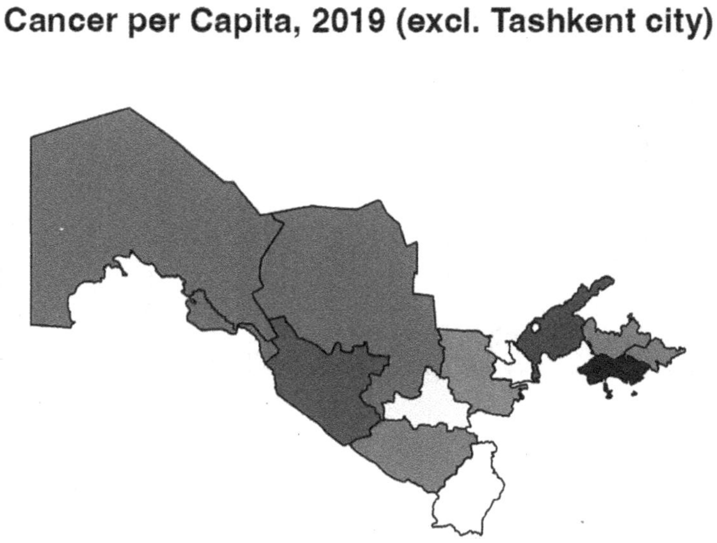

Figure 3.7a All cancer incidence, Uzbekistan 2000–2021, by region and year
Source: Authors' calculations based on the State Statistics Committee of the Republic of Uzbekistan data.

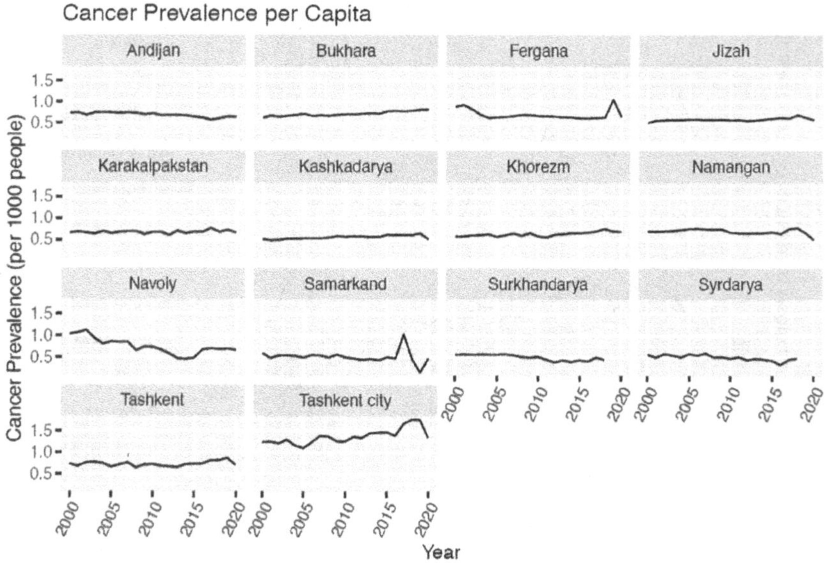

Figure 3.7b All cancer incidence, Uzbekistan 2000–2021, by region and year
Source: Authors' calculations based on the State Statistics Committee of the Republic of Uzbekistan data.

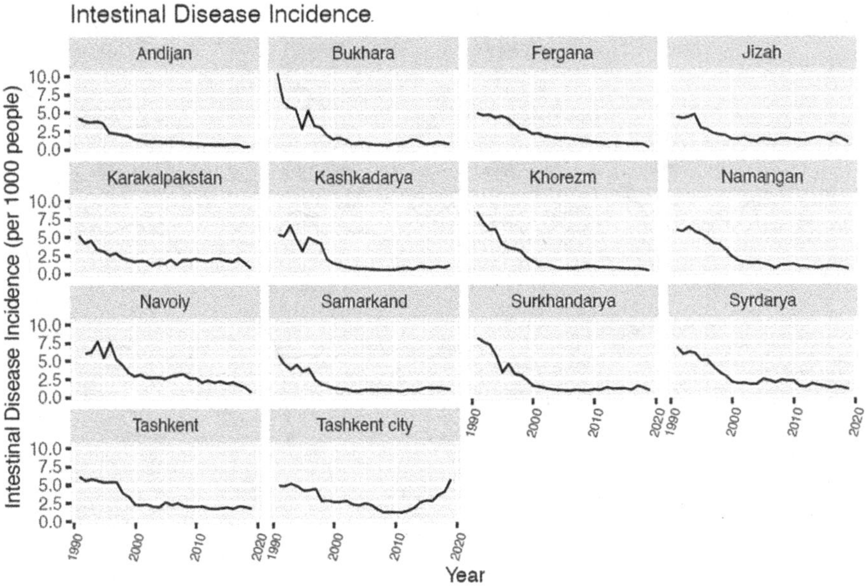

Figure 3.8a Incidence of intestinal disease, respiratory disease, genitourinary tract infections, and hepatitis, Uzbekistan 1990–2020, by region and year

Source: Authors' calculations based on the State Statistics Committee of the Republic of Uzbekistan data.

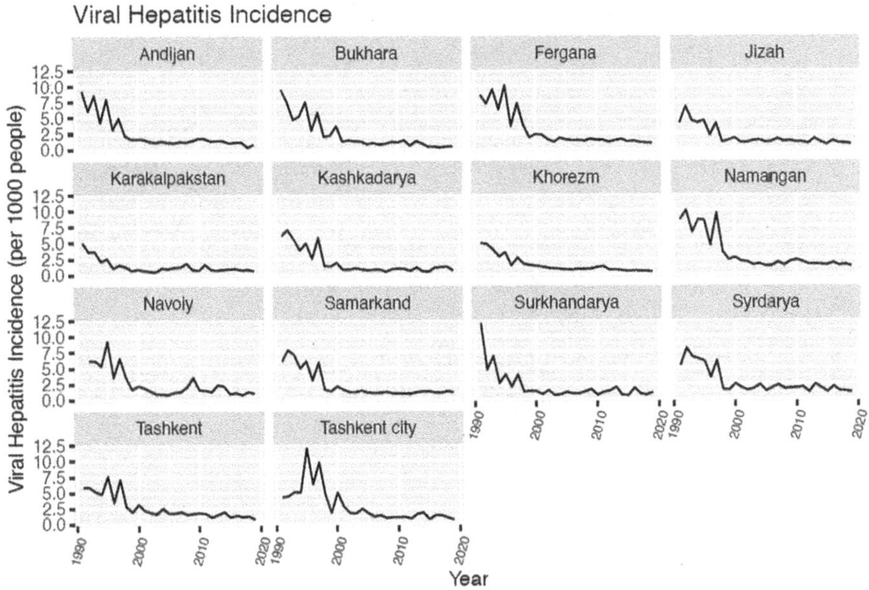

Figure 3.8b Incidence of intestinal disease, respiratory disease, genitourinary tract infections, and hepatitis, Uzbekistan 1990–2020, by region and year

Source: Authors' calculations based on the State Statistics Committee of the Republic of Uzbekistan data.

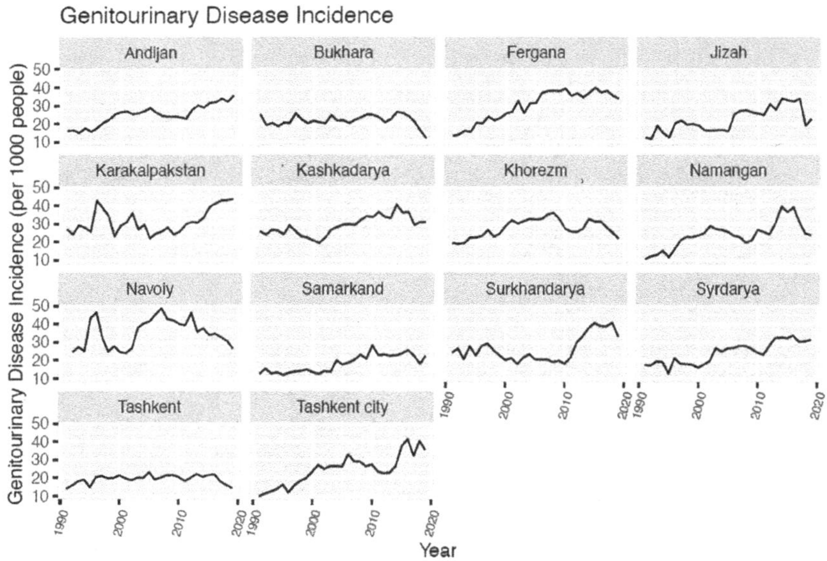

Figure 3.8c Incidence of intestinal disease, respiratory disease, genitourinary tract infections, and hepatitis, Uzbekistan 1990–2020, by region and year

Source: Authors' calculations based on the State Statistics Committee of the Republic of Uzbekistan data.

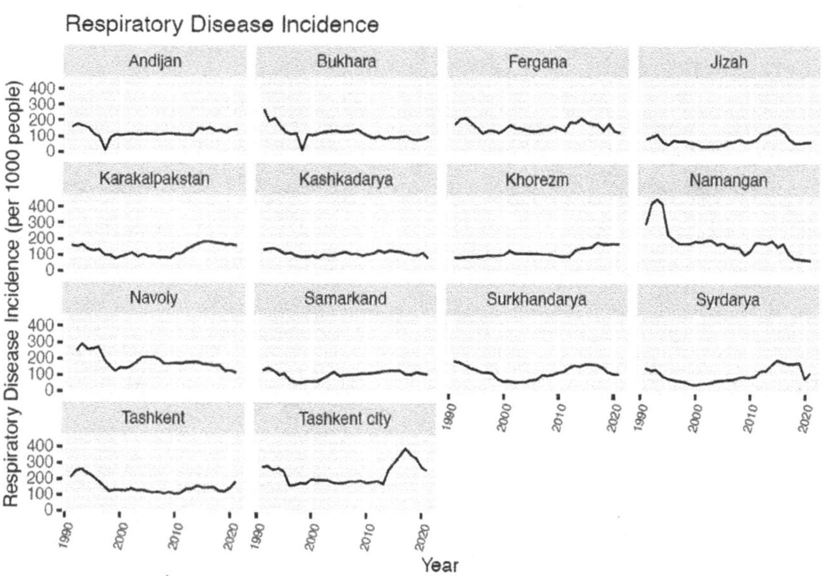

Figure 3.8d Incidence of intestinal disease, respiratory disease, genitourinary tract infections, and hepatitis, Uzbekistan 1990–2020, by region and year

Source: Authors' calculations based on the State Statistics Committee of the Republic of Uzbekistan data.

environmental cofactors. Disentangling these effects is a major future research task. For now, we can only note the rise in cancer incidence in Tashkent – likely but not certainly reflecting population aging – along with an apparent decline in Navoi, and virtual stability elsewhere.

Patterns of other infectious diseases and illnesses that to some degree can be controlled by public health measures tend to be broadly consistent with the illnesses discussed above (Figure 3.8). Respiratory diseases exhibit secular declines in Bukhara, Navoi, and, especially, Namangan provinces, while there have been increases in Karakalpakstan and Khorezm. The incidence is highest in Tashkent City which possibly reflects greater air pollution – but also may reflect better diagnosis. Determining this would necessitate individual diagnosis records, which are not available.

Genitourinary tract infections also appear to be on the upswing in much of Uzbekistan, though not everywhere, and in Bukhara there is a recorded secular decline. While it is conceivable that the nation is experiencing a gradual epidemic, improved diagnosis and treatment strikes us as a more plausible explanation.

In contrast, viral hepatitis has virtually disappeared in Uzbekistan since Independence, constituting a major public health achievement. Most of this decline occurred in the 1990s, making it one of the first major accomplishments. Intestinal diseases have declined more gradually (other than in Tashkent City), but also mark an early post-Independence public health achievement.

3.4 Comparative performance, focusing on neighboring regions in Uzbekistan and Kazakhstan

It is important not only to focus on Uzbekistan's public health achievements and remaining challenges, but also to put it in perspective. Doing so is not straightforward. The quality of health and vital statistics varies across countries, and for some of Uzbekistan's neighbors data are unreliable. On the other hand, while there are much better public health data for Kazakhstan and Russia, these countries have benefited from explosive growth in hydrocarbons and other mineral exports, and have considerably higher per capita income. Climatic conditions and social behaviors also differ greatly as one moves further from the Uzbekistani border.

Our response to this is to compare regions of Uzbekistan near the Kazakhstani border with their immediately proximate counterparts in Kazakhstan. This reduces cultural and climatic variation. In addition, since southwestern Kazakhstan is not as prosperous as Almaty, Astana, and other parts of northern and northwestern Kazakhstan, wealth effects will matter less.

We begin by contrasting Tashkent City (as distinct from the surrounding Tashkent province) with Shymkent, one of three Kazakhstani "cities of Republican significance." The two large cities are only 130 km apart –

roughly a two-hour drive. While Shymkent's population of roughly 1 million is far smaller than Tashkent's roughly 2.7 million, it is the regional center and Tashkent's only obvious comparator.

It is clear from Figure 3.9 that Tashkent has considerably greater medical capacity, perhaps reflecting its Soviet legacy as one of the USSR's most developed cities. Average length of hospital stay has plummeted in both cities, reflecting major and comparable changes in healthcare practices.

Both cities have experienced sharp declines in infant mortality rates, though there is far higher variation in Shymkent (Figure 3.10). Tuberculosis is declining in both cities and, while Shymkent historically had a higher rate, in recent years the rates have converged. The incidence of respiratory illness also has been greater historically in Shymkent, but now is higher in Tashkent. It is unclear whether this reflects changes in diagnosis or the presence of a couple of outliers. The same points hold for diabetes incidence – though this could reflect differences in dietary practices, and merits further study. Finally, it turns out that the peculiar rise in genitourinary tract infections in Tashkent is overshadowed by an even greater level and rise in Shymkent.

Taken together, the contrast between these two large, relatively prosperous cities suggests major changes in health practices and in outcomes. Going from key indicators such as infant mortality rates and average length of hospital stay to various diseases offers less conclusive patterns, and suggests

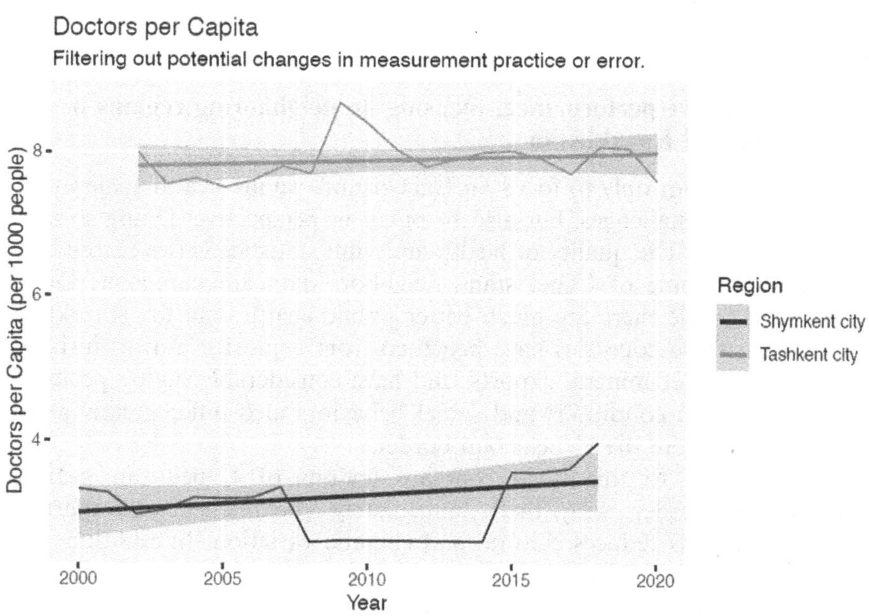

Figure 3.9a Tashkent vs. Shymkent: physicians per capita, average length of hospital stay, and hospital beds per capita

Source: Authors' calculations based on the State Statistics Committee of the Republic of Uzbekistan and MedInform data.

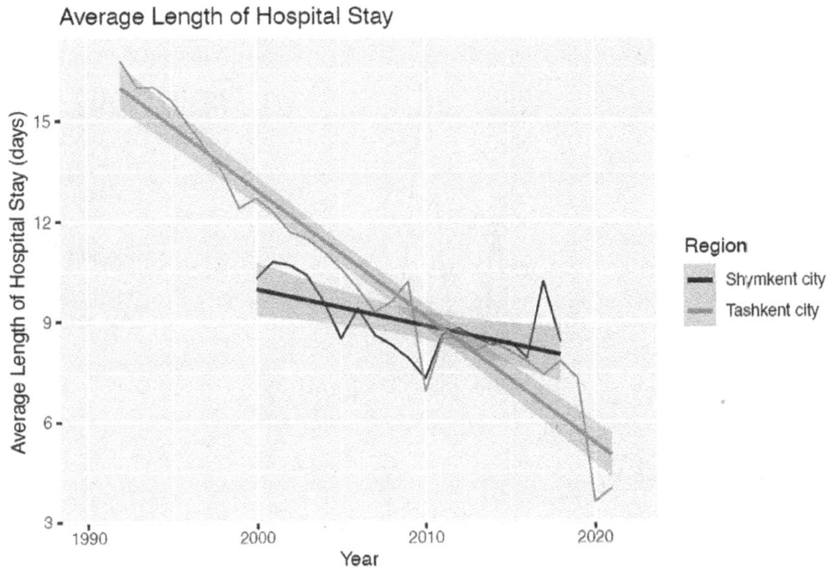

Figure 3.9b Tashkent vs. Shymkent: physicians per capita, average length of hospital stay, and hospital beds per capita

Source: Authors' calculations based on the State Statistics Committee of the Republic of Uzbekistan and MedInform data.

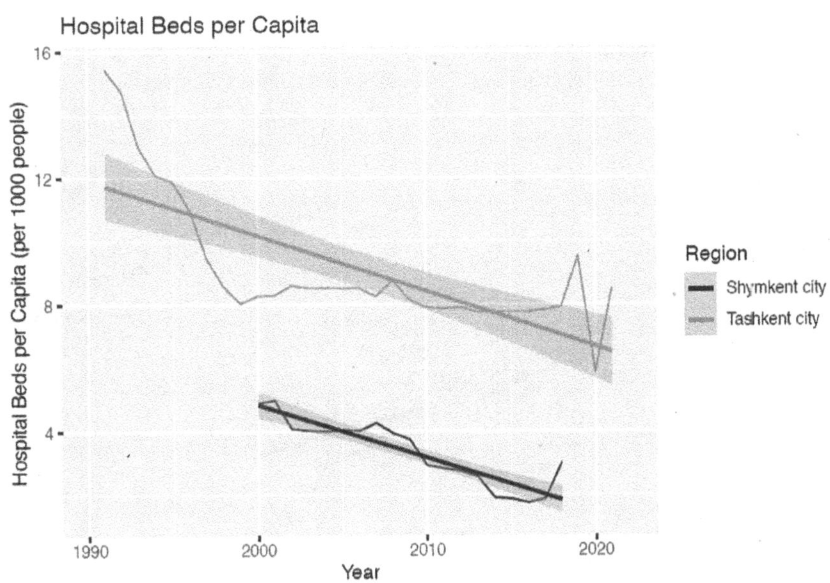

Figure 3.9c Tashkent vs. Shymkent: physicians per capita, average length of hospital stay, and hospital beds per capita

Source: Authors' calculations based on the State Statistics Committee of the Republic of Uzbekistan and MedInform data.

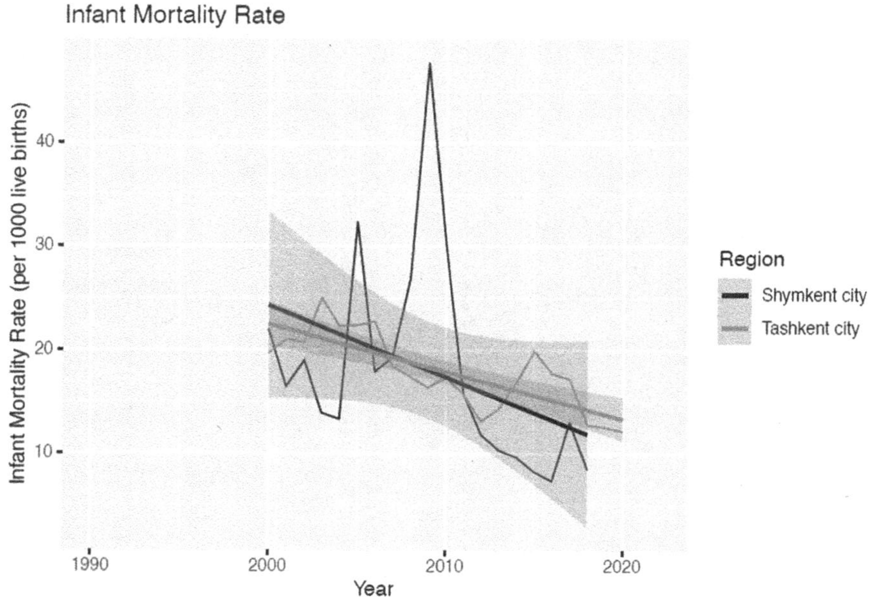

Figure 3.10a Tashkent vs. Shymkent: health indicators patterns over time
Source: Authors' calculations based on the State Statistics Committee of the Republic of Uzbekistan and MedInform data.

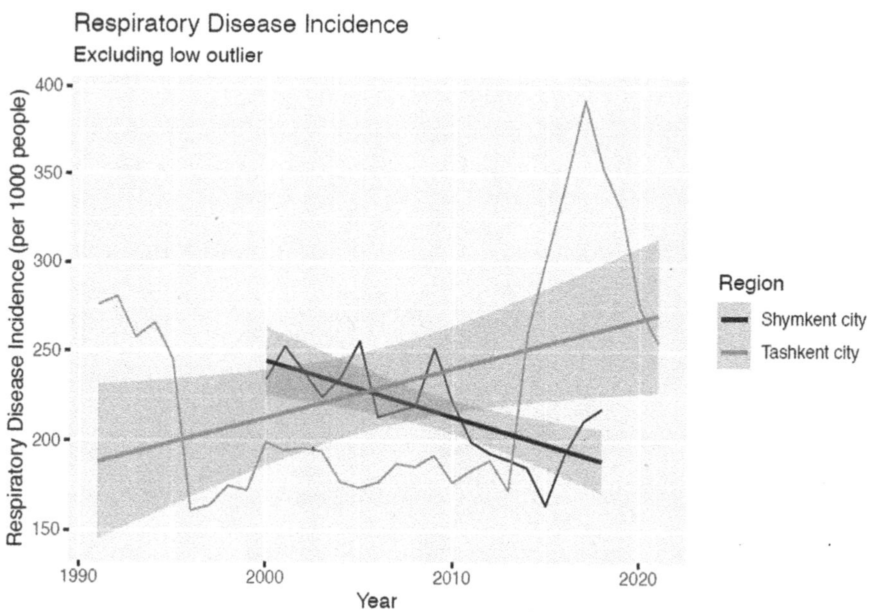

Figure 3.10b Tashkent vs. Shymkent: health indicators patterns over time
Source: Authors' calculations based on the State Statistics Committee of the Republic of Uzbekistan and MedInform data.

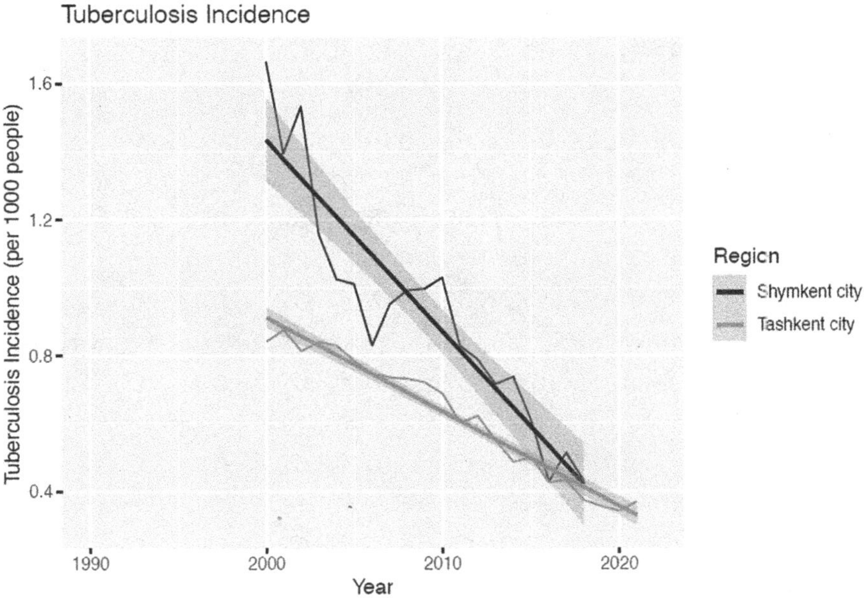

Figure 3.10c Tashkent vs. Shymkent: health indicators patterns over time
Source: Authors' calculations based on the State Statistics Committee of the Republic of Uzbekistan and MedInform data.

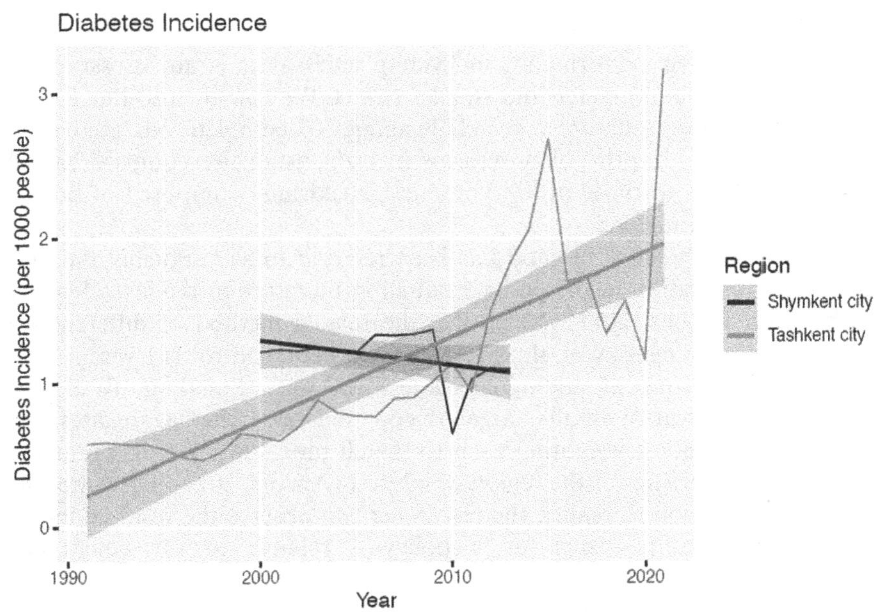

Figure 3.10d Tashkent vs. Shymkent: health indicators patterns over time
Source: Authors' calculations based on the State Statistics Committee of the Republic of Uzbekistan and MedInform data.

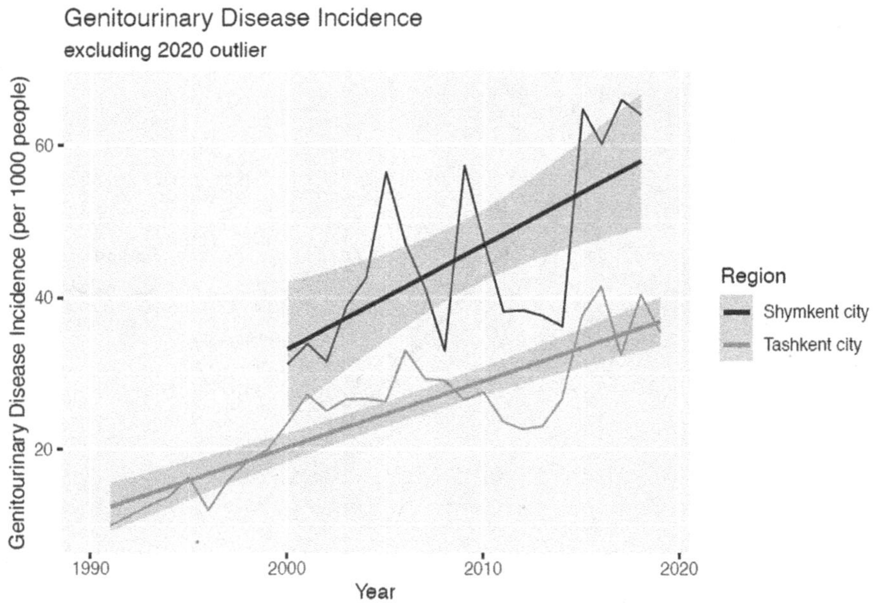

Figure 3.10e Tashkent vs. Shymkent: health indicators patterns over time
Source: Authors' calculations based on the State Statistics Committee of the Republic of Uzbekistan and MedInform data.

topics for more focused research. However, the real test of health systems is not so much their performance in leading cities as it is an assessment of outcomes in the countryside and smaller towns. We now turn to this topic.

Further comparisons are more challenging. To complete our analysis of the effects of the health policy reforms in Uzbekistan, we compare various health indicators to those of a "synthetic Uzbekistan" composed of bordering Kazakhstani regions.

The synthetic control method has been referred to as "arguably the most important innovation in the policy evaluation literature in the last 15 years" (Athey and Imbens, 2017). Much like the related method of difference-in-difference (Arkhangelsky et al., 2021), the synthetic control is leveraged primarily to minimize confounding effects in social science analysis. To create a "synthetic" equivalent of the target region, the researcher aggregates data from similar regions, weighting each to match most closely with the demographic characteristics of the region of interest (Abadie, 2021). By comparing the synthetic region to reality, the researcher can observe the residual impact of an intervention – such as a policy – relative to the constructed counterfactual.

We use a synthetic control model approach following Abadie et al. (2015), Abadie (2021), and Robbins and Davenport (2021). Specifically, we obtain health data at the *raion* (county) level for neighboring districts in Kazakhstan from www.medinform.kz. We chose to center the model on Jizzakh,

Navoiy, and Tashkent provinces, which border Kyzylorda and Turkistan oblasts in Kazakhstan, as these regions were likely to share many characteristics with their Uzbekistani counterparts – both those reflected by our demographic data and confounding factors, as well as the Republic of Karakalpakstan.

For each Uzbekistani province bordering Kazakhstan, we then define a baseline period (either 2000–2005 or, alternately, 2000–2006 – a longer time series would be preferable, but data restrictions do not allow this), and then obtain a combination of comparator regions that best mimics a vector of external characteristics for the chosen province. Coefficients on the comparator regions then serve as weights. To create our synthetic Uzbekistan(s), we weight regions according to ten variables: baseline values of doctors per capita, infant mortality rate, average length of hospital stay, hospital beds per capita, hospitals per capita, and incidences of cancer, diabetes, digestive disease, genitourinary diseases, injury, and tuberculosis per capita. We then run the analysis, observing the estimated impact of 2005-era policies on the same variables. 250 permutations of the synthetic control are also included in each visualization. R offers a variety of packages to conduct synthetic control analysis; we utilize the microsynth package, created by Michael W. Robbins and Steven Davenport, for its ease of use and specification (www.jstatsoft.org/article/view/v097i02).

We estimate these alternately for all Uzbekistani border provinces together, and then alone for Karakalpakstan, which has received particular attention.

Figure 3.11 shows that healthcare trends on either side of the border, with regions matched on initial health sector characteristics, are quite similar. Treatment characteristics (length of stay, and other terms not shown) follow similar trends. While there is considerable oscillation, infant mortality declines are striking and similar as well – though there is a rise in Uzbekistan's provinces in recent years that did not occur in neighboring Kazakhstani raions. Whether this reflects an actual rise or improved monitoring is unclear, and would require a separate paper that tracked rates of recorded very low birth weights (< 1500g), abortion rates, and age 1–5 mortality. In contrast, genitourinary infections rose in Uzbekistan's provinces prior to 2013 and then fell precipitously – while they accelerated across the border.

The most striking distinction is the persistently higher cancer incidence in neighboring Kazakhstan. While this could reflect superior surveillance and diagnosis, that is not an obvious explanation given the similarity of other measures. Taken as a whole, the figures show remarkable similarity, and convergence for tuberculosis, especially when one considers that the data are generated by two distinct health statistical services. The decline in the length of stay is consistently greater in Uzbekistan, which hints at either more rapid healthcare modernization or wasted resources in its more prosperous northern neighbor.

What about Karakalpakstan? Given its remoteness, health consequences of the drying up of the Aral Sea, and lingering effects of weapons tests, the region and adjacent areas in Kazakhstan have been particularly important

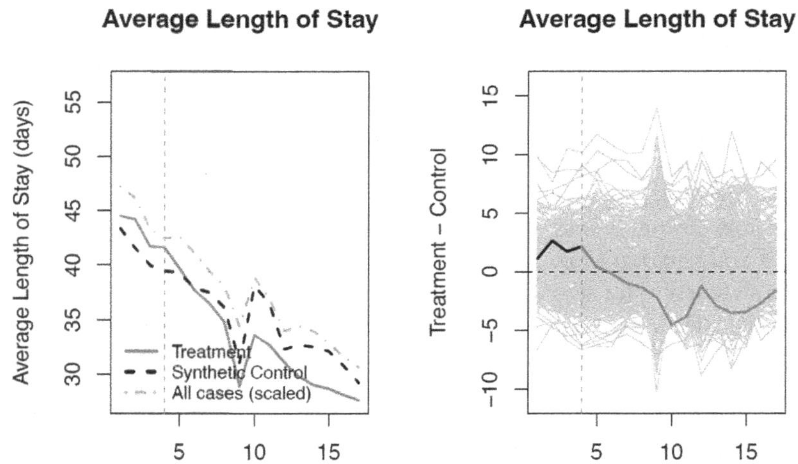

Figure 3.11a Uzbekistan–Kazakhstan border regions matched by synthetic controls: length of stay, infant mortality, tuberculosis, all cancers, and genitourinary infections

Source: Authors' calculations based on the State Statistics Committee of the Republic of Uzbekistan and MedInform data.

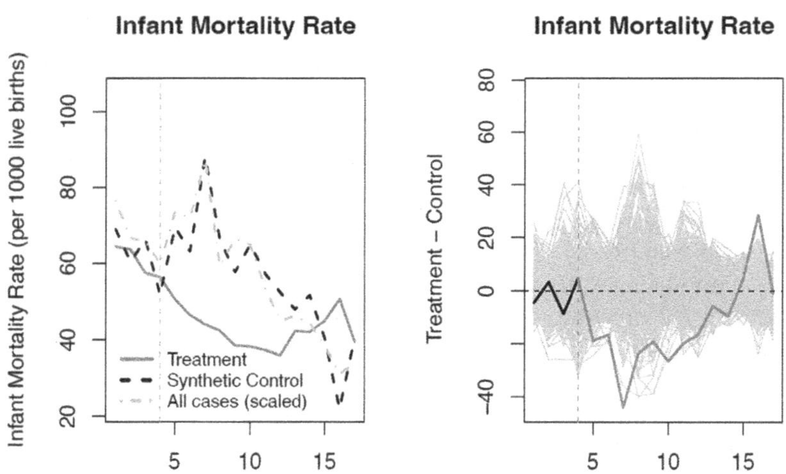

Figure 3.11b Uzbekistan–Kazakhstan border regions matched by synthetic controls: length of stay, infant mortality, tuberculosis, all cancers, and genitourinary infections

Source: Authors' calculations based on the State Statistics Committee of the Republic of Uzbekistan and MedInform data.

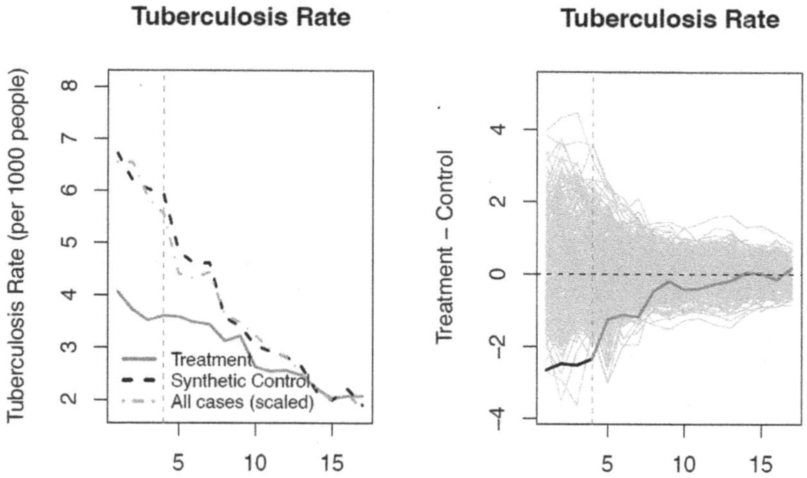

Figure 3.11c Uzbekistan–Kazakhstan border regions matched by synthetic controls: length of stay, infant mortality, tuberculosis, all cancers, and genitourinary infections

Source: Authors' calculations based on the State Statistics Committee of the Republic of Uzbekistan and MedInform data.

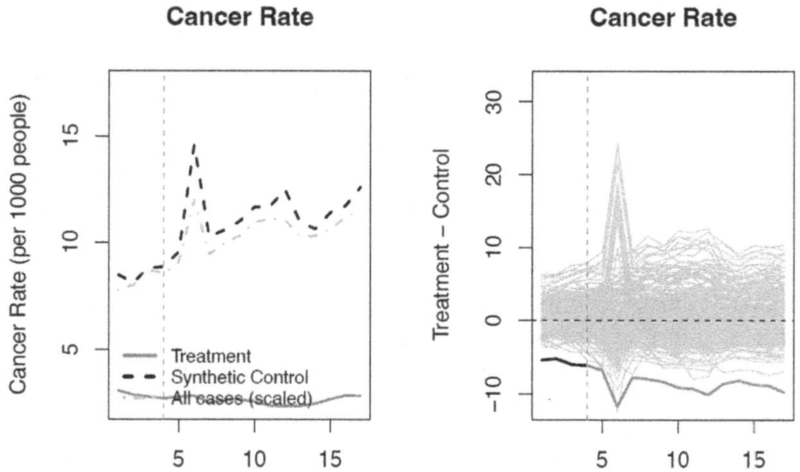

Figure 3.11d Uzbekistan–Kazakhstan border regions matched by synthetic controls: length of stay, infant mortality, tuberculosis, all cancers, and genitourinary infections

Source: Authors' calculations based on the State Statistics Committee of the Republic of Uzbekistan and MedInform data.

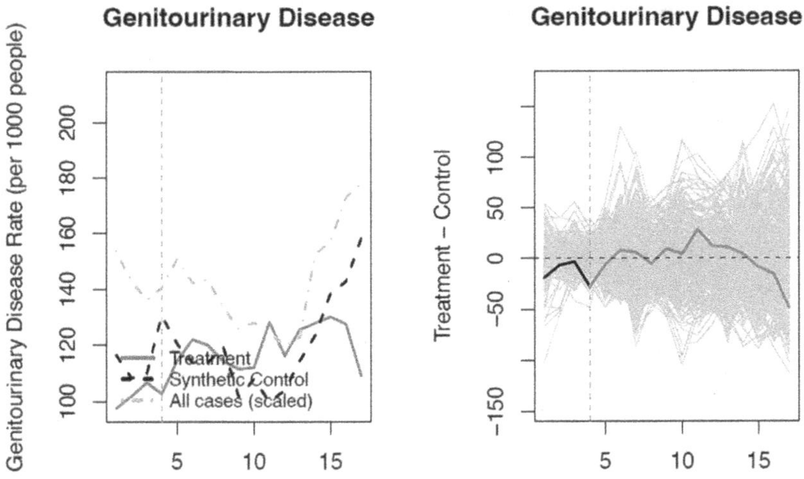

Figure 3.11e Uzbekistan–Kazakhstan border regions matched by synthetic controls: length of stay, infant mortality, tuberculosis, all cancers, and genitourinary infections

Source: Authors' calculations based on the State Statistics Committee of the Republic of Uzbekistan and MedInform data.

focal points. Given the distinct nature of Karakalpakstan, the synthetic control we use is composed of Kyzylorda, Turkistan, and the remaining provinces of Uzbekistan that are *not* Karakalpakstan.

Figure 3.12 justifies Uzbekistan's emphasis on Karakalpakstan. The trends in infant mortality and tuberculosis are similar to its comparator raions in Kazakhstan and other Uzbekistan provinces, but levels remain elevated. While Uzbekistan had advantages in cancer and (slightly) genitourinary tract infections relative to neighboring Kazakhstani regions, Karakalpakstan does not emerge as an advantaged region. Nor does the region exhibit a more rapid decline in the length of hospital stay. Other comparisons not reported also point to the relatively slow progress in Karakalpakstan.

We did not attempt to match more distant regions with Kazakhstani comparators, since differing climatic and cultural differences would make interpretation difficult. However, it is quite possible that Karakalpakstan is not unique, and that other relatively remote and low-density regions also may merit healthcare system focus in the coming years. On the other hand, other relatively high-density regions bordering Kazakhstan have achieved commendable success in the past 15 years.

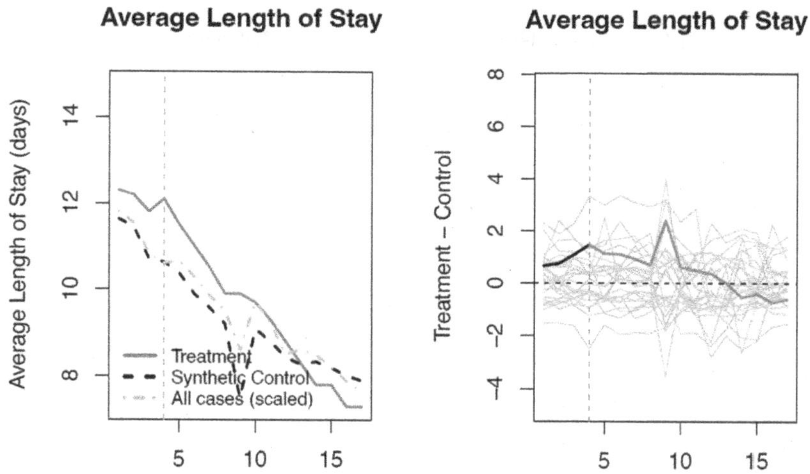

Figure 3.12a Karakalpakstan–Kazakhstan border regions matched by synthetic controls: length of stay, infant mortality, tuberculosis, all cancers, and genitourinary infections

Source: Authors' calculations based on the State Statistics Committee of the Republic of Uzbekistan and MedInform data.

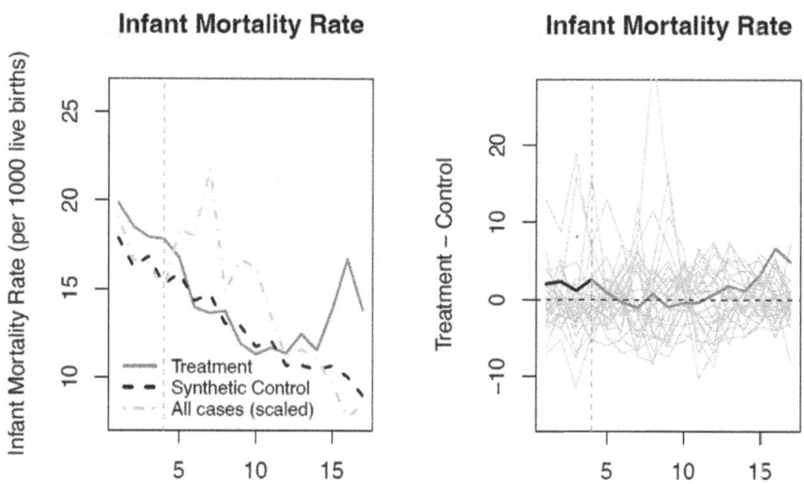

Figure 3.12b Karakalpakstan–Kazakhstan border regions matched by synthetic controls: length of stay, infant mortality, tuberculosis, all cancers, and genitourinary infections

Source: Authors' calculations based on the State Statistics Committee of the Republic of Uzbekistan and MedInform data.

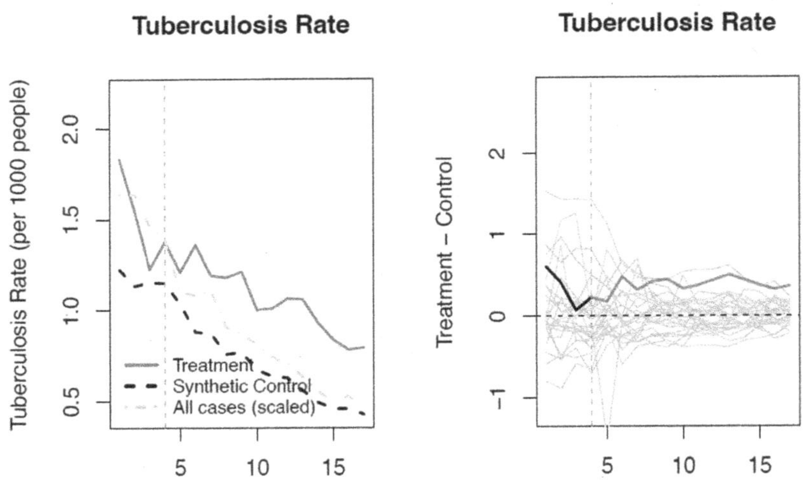

Figure 3.12c Karakalpakstan–Kazakhstan border regions matched by synthetic controls: length of stay, infant mortality, tuberculosis, all cancers, and genitourinary infections

Source: Authors' calculations based on the State Statistics Committee of the Republic of Uzbekistan and MedInform data.

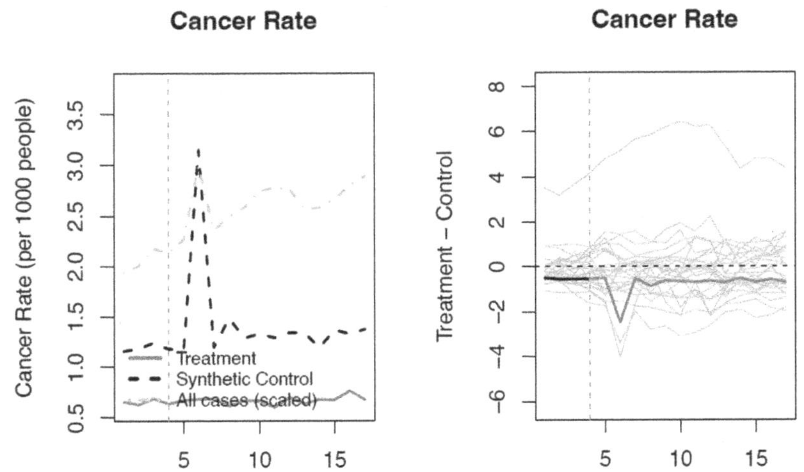

Figure 3.12d Karakalpakstan–Kazakhstan border regions matched by synthetic controls: length of stay, infant mortality, tuberculosis, all cancers, and genitourinary infections

Source: Authors' calculations based on the State Statistics Committee of the Republic of Uzbekistan and MedInform data.

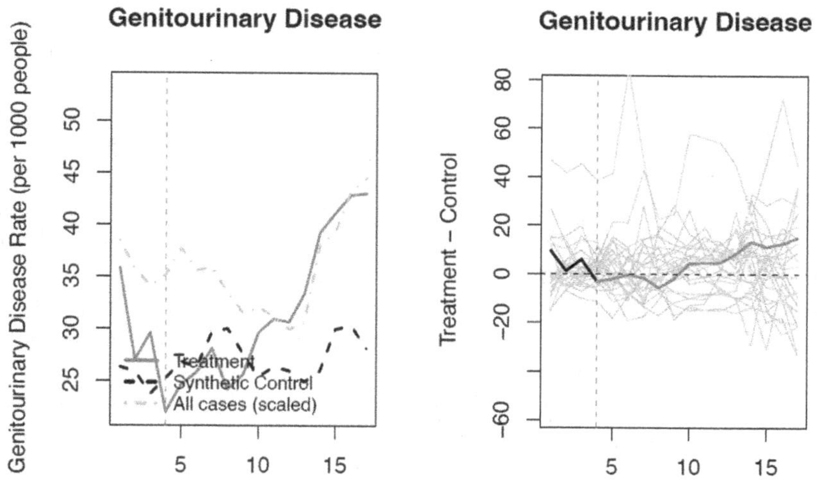

Figure 3.12e Karakalpakstan–Kazakhstan border regions matched by synthetic controls: length of stay, infant mortality, tuberculosis, all cancers, and genitourinary infections

Source: Authors' calculations based on the State Statistics Committee of the Republic of Uzbekistan and MedInform data.

3.5 Summing up: remarkable achievements to date; future gains on the horizon

It is impossible to review the evidence presented and not be deeply impressed with Uzbekistan's accomplishments in the health sphere since independence. Unlike most other post-Soviet states, Uzbekistan's key health metrics did not deteriorate in the 1990s. Many dramatic improvements then followed in the early 2000s. However, given the structural flaws and poor-quality care inherited from the Soviet system, many of these achievements can be regarded as "low-hanging fruit."

With the easy gains largely realized, the Mirziyoyev Administration has embarked on a hugely ambitious set of health sector reforms. While it is still too early to fully assess their effectiveness, especially as many consequences will not be felt for decades, the initial results are promising. Roughly speaking, provinces in Uzbekistan adjacent to Kazakhstan appear to be performing comparably overall to their neighboring regions – even though Kazakhstan also has made major health sector commitments and has the advantage of vast mineral wealth.

The most severe challenge that lies ahead involves reducing the prevalence of "diseases of poverty" in the nation's less developed areas. Of course, this is not a problem unique to Uzbekistan, and it is not as acute a problem in Uzbekistan as in many other countries. Nonetheless, it is a critical task, and it is not obvious that the reforms underway will be fully effective in backward areas.

A second challenge involves curtailing increases in "diseases of new wealth" associated with economic development. Indeed, this term is something of a misnomer, since key "diseases" include death and trauma from motor vehicle accidents. While a detailed discussion is not appropriate here, it is important to recognize that environmental safety and public health policies will play critical roles in future population health gains.

The analysis in this chapter is based on incomplete, highly aggregated data of variable quality. While a great deal is revealed, more refined analysis will require a long, consistent series of disaggregated data and, ultimately, individual records. Collecting and publicly posting data at the district level, as in Kazakhstan, is a first step. Ultimately, surveys that track large numbers of individuals over time – as in the US Center for Disease Control/National Cancer Institute's Surveillance, Epidemiology, and End Results (SEER) Program (seer.cancer.gov) – will be important for making refined estimates of the impact of specific policies.

Notes

1 A Program to Improve the Emergency and Emergency Medical Care System to Be Developed – UzLiDeP.

2 Sources:

- www.uzdaily.uz/en/post/63863
- www.uzreport.news/society/uzbekistan-opens-first-innovative-telemedicine-clinic
- https://kun.uz/en/news/2019/04/12/centers-for-telemedicine-to-be-established-in-uzbekistan
- Ibragimova et al. (2022). Telemedicine in Uzbekistan – https://wos.academiascience.org/index.php/wos/article/view/1561

References

Abadie, Alberto, Alexis Diamond, and Jens Hainmueller. (2015). "Comparative Politics and the Synthetic Control Method." *American Journal of Political Science*, 59 (2): 495–510.

Anthopolos, Rebecca, and Charles M.Becker. (2010). "Global Infant Mortality: Correcting for Undercounting." *World Development*, 38 (4): 467–481.

Arkhangelsky, Dmitry, Susan Athey, David A. Hirshberg, Guido W. Imbens, and Stefan Wager. (2021). "Synthetic Difference-in-Differences." *American Economic Review*, 111 (12): 4088–4118.

Abadie, Alberto. (2021). "Using Synthetic Controls: Feasibility, Data Requirements, and Methodological Aspects." *Journal of Economic Literature*. www.aeaweb.org/articles?id=10.1257%2Fjel.20191450.

Athey, S., and G. W. Imbens. (2017). The State of Applied Econometrics: Causality and Policy Evaluation. *Journal of Economic Perspectives*, 31 (2), 3–32.

Robbins, M. W., and S. Davenport. (2021). Microsynth: Synthetic Control Methods for Disaggregated and Micro-Level Data in R. *Journal of Statistical Software*, 97 (2), 1–31. https://doi.org/10.18637/jss.v097.i02.

Sources for databases and legal documents

World Bank. (2023). www.data.worldbank.org.
Lex.uz. (2023). https://lex.uz/docs/.
OpenBudget.uz. (2023). www.openbudget.uz/ru/outcomesView#RANGE!C8.
Stat.uz. (2023). State Statistics Committee of the Republic of Uzbekistan. *Social Protection.* https://stat.uz/uz/rasmiy-statistika/social-protection-2.
MedInform. (n.d.). www.medinfo.kz/#/dpsraion.
World Health Organization. (2012). *Global Health Expenditure Database (GHED).* https://apps.who.int/nha/database/Select/Indicators/en.

4 The financial system

Davit Babasyan and Martin Melecky[1]

4.1 Introduction

Entering its seventh year of an ambitious market transition, Uzbekistan's reform agenda has the well-being and prosperity of the people at its center. Starting in 2017, the economic transformation entails three major shifts: from central planning to a market economy, from state to private ownership, and from isolation to economic integration. Breaking from policies of statism and relative isolation, the country and its people have embraced a new era of openness and international engagement (World Bank, 2022). Early reforms liberalized the foreign exchange market and most prices, removed heavy-handed regulations on businesses and trade, increased transparency, and relaxed policies that limited personal choice and economic freedom. Six years on, a more open and competitive economy is emerging, with citizens seeing their economic opportunities and freedoms expand. Looking to the next five years, the government has committed to an ambitious plan to reduce poverty by half and make Uzbekistan an upper-middle-income country by 2030.

Financial sector reform is essential to transitioning the Uzbek economy successfully to market principles, supporting economic growth, job creation, and social cohesion. Moving to a market economy requires a fundamental transformation of the financial system from one dominated by state-owned banks—that acted as "development agents" of the state financing state-owned enterprises and priority economic sectors—to a new and commercially oriented system that provides a suitable range of financial services in competitive quality to business and people. Such reforms will improve economic efficiency by enhancing the financial system's ability to intermediate funds to productive investments, strengthening financial stability, and improving access to financial services. These reforms will ultimately support the country's economic growth, boost the productivity of firms and job creation, improve resiliency to shocks, and facilitate the empowerment of marginalized groups, such as women and rural residents.

This chapter assesses the current state of the financial sector in Uzbekistan, the progress achieved since the inception of the economic

DOI: 10.4324/9781003473497-4

transformation program, and highlights the key reform areas that lie ahead in the next, more complex phase of reforms. The remainder of this chapter is organized as follows. Section 4.2 provides an overview of the current situation in all relevant financial subsectors of the country, the progress achieved, and the remaining critical issues. Section 4.3 assesses the financial inclusion of small and medium-sized enterprises and households. Section 4.4 discusses developments in financial sector institutions focusing on oversight and the need for rethinking the currently fragmented supervisory structure for financial subsectors. Section 4.5 concludes and offers some policy recommendations.

4.2 Changing financial sector structure

4.2.1 Banking system

After the breakup of the Soviet Union, the Uzbek government retained its central role in allocating economic resources within the country (World Bank, 2022). The banking system was no exception. In the early 1990s, the state established or reorganized the key state-owned banks on the basis of the banks that used to operate in the USSR era.[2] In the years that followed, the government established several other state-owned banks and reoriented state-owned banks to finance specific economic sectors.[3] As a result, the new Uzbekistan inherited a state-dominated banking system from the start (Figure 4.1, Panel A), largely replicating the state-funded and controlled economy—an economic model operated in the preceding decades.

In addition, while private banks, including foreign banks, appeared as early as the 1990s, they never reached a significant scale over the last three decades. Since 2003, around ten private banks exited the market for financial stability, money laundering, and other reasons, but the number of banks in the system did not change much—hovering between 26 to 33. Lending to state-owned enterprises (SOEs) in industrial sectors dominated the bank lending portfolios while bank lending to individuals—a wider population at large—was almost non-existent (Figure 4.1, Panel B).

By the end of 2018, state-owned commercial banks (SOCBs) still dominated the banking system of Uzbekistan, accounting for more than 95 percent of the total financial sector assets. SOCBs served an important role in the state's highly complex and inefficient approach to financing its industrial policy and industrialization efforts. Banking sector assets and credit stood at 53 percent and 41 percent of GDP by the end of 2018. Having more than 80 percent share in the total banking system assets and funded largely by the government (predominantly through the national sovereign wealth fund—the Uzbekistan Fund for Reconstruction and Development, UFRD) and foreign bank credit lines, the SOCBs *de facto* played the role of the traditional development banks by channeling cheap long-term funding to priority sectors and SOEs at below-market rates. Around 80 percent of total credit was

Panel A. Dynamics of state-owned and private banks' share in banking system in terms of total assets

Panel B. Dynamics of banking system credit portfolio structure

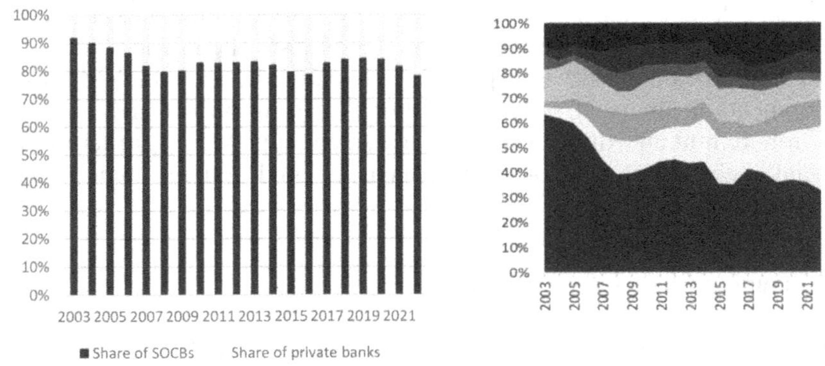

Figure 4.1 The Uzbek banking system was dominated by state-owned banks over the last few decades, which were largely involved in lending to SOEs in industrial sectors. **Panel A.** Dynamics of state-owned and private banks' share in the banking system in terms of total assets. **Panel B.** Dynamics of banking system credit portfolio structure

Source: CBU, authors' calculations.

at preferential rates and around half of the total credit was provided to SOEs and budget organizations (mostly in foreign currency). Interestingly, the agriculture sector—which accounted for about a third of the national economy—received a disproportionally smaller share of the total bank credit.

The state-dominated and funded banking system dampened any incentives to develop client-friendly retail products and provide good quality client service. With a small share in total credit, retail loans to individuals comprised mostly preferential mortgage loans and a smaller portion of loans for purchasing cars produced by the local automobile industry. Mortgage loans, funded by government credit, were mostly provided by SOCBs to individuals for purchasing apartments and houses built by state-led and financed construction companies. While small businesses[4] accounted for around 60 percent of the economy, less than a third of credit was extended to this sector. On top of the low level of financing, small businesses also lacked access to an appropriate range and quality of financial products.

The political mandate to provide credit to priority sectors and SOEs—the main driving force of SOCB activities—resulted in poor corporate governance and risk management practices in SOCBs. Lack of proper capital and liquidity planning in SOCBs and poor profitability—driven by lower net interest margins on the substantial volume of preferential lending—resulted in frequent recapitalizations of SOCBs by the Uzbekistan Fund for Reconstruction and Development (UFRD—Uzbekistan's sovereign wealth fund).

In addition, the restructured large SOE loans—especially after the currency devaluation in 2017—were given regulatory forbearance, obscuring the true non-performing loans (NPL) levels and overstating SOCBs' capitalization levels. SOCBs had largely formalistic and dysfunctional Boards of Directors, populated by state officials with little knowledge and time to devote to their responsibilities. In addition, CEOs of SOCBs were politically appointed, with a lack of transparency and clarity on their appointment process, which resulted in CEOs not being fully accountable to Boards and with inadequate focus on developing the SOCBs' business and risk management function. SOCBs were also engaged in non-core (non-typical) business activities to the detriment of the banks' financial position, bank–client relationships, and overall trust in the banking system. Namely, SOCBs performed tax administration functions, as well as cash monitoring and client account reporting to relevant state bodies. Moreover, SOCBs were in the past often directed by the state to take over the ownership of companies to recapitalize and manage them. Within the overall weak framework for securing property rights, the cases of bank account seizures by the state—with limited recourse for firms and individuals to ensure unbiased rulings—further inhibited trust in the banking system. Finally, the history of cash shortages, restrictions on currency conversion, and disruptions in payment systems eroded the trust of the population in the banking system and reduced demand for deposits. Consequently, the Uzbek banking system suffered from ineffective deposit mobilization from the private sector. The private sector deposits to GDP ratio stood at 13 percent by the end of 2018, with private sector deposits accounting for less than 30 percent of total bank liabilities.

While private banks mostly served the private sector on a commercial basis, they were very small in size. Unlike SOCBs, private banks funded their operations through retail deposits (more than 70 percent of their liabilities) with the remaining liabilities mostly sourced from foreign banks and international development financial institutions. Private banks also consistently outperformed SOCBs on various metrics: private banks were two to three times more profitable than SOCBs, had less dollarized balance sheets, smaller exposure to large borrowers and SOEs, and more independent, foreign, and female board members.

As Uzbekistan embarked on its ambitious program for economic reforms and transitioning to a market economy, the new government realized that the banking sector needed a major restructuring and modernization. The main objective was to transition the banking sector from one that served SOEs to a new one that could provide competitive financial services to the private sector. The banking sector reform aimed to achieve three main objectives: (1) improve financial sector efficiency, (2) enhance financial inclusion, and (3) preserve financial stability. The transformation and subsequent privatization of most SOCBs were envisaged to trigger more efficient allocation of resources to productive investments, wind down the distortive directed lending that enabled the survival of unviable firms, boost the quality of banking services, and level the playing field for all current and prospective competitors in the banking sector. Because SOEs continued to play a crucial role in the Uzbek economy and remained key clients of SOCBs, the success of banking sector reform depended on the parallel reform and privatization efforts in the SOE sector. Banks' business models had to be completely transformed to discourage dependence on public-sector funding and its repercussions for efficient credit allocation and much-needed deposit mobilization. To effectively govern the new business models, strong corporate governance and risk management practices of banks must have taken center stage.

Banking sector reform in Uzbekistan started with a major overhaul of the banking legislation to lay the foundations for modern banking and supervision of the sector. The laws on the Central Bank and Banks and Banking—adopted in the mid-1990s—were outdated and largely non-compliant with international standards (the Basel Core Principles for Effective Banking Supervision). Uzbekistan adopted the two laws in the new edition[5] which were critical for attracting private investors into Uzbekistan's banking system and enabling further improvement of the Central Bank's regulatory and supervisory framework. Along with the adoption of the two laws, Uzbekistan also adopted a new law on Currency Regulation and Payments and Payment Systems. The latter was aimed to meet the diversity of payment preferences in the digital age and to pave the way for electronic money and digital wallets, while bringing the previously unregulated sector of payment providers under the supervisory umbrella of the Central Bank.

In its first important attempt to detach the banking system from the previous SOE-centric model, the government implemented critical reform aimed at stopping the practice of direct on-lending of UFRD funds through SOCBs to SOEs. Moreover, most SOCB loans to SOEs, extended previously using UFRD's resources, were transferred from the SOCB balance sheets to the UFRD. This policy action cleaned up the SOCBs' balance sheets and decreased the foreign currency and concentration risks. Nevertheless, the concentration risk reached the pre-reform levels in the largest SOCBs by the end of 2022 (Figure 4.2, Panel B). The freed-up capital of SOCBs due to the reform was later used to finance private sector loans, mostly on commercial terms. The government further demanded winding down the practice of preferential lending, applying interest rate subsidies only where needed, and concentrating all directed lending programs in three SOCBs that were expected to remain in public ownership for the foreseeable future. As a result, the outstanding preferential loans as a share of total SOCB loans decreased from around 80 percent in 2018 to about 40 percent by the end of 2022 (Figure 4.2, Panel A).

Once the critical pre-conditions for banking sector reform were rolled out, as a next step, the government needed to formulate a banking sector reform strategy to develop and agree on a roadmap of further actions and their sequencing to achieve the three reform objectives: improved efficiency,

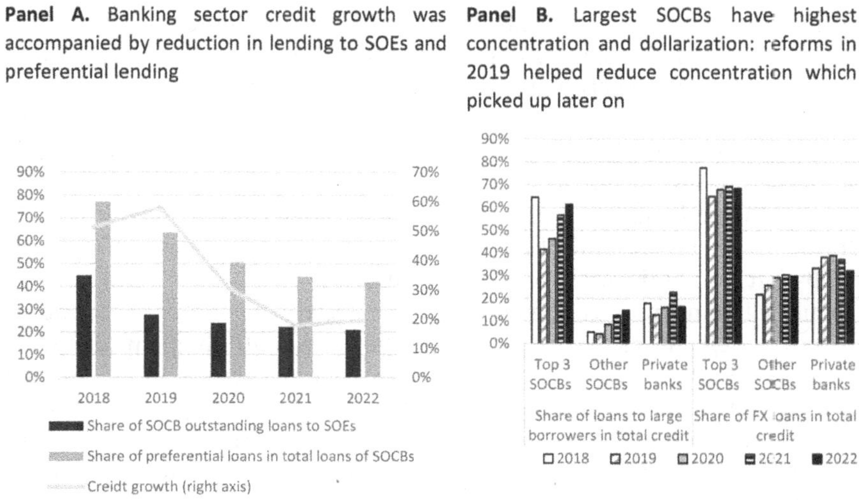

Figure 4.2 Financial liberalization resulted in rapid credit growth of predominantly commercial lending. **Panel A.** Banking sector credit growth was accompanied by a reduction in lending to SOEs and preferential lending. **Panel B.** Largest SOCBs have the highest concentration and dollarization: reforms in 2019 helped reduce concentration which picked up later on

Source: CBU, authors' calculations

financial inclusion, and financial stability. Consequently, in May 2020 and June 2021, the government adopted two critical strategies: (i) Banking Sector Reform Strategy 2020–2025, and (ii) National Financial Inclusion Strategy 2021–2023 (NFIS). The banking sector reform strategy calls for the transformation and commercialization of all SOCBs, and privatization of selected SOCBs. For the largest SOCBs, the privatization should follow a two-stage process with pre-privatization transformation support and an initial partial privatization supported by IFI(s), followed by full privatization of reformed SOCBs to strategic investors through an open and competitive tender. One outcome target of the strategy is increasing the share of private banks in total banking system assets from 15 percent in 2020 to 60 percent by the end of 2025 and their share of deposits in total bank liabilities from 40 percent to 60 percent. This strategy also calls for: (i) further improving the banking legislation to cover Basel III standards, developing the legislation on non-bank credit organizations, the bank resolution framework, the deposit insurance framework, and the capital markets; (ii) moderating dollarization and credit growth; (iii) improving financial and ICT infrastructure; and (iv) upgrading human capital in the banking system. The NFIS defines national financial inclusion objectives, identifies a prioritized set of actions to achieve those objectives, and outlines the main opportunities and obstacles that policymakers should consider during implementation.

It is, however, not the first time that Uzbekistan attempted to privatize its SOCBs. Privatization plans for the largest SOCBs were drawn up several times starting early 2000s, but all of them failed due to a lack of economy-wide reforms, parallel reforms in the SOE sector, restructuring of SOCB's balance sheets, and the continued practice of directed and preferential lending. What makes this time different for Uzbekistan is the fact that the adoption of the banking sector reform strategy was accompanied by critical reforms—both before and after its implementation—that covered not only SOCBs but also SOEs and the economy at large.

While all transition economies have been faced with the need to address SOCB and SOE restructuring as they moved from centrally planned systems to market-based private systems, this process did not always go as smoothly as planned and ended up being implemented at different speeds and under different modalities. Widespread privatization programs were often controversial and difficult to implement for a variety of reasons, such as political opposition—including resistance stemming from the doubtful success of past privatizations; actual or perceived negative distributional consequences; and political economy considerations (Bertay et al., 2020).

Babasyan et al. (2023) synthesize key lessons that have emerged from past privatization reforms: (i) privatization of state-owned banks had a greater positive impact when it was total rather than partial (Ehrlich et al., 1994; Megginson et al., 2005; Bonin et al., 2005; Beck et al., 2005); (ii) privatization in certain cases (such as Hungary and the Czech Republic) required prior cleanup of state-owned bank balance sheets and operational restructuring, making the privatization the last and not the first step in the transformation process (Hawkins and Mihaljek, 2001); (iii) the benefits of privatization are weakest for countries where it was rushed the most, such as in Eastern Europe and where it was not paired with institutional strengthening of the regulatory and supervisory framework (Azam et al., 2004; Reinhart and Rogoff, 2013; Estrin and Pelletier, 2018); and (iv) the success of banking sector reform is dependent on and supports the reform of state-owned enterprises. The above-mentioned elements of successful transformation apply even more when the banking sector is concentrated and underdeveloped, as shown by two papers that examine the privatization of banks in Uganda and Tanzania (Clarke et al., 2009; Cull and Spreng, 2011).

Therefore, privatization of SOCBs shall not be rushed. The government will have one shot at bringing in fit and proper shareholders and if it fails to do so, it would be increasingly difficult to get rid of unfit shareholders in the future (see also Bonin and Wachtel, 2003; Mako, 2020). Throughout the former Soviet Union, in countries such as Ukraine, Russia, Azerbaijan, and Kazakhstan, state failures to bring in fit and proper shareholders bred non-transparent ownership structures, enabling the emergence of oligarchic banking that ultimately set the stage for costly financial crises and inequality in financial access.

Private ownership of banks, however, is not a panacea for reforming a state-owned banking system. Private investors, in their branching strategy for

Uzbekistan, will need to mostly rely on local staff capacity. Local human capital is therefore part of the franchise value when international banking groups strategize about acquisitions in transition countries or greenfield investments. At the same time, low human capital in banking is a general and urgent problem in Uzbekistan's banking system. As SOCBs traditionally acted as public-sector development agencies, the SOCB staff and management lack the necessary skills and knowledge in key competencies—such as credit underwriting, risk management and internal controls, asset and liability management, human resource management, or other aspects of corporate governance. Unfortunately, the problems of the state-dominated banking system spilled over to private banks that suffer from similar issues. The challenge for banks is to quickly enhance the knowledge and capabilities of the existing staff, as well as the possibilities to attract new people with adequate qualifications. Babasyan et al. (2023) point to several studies that highlight the importance of developing human capital for a competitive banking environment to emerge (Borish et al., 1995; Claessens, 1998a; Claessens, 1998b; Brandt and Li, 2003; Bonin et al., 2014). For example, Claessens (1998b) highlights that strong institutions could help substitute for the shortage of banking skills in the initial stages of transition. Foreign investment and participation in banking can be one way to speed up knowledge transfer and the needed upgrade of banking skills in the banking sector of transition economies (Bonin et al., 2014). But counting on future foreign direct investment for skills to upgrade can be counterproductive, and therefore the key focus should be on upgrading the local human capital early in the transition.

The SOCBs that will remain in state hands for the foreseeable future need to operate on competitive neutrality principles—even if they pose a double-bottom line mandate. While there is no strong rationale for having a large public commercial banking sector, there might be justifications for having SOCBs in a market-based financial system. For one, private banks may underserve certain market segments due to market failures or profitability considerations, and SOCBs may help fill in the identified unmet financial needs. They can focus on credit-constrained but viable borrowers or provide finance in rural areas, where private banks and other financial institutions are not well represented, or support financing of large infrastructure projects. As such, fostering access to finance and financial inclusion for specific segments of the population, economic sectors, or asset classes may become a specific mandate for some banks with a development (double-bottom line) mandate. Although the direct provision of public finance may not always be the most optimal solution, this approach may work as a bridging solution while more structural solutions are underway (Gutierrez and Kliatskova, 2021). State-owned banks may also play a critical countercyclical role in lending during periods of crisis (Micco and Panizza, 2006; Bertay, Demirgüç-Kunt, and Huizinga, 2015; Bertay et al., 2020; Bosshardt and Cerutii, 2020; EBRD, 2020). As SOCBs already exist in Uzbekistan, the relevant question is not whether direct state ownership would be an optimal solution to market failures, but rather how to refocus the remaining SOCBs (which will not be privatized) toward well-defined socioeconomic objectives that can complement and crowd in the activity of private banks to complete the banking market. Explicitly defining a clear mandate for state-owned banks along with improved corporate governance and independent oversight are key factors that can help limit the alternative costs related to the SOCB's political remit and lower efficiency.

4.2.2 Non-bank credit organizations

Developing a vibrant ecosystem of specialized non-bank financial sector providers that typically serve micro, small and medium enterprises (MSMEs) and low-income households is important for deepening the financial market and fostering financial inclusion. The subsector of non-bank credit organizations (NBCOs) is underdeveloped in Uzbekistan. Recently, the government has intensified its focus on deepening Uzbekistan's credit markets—including through its financial sector development and inclusion strategies. By the end of 2022, NBCOs in Uzbekistan consisted of 85 Microcredit Organizations (MCOs), 81 pawnshops, and one mortgage refinancing company supervised by the Central Bank of Uzbekistan (CBU).[6] NBCOs accounted for just 0.8 percent of total banking sector assets, of which MCOs (currently called—microfinance organizations; MFOs) accounted for around half of total NBCO assets, and the mortgage refinancing company for another half. The microloans offered by MFOs typically come with short maturities (about three years) and relatively high interest rates (about 60 percent per annum on average), in part due to high operating costs and lack of access of MFOs to debt financing.[7] In addition, around 25 active leasing companies, not regulated by the Central Bank, provide leasing services to commercial entities. They have a combined portfolio of around 1.4 percent of the banking sector's credit portfolio (Leasing Association of Uzbekistan, 2021).

The underdeveloped NBCO sector is largely a result of the fragmented and restrictive legal framework. Strict limitations on the activities of MCOs and their funding sources, coupled with restrictions on new branch openings, have significantly hampered MCO growth and expansion. While MCOs are not allowed to take deposits, they have nonetheless been subjected to relatively strict prudential requirements—such as the 10 percent capital adequacy ratio equivalent to that set for banks.[8] In April 2022, the parliament adopted a new law "On Non-Bank Credit Organizations and Microfinance Activities" that draws on global good practice, provides regulatory oversight proportionate to the size of the sector and the nature of its activities, and protects consumers of financial services provided by NBCOs. While NBCOs will still not be permitted to take deposits—which can be the right approach in the current circumstances—they can now grant loans and leases exceeding the amount for microcredits, provide services such as factoring, guarantee, and Islamic financial services, and issue bonds. The overhauled law is expected to increase the number of NBCOs, their branches, and the volume of their financial intermediation. Over time, with the removal of structural constraints that contributed to higher costs for microcredit organizations, the cost of obtaining microcredit services is also expected to fall.

An acute problem for the further development of the microfinance sector in Uzbekistan remains the weakness in attracting funds by the MFOs to expand activities. Given the small size of individual MFOs in Uzbekistan, a financial apex institution for MFOs could be established jointly by the public and private sectors (including international financial institutions). It would help attract wholesale funding and channel the funding (in the form of grants, loans, partial credit guarantees, etc.) to member MFOs, ideally paired with supporting technical services. A financial apex may also catalyze wholesale financing for green projects and thereby support the greening of the MFO sector and its clients. However, many apex institutions globally have not performed as expected, often due to the lack of a critical mass of good MFOs with capacity to absorb apex funding—a critical issue that often gets underestimated (Levy, 2002).

4.2.3 Insurance sector

Despite numerous insurance companies in the market, insurance penetration in Uzbekistan is very low, including when compared to other countries in the region (Figure 3, Panel B). In 2022, the insurance penetration ratio (GWP to GDP) reached 0.7 percent (Figure 4.3, Panel A), compared with the global average of 7.0 percent of GDP and the Emerging Asia average of 3.7 percent of GDP.[9] The ratio of Uzbek insurance companies' assets to GDP stood at 0.5 percent in 2022.

The number of insurance companies grew from 30 in 2018 to 41 in 2022, of which eight provide life insurance and 33 offer general (non-life) insurance.[10] State participation in the insurance market remains significant with two state-owned insurers (Uzbekinvest and Uzagrosgurta) accounting for about 24 percent of total non-life insurance premiums in 2022. But the share of state insurance companies in the market has been gradually decreasing from 40.5 percent in 2013 to 37 percent in 2017 and 28 percent in 2018. A large state-owned insurance company—Kafolat Insurance—was privatized in 2021. The insurance market in Uzbekistan is concentrated, with the top ten insurance companies accounting for more than 70 percent of total gross written premiums. The rest of the companies are small, having less than 2–3 percent market share. AXCO reports[11] that, except for the occasional very large risks facultatively reinsured overseas, most insurance business is retained in the local market either with the direct insurer or with locally placed reinsurance. In 2022, seven insurance brokers, around 9,000 insurance agents, and just five insurance actuaries were represented in the insurance market.

Panel A. Insurance market in Uzbekistan is growing steadily and rapidly

Panel B. Uzbekistan is well behind its regional peers in insurance penetration ratio

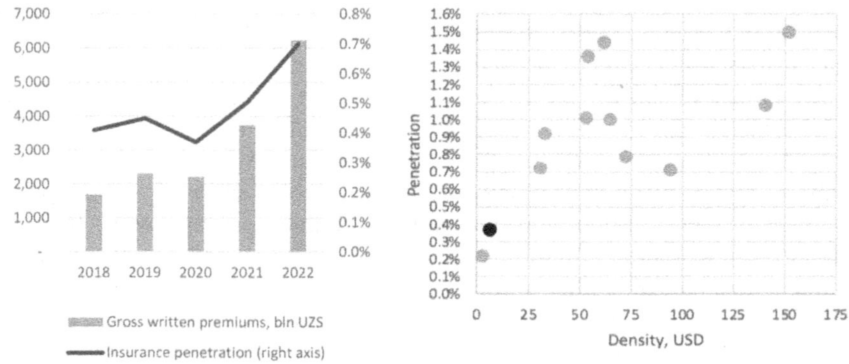

Source: IMDA, AXCO

Source: AXCO (2020)

Notes: Insurance penetration shows gross written premiums (GWP) to GDP ratio. Density shows premiums collected per capita.

Figure 4.3 The Uzbek insurance sector is growing but remains far behind its peers. **Panel A.** The insurance market in Uzbekistan is growing steadily and rapidly. **Panel B.** Uzbekistan is well behind its regional peers in insurance penetration ratio

Notes: Insurance penetration shows gross written premiums (GWP) to GDP ratio. Density shows premiums collected per capita.

Source: IMDA and AXCO (2020).

While the insurance sector grew rapidly with gross written premiums increasing by about threefold over 2020–2022, the product market remains limited, accounting for only a small share of the financial system. Voluntary non-life insurance comprised most gross written premiums in 2022 (68 percent). Voluntary life insurance and mandatory non-life insurance accounted for 24 percent and 8 percent. Major insurance products include property insurance (different classes, 34 percent), long-term life insurance (16 percent), credit risk insurance (12 percent), and transport (motor) insurance (voluntary and mandatory, 13 percent).

The insurance market has been facing a range of interconnected acute issues. The regulatory and supervisory framework is outdated, facing constant shocks to its institutional structure. Data availability to support the development of insurance is limited.[12] There is a scarcity of insurance professionals. For example, eight insurance companies share one actuary which causes insufficient availability of technical knowledge to develop and price products as well as set adequate reserves. Risk assessors are also largely unavailable. Two or three loss adjustors are present in the market limiting the agility in claims settlement and payments—which in turn lowers the confidence of potential clients in the value of insurance. Insurance companies also struggle with outdated ICT systems that negatively affect their business models and solvency positions. Risk management in the insurance sector, with limited reinsurance, high business growth and risk accumulation and no or limited consideration of climate change impacts on the portfolio, needs significant improvement. While there is a wide range of basic insurance products available in the market, product development does not follow a client-oriented approach, and often the products are not suitable to cover the needs of consumers.

Lack of clear legal and regulatory rules for indemnity payments, low financial literacy, and absence of sound consumer protection further aggravate the situation and undermine public trust in private insurance. Due to the increased competition, insurance rates on the market often fall below the cost of risk, resulting in a strong motivation for the insurers to avoid claim payments, which in turn results in the claims processes being cumbersome and lengthy. To reduce the cost of insurance policies, insurers include several exclusions in their policies some of which are unrelated to the covered risks, leaving many claims declined, and consumers frustrated. Consumers are often forced to buy insurance coverage that they do not need or even understand, which leads to unawareness about the contracted protection and unclaimed payments.

Since adopting the 2019–2020 insurance market development roadmap, the government has initiated a few reforms in the sector. A new law on insurance activities was adopted in 2021, and a Presidential Decree on additional measures was signed to digitalize the insurance market. The long-awaited new insurance law, which entered into force in February 2022, draws on national and international expertise to modernize and update insurance regulation. Insurance companies are required to prepare their annual financial statements in accordance with International Financial Reporting Standards. The prudential standards have been strengthened, with the increase of minimum capital requirements and better reserve standards, separated for non-life and life insurers. There are some initiatives to improve product development and offering, specifically in agriculture and export insurance.

A particular issue that the Uzbek insurance market confronts is the lack of disaster risk insurance. It is critical for Uzbekistan that is highly prone to climate-related and geophysical disasters. Uzbekistan faces increasing temperatures, more frequent and extreme droughts, lower precipitation levels and changes in weather patterns (World Bank, 2020b). Floods already threaten a substantial part of the country—they are expected to happen more often.[13] The United Nations estimates the average annual loss from climate disaster events to be US$700 million.[14] The country is also prone to other disasters, such as earthquakes that are infrequent but can cause devastating losses. Disasters can threaten efforts to reduce poverty and build shared prosperity, pushing people back into poverty or leading to poverty traps. Poor and vulnerable people are disproportionally affected by disasters because they have fewer assets and savings to rely on.

Households and businesses have limited access to catastrophe risk insurance and would likely rely on government assistance in case of disasters. Disaster insurance penetration is low, with less than 10 percent of residential dwellings insured against fire, lightning, explosion and aircraft damage risks and natural perils. The penetration varies among regions and is primarily driven by mortgage-linked insurance. This leaves much of the contingent liabilities from disaster damages with the government without much help from the private insurance industry. Nevertheless, even with limited penetration, insurance companies may risk insolvency in cases of major disasters because of insufficient capital and because only a few insurance companies buy reinsurance against such major events or consider how climate change affects the frequency and severity of weather-related disasters.

To strengthen financial preparedness for climate-induced and other disasters, the government should prepare a national disaster risk financing strategy that should be used as a pillar in the development of the private catastrophe insurance market—and establish a risk financing instrument, such as a reserve fund or centralized insurance. It should consider a fiscal reserve pool to reduce the costs of post-disaster financing for affected businesses and households, and support timely and cost-effective response after disasters.

4.2.4 Capital markets

Uzbekistan's capital market is small and underdeveloped. The securities market comprises mainly treasury securities. The corporate bond market is shallow. The equity market is nascent with a very low level of free float of listed companies. There are no pension funds,[15] mutual funds, or collective investment vehicles in Uzbekistan. The local capacity in terms of market professionals is limited as in the case of insurance and other financial subsectors. Capital market infrastructure needs improvements, and the current legislation is fragmented and outdated. The local demand for financial instruments has been weak due to a lack of retail and institutional investors.

In December 2018, the government restarted issuing treasury bills and bonds in local currency after a long pause since 2012. The nominal value of issued government securities reached more than UZS12 trillion in 2022 or 1.4 percent of GDP (Figure 4.4, Panel A).[16] For liquidity management purposes, the central bank has been actively issuing short term (mostly three-month) securities since early 2020—the total volume of which reached UZS70 trillion in 2022. The stock of domestic treasury securities is skewed to the short term, with about 70 percent of domestic debt maturing within one year. However, with every year, the tenor of issued treasury securities has been increasing (Figure 4, Panel B).

Still, as the government continues to meet its financing needs principally by borrowing from abroad, domestic debt comprises only about 10 percent of total state debt and is almost entirely bought by commercial banks (65

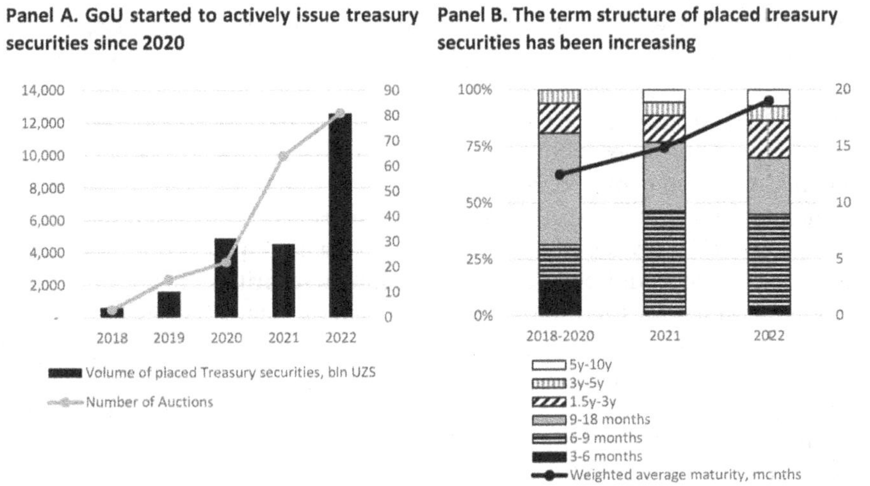

Figure 4.4 The issuance of treasury securities in Uzbekistan gained momentum since 2020 with gradually extended tenors. **Panel A.** GoU started to actively issue treasury securities in 2020. **Panel B.** The term structure of placed treasury securities has been increasing

Source: Uzbek Republican Currency Exchange (UzRCE), authors' calculations.

percent by SOCBs).[17] The biggest challenge for developing a primary government securities market is that the securities rates are linked to the central bank policy rate, with low spreads between short- and long-term tenors. The repo (both with the central bank and interbank) and secondary markets for treasury securities are largely inactive due to relatively low volumes of government securities issuance, absence of proper benchmark issuances, lack of market-making activity, and a shallow investor base with predominantly a buy-and-hold behavior.

The shallow corporate bond market—with the volume of trades registered on the Tashkent Republican Stock Exchange—ticked up from nearly zero in 2018 to UZS110 billion or 0.01 percent of GDP by 2022. The number of issuers has been less than ten over 2018–2022, mostly consisting of a few banks and other financial institutions. The total market capitalization of listed equity securities increased from UZS55 trillion (about 9 percent of GDP) in 2020 to UZS94 trillion or about 11 percent of GDP in 2022. However free-floating shares comprised only around 0.4 percent of GDP. Consequently, trading volumes are low and most of the stocks are not traded daily. Only about ten stocks trade regularly, but with extremely high volatility in prices. There were 45 licensed brokers at the end of 2022, of which about ten brokers were trading actively.

Capital markets need well-organized national infrastructures to operate efficiently. There are four capital market infrastructures serving the market.

Three of them serve the corporate securities market, namely the Republican Stock Exchange of Tashkent (UZSE), the over-the-counter Elsis Savdo market, and the central securities depository. The fourth one, the Uzbek Republican Currency Exchange (UZCE), serves the government securities and foreign exchange wholesale markets. The UZCE is a joint-stock company 51 percent owned by the central bank and 49 percent owned by commercial banks that has a modern and efficient trading system developed in-house, which provides for automated transaction processing and offers low-risk settlement and custody for government securities. The GoU is currently contemplating the establishment of a single central securities depository for government and corporate securities to improve the efficiency of capital market infrastructures functioning.

Shortly after the Capital Markets Development Agency (CMDA) was established in January 2019 and tasked with regulation, oversight, and development of the capital markets, the CMDA was abolished in May 2021. Its functions were transferred to the Ministry of Finance, potentially creating a conflict of interest between the Ministry as issuer of securities and supervisor of the sector. With the same decision a capital market development program and roadmap for 2021–2023 were adopted. They focused on the following key reform areas: (i) increasing the number of issuers and new financial products; (ii) developing capital market infrastructure; (iii) improving the use of ICT in the capital market; (iv) improving capital market legislation and oversight; (v) expanding the investor base and improving the financial literacy of the population; (vi) developing the government securities market; and (vii) improving the skills of capital market participants. With the legal changes enacted in March 2022, resident and non-resident individuals and commercial institutions are now permitted to participate in the primary and secondary market for government securities. While the government is keen to develop the retail investor base, it is a challenging task operationally and contributes little to developing the government securities market. The development of a new capital markets law is underway in early 2023.

The development of capital markets in Uzbekistan, as in any other developing country, is an important but at the same time complex and challenging task, with no quick fixes. The expectations for market development in the short term need to be realistic and balanced against the risks for investors (especially households) arising from market illiquidity, fraud, or mispricing. While the adopted capital markets development strategy of Uzbekistan is comprehensive and ambitious, priority should be given to the development of a fit-for-purpose legal framework—including strong investor legal protection—and of a local government bond market with related infrastructure. The development of the local government bond market is the cornerstone of a broader capital market development that helps risk to be priced appropriately, allows participants in financial markets to better manage their portfolios, and provides a more effective conduit for monetary policy (World Bank and IMF, 2021).

4.2.5 Green finance

The economic development of Uzbekistan is moving toward a less carbon-intensive and more sustainable growth model. Uzbekistan ratified the 2015 Paris Agreement in October 2018. In October 2021, Uzbekistan updated its National Defined Contribution (NDC), committing to curtail its carbon emissions by 35 percent in 2030 compared to 2010 levels. To operationalize the reduction in greenhouse gas emissions, Uzbekistan adopted the 2019–2030 strategy for transition to a green economy,[18] followed by adoption in December 2022 of a Program on transition to a green economy by 2030.[19]

Funding for green transition is key for any country to reach its climate and environmental objectives.[20] The World Bank and IMF (2022) estimate that low-income and middle-income countries will need between USD1.7 and 3.4 trillion per year by 2030 for climate mitigation needs. The funding will need to come from both the public and private sectors, including through the financial sector. This hinges on the availability of a clear, transparent, and consistent definition of what qualifies and what does not qualify as green investment or activity, and how independent verification of greening impacts can be ascertained. One approach that countries can implement early on—following the EU example—is a well-defined and structured green taxonomy that can support better-informed and more efficient decision-making and respond to investment opportunities that contribute to achieving national environmental objectives in the public sector, private sector, and financial sector (World Bank, 2020a). A green taxonomy identifies activities or investments that deliver on environmental and resiliency objectives and can be used to screen and promote financing to priority environmental projects consistent with national commitments and political decisions. Uzbekistan plans to develop a green taxonomy by October 2023. The latter is, however, only one tool that focuses primarily on screening (labeling) investments and activities, and less so on green impact verification. Therefore, it needs to be accompanied by other approaches that can promote transparency and accountability for green impacts such as sustainable reporting standards[21] or the development of an independent (and independently financed) impact verification industry to assure investors and financiers about positive end-green impacts.

In most developing countries, the financial system, and particularly the banking sector that constitutes its core, plays a critical role in funding the transition to a less carbon-intensive economy. Financial institutions can boost the flow of funds toward green and resilient economic activities as well as indirectly stimulate greater transparency by requiring information and public disclosures from businesses and households about green and other sustainable investments that increase resilience to disasters. As countries strategize on the design of climate policy, promoting green finance through banking reform is a critical factor and tool that must be considered to really tilt the balance toward green and sustainable economic activity. Because the political economy and administrative capacity for reform is limited, Uzbekistan's government will need to be selective to achieve meaningful results and must act now on building a solid foundation for green finance to achieve its climate goals.

Actionable reform should focus on two financial policy channels. One channel that can stimulate proper pricing, management, and supervision of climate-change-related risks in the financial sector involves actions by the banking and other financial sector regulators—which oversee banking, insurance, pension, and capital markets. The second channel involves risk-sharing and other financial support from the government through its relevant quasi-fiscal entities to the financial and non-financial markets, most notably through the state-owned Green Fund and possibly other national development finance institutions and programs.

The first channel in the purview of financial regulators needs to consider that technological changes, policy decisions, and even new socioeconomic preferences expose the banking sector to physical and transition risks that should be well-managed to avoid risks to financial stability. For this purpose, the financial sector supervisory authorities need to develop a set of actions, which can be broadly grouped into the following five categories: (i) develop a regulatory framework for managing climate-related risks, as well as mandatory disclosure requirements of climate-related risks; (ii) conduct proper oversight over compliance of financial institutions with the regulatory requirements, including proper reporting of green portfolios; (iii) conduct assessments of financial system's exposure to physical and transition risks and develop green (sustainability) dashboards; and (iv) engage with national and international bodies to keep up to date with the latest developments and move forward in decarbonizing the economy. Although these actions will undoubtedly improve banks' climate risk management framework, the ability of the domestic financial system to allocate and mobilize capital efficiently, avoiding "greenwashing" and "green bubbles" among other risks, could remain a challenge.

Stimulating green investment through the Green Fund operation that could include direct investments (debt or equity), co-investments, or de-risking instruments such as credit and equity risk guarantees can generate widespread positive impacts on making the Uzbek economy more sustainable, set the strategic direction for banking and finance to go beyond environmental, social, and corporate governance considerations, or the application of green taxonomy, and focus capital intermediation on scaled up and verified green impacts. But the Green Fund alone may not suffice, and all government financial support programs will need to be greened.

Drawing on the green taxonomy or by applying impact investing principles, the financial support programs of the Uzbek government can kick-start a virtuous cycle of orienting the operations of the financial industry on verifiable green impacts, including promoting the development of specialized companies/business lines for independent verification of green impacts. A top-down reform of government financial support programs can be complemented by pilot projects that reflect impact investing principles, starting with the focus on climate-change mitigation, adaptation to climate-change-related risks, and a just transition oriented toward people. Furthermore, issuing and earmarking green loans, leasing, equity investments, and insurance support can help the Uzbek Green Fund and government financial support programs at large progress toward raising green bonds through international or later local capital markets.

4.3 Financial inclusion and MSME finance

Financial inclusion is essential for ensuring that individuals and businesses have equitable access to suitable, safe, and affordable financial services to meet their consumption and investment needs and thereby foster socio-economic development. It is an efficient tool to support efforts to increase productivity and reduce poverty and inequality. Financial exclusion, by contrast, inhibits human and physical capital accumulation, household and firm financial stability and social cohesion, thereby contributing to persisting inequality and poverty.

Financial inclusion has long been neglected in Uzbekistan with the near-totally dominant state-owned banking sector historically, limited competition and innovation, shortcomings in the legal and regulatory framework, lack of technological advancement, and nascent NBCO, insurance, and capital markets. Consequently, improving financial inclusion for households and SMEs has been at the heart of financial sector reforms initiated since 2018. However, financial inclusion is not a naturally occurring phenomenon. Achieving greater financial inclusion requires a deliberate and coordinated approach to identify relevant obstacles and opportunities, leverage linkages across financial and non-financial policy areas, and align the efforts of a wide range of stakeholders. To achieve progress, policymakers, and regulators, with support from the private sector, should actively identify and prioritize a set of actions to address multiple (and often interrelated) bottlenecks and market failures which constrain access and usage of financial services.

To this end, Uzbekistan adopted its first National Financial Inclusion Strategy (NFIS) 2021–2023 in June 2021. The NFIS provides an effective instrument to chart a clear and coordinated path toward improving financial inclusion. It focuses on five key policy areas for reform actions: basic financial services, access to finance for SMEs, digital financial services, financial consumer protection, and financial literacy—but it leaves untouched important financial subsectors such as insurance and capital markets. The achievability of targets under the financial inclusion strategy hinges on the successful implementation of the banking sector reform strategy, namely: (i) facilitating the emergence of a commercially oriented financial sector; (ii) restructuring and privatization of state-owned banks; and (iii) phasing out directed and preferential lending shall allow the entrance of new players and the development of an ecosystem of financial providers—that can develop new products to mobilize resources and meet the financial needs of households and business.

4.3.1 Access to financial services

After many years of stagnation, the availability of financial access points began to increase. This was largely driven by a surge in the number of automated teller machines from just 445 in 2017 to more than 11,000 in 2022. The number of point-of-sale terminals doubled since 2017 to more than 430,000, and their intermediated annual volume doubled to UZS120 trillion ($10.6 billion), or 20 percent of GDP. The COVID-19 crisis underscored the importance of digital financial services, providing a strong impetus for innovative contactless payment technologies: around 100,000 business entities have been issued QR codes while another 2,000 use Near-Field Communication.

Since 2017, banks added more than 300 branches to increase their regional outreach and opened more than 1,000 "centers of bank services," a more flexible and cost-efficient access point developed by the Central Bank. The distribution of financial access points across the country is, however, uneven, with only 13 percent of administrative units (with 39 percent of the total population) having at least one financial access point (Figure 4.5, Panel A).

4.3.2 Usage of financial services

Uzbekistan almost doubled the share of adults with bank accounts from 23 percent in 2011 to 44 percent in 2021, according to Global Findex, but remains below some regional peers (52 percent in Armenia, 70 percent in Georgia, 81 percent in Kazakhstan, and 84 percent in Ukraine). Uzbekistan's supply-side data report even larger numbers of 74 percent by the end of 2022.[22] Although the gender gap in account ownership has traditionally been limited in Uzbekistan, it has increased from a 3 to 10 percentage point difference between men and women in 2021 (50 percent versus 39 percent), according to Global Findex data.[23]

The usage of payment cards has also been on the rise, and Uzbekistan ranks well among peer countries.[24] In parallel, the number of users of the remote banking system grew sixfold—reaching about 25 million users, with remote identification of individual clients in place since 2021. Uzbeks use bank accounts mainly for basic operations, and as mentioned earlier, deposit mobilization remains subdued (Figure 4.5, Panel B), albeit growing recently partly due to favorably high interest rates in local currency.

Households and MSMEs benefited from improved access to credit over the last several years. Credit to GDP increased from 36.5 percent at the end of 2017 to 44 percent at the end of 2022, and the overall bank lending portfolio has more than tripled. Around 40 percent of newly extended credit was

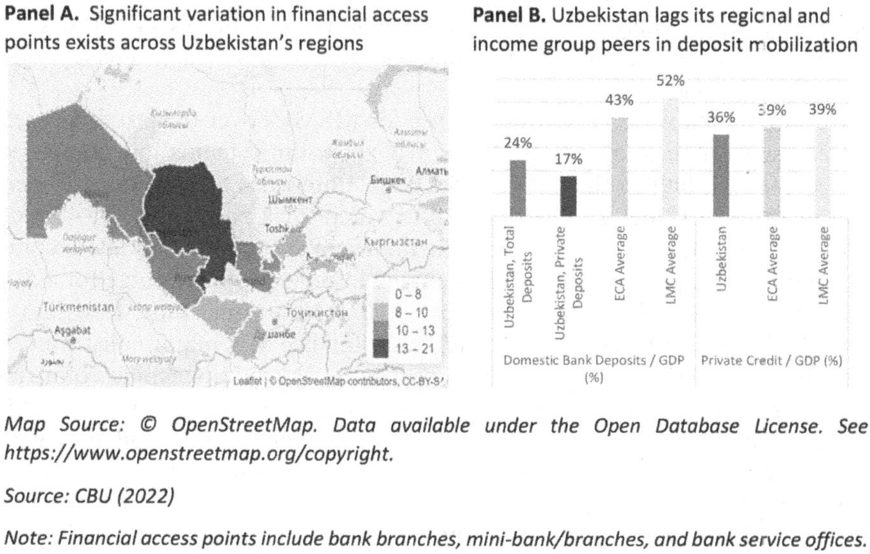

Figure 4.5 Financial access points grew but remained uneven across Uzbekistan's regions while deposit mobilization remains subdued by early 2023. **Panel A.** Significant variation in financial access points exists across Uzbekistan's regions. **Panel B.** Uzbekistan lags behind its regional and income group peers in deposit mobilization

Note: Financial access points include bank branches, mini-bank/branches, and bank service offices.

Source: Map © OpenStreetMap. Data is available under the Open Database License. www.openstreetmap.org/copyright and CBU (2022).

provided to small businesses and entrepreneurs over the last three years, while the share of outstanding loans to individuals has increased from 12 percent at the end of 2017 to 26 percent by the end of 2022.

4.3.3 MSME finance

Small business plays a significant role in the Uzbek economy. By the end of 2021, there were 437,000 registered small businesses in the country (compared to 226,000 by the end of 2017) representing approximately 87 percent of all registered private firms in the country. The contribution of small businesses to GDP has declined from 65 percent in 2017 to 55 percent in 2021, indicating that there are constraints to productivity and growth. The contribution to employment has remained constant at 70–80 percent.

As the Uzbek economy goes through sweeping reforms and opens to international markets, improving access to finance for MSMEs can trigger dynamism in the economy, spur innovation, and create jobs. Advancing financial inclusion of individuals and MSMEs can help many more seize better development opportunities, boost MSME productivity, and share prosperity more widely. It can also improve household and MSME resilience to shocks and help empower marginalized groups, such as women, youth, and rural communities.

Despite the improved access to finance for MSMEs over the last few years, the access to finance among MSMEs in Uzbekistan remains low compared to peers. According to the 2019 World Bank Enterprise Survey data, 22 percent of firms in Uzbekistan had access to a loan or a bank of credit—which is over 5 percentage points lower than the average for lower-middle-income economies (27.6 percent) and 10 percentage lower than the average for Eastern Europe and Central Asia (37.6 percent). At the same time, less than 6 percent of firms in Uzbekistan cite access to finance as a major constraint to their business compared with 25.7 percent in lower-middle-income countries and 17 percent in ECA. While this may appear a sign of financial sector efficiency, it may also reveal a lack of MSME awareness and familiarity with banking products, as well as distrust toward the financial sector.

The main issue is that MSMEs lack access to an appropriate range and quality of financial products. The supply of financing instruments to MSMEs in Uzbekistan is still largely unsophisticated and limited to traditional financing products. Lending to MSMEs has been mostly focused on longer-term credit, while working capital lending is not developed. Factors hampering MSME access to finance include: on supply-side—too much reliance on hard collateral (mostly limited to property and cars) and less focus on cash-flow analyses, absence of innovative and suitable MSME financing products adapted to different stages of MSME growth (including lack of flexible terms for loan repayments), and high cost of bank credit (with a high variability of rates across different banks and among branches of one bank), and on demand side—low financial literacy and high informality among MSMEs.

At the same time, banks should also be careful in MSME lending. With the liberalization of the financial market and the transformation of many state-owned banks, the banking system pays more attention to MSME lending, which is one of the riskiest parts of banking business. High competition and MSME market overheating may coincide with lax lending standards, overindebtedness of MSMEs, and increased credit risks. A balanced approach from banks and regulators is therefore needed.

4.3.4 Financial consumer protection

Uzbekistan's rapid financial sector development and ambitious financial inclusion goals require a comprehensive approach to financial consumer protection. The financial sector is growing rapidly, and recent reforms are expected to enable the deployment of new technology-driven products and delivery channels, including digital credit, e-wallets, and the use of retail agents. Millions of additional consumers are expected to enter the formal financial sector in the coming years for the first time. This rapid pace of financial sector development and innovation holds clear benefits for consumers but also generates significant risks when consumers contract unsuitable financial products or can become victims of predatory lending practices.

In 2019, the new law on the Central Bank of Uzbekistan (CBU) assigned the institutional mandate for financial consumer protection to the Central Bank. It clarified CBU's specific functions in ensuring the rights and protection of consumers of credit institutions, as well as related functions concerning financial access and financial literacy. The laws on banks, NBCOs, payment organizations, and payment systems include provisions on financial consumer protection, and several regulations on financial consumer protection have recently been issued. In February 2022, the Central Bank launched a single online platform aimed at providing comparable and user-friendly information about the financial services of banks to enable consumers to comfortably compare and choose suitable financial products. Financial consumer protection for insurance products and capital markets services rests implicitly with the respective subsectoral supervisor(s). Integrated financial consumer protection for all financial services is yet to be developed in Uzbekistan. The policymakers can consider in this regard two integrated structures to institutionalize financial consumer protection: (i) the single peak model and (ii) the twin peak model. In the current context of Uzbekistan, the single peak model would envisage the placement of consumer protection for all financial services in the central bank where the current consumer protection for the bulk of financial services (payments, deposits, and credits) is housed already. The twin peak model would envisage housing consumer protection (and business conduct oversight) for all financial services in a new independent government agency.

In February 2022, the Central Bank launched a single online platform aimed at providing comparable and user-friendly information about the financial services of banks to enable consumers to comfortably compare and choose suitable financial products. A significant scope remains to improve specificity and coverage in some areas as well as remove inconsistencies across various legislative and regulatory instruments and harmonize rules across similar products and providers. Several key issues that need to be resolved include the need to strengthen rules on fair treatment and business conduct, strengthen the complaints handling and recourse mechanisms ensuring accessible, independent, fair, and accountable treatment, and enhance the consumer protection risk-based supervisory framework over banks and non-bank financial institutions.

4.4 Financial sector oversight and supervisory structure

4.4.1 Main banking sector risks and supervisory response

One important institutional precondition for the successful transformation and privatization of SOCBs is having a sound bank licensing, prudential regulation, supervision, and resolution framework. The experience of many countries shows that for banking transitions to be successful they need to be paired with a proper institutional strengthening of the financial oversight bodies. These studies show that the probability of banking crises conditional on financial liberalization is higher than the unconditional probability of banking crises (Hawkins and Mihaljek, 2001; Angkinand et al., 2010; Reinhart and Rogoff, 2013). Uzbekistan needed to overhaul its banking system regulation and oversight framework for two main purposes: a) to ensure the safety and soundness of SOCBs, which is an imperative for broader financial system stability, economic growth, and protecting fiscal resources (Adams et al., 2022); and b) to ensure entry of fit and proper shareholders into the market and providing adequate oversight over a completely new and private sector-led banking system that is expected to emerge as a result of the implementation of the banking sector reform strategy.

Starting in 2017, economic liberalization triggered a credit boom that increased the risks to financial stability and required increased oversight. Following 110 percent growth in 2017—partly reflecting the 50 percent currency depreciation in 2017—credit grew at 51 percent per annum in nominal terms in 2018 and 58 percent in 2019.[25] Several banks (including a few large banks) doubled and tripled their balance sheets over a span of two to three years. The credit to the private sector in Uzbekistan grew from 12 percent of GDP in 2016 to 30 percent of GDP in 2019—an annual growth of around 6 percentage points. This was more than three times the average annual growth experienced by other transition economies such as Poland, Russia, and Vietnam during the initial years of transition. The rapid credit growth was even more worrisome because of poor credit underwriting standards, risk management capabilities, weak corporate governance, and poor credit quality reporting in the banks, especially in the SOCBs. The limited financial strength of shareholders in small private banks also added to the worries. The highly concentrated and dollarized portfolios of the largest SOCBs were yet another source of financial stability risks.

The rapid and lax lending coupled with the COVID-19 crisis brought the banking system—both SOCBs and private banks—to confront a surge in NPLs from the low and stable level of around 1 to 2 percent during 2018–2020 to 6.2 percent by the end of July 2021 (Figure 4.6, Panel A). Problem loans in about seven banks exceeded 10 percent, while in a couple of banks they reached more than 90 percent. As a result, the Central Bank revoked the licenses of two small private banks in October 2022, which suffered from large credit losses. In parallel, the GoU was forced to recapitalize several SOCBs by injecting in them close to USD1 billion to buffer the increased losses and sustain their lending business. Although the reported NPL ratios gradually declined to 3.6 percent by the end of 2022, the quality of restructured loans because of the COVID-19 pandemic and war in Ukraine is yet to be revealed. The IFRS reports for banks showed a somewhat higher level of problem loans than officially disclosed (Figure 4.6, Panel B).

To respond to these financial sector challenges, the central bank initiated far-reaching reforms in multiple areas to upgrade its regulatory and supervisory framework in line with international standards. Namely, the CBU has: (i) adopted numerous regulations based on the new banks and banking law and in accordance with international standards;[26] (ii) established a financial stability department and improved its internal organizational structure for bank supervision-related departments; (iii) initiated gradual transition to risk-based supervision; (iv) developed a system of early supervisory interventions to address problems at banks early on; and (v) developed and adopted a strategy and roadmap for enhancing and improving the quality of the supervisory data reporting under a supervisory technology initiative.

Transitioning the Central Bank's current supervision model to a new model focusing on the most important risks supported by consistent assessment methodology—to become dynamic, forward-looking, and action-oriented—is not merely a technical exercise. It involves a significant and deep-rooted change management program that should tackle several aspects in parallel (Toronto Centre Notes, 2018). Good supervision involves not only a thorough understating and analyses of risks in individual institutions and across the sector, but also timely, decisive, and proportionate actions to address those risks at an early stage. To achieve this result, supervisors should both be "able" and "willing" to act (Vinals and Fiechter, 2010). In

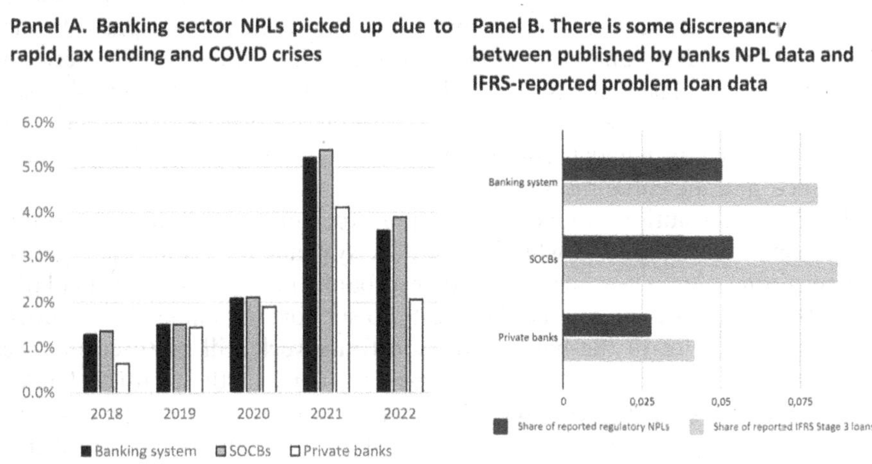

Figure 4.6 Non-performing loans have picked up in Uzbekistan banks, but there is still room to improve the disclosure practices. **Panel A.** Banking sector NPLs picked up due to rapid, lax lending and COVID-19 crises. **Panel B.** There is some discrepancy between published by banks NPL data and IFRS-reported problem loan data

Note: IFRS data in Panel B is provided based on 2021 annual IFRS reports and includes data on 29 out of 33 banks.
Source: CBU, authors' calculations.

particular, the "ability" to act—which requires appropriate resources and information, authority and legal powers, and robust internal decision-making—shall be complemented by "willingness" to act—which requires operational and political independence, healthy relationship with the regulated institutions, and legal protections. It is, therefore, a priority for the government to ensure independent functioning of the CBU and its further development to complete the banking sector reform that it aspires to. But it is more easily said than done in a state-dominated banking system.

4.4.2 Importance of establishing a bank resolution framework

As Uzbekistan transitions to a private sector-led banking sector, having a proper bank resolution and liquidation framework gains importance. The country needs not only a sound bank licensing framework—to enable the Central Bank to ensure its "gatekeeper" function at market entry—and a proper regulatory and supervisory framework—for the central bank to properly monitor risks and apply supervisory measures. It also needs a sound bank liquidation and resolution framework—to ensure that non-viable banks (both large and small) exit the market efficiently and in a way that does not put the entire financial system under threat. While regulation and supervision are essential for preserving a country's financial stability, they do not and cannot guarantee that banks will not run into a financial distress. Even in countries with the most conservative regulations and prudent supervisory practices, bank failures do happen. In the absence of a sound bank resolution framework, the authorities will need to resort to costly public bailouts as was the case during the global financial crisis. Placing a large—or, in some cases, even a medium-sized bank—that runs into serious problems in liquidation may endanger financial system stability, access to finance, and the entire macroeconomy.

The bank resolution regime should apply to banks—including the state-owned ones—the failure of which could have systemic or significant negative repercussions. While less likely, state-owned banks may also fail, particularly when the state has a limited fiscal capacity to support the banks that it owns. The main objective of the bank resolution framework will be to ensure the prevention of systemic financial crisis, the continuity of the troubled bank's critical functions, the protection of the rights and interests of depositors, and the minimization of public costs while achieving all other objectives. To this end and in accordance with international standards, the central bank, as the resolution authority, should be equipped with appropriate tools and powers to properly resolve banks without obtaining the consent of shareholders and other creditors. Adequate safeguards of these powers will also be needed. In addition, the courts must not be entitled to suspend or reverse the resolution authority's decisions taken in good faith. Otherwise, such entitlement would undermine the whole bank resolution framework and render it practically dysfunctional. The court rulings should be limited to awarding monetary compensations to adversely affected parties.

4.4.3 Institutional structure for financial sector supervision

The current institutional structure for financial sector oversight in Uzbekistan is fragmented and subject to constant institutional changes. It demands a rethinking of its suitability for effective supervision and balanced development across financial subsectors. Three different regulators are responsible for the oversight of the following financial subsectors: the Central Bank (banks, non-bank credit organizations and payment system operators/organizations), Insurance Market Development Agency (insurance companies and related entities—during 2020–2022 only), and Ministry of Economy and Finance (capital markets). However, the recent history of the insurance sector and capital markets oversight contains persistent shocks in its institutional design driven by political changes.[27] The lack of institutional development of oversight authorities for insurance and capital markets in Uzbekistan hindered the development of a proper regulatory and oversight framework. The limited financial and operational capacity, and in some cases political dependence of the non-bank supervisory authorities impaired their performance. At the same time, the lack of interagency coordination and consistency of regulatory and supervisory frameworks across financial subsectors hindered effective supervision of risks in the context of local financial groups (conglomerates), where banking, insurance, leasing, and other financial services are intertwined in the ownership and operational activities of various financial institutions. The lack of coordination and consistency also hindered the balanced development of respective financial subsectors.

In addition, there are a few activities and financial companies which, in fact, are not supervised by any of the mentioned financial supervisory authorities. This includes, for example, leasing companies, for which there are no licensing requirements and no ongoing prudential requirements or oversight, while large shops which sell their goods using installment schemes (effectively providing credit) are not overseen even from financial consumer protection perspective by any financial sector authority.

Uzbekistan could benefit from the experience of several EU countries that integrated one or more financial subsectors within the supervisory authority responsible for bank supervision. Among the EU member countries that were once transition economies, the Czech Republic, Hungary, and Slovakia integrated the authority for bank supervision with the authority for supervision of the insurance sector, capital markets, and pension funds under their central banks. Other EU countries, such as Belgium, the Netherlands, Portugal, and Ireland also integrated prudential supervision over all financial subsectors under the central bank. And so did the UK that spearheaded this type of financial sector reform after the 2008 global financial crisis.

Although there may not be a one-size-fit-all model of institutional architecture for all countries (Calvo et al., 2018), integrating prudential oversight across financial subsectors can yield synergies and benefits for countries with relatively simpler and smaller financial systems (Toronto Centre Notes,

2016). The benefits include the following: (i) economies of scale and scope by using a common technical infrastructure and a joint system of support services (statistics, human resources management); (ii) ability to attract, develop and retain a professional cadre of experts within the integrated supervisory authority; (iii) more political independence and safeguards from frequent changes in the political arena, especially if integrated under the national central bank; (iv) a better flow of information and coordination among different supervisors for financial subsectors that will enable a more effective consolidated supervision, enabling a better systemic risk identification and management as well as enhancing the macroprudential supervision and financial stability outcomes; (v) reduction of regulatory arbitrage risks for financial institutions engaged in similar activities; and (vi) improved accountability from a strong and stable institution with consistent approach and institutional history. These arguments led to a new wave of reforms in supervisory structures prompted by the global financial crises, that resulted in prudential integrations, dominated by supervisory integrations under central banks (Melecky and Podpiera, 2013, 2016).

4.5 Conclusion

This chapter summarized the development in key Uzbek financial subsectors from core banking to insurance, to capital markets, and to non-bank credit institutions. It offered some key pointers to what the individual subsectors need for sustained deepening of their markets. One outcome that the sustained deepening needs to support is responsible financial inclusion that connects sound financial access and its framing with financially literate and self-controlled individuals and MSMEs to foster financial well-being in Uzbekistan (Melecky, 2022).

The chapter highlighted the importance of continued strengthening of financial institutions starting with financial support programs and bank supervision, and involving equally important prudential supervision of non-bank financial subsectors (insurance, capital markets, leasing) as well as financial consumer protection for all financial services.

Financial support programs need to be rethought and better institutionalized under strong governance structures such as a development bank and/or financial holding of national development finance institutions to improve consistency of government financial support programs, their transparency and fair access, and accountability for impacts at the level of beneficiaries and the financial market.

While banking supervision needs to steadfastly continue strengthening its capabilities and independence, the prudential oversight over other financial subsectors could be integrated into the Central Bank. First, the integration can be done using a vertical integration—with separate departments for banks, insurance, capital markets, and NBCOs, and then progress to a horizontal integration of licensing, supervision, enforcement, and resolution to cover all financial subsectors. Such integration will boost the potential for capable consolidated supervision and macroprudential oversight (Armenia, Czech Republic, Slovakia, Hungary).

In addition, financial consumer protection needs to cover all financial services, with its placement considering two options following sound international practice: (i) the single peak supervisory structure, i.e., placing financial consumer protection under the central bank as an independent department from prudential supervision reporting to a different vice-governor (Armenia, Czech Republic) or (ii) the twin peak supervisory structure, i.e., establishing a separate financial market institution to oversee financial consumer protection and business conduct issues in the financial sector (Georgia, Slovakia).[28]

The institutional choice should reflect the fact that central banks have proven to be the most independent, technocratic institutions for financial markets across countries—including thanks to the policy advice and technical assistance from IFIs. Although voices in the related policy debates are concerned about creating a too-powerful mega-regulator, they omit the benefits of accountability and less room for blame games when responsibilities for sound financial development and stability are clearly nested into one politically independent institution that can attract and retain talent, build robust infrastructure, and foster strong internal governance. In early 2023, Uzbekistan is at a crossroads with making the right choices about the institutional structure for its financial market oversight.

Notes

1 The findings, interpretations, and conclusions expressed in this chapter are entirely those of the authors. They do not necessarily represent the views of the World Bank and its affiliated organizations, or those of the Executive Directors of the World Bank or the governments they represent. The authors thank the Central Bank of Uzbekistan for support and close cooperation and Mr. Sanjar Nosirov, Head of the Department of Methodology for Regulation of Credit Institutions, for useful and valuable comments on the earlier draft of this chapter.

2 For example, the Uzagroprom bank (later Pakhta bank, now Agro bank) was created in 1990 on the basis of the Soviet Agroprom bank; the UzPromStroy bank (the former Sanoat bank established in 1922) was reorganized into a state joint stock company in 1991; the Xalq bank was reorganized into a state commercial bank in 1995 on the basis of the USSR Savings (Sber) branch, while a new state-owned bank (the NBU) was established on the basis of the Vneshekonombank of the Soviet Union.

3 For example, the Asaka bank was established in 1995 to finance the local automobile production sector and purchases of vehicles by population. The Paxta bank (now the Agro bank) was mainly used to finance the cotton sector. The Aloqa bank was established in 1995 to finance the reconstruction of the telecommunications networks of Uzbekistan. In 2017, the Uzagroexport bank was established to finance the export potential of the country and the producers of agro-industrial products, and the Poytaxt bank was established to finance the construction and purchase of housing (apartments) in Tashkent city. The QQB bank, reorganized in 2009 based on the Galla state-owned bank (established in

1994), was tasked with financing population and legal entities in rural areas for their housing and social needs.

4 Note that the definition of SMEs did not include the "medium-size" category until 2023.

5 The laws on Central Bank and Banks and Banking, adopted in the end of 2019, addressed, among others, the following critical reforms: a) laid the foundations for functioning of an independent Central Bank with sufficient regulatory and supervisory powers, including the ability to exercise supervisory judgment and backed-up by legal protection; b) established a robust "gatekeeper function," providing the Central Bank with adequate powers to ensure that private investors seeking to enter the banking sector meet common fit and proper standards; c) established corporate governance requirements for banks; and d) established a robust set of supervisory enforcement and sanctioning powers.

6 Data as of the end of 2022. The mortgage refinancing company—UzMRC—was established in 2019 by Ministry of Finance (25 percent), several state-owned banks (68 percent) and a few private banks (7 percent). Loans refinanced by UzMRC as of the end of 2022 amounted to 1.9 trillion UZS (i.e., 4 percent of banking sector mortgage portfolio).

7 MCOs' assets are financed by own capital and loans from banks and shareholders. Pawnshops fund their assets almost entirely through their own funds.

8 The leverage ratio (assets to capital) of MCOs stood at below 200 percent as of the end of 2022, indicating that MCOs have been unable to attract sizable funding (apart from own funds) for their operations so far.

9 "World insurance: inflation risks front and centre," Sigma, No 4/2022, Swiss Re Institute.

10 Only 25 out of 41 insurance companies are members of the Motor Guarantee Fund. The fund was established in 2008 to guarantee payments for compulsory insurance of civil liability of vehicle owners in accordance with the Law of the Republic of Uzbekistan "On compulsory insurance of civil liability of vehicle owners."

11 AXCO, Insurance market report: Uzbekistan: non-life (P&C), 2023

12 For example, the meteorologic and weather stations needed to provide data for the implementation of agriculture insurance are limited in coverage. For the life sector to price and develop efficient products, there are no mortality, longevity and morbidity tables available with sufficient credibility.

13 https://climateknowledgeportal.worldbank.org/country/uzbekistan/vulnerability

14 United Nations, Economic and Social Commission for Asia and the Pacific (ESCAP) (2020). The Disaster Riskscape Across North and Central Asia: Key Takeaways for Stakeholders. www.unescap.org/publications/asia-pacific-disaster-report-2019

15 With the exception of the public pension fund which accumulates pension contributions from workers' salaries, deposited in Xalq bank's bank accounts. The minimum requirement is to hold 60 percent of liquidity in government securities and Central Bank bills.

16 In July 2022, the government issued its first-ever inflation-linked bonds worth more than UZS100 billion, with two-year maturity.

17 Holdings of government securities by insurance companies is very small, accounting for about 5 percent of total holdings of commercial banks.

18 Resolution of the President of the Republic of Uzbekistan PP-4477, dated October 4, 2019.

19 Resolution of the President of the Republic of Uzbekistan PP-436, dated December 2, 2022.

20 Including to support sustainable agriculture, avoid deforestation, invest in renewable energy and improve energy efficiency of the industrial production, among other priorities.

21 See, for example, the EU's Corporate Sustainable Reporting Directive or global ISSB Standards.

22 This difference is mostly attributable to difference in measurement, with demand-side data (like Findex) measuring the "perception" people have about their account ownership and usage, i.e., the percentage of adults who think of themselves as "banked" and having access to an account.

23 According to the Central Bank supply data as of the end of 2022, there is a positive 2 percentage points difference on account ownership between adult women and men.

24 The number of debit cards in circulation rose almost 60 percent from 19 million in 2017 to 30 million by July 2022.

25 The credit growth in 2019 was calculated without considering the transfer of UFRD-funded SOE loans from SOCBs' balance sheets in the end of 2019, which would otherwise distort the real credit growth rate.

26 These included regulations on bank licensing (2020), corporate governance (2020), liquidity risk (2020), large exposures framework (2020), internal audit (2021), asset classification (2021), prudential reporting and risk management (2023). A few other regulations have been developed and awaiting adoption at the time of writing this chapter, including regulation on external audit and disclosure requirements of banks. Note that both private banks and SOCBs are subject to the same prudential regulatory requirements in Uzbekistan.

27 In January 2019, the State Committee for the Promotion of Privatized Enterprises and the Development of Competition (and its Center for Coordination and Development of the Securities Market) was abolished, on the basis of which three state agencies were created: Capital Market Development Agency (CMDA); State Asset Management Agency and Antimonopoly Committee. Almost after two years of its existence, the CMDA was abolished in 2021, and its functions were transferred to the Ministry of Finance. The latter was reorganized again in the end of 2022, with little clarity on the future of capital market reforms. In August 2019, a new Insurance Market Development Agency (IMDA) was established on the basis of State Inspection of insurance Sector under the Ministry of Finance, which started its activities in early 2020. As a result of administrative reforms in the end of 2022, the IMDA was again abolished, and its functions were transferred to the reorganized Ministry of Economy and Finance.

28 www.eba.europa.eu/consumer-corner/national-competent-authorities-for-consumer-protection

References

Adams, M., Aydin, H.Y., Kyong Chon, H., Morozova, A., Iskender, I.E. 2022. *Regulating, Supervising and Handling Distress in Public Banks.* IMF, Washington, DC, May.

Angkinand, A., Sawangngoenyuang, W., and Wihlborg, C. 2010. "Financial Liberalization and Banking Crises: A Cross-Country Analysis." *International Review of Finance* 10 (2).

Azam, J.-P., B. Biais, and M. Dia. 2004. "Privatization versus Regulation in Developing Economies: The Case of West African Banks." *Journal of African Economies* 13 (3): 361–394.

Babasyan, D., Gu, Y., and Melecky, M., 2023. "Late Banking Transitions: Comparing Uzbekistan to Earlier Reformers." *World Development Perspectives* 3: 100493. https://doi.org/10.1016/j.wdp.2023.100493.

Beck, T., Crivelli, J.M., and Summerhill, W. 2005. "State Bank Transformation in Brazil— Choices and Consequences." *Journal of Banking and Finance* 29 (8–9): 2223–2257.

Bertay, A.C., Demirgüç-Kunt, A., and Huizinga. H. 2015. "Bank Ownership and Credit over the Business Cycle: Is Lending by State Banks Less Procyclical?" *Journal of Banking and Finance 50 (1)*: 326–339.

Bertay, A.C., Calice, P., Kalan, F.A.D., and Masetti, O. 2020. "Recent Trends in Bank Privatization," *Policy Research Working Paper 9318*. World Bank, Washington, DC.

Borish, M.S., Long, M.F., and Noel, M. 1995. *Restructuring Banks and Enterprises: Recent Lessons From Transition Countries.* The World Bank, Washington, DC.

Brandt, L. and Li, H., 2003. "Bank Discrimination in transition economies: Ideology, Information, or Incentives?" *Journal of Comparative Economics 31* (3): 387–413.

Bonin, J., and Wachtel, P., 2003. "Financial Sector Development in Transition Economies: Lessons from the First Decade." *Financial, Markets Institutions and Instruments* (12), February.

Bonin, J.P., Hasan, I., and Wachtel, P. 2005. "Bank Performance, Efficiency and Ownership in Transition Countries." *Journal of Banking and Finance* 29: 31–53.

Bonin, J.P., Hasan, I., and Wachtel, P. 2014. "Banking in Transition Countries," in A. Berger, P. Molyneux and J. Wilson, eds. *The Oxford Handbook of Banking*. Oxford University Press, Oxford. 1st ed., 2010, Chapter 33, pp. 746–768; 2nd ed., 2015, Chapter 39, pp. 963–983.

Bosshardt J., and Cerutii, E. 2020. "Why Did Public Banks Lend More during the Global Financial Crisis?" *IMF Working Paper WP/20/84*, International Monetary Fund, Washington, DC.

Calvo, D., Crisanto, J.C., Hohl, S., and Gutiérrez, O.P., 2018. "Financial Supervisory Architecture: What Has Changed After the Crisis?" *FSI Insights No 8*. Bank for International Settlements, Basel.

Claessens, S., 1998a. "Banking Reform in Transition Countries." *The Journal of Policy Reform* 2 (2): 115–133.

Claessens, S., 1998b. "Comment on Banking in Transition Economies: Does Efficiency Require Instability?" *Journal of Money, Credit and Banking* 30 (3): 651–655.

Clarke, G.R.G., Cull, R., and Fuchs, M. 2009. "Bank Privatization in Sub-Saharan Africa: The Case of Uganda Commercial Bank" *World Development* 37 (9): 1506–1521.

Cull, R., and Spreng, C. 2011. "Pursuing Efficiency while Maintaining Outreach: Bank Privatization in Tanzania." *Journal of Development Economics* 94 (2): 254–261.

EBRD2020. *Transition Report 2020–21: The State Strikes Back*. European Bank for Reconstruction and Development, London.

Ehrlich, I., Gallais-Hamonno, G., Liu, Z., and Lutter, R. 1994. "Productivity Growth and Firm Ownership: An Analytical and Empirical Investigation." *Journal of Political Economy* 102 (5): 1006–1038.

Estrin, S., and Pelletier, A. 2018. "Privatization in Developing Countries: What Are the Lessons of Recent Experience?" *The World Bank Research Observer* 33 (1): 65–102.

Gutierrez, E. and Kliatskova, T. 2021. *National Development Financial Institutions: Trends, Crises Response Activities, and Lessons Learned.* World Bank, Washington, DC.

Hawkins, J., and Mihaljek, D. 2001. "The Banking Industry in the Emerging Market Economies: Competition, Consolidation and Systemic Stability—An Overview." *BIS Papers* 4, August.

Leasing Association of Uzbekistan. (2021). *Overview of the Leasing Services Sector in Uzbekistan.* Leasing Association of Uzbekistan, Tashkent.

Levy, F. 2002. "Apex Institutions in Microfinance." *CGAP Occasional Paper No. 6*, The Consultative Group to Assist the Poorest.
Mako, W. 2020. *An Efficient Economic Transition: Three Cases.* World Bank, Washington, DC.
Megginson, W., Netter, J. and Chahyadi, C.S. 2005. "Size and Impact of Privatisation-A Survey of Empirical Studies." *CESifo DICE Report* 1.
Melecky, M. 2022. "Economic Stresses And Desperate Financial Choices: How to Nurture Financial Wellbeing in Central Asia." *Eurasian Perspectives*May 13. https://blogs.worldbank.org/europeandcentralasia/how-to-nurture-money-matters-of-people-in-central-asia.
Melecky, M. and Podpiera, A.M., 2013. "Institutional Structures of Financial Sector Supervision, Their Drivers and Historical Benchmarks." *Journal of Financial Stability* 9 (3): 428–444.
Melecky, M. and Podpiera, A. M., 2016. "Central Bank Design and Banking Supervision." *BAFFI CAREFIN Working Papers 1630*, BAFFI CAREFIN, Centre for Applied Research on International Markets Banking Finance and Regulation, Universita' Bocconi, Milano, Italy.
Micco, A., and Panizza, U. 2006. "Bank Ownership and Lending Behavior." *Economics Letters* 93 (2): 248–254.
Reinhart, C.M., and Rogoff, K.S. 2013. "Banking Crises: An Equal Opportunity Menace." *Journal of Banking & Finance* 37 (11): 4557–4573.
Toronto Centre Notes. 2016. "Organizational Alternatives for Supervisors," January 2016.
Toronto Centre Notes. 2018. "Risk-Based Supervision," March 2018.
Vinals J., and J. Fiechter. 2010. "The Making of Good Supervision: Learning to Say 'No'." *IMF Staff Position Note* May.
World Bank2020a. "Developing a National Green Taxonomy." *A World Bank Guide.* World Bank, Washington, DC.
World Bank2020b. *Disaster Property Insurance in Uzbekistan.* World Bank, Washington, DC.
World Bank2022. *Towards a Prosperous and Inclusive Future: The Second Systematic Country Diagnostic for Uzbekistan.* World Bank, Washington, DC.
World Bank and IMF. 2021. "Developing Government Local Currency Bond Markets." *Guidance Notes, 2021/001.* World Bank, Washington, DC.
World Bank and IMF. 2022. *Achieving Climate and Development Goals: The Financing Question.* World Bank and IMF, Washington, DC.

5 Agriculture and rural development reforms

Nodir Djanibekov, Thomas Herzfeld and Martin Petrick

5.1 Introduction

During the first 25 years after the collapse of the Soviet Union, it was the government of Uzbekistan that stood in the way of structural reforms in agriculture. Maintaining many features of central planning, the state continued to play the primary role in determining how economic resources should be allocated (Pomfret, 2008; Zorya et al., 2019). Extractive practices prevailed in the agricultural sector, such as state input and output monopolies, administered pricing, state production plans and quotas, and forced and child labour. Under this agricultural production model, the state was the only purchaser of the two strategic commodities, cotton and wheat. The bulk of agricultural policies were related to increasing the productivity of these two crops and underemphasised other sectors such as horticulture and livestock. Cotton and wheat farmers received stringent output targets and were requested to sell their harvest to parastatal processors at a centrally set price below a potential market level. The state seized the difference between farm-gate and export prices, limiting the income of farmers and wages of farm workers. As part of the state procurement policy, the state provided cotton and wheat growers with subsidised fertilisers, irrigation water, and finance.

Until recently, Uzbekistan's cotton sector was one of the least reformed sectors in any of the Soviet successor states (Djanibekov et al., 2020). Preserving a Soviet type of state dirigisme, the sector featured governmental land allotments and procurement pricing, as well as a sectoral monopoly of parastatal ginneries, input suppliers and exporters. The state taxed cotton growers through artificially low prices for cotton output and currency market controls (Pomfret, 2008). The firm grip of state regulation in the cotton sector resulted in economy-wide inefficiencies, curtailed farm incomes and strangled the ginning and textile companies. Export opportunities for textiles and high-value crops were left untapped. The state control over the cotton sector substantially taxed cotton growers, while subsidies only partly offset this burden (Pomfret, 2008). For instance, in 2000 the net transfers from cotton growers accounted for as much as half of their total cotton revenue, and in subsequent years they were around 22% (Guadagni et al., 2005).

DOI: 10.4324/9781003473497-5

During the 1990s, the government's ability to cushion the transitional recession and maintain public expenditures was largely dependent on the transfers from the cotton farmers to the state budget, which were as high as 5.4% of GDP in 2004 (Pomfret, 2008).

The government's wheat self-sufficiency policy aimed to boost domestic wheat production by expanding sown area and yields of winter wheat and, thus, decreasing the reliance on wheat grain and flour imports. Wheat sector regulation came along with a bread subsidy policy. The state-controlled distribution of domestically produced wheat grains and flour and set ceiling prices to support the poor. Between 1996 and 2017, the government taxed wheat farmers in a similar way as cotton growers. Wheat production expanded through top-down directives and public investments in wheat research. Adoption of domestic high-yield wheat varieties raised per capita production of wheat grains from 118 kg in 1996 to 211 kg in 2017 (Lombardozzi and Djanibekov, 2021). The wheat area expansion led to an exceptionally large rise in overall output, while new wheat varieties and crop management methods drove productivity growth (Yigezu et al., 2022).

The long-standing state regulation of Uzbekistan's wheat sector shows that an increase in national food supply does not automatically translate into improved food access for the poor, adequate nutrient intake, or satisfactory quality of staple food (Lombardozzi and Djanibekov, 2021). Despite the productivity gains, Uzbekistan produces mostly soft wheat varieties that are cheaper but of poor baking quality compared to hard wheat varieties such as those produced in Northern regions of Kazakhstan (Kienzler et al., 2011). As a result, only about half of domestic wheat is used for food, while another half is used as livestock fodder (Lerman et al., 2016). Having declared wheat self-sufficiency, Uzbekistan remains the largest importer of high-quality wheat and flour from Kazakhstan (USDA, 2018).

Along with state-mandated cotton and wheat production, arbitrary expropriations of farmland and terminations of lease contracts have been common and have led to chronic land tenure insecurity among farmers (Djanibekov et al., 2013). The tight control of the agricultural sector depressed wages and productivity in agriculture, curbed rural incomes and caused rural out-migration and labour shortages. To compensate for the latter, the state forcefully mobilised the rural population, students and public workers, as well as children for cotton picking campaigns (Swinkels et al., 2016). Repeated and widespread practice of forced and child labour resulted in an international boycott of Uzbek cotton (ILO, 2022).

The 2016 political changes marked the start of a transformation toward an open society and a market-oriented organisation of the agriculture sector. The new government began to recognise the flaws of the state-led economic model and promoted market-based processes as a more effective way to boost agricultural growth. Although some donor reports document the recent reform path in Uzbekistan's agriculture (World Bank, 2022b, 2022c), there is no comprehensive review of the challenges brought by the recent political changes. This study fills this void by providing an overview of recent agricultural and rural development reforms in Uzbekistan. It analyses the current policy environment for agriculture and rural development. To provide an understanding of persistent and emerging challenges, the study documents the government's actions in agriculture diversification and reforms and their implications for the farming sector.

The study uses desk research of secondary data supplemented by information from face-to-face and online expert interviews in autumn 2022 and national statistical data on agriculture. This chapter also utilises information obtained from the State Statistical Committee and the Ministry of Agriculture, as well as from reports of the international donor community.

5.2 Agri-food development strategy 2020–2030

Agriculture contributes about a quarter of the Uzbek domestic product and employment (UzStat, 2022). Crop and livestock production contribute almost equally to agricultural output. Despite a decrease of 2.2% in the total area of cropland in 2019, the agricultural sector grew by 3.1%, breaking out its two-year stagnation in 2017–2018 (Figure 5.1).

In 2020, during the first waves of the COVID-19 pandemic, Uzbekistan's agriculture contributed to economic resilience (Djanibekov and Herzfeld, 2022), growing by 2.9% and offsetting the contraction in GDP of –0.1%. In

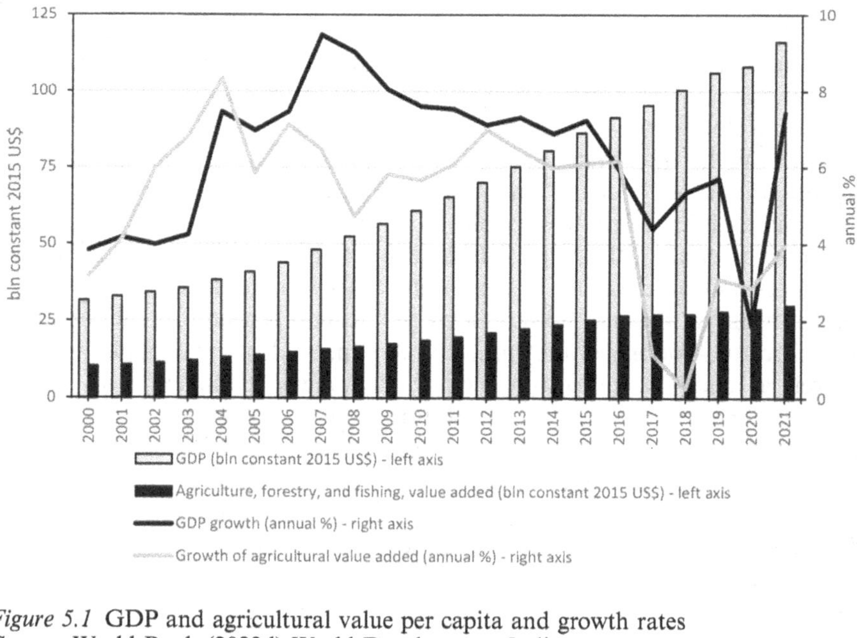

Figure 5.1 GDP and agricultural value per capita and growth rates
Source: World Bank (2022d) World Development Indicators.

2021, agriculture grew by 4%. The recent agricultural growth responded to economic reforms that began in 2017–2018 and eliminated many market-distorting policies in cotton, wheat and horticulture sectors, and restructured agricultural public expenditures (World Bank, 2022b).

By adopting the Agri-food Development Strategy for 2020–2030, the government put forward an ambitious and forward-looking set of reforms to manage the transition from a state-led, staple food-focused, inward-oriented system to a market-based, diversified, outward-oriented agriculture.[1] Notably, the Strategy reduced state involvement in the agricultural sector and thus paved the way for private investments to enhance, diversify, and support the agro-food sector. Furthermore, the Strategy emphasises the productive use of natural resources without overlooking environmental concerns. The main objective of the Strategy is to radically improve public policy directed at deepening ongoing reforms that improve the competitiveness of the agri-food sector. The Strategy includes the following nine priorities (quotes from the Strategy document):

1 *Ensuring food security* by addressing food access for socially vulnerable groups, state procurement of cereals at market prices, gradual abolishment of food price regulation, promoting healthy diets, implementing a food security assessment and monitoring system, expanding production of socially significant food products, and intensifying livestock production.
2 *Improving the agri-business environment and value chains as well as agricultural exports* through aligning the certification system with international standards and facilitating farm cooperation.
3 *Decreasing state intervention in agriculture* to modernise, diversify, and sustainably expand the agri-food sector and to make it attractive for investors.
4 *Ensuring the effective use of natural resources and environmental protection* to strengthen climate change adaptation.
5 *Developing modern public administration systems* by reforming the Ministry of Agriculture, establishing public-private partnership models in agricultural services, and improving communication among policymakers, agricultural producers, processors, and international donors.
6 *Gradual diversification of state expenditures on agriculture* by revising the public agricultural budget, raising public funding for R&D, gradually privatising agri-services, and reducing the tax burden on agricultural producers.
7 *Developing research and education* as well as agricultural information and advisory services to boost rural human capital, agricultural innovation, and labour productivity.
8 *Developing rural areas* by reforming and decentralising rural governments, and introducing new models of rural non-agricultural businesses.

9 *Introducing a transparent system of agriculture and food statistics* that uses data from 'smart agriculture' and the agricultural census.

Through these nine priorities the Strategy set targets in the annual agricultural growth rate of 3% in 2021 and 5% in 2025, and agri-food exports of \$20 billion by 2030. Despite the volatility of national and global agri-food markets, the state kept track of the implementation of the agricultural reforms it had initiated. The COVID-19 pandemic slowed the reform and required some adjustments in the reform plans, e.g. in the wheat sector. In 2022, the Russian Invasion of Ukraine brought new challenges, e.g. in importing high-quality wheat, undermining political support for Uzbekistan's agricultural reform.

Individual farms and small-scale dekhqan farms (smallholders including rural households) are the two primary farm categories in Uzbekistan's agriculture. The former are focused on the production of cotton and grains and operated about 73% of sown area in 2021 (Figure 5.2).[2] Smallholders focus on small-scale horticulture and livestock production and operated about 14% of the sown area in 2021. The dualistic farm structure has recently been reinforced by state-led land transfers from individual farmers to newly created cotton clusters for direct farming. Cotton clusters are recorded as agricultural enterprises, the third farm category. This category operated the remaining 13% of the sown area in 2021. Smallholders contribute over two-thirds of agricultural output, with a dominating role in livestock. Recently, the smallholder share went down slightly as a result of government support of agricultural enterprises.

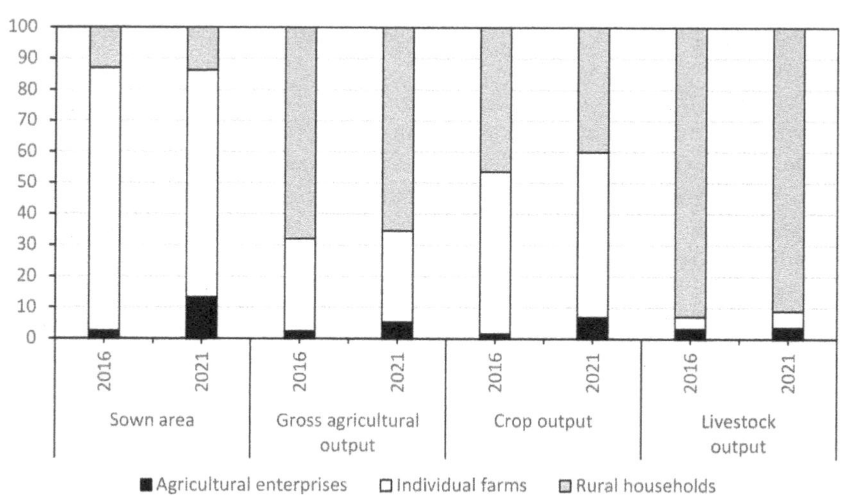

Figure 5.2 Share of farm categories in agricultural output (%)
Source: Based on UzStat (2019, 2022).

5.3 Cotton sector reforms

The price and value-chain liberalisation boosted the sector's performance and resulted in two changes in the structure of cotton cultivation visible in official statistics (Figure 5.3). First, according to the expert interviews and UzStat (2022) agricultural enterprises account now for a much higher share in cotton production since more and more land is being transferred from individual farmers to clusters for 'direct farming'. Second, cotton yields have gone up after the 2011–2018 stagnation. Compared to the 2018 value (2.1 t/ha), in 2021 the average raw cotton yield increased by almost 60% to 3.3 t/ha. One reason is the recorded increase in average farm-gate prices for raw cotton (Figure 5.4). The cotton productivity improvement exceeded the output decline due to the state-directed reduction in cotton cultivation area. As a result, the total cotton output has been rising.

As a major part of the cotton sector reform, the government of Uzbekistan started transforming cotton–textile supply chains into vertically integrated cotton–textile clusters. The cotton–textile clusters are supposed to play a crucial role in the reforms by boosting processing efficiency, supplying farmers with better access to inputs, and investing in new machinery and textile equipment. To promote the modernisation of the cotton sector, the government expects that clusters will expand the adoption of cotton combines and increase wages for cotton pickers. Clusters also serve as financial gatekeepers. While farmers do receive direct public funds, clusters receive low-interest loans from the National Agriculture Fund to supply inputs and services to cotton-growing farmers (Babadjanov and Petrick, 2023). Finally, the government expects that clusters will access international textile markets

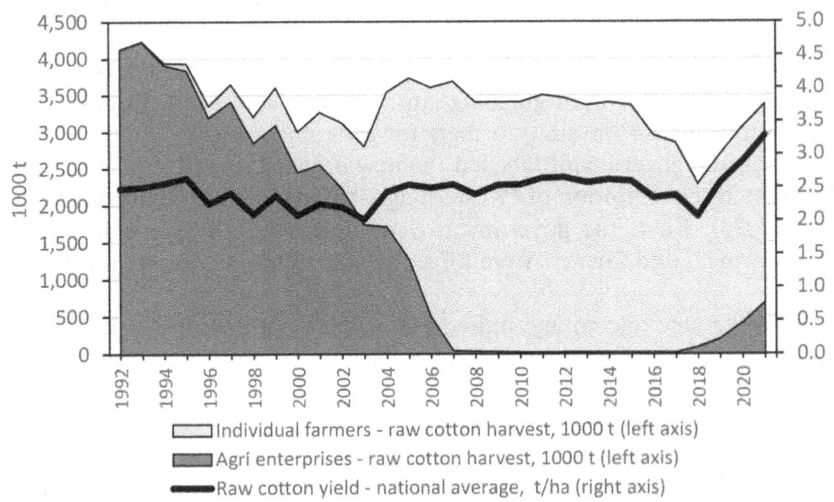

Figure 5.3 Evolution of cotton cultivation in Uzbekistan
Source: Based on data from the State Statistical Committee.

and boost export revenues. According to the latest information, cotton production has been divided among 134 clusters that cover almost 30,000 farmers (Table 5.1). However, their number is changing from year to year due to ongoing reorganisations.

The government liberalised the cotton market and eliminated governmental restrictions on cotton output and pricing, but kept the state mandated land allocation to cotton. State production obligations were replaced by commercial delivery contracts between farmers and clusters (Zorya and Babaev, 2020). State prices were replaced by minimum farm-gate prices to which all cotton buyers must adhere. The average minimum farm-gate price was almost doubled reflecting international price development (Figure 5.4). Previously, the strongly varying gap between international and farm-gate prices for cotton can be related to foreign exchange controls contributing to the isolation of Uzbek cotton markets (Pomfret, 2008). Farmers' implicit taxation has been additionally aggravated by an overvalued exchange rate, visible in the gap between domestic prices measured in official and parallel exchange rates.

The cotton–textile clusters operate through three models.[3] The first, most common model is '*contract farming*' where a cluster makes contracts with local cotton-growing farmers. Farmers retain the land leased from the state and keep management responsibilities. But they commit to growing cotton and delivering it to their cluster. In exchange, the cluster supplies inputs and services to the contracted farmers. Alternatively, the cluster can directly operate land leased from the state. In this case, so-called '*direct farming*' model, the state expropriates land from cotton-growing farmers and transfers it to clusters. The cluster management directly operates the cotton production and former farmers are employed by the cluster as wage labour. The third model represents a combination of direct and contract farming. According to anecdotal evidence, some private clusters under direct farming or '*mixed models*' have been grabbing large areas of land from cotton-growing farmers without compensating farmers for economic losses.[4]

Although the government labelled the new organisations as 'clusters', they do not match the definition of 'Western agri-based clusters' (Babadjanov and Petrick, 2023). First, the government determined the places where clusters must be formed, and farmers were forced to join clusters (Zorya and Babaev, 2020).

Second, the new reform legitimised the clusters' monopoly on the delivery of inputs and services to farmers within their territory. Clusters are the sole buyers of raw cotton and the only processors and exporters of final textile products. State orders attached farmers to a cluster within their district. This implies that farmers should sell their cotton harvest to a single monopsonist buyer and purchase inputs and services from a single monopolist designated by the state. As one district usually has only one cluster, clusters do not compete for cotton-growing farmers. Farmers have no choice over the crops they produce or the inputs they use on land allocated to them. Furthermore,

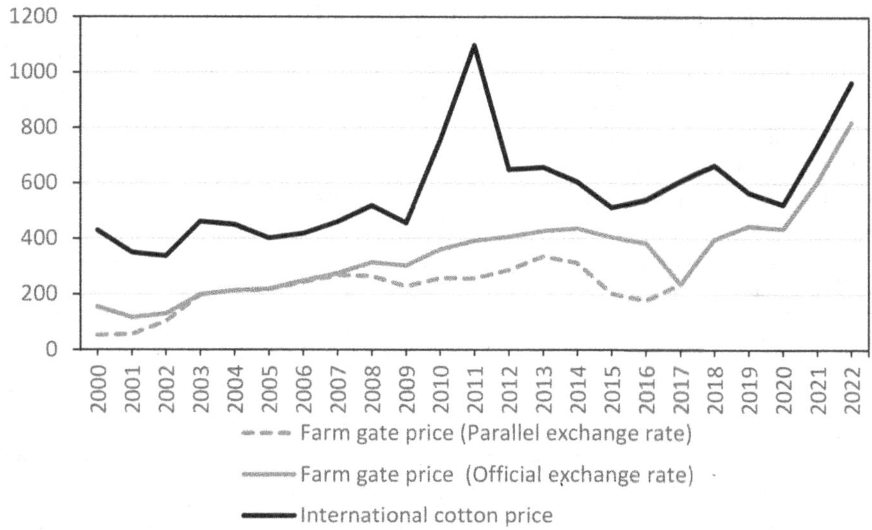

Figure 5.4 Average farm-gate prices for raw cotton, US$/t in nominal US$

Notes: The farm-gate price under the official exchange rate is the price paid to farmers converted to US$ using official exchange rates from the CBU. The parallel exchange rate is an unofficial (black) market exchange rate in Uzbekistan which in some years was much higher than the official exchange rate. The international cotton price for raw cotton is calculated as Cotton A Index price from World Bank Commodity Price Data (The Pink Sheet) multiplied by a ratio of 0.33 which is an approximate rate of converting raw cotton to cotton fibre.

Source: Uzbekistan's cotton prices from the Ministry of Agriculture. International cotton price is calculated using annual prices for 2000–2021 and as average monthly prices for January–November 2022 of World Bank Commodity Price Data (The Pink Sheet).

they still have no freedom in selecting marketing and input/service supply channels.

Finally, the transition of parastatal ginneries to private clusters has neither abolished the output quota nor the government's control over cotton pricing. The clusters impose contracted amounts of cotton based on targets assigned by the state, while the latter administers a minimum farm-gate price, which usually becomes the maximum price that clusters pay to farmers. As a result, the regulations governing the cluster system are associated with severe market distortions that reduce the bargaining power of farmers. Despite the announced desire to transition to a more liberalised cotton sector, the state remains the major implementer of changes.

To address the issue of cluster monopsony and to establish competition in the cotton sector, a presidential decree of November 2021 granted farmers the freedom to voluntarily enter into 'futures' (pre-financing) contracts with any cotton–textile cluster within their province (viloyat). Each province

Table 5.1 Number and Area of Cotton–Textile Clusters

	2018	*2019*	*2020*	*2021*	*2022*
Number of cotton-textile clusters	13	77	97	122	134
Total sown area of cotton-textile clusters, 1,000 ha	NA	668	917	1,034	1,034
Number of farms contracted by cotton-textile clusters	NA	20,981	25,150	28,206	28,206
Total raw cotton output in clusters, million tonnes	NA	1.8	2.7	3.4	3.6

Source: Based on unpublished data from the Ministry of Agriculture.

covers several clusters.[5] However, the implementation of the legislation in the 2022 contracts turned out to be arbitrary or was simply disregarded.[6]

The agricultural reforms also foresee the establishment of farm cooperatives as another major form of organised agriculture.[7] The new cooperative legislation permitted the voluntary participation of farmers in cooperatives. The government exempted land leases to cooperative participants from expropriations and reallocations. Furthermore, cooperative participants were granted the freedom to independently select their crop portfolio (Niyazmetov et al., 2021). Farmers are permitted by law to create cooperatives as an alternative to contracting individually with clusters. The minimum number of farmers necessary to organise a cooperative is five, and the procedures regulating cooperative registration are straightforward.

In reality, however, local authorities prohibited the registration of cooperatives or impeded their operation by barring farmers from establishing cotton producer cooperatives in several districts (Niyazmetov et al., 2021). In 2019, following the government resolution, over 30 agricultural cooperatives were established in four regions (Asfaw, 2020). Along with the rapid proliferation of monopolistic cotton clusters, the top-down introduction of cooperatives involving the forced participation of farmers has reduced trust in state-mandated collective action (Niyazmetov et al., 2021). Acknowledging the problems in the top-down establishment of cooperatives, the government abandoned the old decree. It now tabled a new law on agricultural cooperatives that is based on international experience in forming voluntary cooperatives.

5.4 Labour and mechanisation

The new government's aim to modernise the old agricultural economic model also targeted child and forced labour in cotton picking. The reforms introduced fair recruiting methods and acceptable monetary remuneration to attract volunteer cotton pickers. As a result, the systematic mobilisation of students and public servants in cotton picking has disappeared. The abolishment of forced labour in cotton picking has been supported by the state programme on mechanising cotton harvesting in cotton-textile clusters.

According to observations of the International Labour Organization (ILO, 2022), the reforms continue to have a beneficial effect and the practice of forced labour has been rapidly eliminated. Through awareness-raising campaigns on labour rights, criminalising child and forced labour, and steadily increasing the minimum wage for cotton pickers, rural workers have been empowered to negotiate higher wages with farmers and clusters. The Cabinet of Ministers jointly with the Ministry of Labour, the Federation of Trade Unions and the Employers Association announces the minimum wage for manual cotton picking (ILO, 2022). Furthermore, within cotton clusters, cotton pickers are reported to engage in different forms of collective bargaining at the brigade level (ILO, 2022). The government systematically eradicated forced and child labour used during the 2021 cotton production cycle (ILO, 2022). Yet, despite higher wages for cotton pickers, they are still determined by the state mandates, but not by market mechanisms (World Bank, 2022b).

As forced and child labour disappeared from Uzbekistan's cotton fields, the Cotton Campaign, a global network of retailers, abolished the international boycott of Uzbek cotton in March 2022.[8] This move became a milestone for improving trading relations with Western partners not only in textile, but also in horticulture exports. The decision should thus provide Uzbek cotton processors access to hitherto blocked markets of global clothing retailers.

In recent years, the government has made various steps to expand the mechanisation of cotton harvesting, although its adoption rate has been hampered by several structural reasons. First is that planting and cultivation of cotton for manual harvesting significantly differ from the agronomic practices applied for mechanically harvested cotton. The use of cotton combine services requires that cotton-growing farmers have access to reasonably priced complementary services for sowing cotton seeds and spraying defoliants before harvesting. Furthermore, hiring cotton combine services becomes cheaper with the adoption scale and thus requires that cotton growers coordinate in cotton cultivation and harvesting. For this reason, the use of cotton combines has been expanding on 'direct farming' fields, which are controlled and operated by cotton clusters. The mechanised cotton harvesting of 'contract farming' fields, which are operated by individual farms is still uncommon (ILO, 2022).

5.5 Wheat sector reforms

In contrast to the cotton sector, the total area under wheat has been declining during the last six years. Since 2007, wheat production has been concentrated in individual farms, while smallholders' contribution accounts for approximately 8%. In recent years, the share of the 'rural households' category of producers, which comprises household plot owners and dekhqan farms, declined, from 15% in 2016 to 7% in 2021, and that of agricultural enterprises went up again (Figure 5.5). Similar to the cotton sector, the expansion of wheat clusters and cooperatives increased the production in agricultural enterprises almost tenfold from 64,000 tonnes in 2016 to 560,000 tonnes in 2021. However, the delays in liberalising the wheat sector slowed down the sector's performance. The low farm-gate prices offered failed to incentivise the growth of wheat productivity. As a direct consequence of this, wheat output stagnated between 2016 and 2021, except for the drought year 2018. In 2016, the total wheat output was almost 7 million tonnes, while in 2021 it was as high as 6 million tonnes. With the exception of 2018, wheat yields are stagnating around the average of 4.6 t/ha (2012–2021).

In September 2018 price regulation on bread (i.e. the bread subsidy programme) was abolished, resulting in an increase in bread prices by 30%.[9] To compensate for this bread price inflation the government introduced monthly financial compensation to poor households equivalent to 10% of the minimum wage in October 2018.[10] In March 2020, the government declared that similar to the cotton sector liberalisation the state quota system for wheat would be terminated.[11] Yet, due to the COVID-19 pandemic the implementation of this reform has been delayed. The presidential resolution from November 2021 announced that the reform should begin in 2022 with a liberalisation of wheat prices.[12] In 2022, the wheat procurement prices went up

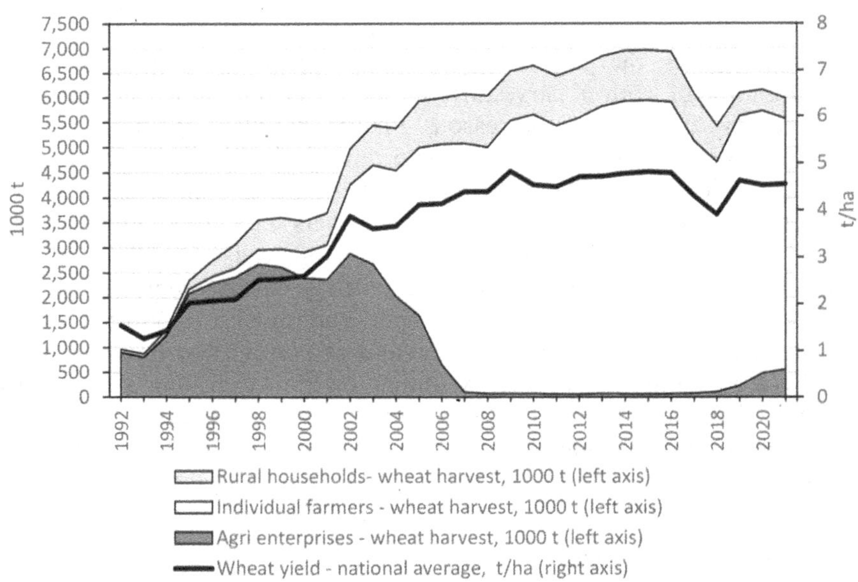

Figure 5.5 Evolution of wheat cultivation in Uzbekistan
Source: Based on data from the State Statistical Committee.

by 50% (Figure 5.6).[13] The abolition of state procurement targets in the wheat sector is seen as a complementary step in line with the liberalisation of bread prices in 2018 and wheat flour prices in 2019. While implementing the liberalisation of the wheat sector, the government does not expect price shocks for domestic flour and bread markets. The wheat price liberalisation is expected to affect only the price of subsidised bread loaves as the bread subsidy has already been cut in 2018.[14] Types of bread of higher quality request higher quality wheat which has been always more expensive than the procurement price level.

To respond to the concerns of excessive wheat price volatility, the government announced that the old state procurement system would be replaced by a public grain reserve. Furthermore, the new public grain reserve is envisaged to address the long-standing dependency on imports of Kazakh wheat grain and flour. According to the expert interviews, the state will purchase wheat and store it in public reserves to stabilise the domestic wheat market. Assessing the effectiveness of the new public wheat reserves will have to await

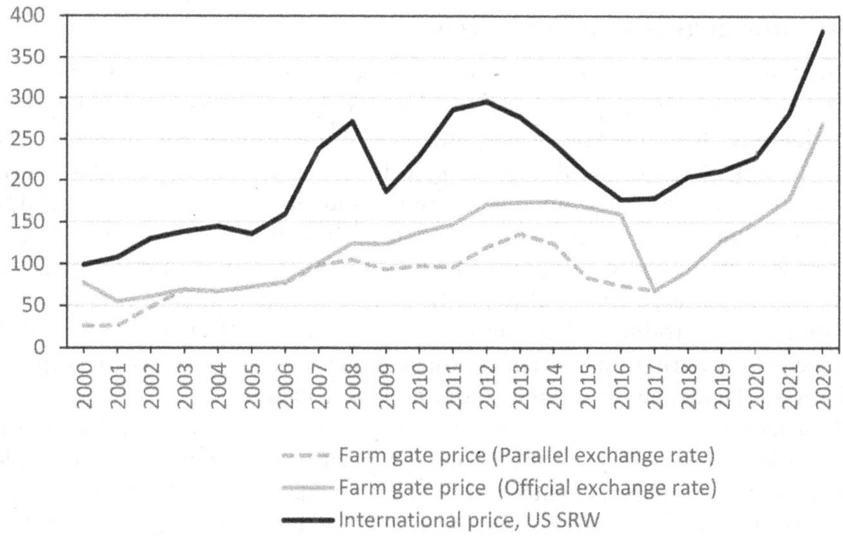

Figure 5.6 Farm-gate prices of wheat grain, US$/t in nominal US$.
Note: The farm-gate price under the official exchange rate is the price paid to farmers converted to US$ using exchange rates from the Central Bank of Uzbekistan. The parallel exchange rate stands for the unofficial (black) market exchange rate in Uzbekistan which in some years was much higher than the official exchange rate. International price is the US soft red wheat price from World Bank Commodity Price Data (The Pink Sheet).
Source: Uzbekistan's wheat prices from Lombardozzi and Djanibekov (2021) and the Ministry of Agriculture. International price is calculated using annual prices for 2000–2021 and as average monthly prices for January–July 2022 of World Bank Commodity Price Data (The Pink Sheet).

implementation and funding. Given the global wheat market uncertainties after Russia invaded Ukraine, smoothing the food price volatility in the Uzbek consumer market will be challenging.

Similar to the cotton sector reform, the liberalisation in the wheat sector also aimed at increasing wheat exports. The location of Uzbekistan next to Afghanistan and Tajikistan allows it to export cheaply blended flour that competes with more expensive high-quality Kazakh wheat flour. In August 2018, a governmental decree allowed exporting up to 75% of wheat flour produced from imported grains which previously was fully restricted. This reform is complementary to the liberalisation of imported wheat grain, freed from customs duties until 2020 and then exempted again from January 2022 until July 2023. As a result of these two reforms, the production and trading activities of the Uzbek milling sector, both private and public, have boomed. For instance, Kazakh businesses have invested in Uzbekistan's milling sector to access Afghan and Tajik markets in response to the new wheat regulatory framework.[15]

5.6 Horticulture and livestock sectors

With the Strategy, the government announced ambitious goals to increase fruit and vegetable exports and to diversify Uzbekistan's export markets. Horticulture has quickly gained increasing importance and became the second biggest agricultural exporting sector after cotton. The horticultural sector delivers half of crop output value and 40% of overall agricultural output, while being cultivated on roughly 10% of all arable land (World Bank, 2022a). Despite the government's new attention to horticulture, the sector is dominated by small-scale farmers and smallholders (Figure 5.7). Medium-scale producers have appeared only recently (Larson et al., 2015). Concerning international certification standards, such a structure imposes additional challenges and might require market facilitation.

Horticulture has been less regulated than cotton and wheat and thus was not under the scrutiny of the farm optimisation campaigns. As a result, horticultural farmers benefited from decision-making freedom and tenure security. Horticulture incomes substantially exceeded those of wheat and cotton producers. Furthermore, horticulture requires more permanent labour than cotton and wheat. Therefore, the recent production expansion also benefited low-wage rural workers (Asfaw, 2020). By supplying food and cash directly to smallholders and increasing agricultural employment, horticulture contributes to rural incomes and poverty alleviation (Larson et al., 2015).

Livestock production is almost entirely done by smallholders where cattle serves as a social safety net for many rural households (Figure 5.8). In 2021, about 4.7 million households possessed over 12.4 million cattle and contributed about 91% of total livestock output. About a quarter of the agricultural labour force is engaged in livestock production (World Bank, 2020). Due to farm restructuring in the 1990s, agricultural enterprises account for

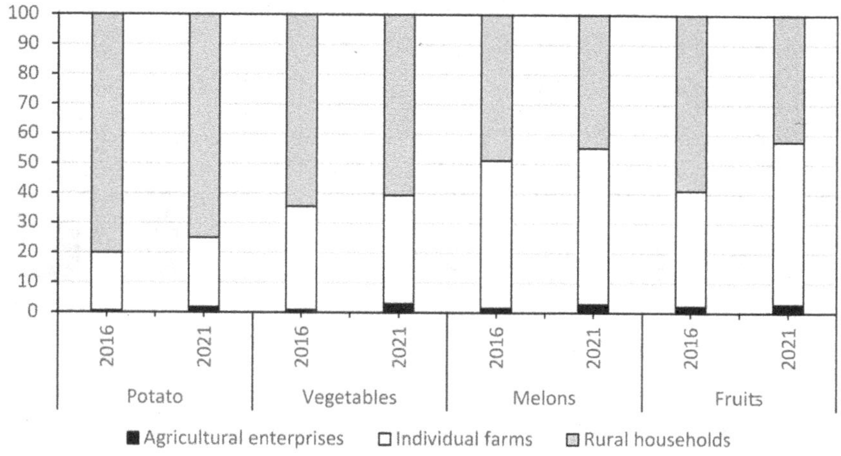

Figure 5.7 Share of agricultural producer categories in horticulture (%)
Source: Based on UzStat (2019, 2022).

only a small share of meat and milk production today. In 2021, they produced 3.6% of livestock output. Individual farms, while operating over 80% of the sown area, contribute only 5.3% of livestock output.

Recent state support programmes aimed at increasing the share of individual farms and agricultural enterprises in livestock production. Starting from a very low level, meat production in individual farms rose by 120% and milk production increased by 60% between 2016 and 2021. Agricultural enterprises increased meat production in the same five-year period by 137% and milk production by 60%. But also smallholders reported an increase in livestock output over the same period. Meat production increased by 15% and milk production by 14%.

While smallholder-based horticulture and livestock sectors benefit the rural population, their fragmentation puts limits on their further development. Almost no public initiatives were aimed at smallholders, and when they did, they were neither well-planned nor well-supported (Asfaw, 2020). In addition, the state has rarely been engaged with smallholder production and hardly provided them with public support, except for a few spillover effects (Asfaw, 2020). For instance, smallholders are restricted in access to improved farming methods and technology that are mostly developed for the large-scale farming system (Larson et al., 2015). Smallholders engage in low-cost traditional methods of horticultural production due to poor access to financial resources and services which are channelled entirely to bigger farms. Smallholders have almost no access to processors, storage, and packaging facilities for perishable fresh horticultural and livestock products (Asfaw, 2020). Absent connections to marketing channels, missing role models and complete inexperience with alternative farming technologies have been

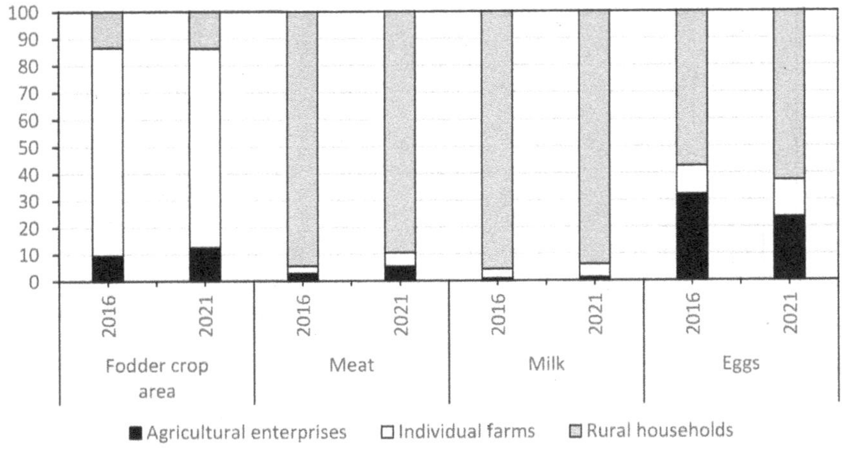

Figure 5.8 Share of agricultural producer categories in livestock production (%)
Source: Based on UzStat (2019, 2022).

impeding the further expansion of crops other than cotton or wheat (Petrick and Djanibekov, 2016). As land transactions have been restrained until recently, smallholders could access additional agricultural lands only by engaging in informal sharecropping or informal land rent arrangements with individual farms (Djanibekov et al., 2013; Mukhamedova and Pomfret, 2019). Active organisations for collective learning and participatory knowledge exchange that target smallholders and could improve their access to inputs and capital are absent (Asfaw, 2020).

There is a significant gap in the skills and capacity needed for the functioning of a modern horticulture subsector across the entire value chain, as smallholders have no access to modern production technologies and knowledge (Larson et al., 2015). Smallholders gain little from market participation as they are cut off from higher-paying retailers and exports due to low capacity to maintain consistent supply volume, quality, and safety requirements. Smallholders have been used to selling their harvests locally through traditional markets and retailers who buy on the spot and without written contracts. Retailers and exporters avoid the significant transaction costs associated with contracting fragmented smallholders. Small-scale horticulture producers have limited capacity to comply with international sanitary and phytosanitary regulations and food safety standards to access international markets.

The Strategy addresses these challenges and aims at improving market access and attracting public investment in productivity-enhancing initiatives for smallholders. In 2021, to support the smallholder sector in accessing additional land, new legislation formalised sub-rental arrangements from individual farms and agricultural enterprises.[16] More precisely, individual farms or other agricultural enterprises were granted rights to sublease their lands of up to 10 ha to smallholders for one year. Furthermore, in September 2022, the new legislation specified that smallholders, particularly from vulnerable groups, can receive 1 to 2 ha of additional land through a long-term lease.[17]

A lack of adequate fodder supply hinders livestock expansion, particularly for smallholders, through intensive large-scale production. The continuous growth of Uzbekistan's livestock herd has yet to be accompanied by an adequate increase in fodder production (Robinson and Petrick, 2021; Shapiro et al., 2022). The wheat self-sufficiency policy was introduced at the expense of area under perennials and high-quality fodder crops. Pasture management was shifted to individual farmers and clusters who restrict smallholders' livestock grazing on these lands. As the demand for feedstuff has been outstripping its production, livestock keepers mix relatively affluent metabolisable feedstuff such as wheat bran and maize or sorghum straw with crude protein-rich feedstuff which comes mostly from cottonseed cake (Djumaeva et al., 2009). Furthermore, smallholders lack access to high-quality veterinary services, high-performing genetic breeds, instruments to secure hygienic conditions, and expertise to boost livestock output (Asfaw, 2021).

Acknowledging the problems of livestock sector development, particularly the lack of fodder production areas, the government has increased the subsidies for livestock producers in 2021 and approved a programme for livestock sector development in early 2022.[18] The latter emphasises the modernisation of livestock technologies and value chains through agricultural enterprises and cooperatives. In February 2022, new legislation earmarked additional subsidies for meat and milk producers, to be disbursed during the coming two years.[19] The legislation promotes outgrower contractual arrangements in livestock between individual farms and rural households. It is expected that large individual farms and clusters will outsource livestock growing to small family-based growers. The legislation also instructs cotton-textile, grain, and rice clusters to establish livestock feedlots of between 500 to 1,000 cattle heads. Abandoned and unused arable lands will be leased to meat and dairy companies for fodder crop cultivation.

5.7 The future of individual farms

While increasing the level of farm subsidies on the one hand, the state keeps controlling farmers' decision-making on the other. It forcibly terminates farm businesses by revoking land leases through repeated farm optimisation campaigns. For instance, the last wave of farm optimisation in 2019 cut the number of individual farms by 40%. The establishment of the cluster system put farmers at a new risk that the state will expropriate their land and pass it to clusters. Weak land tenure security disincentivises farmers' investments in soil fertility, irrigation and sustainable technologies, eventually decreasing land productivity and increasing its vulnerability to climate change in the long run.

Cotton sector liberalisation meant that farmers would be permitted to select which crops they produce.[20] However, farmers, notably those specialised in cotton and wheat, perceive low levels of decision-making freedom in choosing which crops to farm and the marketing channels through which to sell their output (Kurbanov et al., 2022). Furthermore, several policies aiming at the diversification of the crop portfolio and exports recently mandated the cultivation of high-value crops but failed to provide proper services to deliver the harvest to markets. Recent examples include the 2022 state order that requested individual farmers to cultivate potatoes and soya beans for food security regardless of farmland suitability,[21] the 2018 order concerning chilli peppers, and the 2017 order concerning pumpkin production for export markets and crop diversification.[22] The continuous interference with farmers' decision-making, the risk of land expropriation and the incapacity of land titles to mitigate this risk endanger the future of individual farms.

The authorities continue to prescribe *de facto* production targets and require farmers to cultivate cotton and sign 'futures' (pre-financing) contracts with cotton–textile clusters (Asfaw, 2021). These 'future' contracts do not inform farmers of their final output payment and most importantly, their ability to meet production costs. Local administrators require that farmers sign contracts with specified clusters and restrict farmers in selecting clusters based on the highest price offered for raw cotton. Due to the inconsistency between land tenure regulations and the production targets, Uzbek farmers underuse their rights in income generating and crop harvesting, as they do not have full autonomy on the choice of crops to cultivate and marketing channels, which in turn affects their willingness to increase crop production (Akhmadiyeva and Herzfeld, 2021).

Furthermore, the cotton sector reform puts Uzbek farmers at a severe economic disadvantage against clusters and reduces farmers' bargaining power over contract conditions (World Bank, 2022b). Anecdotal evidence suggests that farmers are threatened by illegal land confiscations, blank contracts without indication of cotton prices or inflated output targets. Moreover, they may not receive adequate payments for their harvests and face cluster monopolies in input supplies and marketing channels. To obtain bargaining power over the existing cotton clusters, according to expert interviews, cotton farmers have been banding together to form independent production cooperatives.[23] However, the operation of these cooperatives has been prevented by local authorities. By denying cooperatives access to preferential loans from the Agriculture Fund, the state is barring farmers from operating independently from clusters.

5.8 Ways forward

Since 2017, the government of Uzbekistan has implemented bold and historically unprecedented reforms to increase agricultural production and competitiveness. The Strategy brought substantial changes to the sector, such as the abolition of state output targets for cotton and wheat, the termination of the systematic use of forced labour in cotton harvesting, and the liberalisation of horticulture exports. Price liberalisation and the admission of private investors into the cotton ginning sector had a favourable impact on the performance of the sector. Cotton output increased and farm-gate prices went up.

Rising food prices due to the global pandemic and the war in Ukraine have introduced additional threats, as food access for low-income households may deteriorate. In the face of global crises, the government implemented the wheat sector reform only partially to maintain low bread prices and avoid price volatility for staple foods. Since wheat is still the most significant source of food, a strategy that maintains both the stability of supply and strives to cushion price volatility is seen as an alternative with lower political costs. Liberalising wheat prices quickly would almost surely harm low-income consumers.

The first years of agricultural reforms in Uzbekistan also revealed new challenges threatening the sector's long-term sustainable and inclusive growth. The speed and actual execution of the agrarian reforms have been prioritised more than their thorough implementation which would take into account unintended negative outcomes and externalities. One visible and often reported concern amid the reforms is that farmers do not have bargaining power within the newly established cluster system. Farmers have little control over the crops they cultivate or the inputs they use. The state administration continues to oversee the allocation of land for wheat and cotton cultivation. Farmers are still compelled to sell cotton to a single monopsonist buyer selected by the state, and farm-gate pricing for cotton continues to be regulated. Without effective organisations through which they could contract or own the ginning sector, farmers fall under the strict control of powerful private clusters. The inadequacy of farmers' autonomy over decision-making and their lack of bargaining power may harm not only individual farmers but also the entire cotton sector. One solution may come through introducing a strong association to advocate farmers' interests or allow collective negotiation of more favourable conditions. The current 'Council of Farmers, Dekhqan Farms, and Household Plot Owners' is busy with monitoring and exercising public supervision over farmers and households rather than representing and defending their interests.[24]

After the government abolishes cotton and wheat output quotas it will need to formalise the 'freedom to farm' and terminate the crop placement system (Petrick and Djanibekov, 2019). The experiences of Kazakhstan and Kyrgyzstan's liberalised cotton sectors prove that cotton may be economically competitive with other high-value crops (Petrick et al., 2017). Cotton production will not disappear after eliminating the state procurement targets or under a *laissez-faire* economic model. In reality, sectoral development is highly dependent on the prices obtained by cotton farmers and their ability to independently choose marketing channels, i.e. the competition between cotton gins for the cotton harvest. The open competition among gins in an export-oriented cotton value chain can also benefit small-scale cotton growers. Any production mandates on high-value crops, e.g. to improve exports, crop diversification or food security, will only impose an additional burden on farmers.

Repeated farm optimisation by decrees and weak land tenure rights curtail farmers' management and investment incentives and raise issues for smallholders in accessing productive land. The cotton sector liberalisation has not paid attention to the weak land rights and their effects on the farming sector. The 'clusterisation' of agriculture created new threats of farmland expropriation by allowing newly emerged clusters to implement 'direct farming'. Without stronger land tenure security, the subsidies to incentivise farmers' investments in sustainable land and water management technologies will have little other effect than draining the public budget. Agricultural growth can be sustained and brought to the next level by hardening farmers' property rights through more flexibility in land transactions, allowing land rentals to more productive users. In contrast to top-down farm optimisation campaigns, secondary land markets will serve market-driven farm consolidation. The land market liberalisation does not require the complete privatisation of farmland, but rather formalised and secured voluntary land rental agreements. The government must make farmers believe in an end to public and private land seizures.

How a future and still growing rural population will be employed and secure its income is one of the essential questions the government needs to address (Varis, 2014). In addition to land, smallholders are also lacking access to financing and training tailored to their needs. Rural out-migration complicates the situation further, as it causes the loss of young and skilled workers leading to the ageing and feminisation of agricultural labour and thus challenging the future of smallholders (Asfaw, 2020). Improving the public sector's responsiveness to the needs of smallholders will be crucial for creating more sustainable and inclusive development. Capacity-building programmes focusing on technical and business skills, reduced transaction costs in land, service and credit access and technological research on high-yielding crop varieties, breeds, and fertiliser applications can contribute to the modernisation of smallholder farming and support its further growth.

Yet in the longer run, improving smallholder incomes requires action beyond the agricultural sector. Raising labour productivity in agriculture will be impossible without releasing a major share of workers from the sector (Petrick and Djanibekov, 2019). Allowing private investment into up- and downstream rural industries and private intermediation with export markets has the potential to create new jobs for the rural population and broaden the tax base for the government. Off-farm employment opportunities will reduce the pressure to leave rural areas and allow in particular smallholders to combine farming with additional sources of income. But a fundamental modernisation of the agricultural sector will also depend on comprehensive reforms to vitalise the non-farm economy.

Taking a systemic perspective on rural development could be based on IFAD's definition of rural transformation as a process which involves rising agricultural productivity, commercialisation, and diversification of production patterns on the one hand but a diversification of livelihoods and expanded off-farm employment on the other hand (IFAD, 2016). Besides a more diversified agricultural production of non-grain or high-value products, it will be crucial to have new employment opportunities outside of the agricultural sector. This will not only accompany structural change in agriculture, but can help to increase rural incomes, have more resilient rural economies, and, ultimately, provide people incentives to stay in rural areas. For instance, in China the share of rural non-farm employment increased from 7% in 1978 to 51% in 2018 (Huang, 2022). The sources of non-farm employment growth can be multiple. In the case of China, the government stimulated the emergence of so-called Township and Village Enterprises which absorbed labour in particular in the 1980s (Zhang, et al., 2018). Later, employment growth in smaller cities allowed rural people to commute to non-farm work (Sheng et al., 2022). Investments in public infrastructure and transport might be a precondition to enlarge the mobility of rural people.

Notes

1 Presidential decree 5852 (23 October 2019) on approval of the Strategy for Agricultural Development of the Republic of Uzbekistan for 2020–2030. https://lex.uz/ru/docs/4567337.
2 It is impossible to assess the structure of individual farms by farm size as the official statistics' category 'individual farms' (*fermer xo'jaliklar*) aggregates over all individual farms including small-scale individual farms.
3 Resolution of the Cabinet of Ministers №733 (4 December 2021) on approval of regulations on the procedure for organising activities of cotton-textile clusters. https://lex.uz/uz/docs/5760091.
4 Land-grabs—the new red flag for Uzbek cotton sector. www.uzbekforum.org/land-grabs-the-new-red-flag-for-uzbek-cotton-sector/.
5 Presidential decree (16 November 2021) on measures to regulate activities of cotton-textile clusters. https://lex.uz/ru/docs/5731036.
6 Uzbekistan's cotton sector cannot thrive without autonomy for farmers. https://labourcentralasia.org/en/news/uzbekistan-s-cotton-sector-cannot-thrive-without-autonomy-for-farmers/
7 Presidential resolution 4239 (14 March 2019) on measures for development of agricultural cooperation in fruit and vegetable sector. https://lex.uz/ru/docs/4242012.
8 https://thediplomat.com/2022/03/the-boycott-of-uzbek-cotton-is-over/.
9 State regulation of prices for flour is terminated. Why did the government take this step? (in Russian). www.gazeta.uz/ru/2019/10/15/flour-liberalization/.
10 The President instructed to reduce the cost of bread (in Russian). www.gazeta.uz/ru/2019/11/08/bread/.
11 Presidential resolution 4634 (6 March 2020) on measures for wide implementation of market principles in production, procurement and sale of grains. https://lex.uz/ru/docs/4757015.

12 Presidential resolution 10 (15 November 2021) on introduction of market principles to ensure free competition in production and sale of grains. https://lex.uz/uz/docs/5729391
13 Grain prices will begin to 'release' from 1 June (in Russian). www.gazeta.uz/ru/2022/05/11/wheat/.
14 How reforms in grain production will affect the cost of flour and bread (in Russian). www.gazeta.uz/ru/2022/05/12/wheat-reform/.
15 Mills of Kazakhstan transfer business to Uzbekistan (in Russian). https://forbes.kz/finances/markets/mukomolyi_kazahstan_perenosyat_biznes_v_uzbekistan/.
16 Law on Dekhqan farm 680 (1 April 2021). https://lex.uz/pdfs/5351640.
17 Presidential resolution 373 (10 September 2022) on additional measures to increase income of population by supporting establishment of dekhqan farms. https://lex.uz/docs/6188635.
18 Presidential resolution 4243 (18 March 2019) on measures for further development and support of livestock sector, 4576 (29 January 2020) on additional measures of state support of livestock sector, 5051 (3 March 2021) on additional measures of further state support of livestock sector, 120 (8 February 2022) on approval of livestock sector development programme for 2022–2026. https://lex.uz/ru/docs/5858730.
19 Presidential resolution 121 (8 February 2022) on measures for further development of livestock and strengthening forage base. https://lex.uz/ru/docs/5851477.
20 Presidential resolution 4633 (6 March 2020) on measures for wide implementation of market principles in cotton sector. https://lex.uz/docs/4756992.
21 Uzbekistan's cotton sector cannot thrive without autonomy for farmers. https://labourcentralasia.org/en/news/uzbekistan-s-cotton-sector-cannot-thrive-without-autonomy-for-farmers/.
22 Ordered to grow red-hot chili peppers, Uzbek farmers may as well give 'em away now. www.rferl.org/a/uzbekistan-ordered-to-grow-chili-peppers-farmers-may-as-well-give-em-away-now/29292953.html.
23 'Significant risks' remain in Uzbek cotton sector. https://apparelinsider.com/significant-risks-remain-in-uzbek-cotton-sector/.
24 'Get out of here, you won't work anymore'. The head of the Federation of Trade Unions of Uzbekistan rebuked the deputy head of the Farmers' Council. www.gazeta.uz/ru/2021/03/10/farmers-council/.

References

Akhmadiyeva, Z., and Herzfeld, T. (2021) How does practice match land laws in Central Asia? *Land Use Policy* 109, 105726.

Asfaw, E.B. (2020) 'Dehqan' farms: Uzbekistan's underserved 70 Percent. *CPRO Policy Brief 2020–08*, Tashkent.

Asfaw, E.B. (2021) State-led cotton deregulation in Uzbekistan: Reforms and effects. *Central Asian Journal of Water Research* 7 (2), 1137–1210.

Babadjanov, J., and Petrick, M. (2023) Uzbekistan's cotton clusters in the context of the industrial policy debate. *Eurasian Geography and Economics*, 1–30. doi:10.1080/15387216.2023.2267093

Djanibekov, N., Charyyeva, S., and Sanaev, G. (2020) Cotton sector reforms in Central Asia. *IAMO Annual* 22, 46–54.

Djanibekov, N., and Herzfeld, T. (2022) The impact of COVID-19 on agrifood systems and rural areas in Central Asia and Caucasus countries: Final report of a study commissioned by FAO. *IAMO Discussion Paper* 198, Halle (Saale).

Djanibekov, U., Van Assche, K., Boezeman, D., and Djanibekov, N. (2013) Understanding contracts in evolving agro-economies: Fermers, dekhqans and networks in Khorezm, Uzbekistan. *Journal of Rural Studies* 32, 137–147.

Djumaeva, D., Djanibekov, N., Vlek, P.L.G., Martius, C., and Lamers, J.P.A. (2009) Options for optimizing dairy feed rations with foliage of trees grown in the irrigated drylands of Central Asia. *Research Journal of Agriculture and Biological Sciences* 5 (5), 698–708.

IFAD (2016) *Rural Development Report 2016: Fostering Inclusive Rural Transformation.* IFAD, Rome.

International Labour Office (ILO) (2022) *2021 Third-Party Monitoring of Child Labour and Forced Labour During the Cotton Harvest in Uzbekistan.* International Labour Office, Geneva.

Guadagni, M., Raiser, M., Crole-Rees, A., and Khidirov, D. (2005) Cotton taxation in Uzbekistan: Opportunities for reform. *ECSSD Working Paper* 41. World Bank, Washington, DC.

Huang, J. (2022) China's rural transformation and policies: Past experience and future directions. *Engineering* 18, 21–26.

Kienzler, K.M., Rudenko, I., Ruzimov, J., Ibragimov, N., and Lamers, J.P.A. (2011) Winter wheat quantity or quality? Assessing food security in Uzbekistan. *Food Security* 3 (1), 53–64.

Kurbanov, Z., Tadjiev, A., and Djanibekov, N. (2022) Adoption of sustainable agricultural practices and investments in productive assets in irrigated areas of Central Asia: Farm-survey evidence from Kazakhstan and Uzbekistan. *IAMO Annual* 24, Halle (Saale), 69–79.

Larson, D.F., Khidirov, D., and Ramniceanu, I. (2015) Uzbekistan: Strengthening the horticulture value chain. *Uzbekistan Vision 2030 Background Paper Series.* World Bank, Washington, DC.

Lerman, Z., Sedik, D., Yusupov, Y., Stanchin, I., and Kazakevich, I. (2016) Wheat Production and Regional Food Security in CIS: The Case of Belarus, Turkmenistan and Uzbekistan. *FAO Policy Studies on Rural Transition No. 2016–1*, FAO Regional Office for Europe and Central Asia, Budapest.

Lombardozzi, L., and Djanibekov, N. (2021) Can self-sufficiency policy improve food security? An inter-temporal assessment of the wheat value-chain in Uzbekistan. *Eurasian Geography and Economics* 62 (1), 1–20.

Mukhamedova, N., and Pomfret, R. (2019) Why does sharecropping survive? Agrarian institutions and contract choice in Kazakhstan and Uzbekistan. *Comparative Economic Studies* 61 (4), 576–597.

Niyazmetov, D., Soliev, I., and Theesfeld, I. (2021) Ordered to volunteer? Institutional compatibility assessment of establishing agricultural cooperatives in Uzbekistan. *Land Use Policy* 108, 105538.

Petrick, M., and Djanibekov, N. (2016) Obstacles to crop diversification and cotton harvest mechanisation: Farm survey evidence from two contrasting districts in Uzbekistan. *IAMO Discussion Paper* 153, Halle (Saale).

Petrick, M., Oshakbayev, D., Taitukova, R., and Djanibekov, N. (2017) The return of the regulator: Kazakhstan's cotton sector reforms since independence. *Central Asian Survey* 36 (4), 430–452.

Petrick, M., and Djanibekov, N. (2019) Farm restructuring in Uzbekistan: What next? *IAMO Policy Brief No.* 36, Halle (Saale).

Pomfret, R. (2008) Tajikistan, Turkmenistan, and Uzbekistan. In Anderson, K., Swinnen, J.F.M. (Eds.) *Distortions to Agricultural Incentives in Europe's Transition Economies.* World Bank, Washington, DC, pp. 297–338.

Robinson, S., and Petrick, M. (2021) Trade-offs among sustainability goals in the Central Asian livestock sector: A research review. *SDGnexus Network Working Paper, 01–2021.* Center for International Development and Environmental Research (ZEU), Gießen.

Shapiro, B.I., Bahta, S., Nigussie, K., Gebru, G., Shaumarov, M., Desta, S., and Kuziyev, B. (2022) Uzbekistan livestock sector analysis: Baseline report. *ILRI Project Report.* ILRI, Nairobi.

Sheng, Y., Zhao, Y., Zhang, Q., Dong, W., and Huang, J. (2022) Boosting rural labor off-farm employment through urban expansion in China. *World Development* 151, 105727.

State Committee on Statistics of Uzbekistan (UzStat) (2019) *Agriculture of Uzbekistan.* State Committee on Statistics of Uzbekistan, Tashkent.

State Committee on Statistics of Uzbekistan (UzStat) (2022) *Agriculture of Uzbekistan.* State Committee on Statistics of Uzbekistan, Tashkent.

Swinkels, R., Romanova, E., and Kochkin, E. (2016) *Assessing the Social Impact of Cotton Harvest Mechanization in Uzbekistan.* World Bank, Washington DC.

USDA (2018) Kazakhstan grain and feed update report. USDA Foreign Agricultural Service. GAIN Report KZ03.

Varis, O. (2014) Comment: Curb vast water use in Central Asia. *Nature* 514, 27–29.

World Bank (2020) *Uzbekistan: Agri-Food Job Diagnostic.* World Bank, Washington, DC.

World Bank (2022a) *Towards a greener economy in Uzbekistan.* World Bank, Washington, DC.

World Bank (2022b) *Toward a Prosperous and Inclusive Future: The Second Systematic Country Diagnostic for Uzbekistan.* World Bank, Washington, DC.

World Bank (2022c) *Uzbekistan: Review of Agricultural Strategy Implementation 2020/2021.* World Bank, Washington, DC.

World Bank (2022d) *World Development Indicators.* World Bank, Washington, DC.

Yigezu, Y., Bishaw, Z., Niane, A.A., and Nurbekov, A. (2022) *Political Economy of the Wheat Sector in Uzbekistan Seed Systems, Variety Adoption and Impacts.* ICARDA, Beirut.

Zhang, L., Dong, Y., Liu, C., and Bai, Y. (2018) Off-farm employment over the past four decades in rural China. *China Agricultural Economic Review* 10 (2), 190–214.

Zorya, S., and Babaev, S. (2020) *Cotton-textile Clusters in Uzbekistan: Status and Outlook. Policy Dialogue on Agricultural Modernization in Uzbekistan.* World Bank, Washington, DC.

Zorya, S., Djanibekov, N., and Petrick, M. (2019) *Farm Restructuring in Uzbekistan: How Did It Go and What is Next?* World Bank, Washington, DC.

6 Land tenure change and agricultural production and productivity in Uzbekistan

Lijie Ni, Kamiljon Akramov and Shenggen Fan

Overview

Agriculture is one of the most important sectors of the economy in Uzbekistan, accounting for a quarter of the country's GDP and employment (UzStat, 2022). Studies show that proper land systems and land tenure are the key to improving agricultural production and productivity (Lin, 1992; Fan, 1991). Following the declaration of Uzbekistan's independence in 1991, various reforms have been implemented in agriculture, the most significant of which was the farm restructuring (Lerman, 2008b; Djanibekov et al., 2012; Spoor, 2012). This study tries to assess the impact of land restructuring in the country based on existing studies, review other country's experiences and offer ways forward for Uzbekistan to further strengthen its land policy to further improve agricultural production and productivity to benefit smallholder farmers, consumers, and overall economic efficiency.

6.1 Historical evolution of agricultural land policy and tenure in Uzbekistan

6.1.1 Land policy and land tenure before independence

Early agricultural land system

Agriculture in Uzbekistan has inherited the dualistic system of the Soviet Union. Under this system, large collective and state farms coexist with quasi-private individual agriculture on subsistence household plots (Lerman, 2008b). These two forms of agricultural organization made up the basic framework of Uzbekistan's traditional agricultural system. The October uprising in 1917 had a fundamental impact on the Uzbek people's lives, including land policy and tenure change. Between 1917 and 1924, a large amount of land was violently nationalized. The process of collectivization in Uzbekistan began in the 1920s and was fully completed by the end of the 1940s. Analyses show that in 1928, 1.2% of peasant farms were collectivized, and in the summer of 1947, this figure rose to 100% (Topildiev et al., 2021). During this

DOI: 10.4324/9781003473497-6

period a large number of collective farms and state farms were established on the basis of peasant farms and land became state-owned.

Early agricultural production systems

Before the transition in the late 1980s and early 1990s, agricultural production and distribution in Uzbekistan was mainly controlled by the state. Cotton and grains were of strategic importance. They were usually produced on a large scale, and required substantial upfront investments for improving infrastructure and obtaining agricultural machinery. Household plots did not have the conditions for large-scale production. Therefore, cotton and cereals were mainly grown by large collective and state farms. Although small in size, household plots were vital to Uzbekistan's agriculture. During the decades of the Soviet era, households produced 20–25% of Uzbekistan's gross agricultural output with 3% of the arable land (Lerman, 2008b). Most of Uzbekistan's livestock is produced by households. Since 1970, the absolute number of cattle owned by families has exceeded half of that in Uzbekistan. In addition, family farms were also engaged in labor-intensive horticultural production. In the decade 1980–1989, family farms produced 30% of the country's potatoes, 45% of vegetables, and 60% of fruits and berries (Lerman, 2008b). Agricultural products produced by family farms beyond their subsistence needs were often sold to large farms, to a network of state-controlled consumer cooperatives, or to nearby towns with established marketplaces.

6.1.2 The process of land reform

Land policy

Since the late 1980s, Uzbekistan has been exploring farm restructuring and land reform. Several waves of farm restructuring and land redistribution processes experienced in the past were mainly aimed at increasing the efficiency of agricultural production and ensuring food security, while promoting economic development. However, the reform process rarely involves markets and has no impact on farmers' incomes (Zorya et al., 2019).

The current phase of agricultural reform began in 1989, when Uzbekistan was part of the Soviet Union. Before that, Gorbachev initiated reforms at the central level aimed at increasing food production and improving farm efficiency. 1989 land reform in Uzbekistan was an extension of this reform and was adapted to the actual situation. This phase of agrarian reform and farm restructuring embarked on an attempt to de-collectivize. More land was allocated to individual producers, for example, by establishing autonomous subdivisions and intra-farm family tenancy rights on large collective and state farms. The Soviet Land Law, adopted in February 1990, legalized the leasing of agricultural land in order to create independent individual farms, but did not legalize land ownership (Wegren, 1998). Overall, this phase of reform followed a dual-track approach that allowed families to own more land while encouraging large-scale farms to reorganize for greater efficiency. As a result, this reform led to a 60% increase in the area of land owned by households within two years (Lerman, 2008b).

During 1992–1997, state farms were restructured with 224 inefficient state farms converted to collective farms in 1992 (Topildiev et al., 2021). At the same time, agricultural property rights were transferred from state farms (*sovkhozes*) to collective farms (*kolkhozes*). At this stage, individual farms also began to appear, but their number and size were small. They leased abandoned or unused land from kolkhoz or *sovkhoz* for agricultural production over a period of up to 50 years. Individual farms had limited freedom to make production decisions. They had to grow crops that matched the infrastructure of the *kolkhoz* or *sovkhoz* and sell their products to them under contracts.

In the period 1998–2002, the state further promoted farm restructuring. Collective farms (*kolkhozes*) were further transformed into agricultural production cooperatives (*Shirkats*). However, this reorganization did not have a substantial impact on agricultural production. *Shirkats* continued to use the system of collective farms and were simply re-registered under a new category. In 1998, the government officially defined three categories of agricultural producers that coexist in Uzbekistan: *Dekhkan hojalik* (based on agricultural production on household plots), *Shirkats* (agricultural enterprises), and *Fermer hojalik* (individual farms). Individual farms started to appear as early as the early 1990s. However, the increase in the number of individual farms was slow in 1992–2002, and during 1998–2002, the government started to try to divide some of the low-performing large-scale farms (agricultural cooperatives) into smaller individual farms. At the same time, the law on individual farms gave them the right to independently make production decisions, which did lead to some fundamental changes.

In 2003–2008, the government accelerated the process of de-collectivization. During this period, *Shirkats* were divided into small-scale individual farms with an average area of less than 30 hectares. The fragmentation of agricultural land led to a rapid increase in the number of individual farms, which reached 218,600 in 2008 when the process was largely completed. Meanwhile, individual farms cultivated 84.36% of the country's arable land and became the main producers in the agricultural sector. However, this phase of fragmentation and reorganization ignored the applicability of existing agricultural infrastructure. For example, the agricultural irrigation system built in the Soviet era was suitable for large-scale farms, so the excessive fragmentation of individual farm reforms made irrigation less efficient, thus affecting agricultural productivity. In order to better adapt the scale of farm operations to the existing irrigation system and improve agricultural production efficiency, the state initiated a new round of restructuring in 2008 to appropriately expand farm scale. In the new round of restructuring, farmers with an area of less than 30 ha were forced to return their land without any compensation (Melnikovová and Havrland, 2016).

During 2009–2016, farm size was further optimized. The number of individual farms decreased by 53% in 2009 compared to 2008, and this number was further reduced to around 70,000 in 2010–2012. The new norms for farm reorganization in 2012 removed the restriction on the minimum size of land, making it possible to reduce the size of land. As a result, the average size of individual farms decreased, while their number increased. *Dehkan* small farmers coexisted with large individual farms in this period. *Dehkan*, with an average size of about 1 hectare, mainly produced livestock and horticultural products. The readjusted large individual farms, with an average size of about 40–60 hectares, mainly produced cotton and wheat under the state order system, which accounted for approximately more than 80% of the sown area in the country.

In January 2019, Uzbekistan started a new farm restructuring. It sought to optimize the use of farmland by increasing the size of farms producing wheat and cotton, reallocating land to more efficient farmers and even clusters, and improving crop rotation options.

Ownership and tenure of land

Land tenure in Uzbekistan was inherited from the Soviet land system. After independence, the new Constitution of Uzbekistan, adopted in December 1992, established exclusive state ownership of land, which was reaffirmed in the Land Code, adopted in 1998. For agriculture, the land is uniformly allocated to users by the state, which means that farmers are granted the right to use the land, but this right is not transferable. The law states that land owned by families for life can be inherited, but not sold, given away, or exchanged; and land leased from the state by individual users cannot be subleased. However, intra-farm leasing is allowed within a shirkat, which means that worker families can lease land for agricultural production from the shirkat where they work. When a shirkat is restructured into individual farms, the individual farm acquires the right to use the land on a lease basis. Farmers pay for land use by paying land taxes or lease fees (Lerman, 2008b).

6.2 Main forms and characteristics of current farms

Agricultural producers in Uzbekistan can be now divided into three categories, which are individual farms, *Dekhkan* farms and agricultural enterprises. Table 6.2 presents their main characteristics.

Currently, agricultural production in Uzbekistan mainly relies on two types of producers, namely, individual farms and *Dekhkan*. The individual farm, a new type of farm independent of the collectivist framework, emerged in 1991, mainly producing cotton and wheat. It was the workers of the large collective farms and state farms who initially ran individual farms and were

Table 6.1 Salient Characteristics of the Farm Restructuring Stages in Uzbekistan Since 1991

	First stage 1992–1997 De-collectivization of state farms	*Second stage 1998–2002 Partial fragmentation*	*Third stage 2003–2008 Complete fragmentation*	*Fourth stage 2008/2009–2015 Farm consolidation*	*Fifth stage 2016–present Production specialization*
Main transformation process	Transformation of *sovkhozes* into *kolkhozes*	Transformation of kolkhozes into *Shirkats*. Land lease to individual farms	Complete transformation of *Shirkats* into individual farms	Farm reconsolidation (farm-size optimization)	Fragmentation and optimization of production
Dominant farm types	*Kolkhozes, sovkhozes*	*Shirkats*, individual farms	*Shirkats*, individual farms	Individual farms, mainly cotton-grain producers	Individual farms of different specialization
Main policy objectives	Expansion of wheat area & yields, reorganization of state farms	Specialization of newly established individual farms	Development of non-cotton/wheat-producing sectors, and livestock farms	Increasing and stable cotton yields, relocating cotton fields	Relocation of cotton and wheat fields, increased area of high-value crops, multi-profile farms

Source: Djanibekov et al., 2015; Zorya et al., 2019

Table 6.2 Main Characteristics of Different Types of Farms in Uzbekistan

	Individual farm (Fermer hojaligi)	*Dekhkan farm (Dekhkan hojaligi)*	*Agricultúral enterprises (Shirkats)*
Basic definition	Individual commercial farms organized as a legal entity operating leased land	Small-scale family-based farm, based on household plot operation	A large-scale corporate farm based on membership shares with private ownership of assets
Labor	Family members, as well as permanent and seasonal workers	Mainly family members, with an option to hire seasonal workers	Members, hired workers
Land tenure	Long-term land lease (up to 50 years). The land lease duration depends on the fulfillment of the state procurement target. Farm size can vary with respect to production specialization	Lifetime inheritable possession. Sizes of allocated land: 0.35 ha for irrigated land; 0.5 for rainfed land. This includes also an area for buildings	Permanent possession for agricultural purposes
Ownership	Any adult person with sufficient agricultural qualification	Former workers of agricultural enterprises, rural families	Members-shareholders
Production specialization	Only agricultural produce is indicated in the land lease contract. Mainly cotton and wheat	Any agricultural produce, mainly wheat, vegetables, fruits, livestock	Mainly scale crops (wheat, cotton)

Source: Lerman, 2008; World Bank Group, 2019.

allowed to leave the farms they worked on with their share of land and assets. In 1991, the number of individual farms did not exceed 2,000. This new form of farming was officially recognized by the Law on Peasant Farms adopted in July 1992, which led to an increasing number of people registering individual farms. In 2001, the number of individual farms soared to 50,000. With the ongoing restructuring of agriculture, this number reached nearly 200,000 in 2006 (Lerman, 2008b). Individual farms receive production materials and public services from the government, but they are also constrained by procurement quotas and unstable land tenure. As a result, individual farm production was not very efficient.

With agricultural reform, small-scale *Dekhkan* farms have become the main producers of horticultural and livestock products. *Dehkan* farms are less subject to government intervention and have the freedom to decide what crops to produce. However, they also have little access to public services provided by the government. In this case, the production of *Dekhkan* farms is still increasing. Therefore, the agricultural productivity of *Dekhkan* farms in Uzbekistan is higher than that of large (individual) farms. There are two main reasons for this. On the one hand, *Dekhkan* farms can sell the produced products at market prices and use less water, thus making them relatively more profitable. On the other hand, *Dekhkan* farms have relatively stable land tenure, so they are willing to invest in their land to improve the quality of their land and thus increase their productivity. However, *Dekhkan* farms also have some limitations, such as their small size, which prevents them from producing at scale to reduce market transaction costs and improve the quality of output.

The third category of agricultural production organization is agricultural enterprises. The agricultural enterprises originated from state farms and collective farms in the Soviet period. With the development of farm restructuring, these farms were gradually transformed into agricultural cooperatives (*Shirkats*). With further de-collectivization, some *Shirkats* were reorganized into different types of specialized enterprises, such as parastatal export-oriented producers or large poultry-specialized enterprises. In addition, agribusinesses also include agricultural companies that have been established since 2006 (Larson et al., 2012). In general, agribusinesses are mainly private companies with vertically integrated characteristics, and processing companies that are also engaged in agricultural production (Zorya et al., 2019).

6.3 Impact of land policy and tenure on production and productivity

The change has had a significant impact on the country's land tenure, crop structure, and agricultural production and productivity.

6.3.1 How shares of different land tenure have changed over time

The land reform in Uzbekistan has completed the "de-collectivization" of land on the legal basis of public ownership of land. The "de-collectivization" of state farms began in 1992–1997. In 1998–2002, *Shirkats* land was allocated to individual farms and the farms were fragmented into small-scale production units. The rate of land transfer from agribusiness to newly established individual farms was slow in the period 1992–2002. However, in 2003–2008, there was a rapid transfer of *Shirkats* land to individual farms, and the "de-collectivization" was rapidly completed. During the "de-collectivization" process, the number of farms rose sharply to 218,645, while the average size of individual farms continued to decline. However, the productivity of these farms has not been as efficient as expected because farm reorganization has led to land fragmentation. An individual farm consists of scattered fields, often far from each other. These along with other issues triggered decisions of the state to reduce the number of farms and increase ("optimize") the size of their land. During the farm optimization process, the minimum size of cotton and wheat farms, and gardening and horticulture farms, were adjusted. The minimum size of cotton and wheat farms was increased from 10 ha to 30 ha, and for horticultural and gardening farms from 1 ha to 5 ha. This process started in 2008/2009 and continued until 2015. It culminated in a dual system of small *Dekhkan* farmers producing livestock and horticultural products on an average of 1 hectare, and large individual farms producing cotton and wheat on an average of 40 ~ 60 hectares under the state order system (Zorya et al., 2019). The 2019 restructuring aims to double the size of cotton and wheat farms to an average of 100 ha.

The share of the individual farming sector – both the traditional household plots and the new peasant farms that began to emerge in the second phase of reform after 1998 – increased dramatically. Overall, the change in land use in Uzbekistan since 1992 is mainly reflected in the transfer of land from farm enterprises to the individual sector. During this period, the share of land owned by *Dekhkan* smallholders increased only slightly, from 8% to 14%. In 1992, the share of arable land owned by farm enterprises (then state farms and collective farms) was as high as 90%. In other words, they cultivated almost all the land in the country. As farm restructuring progressed, the category evolved from Soviet-style collective farms and state farms to agricultural cooperatives (shirtkats) and further into different forms of specialized enterprises, including parastatal export-oriented producers or large poultry farms registered as enterprises. After that, the land of farm enterprises gradually flowed to individual farms. This process was completed in 2007. In 2008, the area sown by individual farms reached 3.045 million hectares, accounting for 84.36% of the country's planted area. The individual farms inherited the burden of fulfilling the national cotton and wheat orders that had traditionally been borne by collective and state farms. Farm workers became the official suppliers of two strategic commodities to the state. Any deviation from the sowing practices stipulated in the land lease contract was a serious violation and constituted grounds for termination of the farm lease (Lerman et al., 2016). On the other hand, family land is not subject to state order. They are free to grow and produce whatever they want on their small plots of land.

Broadly similar changes were observed for all agricultural lands (Lerman, 2008a). In addition to cropland, the agricultural land area includes pasture, grassland, perennial orchards and vineyards. Another striking feature of the change in agricultural land use is the overall decrease in land use for all categories of agricultural users. This is due to the increasing abandonment of land in recent years, mainly pastureland, as all arable land is allocated to users. In the process of reform of agribusiness to individual farms mainly arable land was redistributed rather than pastures. The decline in the area of

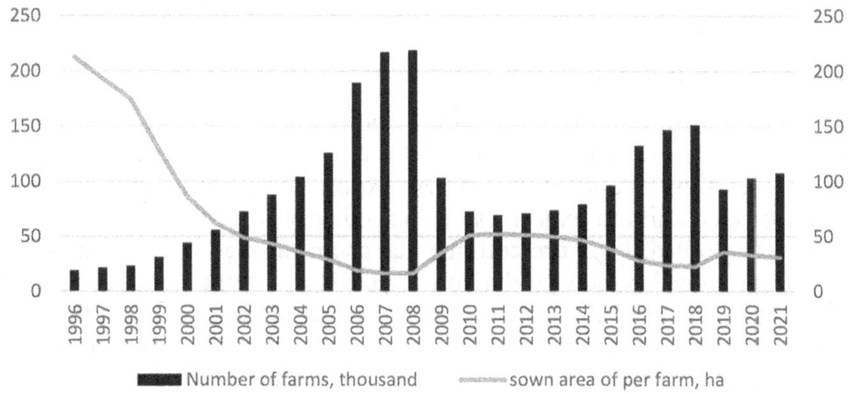

Figure 6.1 Number of farms and sown area per farm
Source: State Statistics Committee of the Republic of Uzbekistan, Authors' calculations.

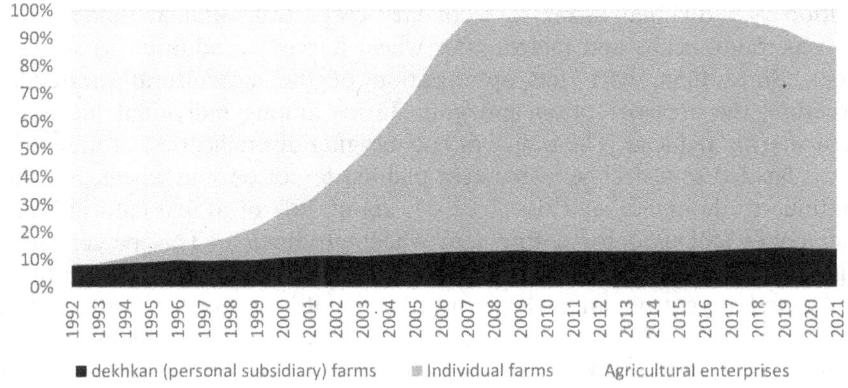

Figure 6.2 Total sown area by categories of farms
Source: State Statistics Committee of the Republic of Uzbekistan, Authors' calculations.

agricultural land in agribusiness is therefore less pronounced than in arable land, because of its relatively high proportion of pastureland.

Impact on crop structure

Among all agricultural products, cotton and wheat are the two most important strategic crops in Uzbekistan, which use most of the country's arable land. Uzbekistan is one of the largest exporters of cotton in the world. Cotton production and export has a long history in Uzbekistan. The government controlled the entire cotton value chain through centralized pricing and setting annual cotton production targets through the national procurement system. To meet the annual cotton production targets set by the state, more than 50% of the country's arable land needs to be devoted to cotton cultivation (Djanibekov et al., 2010). However, the government has been encouraging market-oriented transformation and diversification of agricultural production in recent years.

With the advancement of farm restructuring, the production of cotton and wheat was transferred from the former collective farms to individual farms. Currently, 99% of the country's cotton fields and 84% of the country's wheat area are cultivated by individual farms (Zorya et al., 2019). *Shirtkats* completed the transition to individual farms in 2006. Of the total land allocated to individual farms, cotton and grain farms accounted for 71% of the area. With the continuous advancement of land consolidation, this percentage increased to 87% in 2011. In 2012 the state recommended a shift to diversification of individual farms to secondary crops (e.g., annual fodder crops such as mung beans and maize) after wheat harvest in addition to strategic crops. Since then, with the optimization of the agricultural production structure, the area of cotton and grain farms among individual farms has been sharply reduced. The policy of encouraging diversification of individual farms has led to a decline in the area planted to cotton and wheat, but they continue to dominate land use. In 2021, about 70% of arable land in Uzbekistan was still used for cotton and wheat production. This percentage is higher in individual farms. Almost 80% of the sown area of individual farms is devoted to cotton and wheat production: 40% cotton and 40% wheat (Zorya et al., 2019). Among them, there is a decreasing trend in the area planted to cotton, while the proportion of area planted to grain crop is gradually increasing.

The structure of vegetable and fruit cultivation in Uzbekistan has also undergone some changes. In the early years of independence, almost half of the total area of vegetable production was in agricultural enterprises and the other half in farmers. The first stage of farm restructuring in 1992–1998, when state and collective farms underwent organizational changes and marketing channels were not developed, led to a stagnation of vegetable acreage (Zorya et al., 2019). 2007 saw the completion of farm restructuring and the resumption of vegetable production. In fact, the expansion of vegetable areas

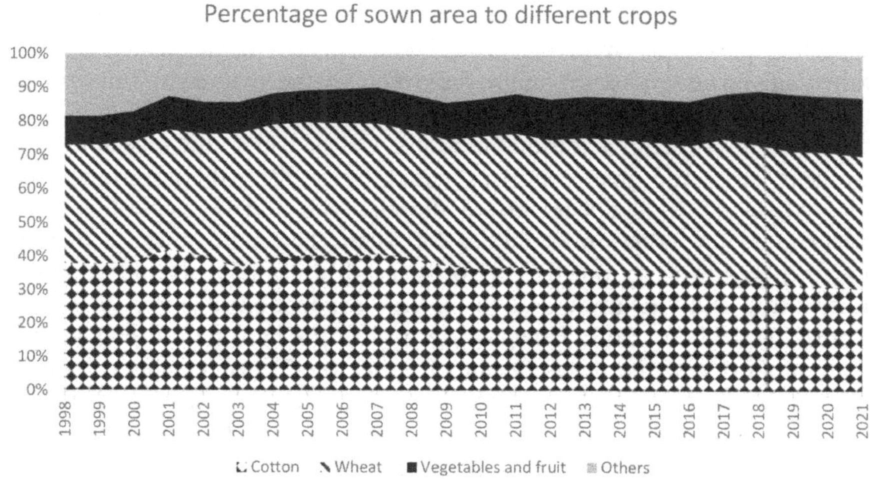

Figure 6.3 Percentage of sown area to different crops
Source: State Statistics Committee of the Republic of Uzbekistan, Authors' calculations.

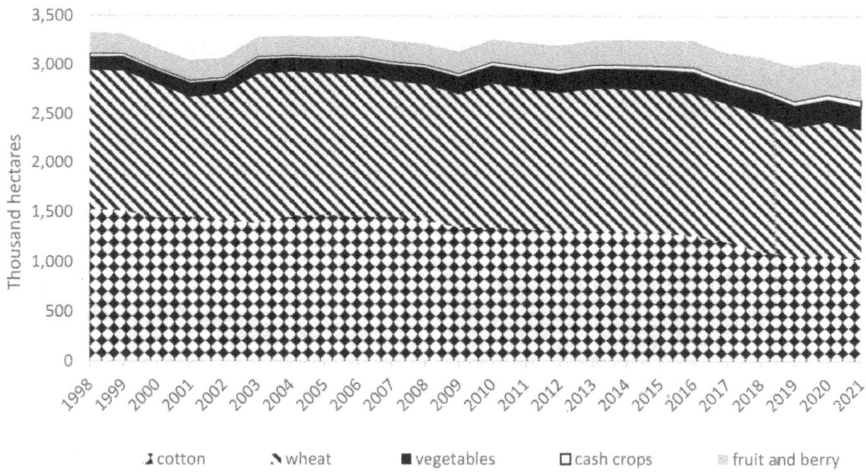

Figure 6.4 The sown area of different crops
Source: State Statistics Committee of the Republic of Uzbekistan, Authors' calculations.

in *Dekhkan* farms contributed the most to the recovery and further increase of vegetable sown area after 2006. At the national level, the area sown to vegetables accounted for 5.6% of the total sown area in 2016: the largest share was in Tashkent province. In the early years of independence, fruits were mainly grown by agribusiness, which accounted for 70% of the total area under fruit cultivation, while the remaining 30% came from households. The share of families in the area under fruit cultivation has hardly changed and has always remained at about 30%. With the restructuring of farms, the main body of fruit planting gradually changed from agricultural enterprises to individual farms. With the completion of farm restructuring in 2006, individual farms took over more than 60% of the country's fruit-growing area.

Due to the superior natural conditions, Uzbek fruits and vegetables have excellent flavor and great export potential. Since 2015, the government has adopted several legal documents to support fruit and vegetable farms and create more favorable opportunities for them. The main purpose of these documents is to carry out deep reforms in all areas of fruit and vegetable, horticulture and viticulture and to increase production in order to increase exports (Azizkhon, 2017; Umarxodjaeva, 2020). Thanks to strong government support and the development of agricultural clusters, the area under fruit and vegetable cultivation has increased significantly since 2015. In recent years, vegetables are mainly produced by small *Dekhkan* farms, while fruits are mainly produced by specialized individual farms. In 2021, more than 70% of the total area of vegetables in the country is cultivated by *Dekhkan* farms. On average, *Dekhkan* farms allocate slightly more than 25% of the sown area to vegetables (Zorya et al., 2019). agribusiness has contributed the most to the increase in the area planted to fruits after 2015. However, individual farms continue to dominate fruit production, accounting for 54% of the area planted to fruit in 2021.

Livestock products are one of the main branches of agriculture in Uzbekistan. Livestock farming in Uzbekistan has traditionally been dominated by rural families. During the Soviet period, more than 50% of livestock was

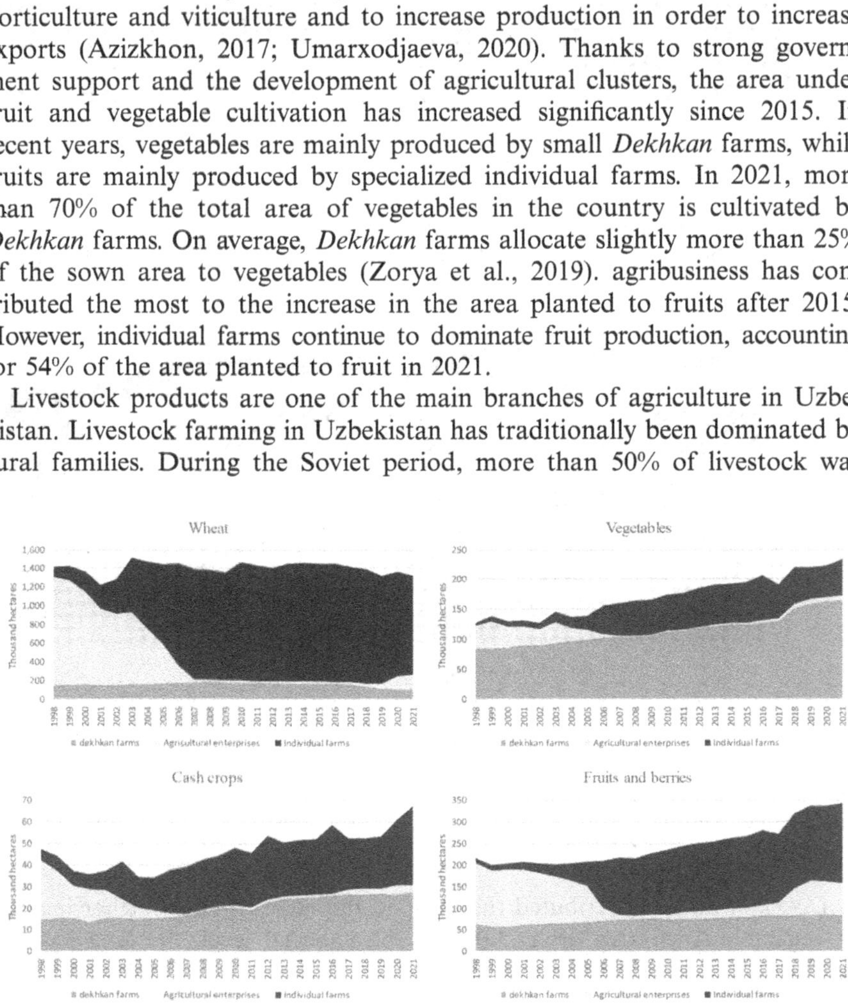

Figure 6.5 Crops area by categories of farm

Source: State Statistics Committee of the Republic of Uzbekistan, Authors' calculations.

raised by rural families (Lerman, 2008c). The reforms carried out in 1993–1994 to liquidate the country's collective and state farms abolished livestock facilities, hundreds of farms, breeding and breeding farms, and hundreds of genealogical, prolific herds (Dosmukhamedova, 2022). According to the decisions taken in 1996–1998, specific measures for the development of livestock farming were taken on farms, *Dekhkan* farms, and individual subsidiary lands of the population. Among them, livestock farming is better developed only on *Dekhkan* farms, while individual farms play a marginal role. In 2020, livestock farming in Uzbekistan accounted for 50.5% of national agricultural production, which is mainly concentrated on *Dekhkan* farms. The share of livestock ownership on *Dekhkan* farms has declined in recent years, but is still much higher than on other types of farms. 92.8% of the country's cattle, including 93.2% of cows, 81.4% of sheep and goats, 76.3% of horses, and 58.9% of birds, were owned by *Dekhkan* farms in 2020, contributing 90.1% of the country's meat, 94.1% of the country's meat, and 94.9% of the country's livestock. The country's cattle production is 92.8%, including 93.2% of cows, 81.4% of sheep and goats, 76.3% of horses and 58.9% of birds, contributing 90.1% of meat, 94.3% of milk and 58.5% of eggs (Ashurmetova, 2021; Urdushev, 2021).

Impact on production and productivity

Since 1992, agriculture has grown at a higher rate, leading to an increase in average productivity. In particular, agricultural labor productivity grew at an average annual rate of 1.5% from 1996–2016 (Zorya et al., 2019). However, agricultural productivity growth has slowed down over time despite farm restructuring. At the same time, the share of agriculture in the total labor force decreased from 43% in 1996 to 25% in 2021. In other words, the growth of agricultural labor productivity is the result of a significant decrease in the number of agricultural laborers rather than a significant increase in the value-added of agriculture. The ratio of agricultural gross output of the sector (billions of soums) to the sown area (thousand ha) is used to express land productivity. agricultural land productivity grew at an average annual rate of 3.5% from 1998 to 2021. Agricultural land productivity has increased rapidly since 2010, and the difference between different farms is becoming more pronounced. Among them, *Dekhkan* farms have the fastest growth rate of land productivity, with 133 million soums/ha in 2021, which is almost 500 times higher than 0.27 million soums/ha in 1998.

During the land reform process, a large amount of land was transferred from agribusiness to individual farms, but the productivity of individual farms did not match the proportion of land they occupied. In 1992, *Dekhkan* farms produced about 30% of GAO, while the rest of the output came from agribusiness (Zorya et al., 2019). The proportion of households in GAO increased consistently over the next few years, reaching two-thirds in 2000–2001. As farm restructuring progressed, the contribution of individual farms

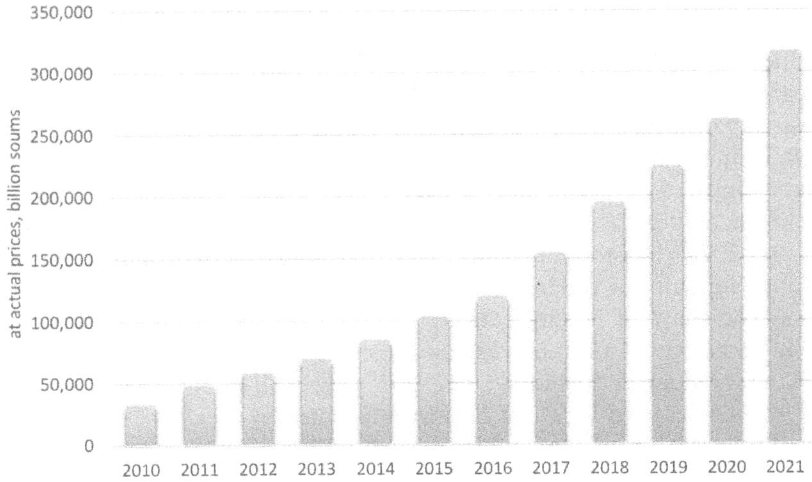

Figure 6.6 Volume of products (services) of agriculture, forestry and fisheries
Source: Preliminary data for 2022.

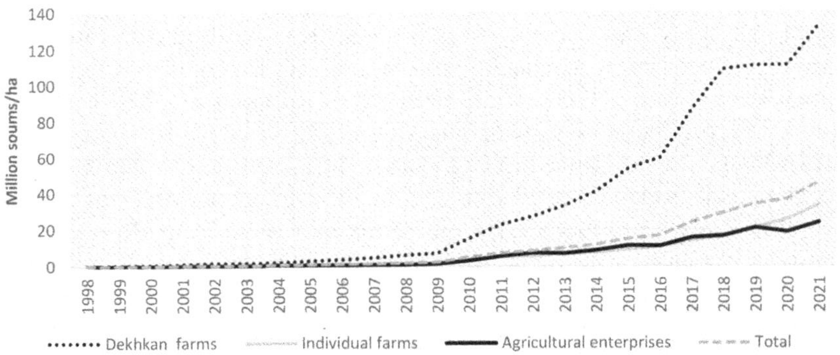

Figure 6.7 Land productivity of crop by categories of farms
Source: State Statistics Committee of the Republic of Uzbekistan, Authors' calculations.

to GAO increased: it reached 31% in 2006 and stabilized at around 29–35% in subsequent years. In 2021, individual farms, which cultivate about 73% of the sown area, produced only 29.3% of agricultural production. In contrast, *Dekhkan* farms, with 13.7% of the sown area, produced about 65% of the country's agricultural production in 2021, including 40% of crops and 91.1% of livestock.

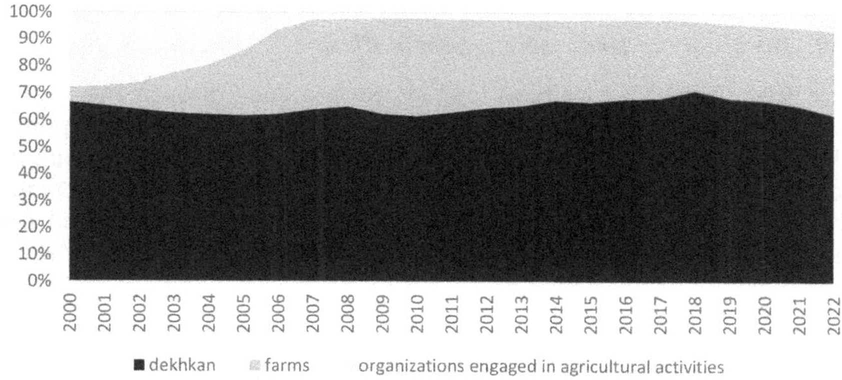

Figure 6.8 Structure of agricultural production
Source: The data for 2000–2009 are given by classification OKONH. The data for 2010–2022 are given taking into account the updated (revised) data.

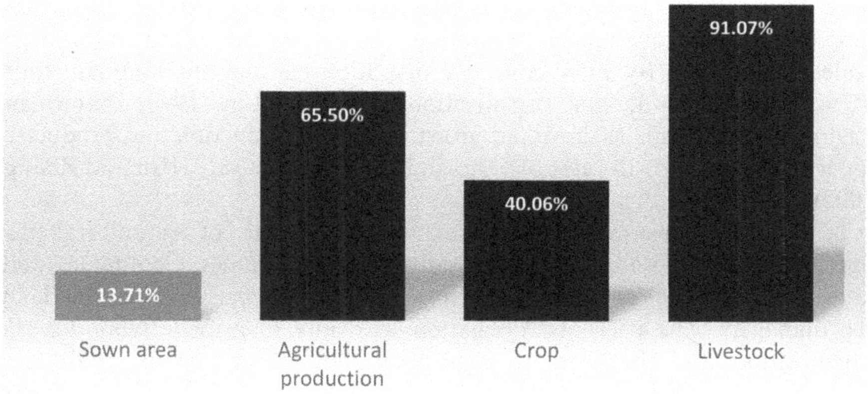

Figure 6.9 Production and land use share of *Dekhkan* farms
Source: State Statistics Committee of the Republic of Uzbekistan, Authors' calculations.

6.4 China's land tenure changes and the impact on production and productivity

6.4.1. The history of land tenure reform in China

Since 1952, China's agricultural land system has gone through two distinct phases. From 1952 to 1977, China followed the Soviet Union in adopting a collective form of land organization. To improve the efficiency of agricultural production, China has adopted a series of reforms since 1978, which gradually transformed the agricultural land system into a market-oriented one. This shift is critical to the development of China's national economy.

6.4.1.1 Early land reform (Prior to 1978)

Traditional land ownership in China was feudal. Landowners, who accounted for 10% of the rural population, owned about 70–80% of the agricultural land. Therefore, when the People's Republic of China was founded in 1949, one of the priorities of the Communist government was to implement large-scale land reform nationwide (Fan, Zhang and Zhang, 2002).

The Chinese government announced the Land Reform Law in June 1950, which launched a massive nationwide land reform aimed at abolishing land ownership and redistributing land to farmers. The land reform completed at the end of 1952 allocated land to more than 300 million landless peasants. After that, some peasants with smaller landholdings tried to pool their land and other production resources for joint production. At that time, peasants were allowed to join or leave the cooperatives freely and without any penalties. Later, with government promotion, there were more and more large-scale cooperatives. By 1956, collective operation became the dominant form of agricultural production organization in China (Lin, 1990; Putterman, 1990). These reforms led to rapid growth in both production and productivity, with annual growth rates of 5.3% and 2.7%, respectively (Fan and Zhang, 2002).

In 1958, the government further expanded the scale of agricultural production by merging advanced cooperatives into communes. Communes were unified management organizations whose production decisions were made by the managers. The peasants' obligation was only to provide labor for the organization, and they had no right to participate in making production decisions. In addition, peasants were not allowed to engage in productive activities on private land. In other words, peasants' income and welfare are not correlated with their efforts. Therefore, the forced collectivization failed to motivate farmers to be more efficient. As a result, Chinese agriculture experienced a sharp decline in production and productivity, and this situation was further exacerbated by the Great Famine of 1959–1961(Lin, 1990; Lin and Yang, 2000). In 1962–1965, the government implemented a corresponding policy of restructuring and consolidation by decentralizing the communes into smaller units called "production teams". Production teams, consisting of 20–30 neighboring farm households, constituted basic units of operations and accounting in rural areas.

During the Cultural Revolution of 1966–1976, the government reinstated its control over agricultural production. These policies inhibited production and productivity growth once again. During this period, agricultural output grew slowly, while total factor productivity was virtually no gain (Fan, Zhang and Zhang, 2002).

6.4.1.2 Recent land reform (1978–present)

It was acknowledged in 1978 that the key to improving the farmer's incentives was to solve the managerial problems in the team system. However, the division of collectively owned land to individuals was considered at that time to be opposed to the principles of socialism. However, at the end of 1978, a few production teams secretly began to carry out internal reforms. Their land, other production materials, and production quotas were distributed to each household. Production exceeding the quota could be freely consumed by peasant families or sold at the market. A year later, the dramatic increase in crop yields proved that this reform was conducive to increased production efficiency. It was later known as the household responsibility system. Local authorities and the central government gradually recognized this new form of agricultural production organization. In 1981, the government began to extend the reform on a large scale throughout the country by distributing communal land to households, and by 1984, more than 99% of production teams nationwide had completed the reform of the household responsibility system (Fan, Zhang and Zhang, 2002). Under this system, land ownership was still vested in the collective, but the use rights of land were transferable. Provided that the government's grain procurement quota is met, peasants can freely make production decisions based on their demands and market prices. As a result, farmers' incentive to produce is significantly increased.

After that, the land contract period was extended several times. The continuous improvement of the household contract responsibility system since the 1990s played a catalytic role in agricultural growth. At the beginning of the reform, farmers had a land contract period of less than three years. To incentivize farmers to invest in their land for productivity improvement, the central government extended the contract period to 15 years in 1984. The contract period was extended to 30 years in 2002 to stabilize farmers' land contract rights. In 2011, this system was further standardized. The central government launched land registration and certification while allowing land to be subcontracted among rural households.

In recent years, the government has strongly supported the transfer of land from small farmers to large-scale farmers or agricultural organizations. In 2014, the separation of the three rights of land began to be piloted, specifically, the separation of ownership, contracting, and management rights. This policy has created good conditions for moderate-scale agricultural operations. Farmers or agricultural enterprises can expand their production scale by renting other farmers' land, thus improving production efficiency. Those who sublet their land are mainly farmers who work outside and elderly farmers who are unwilling or unable to continue farming. The purpose of this policy is to guide the orderly transfer of rural land management rights and promote moderate-scale agricultural management. In 2017, agricultural land rights were extended for another 30 years, which helped stabilize farmers' land tenure. Previously, most farmers chose to lease their land to relatives or friends when subleasing. With the reform of land transfer rules and the completion of land titling, leases have become more formalized, facilitating the assignment of land to more productive users and improving the efficiency of the land rental market (Cheng et al., 2019). As a result, more and more farmers are transferring their land to agribusinesses and cooperatives rather than other households. These policies have contributed to the emergence of "new types" of farms, such as large family farms, cooperative farms, and farms operated by agribusinesses.

6.4.2 *Accompanied policy and investment*

While deepening the reform of the agricultural land system, China had also been pushing forward a series of other rural system reforms.

The first is the reform of agricultural marketization. The liberalization of agricultural markets and price systems increased farmers' incomes while improving allocative efficiency (Huang and Rozelle, 2018). At the beginning of the reform, the market economy was seen as a complement to the planned economy and was not the main form of economic organization. Later, the planned economy system was gradually withdrawn and the marketization of the agricultural sector increased significantly. For staple agricultural products such as grain, cotton, oil and sugar, the country adopts a dual-track market-oriented reform model. Under the dual-track system, the state sets minimum production quotas and buys these agricultural products at a fixed price, while the remaining production is sold at a higher market price. When China applied to join the World Trade Organization (WTO) in 2001, the dual-track pricing system was gradually transformed into a "guaranteed minimum price" to protect farmers' incomes. Currently, Chinese agricultural prices largely reflect market conditions, but for critical commodities, input subsidies, and price support significantly affect product prices (World Bank, 2022).

Second, agricultural taxes shifted to agricultural support policies. In ancient times, agricultural taxes were the prime source of government revenue. After 1949, agricultural taxes continued for several more decades to support the country's industrial development (Naughton, 2018). The wide variety of agricultural tax expenditures was a huge burden for farmers, especially those poor. With the rapid development of industry, the role of agricultural taxes in increasing fiscal revenue has been decreasing. To narrow the gap between urban and rural areas, China abolished all agricultural taxes in 2006. Moreover, since the late 2000s, the government has developed a series of transfer programs targeting poor rural areas to raise farmers' incomes and promote rural development.

Third, substantial investment in agricultural R&D, extension, and infrastructure. It is well known that agriculture is vulnerable to weather and natural disasters. Therefore, investing in infrastructure development is beneficial for securing agricultural production. In China, Agricultural infrastructure construction has been the largest expenditure project of national financial support for agriculture. Among them, farmland water conservancy facilities are one of the crucial agricultural infrastructures. In China, more than 70% of grain, 80% of cotton, and 90% of vegetable production depend on irrigation (Wang et al., 2020). With the investment and construction of farmland irrigation facilities, China's irrigated area of arable land has increased from 449.65 million ha in 1978 to 691.6 million ha in 2020 (National Bureau of Statistics, 2021), effectively increasing the productivity of the land. In addition, China has strongly supported the research, development, and promotion of agricultural films, fertilizers, pesticides, high-quality seeds, and agricultural machinery. These efforts have enabled farmers to learn more about modern agronomic practices, thereby increasing agricultural productivity and their incomes.

Finally, promote the development of agricultural industrialization. In recent years, China has promulgated a series of policies to promote the integration of agriculture's primary, secondary, and tertiary industries and to encourage the development of agricultural processing industries to increase the added value of agricultural products. Local governments have established wholesale markets for agricultural products and invested in agricultural processing, storage, and marketing facilities to promote the industrialization of agriculture. In addition, the government encourages farmers to form cooperatives to share fixed costs such as agricultural machinery and improve operational efficiency. 53% of farmers' cooperatives already had their own processing and marketing facilities at the end of 2016 (World Bank, 2022). The processing rate of agricultural products in cooperatives and farms reached 65%, and the added value of agricultural products increased by 2.2 times. To promote the development of rural markets, the Chinese government has introduced a series of policies since 2014 to support the development of agro-related e-commerce and to conduct comprehensive e-commerce demonstrations in rural areas (Luo and Niu, 2019).

6.4.3 The impact of land reform

The rural reforms that began in 1978 and culminated in the universal adoption of the household responsibility system had a significant positive effect on grain output and food availability in China (Gibson, 2020). As a result of the reform policies, national GDP grew at about 10% per annum from 1978 to 1997 and per capita income increased more than fourfold, or 7.8% per annum (Fan, Zhang and Zhang, 2002). The dual-track system, together with the household responsibility system, dramatically improved farmers' terms of trade and led to a sharp increase in agricultural output and incomes.

Since the reform, the average annual growth rate of agricultural GDP at constant prices has increased from 2.2% in 1952–1978 to 4.4% in 1978–2021; grain production has increased from 305 million tons in 1978 to 683 million tons in 2021, with an annual growth rate of 2%. The fastest growth rate of agricultural GDP occurred in the early reform period (1978–1984) (Figure 1). From 1979 to 1984, farm output and productivity grew by 5–10% (McMillan, Whalley and Zhu, 1989; Lin, 1992; Fan, Zhang and Zhang, 2002). The dramatic growth during 1978–1984 was a result of a package of market-oriented reforms. Among them, the shift to the household responsibility system accounted for 30% to 50% of the total rise in agricultural output (Fan, 1991; Lin, 1992; Huang and Rozelle, 1996; Gibson, 2020). Since the mid-1980s, the average annual growth rate has remained at around 4% (Huang, 2018).

The rise in agricultural productivity contributed to poverty reduction through two main channels. First, higher productivity led to increased farmer incomes. Since the reform in 1978, the per capita net income of rural residents in China has increased from 133.6 yuan in 1978 to 18,930.9 yuan in 2021, which has increased more than 20 times in real terms after deducting price factors, with an average annual growth rate of 7.45%. In the net income per capita of rural residents, although the proportion of agricultural income decreased from 80% in 1978 to 26.4% in 2016, the net income from agriculture increased from 107 yuan in 1978 to 3,270 yuan in 2016, which increased nearly four times in real terms after deducting the price factor, with an average annual growth rate of 4.3%, playing an important role in the stable increase of farmers' income (Huang, 2018). Second, it released surplus

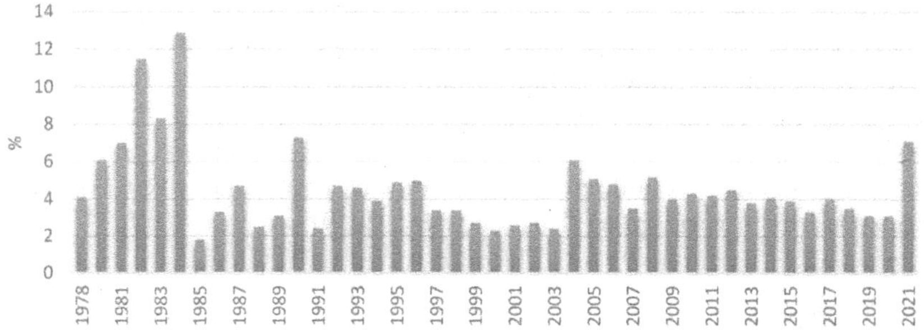

Figure 6.10 The growth rate of China's agricultural GDP
Source: China Statistical Yearbook, National Bureau of Statistics.

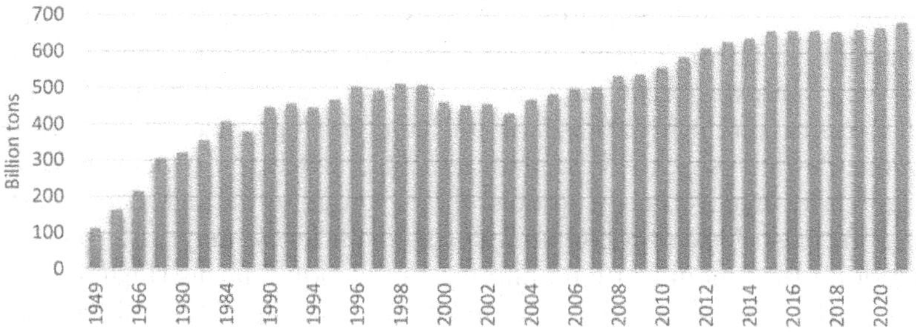

Figure 6.11 China's grain output from 1949 to 2021
Source: China Statistical Yearbook and Brilliant 70 years: The Achievements of New China's Economic and Social Development (1949–2019), National Bureau of Statistics.

labor to other sectors and urban areas. Thus, it allowed households to diversify income sources (and thereby reduce household risk) and to take advantage of better-paid nonagricultural labor opportunities, locally and through migration.

In fact, this reform had positive effects on both efficiency and equity. In other words, it not only contributed to rising agriculture factor productivity (Jin et al., 2002), but also helped to reduce the gap between poorer and richer areas (Gibson, 2020).

6.5 How to further strengthen land policy and tenure in Uzbekistan

From the previous analysis, it is clear that land reform has improved agricultural production efficiency and contributed to Uzbekistan's economic development. However, the majority of total agricultural output currently comes from *Dekhkan* farms with a small amount of land, and this is a clear indication that there are still some obstacles to the current agricultural land use and agricultural productivity improvement, which are mainly from three aspects: land tenure, state procurement targets, and public services.

First, the current land tenure is insecure. According to the Land Code of Uzbekistan, land in Uzbekistan is solely owned by the government, and farmers only have usufruct rights (Lerman, 2008a; Djanibekov et al., 2012; Melnikovová and Havrland, 2016; Akhmadiyeva and Herzfeld, 2021). In accordance with this premise, individual farms are permitted to lease land through a lease contract for a term of up to 50 years, with a minimum of ten years and typically not less than 30 years (Law on Peasant Farms, 1998). It seems that the tenure of the individual farm is stable given the length of the lease. In reality, however, this is not the case, and individual farms face a lot of uncertainty over land leases and tenure. At first, the individual farmer who leases the land is obligated to fulfill the contract's cotton and wheat quotas.

Any deviation from the sowing practices specified in the land lease contract is a serious violation and constitutes grounds for termination of the farm lease (Lerman et al., 2016). Second, under specific conditions, the state, as a single landowner, can expropriate land from farmers (Djanibekov et al., 2012), such as farm restructuring in 2008–2010 and land size optimization in 2019. Furthermore, despite using the best management practices, crop yields remain low and fall short of government quotas due to agriculture's high dependence on natural factors. This non-human-induced inefficiency may also result in a reduction in the amount of land allotted to individual farms (Djanibekov and Finger, 2018). The aforementioned are all effects of unstable land tenure.

One of the most significant factors affecting farmers' agricultural productivity and investment decisions is the degree of tenure security (Spoor, 2007; Akhmadiyeva and Herzfeld, 2021). Farmers' incentives to produce are reduced by the instability of their land leases and tenure, and they are deterred from making long-term investments in their property that might enhance the soil's quality. Also, this will lower individual farms' production and consequently their crop yield. *Dekhkan* farms, which are leased for life and are inheritable, have substantially more secure land ownership than individual farms. They are therefore more motivated to make larger investments in the land to increase soil fertility. This is one of the factors contributing to *Dekhkan* farms' present high levels of productivity. *Dekhkan* farms, however, are often modest, measuring 0.17 ha on average, or no more than 0.35 ha if they are irrigated, or 1 ha if they are not, and they are not necessarily located close to the family home (FAO, 2019). Land resource limitations are a significant obstacle for *Dekhkan* farms and the production of agricultural and livestock goods. They are unable to produce enough returns to lower market transaction costs (Zorya et al., 2019). As a result, they have relatively little potential to boost agriculture's economy.

Transferability of land tenure rights is another problem that needs to be solved. The Land Law of 1998 states that only the land rights of *Dekhkan* farms can be passed down through the generations; all other land usufructs are prohibited from being traded, sold, or mortgaged. Users (agricultural entities) do not have the flexibility to adjust the size of their leased land when needed. They cannot acquire more land from less productive farmers or farmers who are not willing or able to cultivate. Under the above circumstances, the land market cannot function adequately (Melnikovová and Havrland, 2016). The lack of a land exchange market is a serious obstacle to improving the efficiency of individual farm agriculture and the economy as a whole. This situation has improved in recent years, but some limitations remain. Under an amendment to the Land Law introduced on September 29, 2020, commercial farmers can sublease their land for up to one year for agricultural purposes. Upon expiration of the land lease, the lessee has the primary right to renew the land lease.

Second, individual farms do not have freedom of production decisions and freedom of marketing. Individual farms inherit the burden of fulfilling state cotton and wheat orders traditionally borne by collective and state farms, and they do not have the right to use the land allocated for cotton and wheat for other purposes (Bobojonov et al., 2013). For individual farms producing cotton and wheat, the state also controls the water supply and delivery of production factors, commodity prices, processing, and export. In January 2019, a new cabinet resolution called for further restructuring of the agricultural sector, aiming to double the size of cotton and wheat farms to an average of 100 hectares (Zorya et al., 2019). Until recently, these two main crops were subject to state orders. However, since a presidential decree on January 28, 2020, the state has been shifting from state orders on grains to market rules in the agricultural sector, hoping to reduce inefficiency and corruption. In March 2020, quotas for the cultivation and sale of cotton were canceled altogether, giving farmers the flexibility to plant other cash crops.[1] Although the state quota for cotton was abolished, the cotton quota still exists in the form of contractual obligations for farmers to grow a certain amount of grain and cotton for so-called clusters, registered as limited liability companies (LLCs).[2] As of February 2021, the government had approved 96 clusters covering nearly 1 million hectares of cotton.[3] Despite the privatization, government involvement in the cotton sector persists in the setting of quotas. In other words, the situation of individual farms or farmers has not been substantially improved. The control over the production system has simply shifted from the state to the production clusters. Under the existing state order formation mechanism and price system (government procurement prices are lower than market prices), most farmers grow cotton and wheat unprofitably (Khakimov et al., 2022). This leaves farmers with insufficient incentive to increase cotton and wheat production. In addition, the long cotton-wheat rotation reduces the humus layer of irrigated land and decreases soil fertility (Zorya et al., 2019). At the same time, the reduction of fodder crops has resulted in a reduction in livestock numbers, which has led to a significant reduction in manure placement in the field, below the total annual demand, further reducing soil fertility (Yuldashev et al., 2020). This production model is unsustainable in the long term. According to official World Bank sources, reducing the area under cotton and wheat in Uzbekistan to about 45% would lead to a 52.2% increase in total agricultural output and a 17% increase in employment in the agricultural sector, saving water 10.5%.

Dekhkan farms, on the other hand, have absolute freedom of production decisions and marketing. In Uzbekistan, *Dekhkan* farms are more efficient in the use of land and labor than individual farms, partly because of their secure land ownership and partly because of the freedom of production decisions and trade of *Dekhkan* farms. They can choose the crops they want to grow according to the market demand or their own wishes, and then sell the excess products at market prices. In this case, farmers can choose crops that are more profitable, use less water, and help maintain soil fertility. However, *Dekhkan* farms are disconnected from food value chains and agribusinesses.

Third, public services are inadequate and resources are poorly allocated. Much of Uzbekistan's existing agricultural infrastructure and production system, inherited from the Soviet Union and not adapted with land reform, was designed for state-owned farms and collective farms and was therefore considered suitable for large-scale farms producing mainly cotton. Thus, while horticultural, horticultural, and livestock farms have better freedom of decision-making compared to cotton and grain-producing farms, cotton and wheat farms have privileged access to irrigation water, fertilizers, fuel, machinery, credit, value chains, and export channels (Djanibekov et al., 2012; Zorya et al., 2019). Thus, strategic crops still dominate the sown area of individual farms. In contrast, individual farms and *Dekhkan* farms producing high-value crops have limited access to resources such as seeds and equipment, and the market for processing and marketing of products is not well developed (Bobojonov et al., 2013). Livestock production, like horticulture, operates within the framework of a free-market economy and is dominated by *Dekhkans.* Government intervention in these sectors is minimal, but the government also does not provide any significant support (Melnikovová and Havrland, 2016). In addition, the use of public expenditure in the agricultural sector in Uzbekistan is inefficient. Public spending in Uzbekistan's agricultural sector as a share of GDP is high, at 1.7% in 2018 (over 2% in 2016 and 2017), well above the 0.6% of middle-income countries, 0.2% of Organization for Economic Cooperation and Development (OECD) high-income countries, and 0.8% of Kazakhstan and 0.5% of Vietnam (Yuldashev et al., 2020). However, the high proportion of government spending in the agricultural sector has not significantly increased the efficiency of agricultural production in the country. This is because a large amount of public funds is currently used to pay for electricity, which is necessary to pump irrigated crop areas and to operate and manage irrigation systems that supply water to cotton and wheat producers. At the same time, little money is spent on upgrading irrigation and reclamation infrastructure, agricultural research and innovation, and technology extension.

6.6 Conclusions and policy recommendations

Uzbekistan attaches great importance to agriculture and rural development and has undertaken a series of reforms in recent years, especially after 2016, dedicated to shifting agriculture from a state-oriented to a market-oriented approach. However, farm restructuring by decrees and weak property rights in land use curtail management and investment incentives and raise issues of the just access to farmland for the rural population. In order to achieve better and faster development of agriculture in Uzbekistan, we propose the following recommendations, taking into account the actual situation in Uzbekistan and the experience of land reform in China.

First, the land market should be further liberalized and land should be allowed to circulate freely among farmers. In Uzbekistan, the land market is currently essentially nonexistent. The long-term leases do not protect farmers' land tenure. Improving the organization of land would help increase crop yields, increase international market demand, and improve the export capacity of agricultural products, thus ensuring economic stability for farmers and efficient agricultural development (Khakimov et al., 2022). Therefore, the government should reduce its intervention in the land market and give farmers more freedom. Liberalizing the land market aims to enable market-driven land leasing and subleasing, not to complete privatization of agricultural land property. The government should encourage the transfer of land (use rights, or even ownership rights) among farm households. This can, on the one hand, increase the family's land size, reduce fragmentation, and contribute to more efficient irrigation. On the other hand, land can be transferred from inefficient farmers to efficient farmers, improving the efficiency of agricultural production. In addition, in order to effectively safeguard farmers' land tenure, the government should do away with the threat posed by illegitimate land acquisition. The appropriate scale of agricultural production is determined by many factors, such as geographic location, climatic conditions, degree of land fragmentation, agricultural infrastructure, and even off-farm job opportunities and compensation. It is not necessarily the larger the scale, the better. The optimal scale of production varies from region to region and from crop to crop, so the market, not the government, should decide what is the optimal scale of agricultural production.

Second, marketization should be further strengthened. First, the government should gradually abolish production quotas, abstain from any other production interventions, and give farmers more rights to make production decisions. Market demand and farmers' wishes should determine the cropping patterns. With the progress of science and technology, many alternatives to cotton have been invented and cotton is gradually becoming less competitive in the international market. Secondly, for Uzbekistan, it is possible to consider reducing wheat cultivation to more profitable high-value crops. Thirdly, reducing price intervention in agricultural products such as cotton and wheat and allowing farmers to trade at market prices to increase their profits could increase the incentives for farmers. In addition, factor markets and product processing and marketing infrastructure should be strengthened to accommodate new production needs. Finally, links with international markets should be strengthened to promote international trade in agricultural products. Increased marketization of agricultural production and trade might help Uzbekistan to join the World Trade Organization sooner.

Third, public services in agriculture must be strengthened. First, the government should improve the efficiency of public spending in the agricultural sector to help farmers increase the return on their land and labor. This will require shifting agricultural subsidies to the provision of public goods and empowering national and local governments to allow more efficient service delivery. Specifically, the main focus would be to provide adequate financial support for agricultural research and innovation, technology extension, water conservation techniques, market infrastructure and logistics, education, and soil fertility. This will help to develop a large number of professional farmers with knowledge and skills. Second, the government should improve agricultural infrastructure. The existing agricultural infrastructure is no longer adequate for the current production needs. For example, the government should build more resilient, environmentally friendly, and efficient modern agricultural irrigation infrastructure, which not only improves crop yields but also helps conserve water and improve soil fertility. Finally, equity in the distribution of agricultural factor resources should be improved. Fruits, vegetables, and livestock have great production potential, but the current public service support for these products is weak. *Dekhkan* farms and individual farms producing these crops should receive more government support. Moreover, the government should provide different extension services according to the actual situation of each type of farm in order to maximize the benefits.

Notes

1 (2020, March 6). Uzbekistan scraps cotton state-order system. https://eurasianet.org/uzbekistan-scraps-cotton-state-order-system
2 (2022, July 17). Illegal Land Confiscations in Uzbekistan Farmers in Namangan Fight for Their Rights and Livelihoods. www.uzbekforum.org/illegal-land-confiscations-in-uzbekistan-farmers-in-namangan-fight-for-their-rights-and-livelihoods/
3 Schweisfurth, L. (2021, February 19). Land-Grabs – the New Red Flag for Uzbek Cotton Sector. Apparel Insider. https://landportal.org/blog-post/2021/05/land-grabs-%E2%80%93-new-red-flag-uzbek-cotton-sector

References

Akhmadiyeva, Z. and T. Herzfeld (2021) "How does practice matches land laws in Central Asia?", *Land Use Policy* 109, 105726. Available at: https://doi.org/10.1016/j.landusepol.2021.105726.

Ashurmetova, N.A. (2021) "Condition and factors of development of the stock-raising industry in Uzbekistan", *E3S Web of Conferences* 254, 08020. Available at: https://doi.org/10.1051/e3sconf/202125408020.

Azizkhon, K. (2017) "The peculiarities of statistical analysis on fruit and vegetable farming (Fergana region is as an example)", *Бюллетень науки и практики* 8 (21), 188–193.

Bobojonov, I., J.P.A. Lamers, M. Bekchanov, and N. Djanibekov (2013) "Options and Constraints for crop diversification: A case study in sustainable agriculture in Uzbekistan", *Agroecology and Sustainable Food Systems* 37 (7), 788–811. Available at: https://doi.org/10.1080/21683565.2013.775539.

Cheng, W., Y. Xu, N. Zhou, Z. He and L. Zhang (2019) "How did land titling affect China's rural land rental market? Size, composition and efficiency", *Land Use Policy*, 82, 609–619. Available at: https://doi.org/10.1016/j.landusepol.2018.12.037.

Djanibekov, N., I. Rudenko, J.P.A. Lamaers and I. Bobojonov (2010) "Pros and cons of cotton production in Uzbekistan", *Study Case #7–9 of the Program: Food*

Policy For Developing Countries: The Role of Government in the Global Food System, Cornell University. Available at: https://ecommons.cornell.edu/handle/1813/55707 (Accessed: March 5, 2023).

Djanibekov, N., K. van Assche, I. Bobojonov and J.P.A. Lamers (2012) "Farm restructuring and land consolidation in Uzbekistan: New farms with old barriers", *Europe-Asia Studies* 64 (6), 1101–1126.

Djanibekov, U., K. van Assche, D. Boezeman and G.B. Villamor (2015) "Revealing the role of agricultural contracts in rural livelihoods in Uzbekistan", in A. Kimhi and Z. Lerman (Eds.) *Agricultural Transition in Post-Soviet Europe and Central Asia after 25 Years.* IAMO, Halle (Saale), 141–158. Available at: https://repository.ubn.ru.nl/handle/2066/140606 (Accessed: January 12, 2023).

Djanibekov, U. and R. Finger (2018) "Agricultural risks and farm land consolidation process in transition countries: The case of cotton production in Uzbekistan", *Agricultural Systems*, 164, 223–235. Available at: https://doi.org/10.1016/j.agsy.2018.03.009.

Dosmukhamedova, M.H. (2022) "Development factors of the state of the livestock sector in Uzbekistan", *IOP Conference Series: Earth and Environmental Science* 1068 (1), 012034. Available at: https://doi.org/10.1088/1755-1315/1068/1/012034.

Fan, S. (1991) "Effects of technological change and institutional reform on production growth in Chinese Agriculture", *American Journal of Agricultural Economics*, 73 (2), 266–275.

Fan, S., L. Zhang, and X. Zhang (2002) *Growth, Inequality, and Poverty in Rural China: The Role of Public Investments.* International Food Policy Research Institute. Available at: https://doi.org/10.2499/0896291286rr125.

Fan, S. and Zhang, X. (2002) "Production and productivity growth in Chinese agriculture: new national and regional measures", *Economic Development and Cultural Change*, 50 (4), 819–838.

FAO (2019) *Gender, agriculture and rural development in Uzbekistan – Country Gender Assessment Series.* Food and Agriculture Organization of the United Nations. Available at: www.fao.org/3/ca4628en/ca4628en.pdf.

Gibson, J. (2020) "Aggregate and distributional impacts of China's household responsibility system", *Australian Journal of Agricultural and Resource Economics* 64 (1), 14–29.

Huang, J. (2018) "Forty years of China's agricultural development and reform and the way forward in the future", *Journal of Agrotechnical Economics* (3), 4–15. Available at: https://doi.org/10.13246/j.cnki.jae.2018.03.001.

Huang, J. and S. Rozelle. (1996) "Technological change: Rediscovering the engine of productivity growth in China's rural economy", *Journal of Development Economics* 49 (2), 337–369.

Huang, J. and S. Rozelle. (2018) "China's 40 years of agricultural development and reform". R. Garnaut, L. Song, C. Fang (Eds.) *China's 40 Years of Reform and Development: 1978–2018.* 1st ed. ANU Press, pp. 487–506.

Jin, S., J. Huang, R. Hu and S. Rozelle (2002) "The creation and Spread of Technology and total factor productivity in China's agriculture", *American Journal of Agricultural Economics* 84 (4), 916–930.

Khakimov, R., B. Sarsengaliy, J. Rozikov, M. Mamatkulov, K. Ismailov and A. Durmanov (2022) "Current state of agriculture in the republic of Uzbekistan and the need for improving the efficiency of agro-clusters in the fruit and vegetable industry", *IOP Conference Series: Earth and Environmental Science* 1043, 012043. Available at: https://doi.org/10.1088/1755-1315/1043/1/012043.

Larson, D.F., Khidirov, D., & Ramniceanu, I. (2012). *Uzbekistan Strengthening the Horticulture Value Chain.* World Bank, Washington, DC. Available at: https://openknowledge.worldbank.org/handle/10986/21495.

Lerman, Z. (2008a) "Agricultural development in Central Asia: A survey of Uzbekistan, 2007–2008", *Eurasian Geography and Economics* 49 (4), 481–505.

Lerman, Z. (2008b) Agricultural development in Uzbekistan: The effect of ongoing reforms, *Discussion Paper 7.08*, The Center for Agricultural Economic Research, The Hebrew University of Jerusalem. Available at: https://doi.org/10.22004/ag.econ.37945.

Lerman, Z. (2008c) "Sustainable development of the livestock sector in Uzbekistan: Status and policy recommendations", *UNDP Uzbekistan Policy Brief: The Executive Series*, 1–11.

Lerman, Z., Sedik, D., Yusupov, Y., Stanchin, I., & Kazakevich, I. (2016). 'Wheat production and regional food security in CIS: the case of Belarus, Turkmenistan and Uzbekistan'. *FAO Policy Studies on Rural Transition* 1.

Lin, J.Y. (1992) "Rural reforms and agricultural growth in China", *American Economic Review* 82 (1), 34–51.

Lin, J.Y. (1990) "Collectivization and China's agricultural crisis in 1959–1961", *Journal of Political Economy* 98 (6), 1228–1252.

Lin, J.Y. and D.T. Yang (2000) "Food availability, entitlements and the Chinese famine of 1959–61", *The Economic Journal* 110 (460), 136–158.

Luo, X. and C. Niu (2019) E-Commerce participation and household income growth in taobao villages. *Working Paper*, World Bank, Washington, DC. Available at: https://doi.org/10.1596/1813-9450-8811.

McMillan, J., J. Whalley and L. Zhu (1989) "The impact of China's economic reforms on agricultural productivity growth", *Journal of Political Economy* 97 (4), 781–807.

Melnikovová, L. and B. Havrland (2016) "State ownership of land in Uzbekistan – an impediment to further agricultural growth?", *Agricultura Tropica et Subtropica* 49 (1–4), 5–11. Available at: https://doi.org/10.1515/ats-2016-0001.

National Bureau of Statistics. (2021) *China Statistical Yearbook – 2021.* China Statistics Press, Beijing.

Naughton, B.J. (2018) *The Chinese Economy: Adaptation and Growth.* 2nd edition. MIT Press.

Putterman, L. (1990) "Effort, productivity, and incentives in a 1970s Chinese People's commune", *Journal of Comparative Economics* 14 (1), 88–104.

Spoor, M. (2007) *Ten Propositions on Rural Poverty and Agrarian Transition in Central Eurasia.* Institut Barcelona d'Estudis Internacionals (IBEI). Available at: www.jstor.org/stable/resrep14194 (Accessed: March 9, 2023).

Spoor, M. (2012) "Agrarian reform and transition: what can we learn from 'the east'?", *The Journal of Peasant Studies* 39 (1), 175–194.

Topildiev, S., S. Toshmatov, A. Rasulev, and M. Abdullayeva (2021) "The evolution of agrarian relations over a century and their future development ways in Uzbekistan", *Journal of Hunan University Natural Sciences* 48 (10), 704–713.

Umarxodjaeva, M. (2020) "Export potential development and export diversification of fruit and vegetable products in Uzbekistan's economy", *Архив научных иccледёваний* 35. Available at: https://tsue.scienceweb.uz/index.php/archive/article/view/3549 (Accessed: March 5, 2023).

Urdushev, K. (2021) "About formation of agrarian clusters in Uzbekistan", *International Journal of Multicultural and Multireligious Understanding* 8 (11), 409–415. Available at: https://doi.org/10.18415/ijmmu.v8i11.3222.

Uzbekistan. (1998). *Law On Peasant Farms.* Tashkent. Available at: https://faolex.fao.org/docs/pdf/uzb70917.pdf (Accessed: June 5, 2023).

State Committee on Statistics of Uzbekistan (UzStat). (2022). *Agriculture of Uzbekistan.* State Committee on Statistics of Uzbekistan Tashkent.

Wang, J., Y Zhu, T. Sun, J. Huang, L. Zhang, B. Guan and Q. Huang (2020) "Forty years of irrigation development and reform in China", *Australian Journal of Agricultural and Resource Economics* 64 (1), 126–149.

Wegren, S. (1998) *Agriculture and the State in Soviet and Post-Soviet Russia.* University of Pittsburgh Press.

World Bank and Development Research Center of the State Council of the People's Republic of China (2022) *Four Decades of Poverty Reduction in China: Drivers, Insights for the World, and the Way Ahead.* World Bank, Washington, DC. Available at: https://doi.org/10.1596/978-1-4648-1877-6.

Yuldashev, N.K., V.I. Nabokov, K.V. Nekrasov and B.O. Tursunov (2020) *"Modernization and intensification of agriculture in the republic of Uzbekistan,"* in E3S Web of Conferences. Available at: https://doi.org/10.1051/e3sconf/202022206033.

Zorya, S. with N. Djanibekov, M. Petrick, S. Hasanov, N. Mukhamedova, O. Durand and D. Khidirov (2019) *Farm Restructuring in Uzbekistan: How Did It Go and What is Next?* World Bank, Washington, DC. Available at: https://doi.org/10.1596/31248

7 Trade and logistics

Richard Pomfret and Jamshid Normatov

A dramatic feature of New Uzbekistan has been the shift from a closed economy to a situation where trade and logistics conditions have been substantially improved. The renewed openness to the world was signalled by Shavkat Mirziyoyev's travel agenda in the last four months of 2016 and in 2017 (Pomfret, 2019, pp. 117–118). Working meetings with the presidents of Russia and Kazakhstan in September 2016 indicated Mirziyoyev's priorities; Russia is too important for a Central Asian leader to ignore, and Uzbekistan and Kazakhstan are the leaders of Central Asia. They were followed by the leaders of Belarus in October, Turkey in November, and the Kyrgyz Republic in December.

In 2017, the president made state visits in March and April to Turkmenistan, Kazakhstan and Russia. In May he was in Beijing for the launch of the Belt and Road Initiative and in Riyadh for the Arab Islamic Summit. Mirziyoyev attended in June the Shanghai Cooperation Organization summit in Astana, where he met, inter alia, the Prime Ministers of Pakistan and India, in September the United Nations General Assembly in New York, and in October the Commonwealth of Independent States summit in Sochi, followed by state visits to Turkey, Korea and Tajikistan in October and November. The travel agenda spoke of opening the Uzbek economy, reconnecting with international partners, and leadership in the reintegration of Central Asia.[1] At Uzbekistan's initiative, a Central Asian leader's summit was held in 2018, the first since 2009. Since 2017, relations between the leaders have much improved and are institutionalized in Central Asian Summits and concerted actions in other fora.[2]

This chapter analyzes trade and logistics in the New Uzbekistan. After a brief review of trade and trade policy before 2016, emphasizing the initial conditions for new policies, the second section documents changes in tariffs and other trade policies and in the level and composition of trade between 2015 and 2019/2020. The third section examines external institutional arrangements. The fourth section on connectivity and logistics emphasizes the importance of trade facilitation. COVID-19 caused a slowdown in trade, tourism, and transportation in 2020, although real growth remained positive at 1.9% and rebounded to 7.4% in 2021 (IMF, 2022). The final section concludes.

DOI: 10.4324/9781003473497-7

7.1 Background

Islam Karimov was First Secretary of the Communist Party of Uzbekistan from 1989 to 1991 and President of Uzbekistan from 1991 until his death in September 2016. After the dissolution of the Soviet Union in December 1991, Karimov pursued an economic strategy of cautious gradualism in replacing central planning with a market-based economy.[3] The strategy was successful in ameliorating the transitional recession of the 1990s, but after 1996 restrictions on international economic interactions constrained efficiency (Pomfret, 2000). In the twenty-first century, Karimov focused on state-led investment in capital-intensive sectors and failed to facilitate a more sustainable market economy, as "the government became increasingly isolationist in its international relations and authoritarian in its domestic affairs" (Ruziev, 2021, p. 1303).[4] Karimov's positive legacy of a more sophisticated and diversified economy than in 1991, plus sound macroeconomic fundamentals including moderate inflation, low government debt and a large stock of international reserves (Holzhacker, 2018) provided a foundation for economic reforms, but Mirziyoyev also inherited fundamental challenges due to the inefficiency associated with economic isolation.

7.1.1 Trade in the Karimov era

In a brief initial era of more open policies, Uzbekistan applied to join the World Trade Organization in 1993, but negotiations stagnated after the 1990s (Pomfret, 2020). Uzbekistan maintained free trade and visa relations with other members of the Commonwealth of Independent States, but such rights were often terminated administratively without recourse. In this setting, both general and preferential tariff rates were uncertain, reducing the attractiveness of international trade (and increasing incentives for smuggling).

Published tariff rates (Table 7.1) indicate public policy. Uzbekistan's average tariff in 2015, the last year before Karimov's death, averaged 14%, more than double that of neighbouring Tajikistan or Turkmenistan and 75% higher than the tariff of the Eurasian Economic Union countries. Moreover, these numbers understate the protection granted to import-competing industries like motor vehicle production.[5]

Relations with neighbouring countries were problematic due to political tensions, which further restricted Uzbekistan's foreign trade. Uzbekistan opposed the construction of water reservoir projects in neighbouring countries Tajikistan and the Kyrgyz Republic, fearing that they would create environmental and economic risks for Uzbekistan. Uzbekistan limited the transit of goods to Tajikistan through its territory and applied similar restrictions to the Kyrgyz Republic. Moreover, Uzbekistan feared that religious extremists found refuge in those countries and believed they caused an existential threat to the government, leading to further restrictive border control measures. Border crossings of people and goods were challenging and time-consuming.

Table 7.1 Uzbekistan's Import Tariff Rates in Regional Comparison, 2015

Country	*Average tariff rate, all products %*	*Average applied tariff rate, all products %*
Kazakhstan	7.8	6.91
Kyrgyz Republic	7.8	5.33
Russia	7.8	5.33
Tajikistan	6.14	6.14
Turkmenistan	5.43	n/a
Uzbekistan	14.2	13.66

Source: World Bank.

International logistics were also complex and low priority in the Karimov era. Delays and charges at border crossing points were substantial. Transit traffic was discouraged by requirements for trucks to form escorted convoys and by often unpredictable traffic fines. Rail traffic on the main line north to Russia could be delayed at the border for over a week. Uzbekistan Airways which had been revamped in 1993 and Tashkent airport which was marketed as the Crossroads of Asia both lost their gloss in the twenty-first century as Air Astana emerged as the leading Central Asian airline and Almaty (or Istanbul) as the regional hub.

The major restriction on international economic transactions was the system of foreign exchange controls introduced in October 1996 which was revised several times over the next 20 years, but never eliminated. After remittances from workers in Russia dropped in 2008–2009, controls were

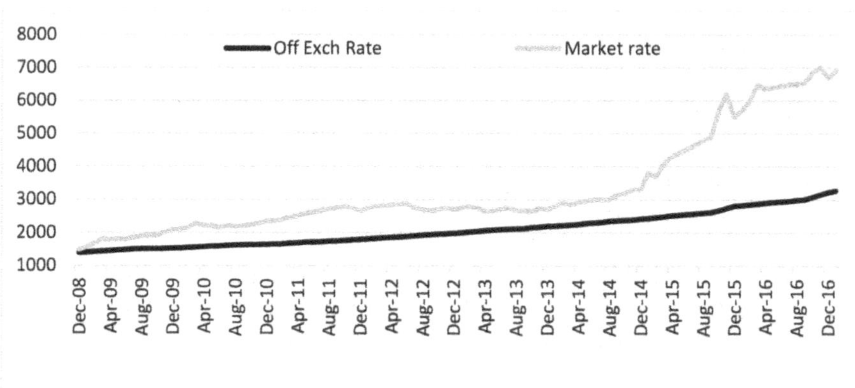

Figure 7.1 Official exchange rate and market rate, sum/US dollar, 2008–2016
Source: Ben Slay, based on Central Bank of Uzbekistan data and UNDP calculations; reported in Pomfret (2019, p. 113).

tightened, and the black-market premium on foreign exchange increased substantially after the end of the resource boom in 2014 (Figure 7.1).

Foreign exchange controls reduced the attractiveness of exporting, as earnings had to be surrendered for domestic currency at a poor exchange rate, while import-competing industries were protected. These patterns were reinforced by administrative measures such as control over prices received by cotton producers, the principal export after independence, or distorted by directing investment to specific export activities or by allocating licences to preferred imports. The banking sector was focused on implementing state programmes (including the exchange controls) and collecting government revenues, rather than attracting deposits and evaluating investment projects. More generally, the foreign exchange system diverted attention away from productive activities and towards rent-seeking activities, such as obtaining import licences and foreign currency to import goods that could be resold profitably.

7.2 Tariff and other trade policies since 2016/2017

The *Strategy of Actions for the Development of Uzbekistan for 2017–2021*, adopted in February 2017, included measures to liberalize the economy and trade, identifying goals such as the "liberalisation and facilitation of export activities, diversification of the export structure and geography, and the expansion and mobilisation of the export potential of economic sectors and territories". The strategy aimed at a full liberalization of foreign economic activities related to exports and the removal of existing obstacles for exporting firms. It envisaged programmes for the identification and development of prospective export-oriented products, export market diversification and trade infrastructure development.

By far the most significant economic reform measure came on 5 September 2017, when the Central Bank of Uzbekistan reunified Uzbekistan's exchange rates, and President Mirziyoyev promised freely floating market-determined rates for the future. The soum immediately dropped from the official rate of 4,210/USD to 8,100, and the black market disappeared. Simultaneously, restrictions were lifted for legal entities and individuals to convert currency. Individual entrepreneurs and farmers in Uzbekistan were allowed to withdraw foreign currency from their bank accounts. Legal entities could purchase foreign currency in banks without restrictions for payment on current international transactions, i.e. the import of goods, workers and services, repatriation of profits and remittances, repayment of loans, travel expenses and other non-trade transfers. In December 2017, banks in Uzbekistan launched a service to transfer money abroad, e.g. for relatives who are studying or being treated abroad. If rigorously implemented over the long term, a unified market-determined exchange rate will remove the single largest obstacle to the efficient operation of a market-based economy in Uzbekistan.[6]

7.2.1 Tariff levels, tariff structure, and non-tariff barriers to trade

Tariff rates in Uzbekistan before 2017 were among the highest in the region. President Mirziyoev took measures to lower tariffs (Pomfret, 2022). First, the new government drastically reduced import duties in 2017. Later in 2018, the government revised tariff rates and increased rates for several products (primarily electric goods and home appliances) with effect from 2019. New rates were still lower than rates for the period before 2016 (Table 7.2).

The government reduced import duties for practically all categories of goods. The share of duty-free imports increased significantly. The lowest rates on imports apply to categories of goods such as petroleum (average 0.4%), chemicals (2.5%), non-electrical machinery, minerals, and metals (5.2%). Relatively high rates still apply for categories such as beverages and tobacco (average MFN rate 29.8%), clothing (28%), and textiles (13.1%). The latter two include the highest rates in some subcategories maxing at 279% in textiles and 900% in clothing. Some categories of imported products are subject to specific duties and ad valorem tariffs. For example, automobiles are subject to a 15% import duty and a specific duty depending on the engine volume of the car, which may effectively add from 40% to 70% to the imported value of the vehicle. Although these rates may appear high, they are still much lower than those during the pre-reform period.

7.2.2 Level and composition of Uzbekistan's international trade

Reductions in import rates and removal of currency exchange restrictions had a profound effect on foreign trade volumes in Uzbekistan, resulting in a two-fold increase in 2020 compared with 2015 (Figure 7.2). The share of trade in GDP, an indicator of trade openness, increased from 30% in 2015 to 73% in 2019.

The import structure of Uzbekistan has changed after 2016. By 2019, there had been a significant increase in importation of construction machines and equipment, prefabricated buildings, planes and helicopters, and cars and motor vehicle parts and accessories compared with 2015 (Table 7.3). Imports by country of origin did not change significantly (Table 7.4). The top six exporters to Uzbekistan remained unchanged from 2015 to 2019, and volumes of imports increased substantially from all leading partners. Uzbekistan is increasingly trading with neighbouring countries of Central Asia;

Table 7.2 Import Duties Before and after President Mirziyoev's Reforms

	Pre-reform (2015)	*After reform (2020)*
Weighted average, MFN, all products	9.3%	4.5%
Simple average, MFN applied	14.9%	7.5%

Source: WTO.

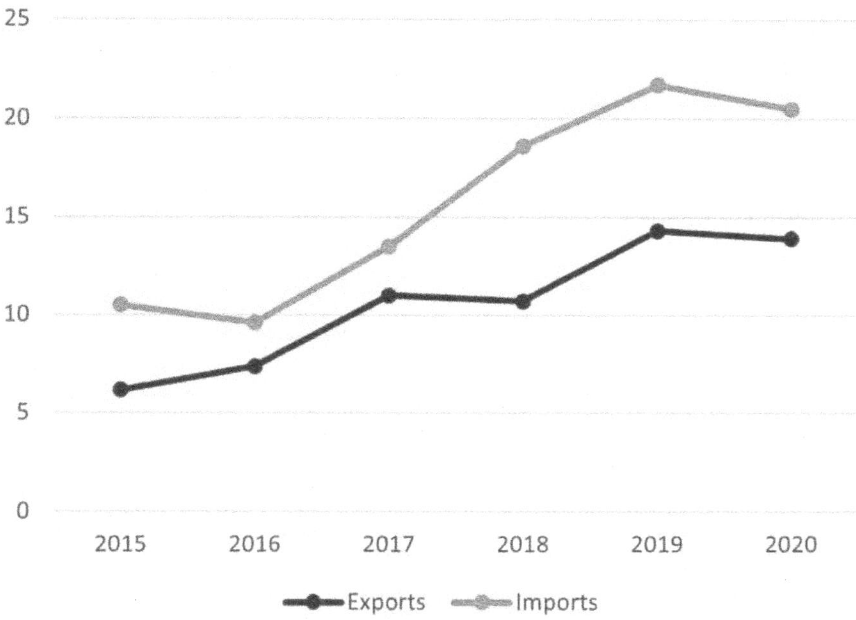

Figure 7.2 Foreign trade of Uzbekistan, 2012–2020, billion US dollars
Source: World Bank, WITS database.

compared with 2015, trade volumes with neighbours increased almost threefold by 2019, and the number of goods traded also increased.

Uzbekistan keeps local industries protected, although the government is gradually allowing more foreign competition. The government has plans to privatize state-run enterprises, and the car industry is expected to be first in the line. The government subsidizes enterprises providing benefits in one way or another. For instance, the government supports exporters by covering transportation expenses, etc. In exports, Uzbekistan enjoys duty-free treatment to CIS countries. The country enjoys preferential access to the EU market within the GSP+ scheme for a large group of products.

Uzbekistan exports mostly primary goods, though the share of processed products has been increasing. Gold is the top export of Uzbekistan. Other important categories include natural gas, copper, zinc, and uranium, and agricultural products such as cotton, grapes, pitted fruits, and dried legumes. Volumes of exports of these products increased compared with 2015, except for raw cotton, due to local consumption by the domestic textiles industry. It is worth mentioning that Uzbekistan has been developing its chemical industry to process natural gas. Recently, we have seen a massive increase in ethylene polymers exports, a new product in Uzbekistan's exports.

Switzerland is Uzbekistan's number one export destination. Gold is traded in metal exchanges in Switzerland and, to a lesser degree, in the UK. Apart from the gold, Uzbekistan exports mainly to countries in the region. Due to geographical proximity, Russia, China, Kazakhstan, Turkey, the Kyrgyz

Table 7.3 Top Ten Imported Goods in 2015 and in 2019

Top 10 imported goods in 2015			*Top 10 imported goods in 2019*			
		million USD			*million USD*	*% Change from 2015*
1	Packaged Medicaments	571	1	Motor vehicles, parts and accessories	985	78%
2	Motor vehicles, parts and accessories	554	2	Packaged Medicaments	748	31%
3	Refined Petroleum	442	3	Refined Petroleum	551	25%
4	Coated Flat Rolled Iron	249	4	Cars	533	328%
5	Sawn Wood	212	5	Planes, Helicopters	424	454%
6	Wheat	207	6	Coated Flat Rolled Iron	389	56%
7	Wheat Flours	195	7	Stone Processing Machines	388	523%
8	Vinyl Chloride Polymers	193	8	Large Construction Vehicles	377	505%
9	Air Pumps	165	9	Wheat	372	79%
10	Rubber Tires	132	10	Prefabricated Buildings	338	34 fold

Table 7.4 Imports by Country of Origin

Top 10 exporters to Uzbekistan in 2015		*Top 10 exporters to Uzbekistan in 2019*		
	million USD		*million USD*	*% Change from 2015*
China	2,228	China	5,236	135%
Russia	2,221	Russia	3,844	73%
South Korea	1,283	South Korea	2,483	93%
Kazakhstan	940	Kazakhstan	1,956	108%
Turkey	517	Turkey	1,255	143%
Germany	429	Germany	920	115%
United Arab Emirates	273	United States	538	563%
Japan	248	Turkmenistan	375	NA
Iran	238	Italy	369	139%
Ukraine	174	Japan	309	25%

Source: World Bank, WITS database.

Table 7.5 Top Ten Exported Goods in 2015 and in 2019

Top 10 exported products in 2015		*Top 10 exported products in 2019*		
	million USD		*million USD*	*% Change from 2015*
Gold	1,881	Gold	5,255	179%
Raw Cotton	575	Petroleum Gas	2,321	303%
Petroleum Gas	575	Non-Retail Pure Cotton Yarn	923	90%
Non-Retail Pure Cotton Yarn	486	Refined Copper	595	76%
Radioactive Chemicals	433	Ethylene Polymers	389	1,197%
Refined Copper	339	Raw Cotton	287	–50%
Grapes	141	Grapes	226	60%
Copper Wire	136	Raw Zinc	218	117%
Utility Metres	114	Pitted Fruits	196	360%
Raw Zinc	100	Dried Legumes	185	257%

Source: World Bank, WITS database.

Table 7.6 Top Ten Export Destinations in 2015 and 2019

Top export destinations of Uzbekistan in 2015			*Top export destinations of Uzbekistan in 2019*			
		million USD			*million USD*	*% Change from 2015*
1	Switzerland	1,870	1	Switzerland	2,611	40%
2	China	1,212	2	United Kingdom	2,388	95,234%
3	Turkey	718	3	Russia	2,041	258%
4	Kazakhstan	688	4	China	1,911	58%
5	Russia	570	5	Kazakhstan	1,210	76%
6	Bangladesh	242	6	Turkey	1,157	61%
7	Afghanistan	191	7	Kyrgyz Rep	634	1,021%
8	France	177	8	Afghanistan	604	217%
9	Ukraine	59	9	United Arab Emirates	368	1,733%
10	Kyrgyz Rep	57	10	Iran	209	387%

Source: World Bank, WITS database.

Republic, Afghanistan, and Iran are major export destinations for Uzbekistan.

7.3 External institutional arrangements

Under President Karimov, steps towards WTO membership and agreements with the EU had become frozen during the 2000s. Although Uzbekistan remained a member of the World Bank, the International Monetary Fund and other multilateral institutions, relations were generally cool. Relations were warmer with the United Nations and other organizations requiring little commitment, such as the Shanghai Cooperation Organization (SCO) and Central Asia Regional Economic Cooperation (CAREC). Uzbekistan remained a member of the Commonwealth of Independent States (CIS) but was reluctant to participate In the Collective Security Treaty Organization (CSTO).[7]

7.3.1 Bilateral agreements up to 2016

Uzbekistan in 2016 had bilateral trade agreements with over 40 countries, of which the most important were with former Soviet republics. A protocol establishing a free trade area between CIS members (Armenia, Belarus, Kazakhstan, the Kyrgyz Republic, Moldova, Russia, and Ukraine) and Uzbekistan came into force in May 2014.[8] This protocol grants Uzbekistan duty-free access to the markets of all the signatories and vice versa, although the protocol contains several exemptions related to the import regime, national treatment, and a dispute settlement mechanism.[9]

President Karimov was suspicious of closer ties with Russia, and stayed apart from the customs union between Russia, Belarus and Kazakhstan that in 2015 was deepened and extended (by accession of Armenia and the Kyrgyz Republic) to become the Eurasian Economic Union (EAEU). An agreement between Uzbekistan and Russia on the main directions of development and deepening of economic cooperation for 2015–2019 came into force in April 2015. The agreement aimed to promote the deepening of bilateral trade relations, diversification of goods traded, and expansion of trade in agricultural products and high-value-added goods of mutual interest.[10]

In Karimov's later years, relations with neighbouring Central Asian countries were poor, and personal relations with the leaders of Tajikistan and Turkmenistan were particularly fractious. President Mirziyoyev quickly engaged with neighbouring countries to defuse tensions, e.g. on water management issues (relaxing opposition to the Rogun and Farkhad dams in Tajikistan, and the Kambarata dam in the Kyrgyz Republic) and on border demarcation with Tajikistan and the Kyrgyz Republic. Meetings with the presidents of Turkmenistan and Kazakhstan in March 2017 highlighted connectivity and Uzbekistan's reintegration into a regional (and wider) economic circle.[11]

7.3.2 The World Trade Organization

In December 1994, Uzbekistan was the first Central Asian country to apply to join the World Trade Organization (WTO). The 1996 introduction of foreign exchange controls, which contravened both the spirit and the letter of WTO rules, stalled the accession negotiations. In 2003, the government's announcement of the end of forex controls was followed by workshops and other projects to analyze the impact of WTO accession (Normatov, 2018). Despite recommendations to include WTO accession in a programme of economic reform, the government tightened exchange controls and WTO negotiations lapsed after 2005. Apart from the Kyrgyz Republic, such delays in negotiations were not uncommon in Central Asia (Table 7.7). However, Tajikistan in 2013 and Kazakhstan in 2015 acknowledged the benefits of committing to WTO trade law, which is especially useful if major trade partners also accept those rules – China had joined the WTO in 2001 and Russia in 2012. Consistent with Karimov's stance of resisting constraints on national policymaking, Uzbekistan showed no interest in restarting accession negotiations.

President Mirziyoyev reactivated the WTO accession process. After the currency became convertible in September 2017, negotiations resumed. The Working Party on Uzbekistan's accession met in July 2020, the first meeting since 2005, and again in June 2022. When accession happens, Uzbekistan will hold the record for the longest delay between application and membership of any country in the world.

WTO accession will enable Uzbekistan to take greater advantage of the multilateral trading system. The main benefit of membership is the commitment to observe the same rules for conducting international trade that are recognized by almost all trading nations; such certainty and transparency make trading with and investment in Uzbekistan more attractive to prospective partners. Membership also provides a forum for resolving trade issues through participation in Agriculture, Sanitary and Phytosanitary (SPS), and other WTO Committees and by using dispute settlement mechanisms.

Table 7.7 Status of WTO Accession Negotiations

	Applied	*Member*
Kazakhstan	January 1996	November 2015
Kyrgyz Republic	February 1996	December 1998
Tajikistan	May 2001	March 2013
Turkmenistan	November 2021	
Uzbekistan	December 1994	
China	July 1986	December 2001
Russian Federation	June 1993	August 2012

Source: updated from Pomfret (2021, p. 2), based on data at www.wto.org.

7.3.3 The Eurasian Economic Union

Among Mirziyoyev's first official business after re-election in October 2021 was a state visit to Russia in November. One item on the agenda was the Eurasian Economic Union accession, which would secure duty-free access to the Russian market and improve the security and status of the 2 million Uzbeks working in Russia. Tashkent had observer status in the EAEU since December 2020, and in 2021 the government was already undertaking steps on the path toward membership as several government agencies were drafting national documents to align with EAEU technical regulations and to synchronize areas such as tax collection and customs procedures. Policy statements also mentioned negotiations for WTO accession and with the EU, but the EAEU appeared to have priority in 2021 (Hashimova, 2021). However, the initiative faltered in 2022 after Russia invaded Ukraine.

7.3.4 The European Union and the United Kingdom

Uzbekistan's trade with the EU benefits from the 1999 Partnership and Cooperation Agreement (PCA) which grants MFN treatment, the Generalised Scheme of Preferences (GSP) which allows developing countries to pay fewer or no duties on exports to the EU, and the EU-Uzbekistan Textile Protocol.[12] In November 2018, the EU and Uzbekistan formally started negotiations on an Enhanced Partnership and Cooperation Agreement (EPCA), reflecting President Mirziyoyev's priority of kickstarting Uzbekistan's economy and attracting foreign investment.

In April 2021, the EU admitted Uzbekistan to its GSP+ scheme, and later in the year Uzbekistan signed up to Britain's Generalised System of Preferences Enhanced Framework (GSP EF). Under the UK deal, Uzbekistan will be able to export 3,000 products to Britain tariff-free and another 3,200 with reduced tariffs. The main products exported to Britain from Uzbekistan under the deal will be fabrics and agricultural products.

In July 2022 the EU and Uzbekistan concluded the EPCA negotiations, which included new areas of cooperation and upgraded the regulatory framework for trade and economic relations. The EPCA ensures a better regulatory environment for economic operators in areas such as trade in goods and services, state-owned enterprises, procurement, and intellectual property rights, and enhanced cooperation in other policy areas, including economic and financial cooperation, energy, transport, environment and climate change, digital economy, agriculture and rural development, employment and social affairs, culture, education and youth, and research. The EPCA also covers political cooperation and reforms (with emphasis on shared values, democracy and the rule of law, human rights and fundamental freedoms, and sustainable development), enhanced cooperation in foreign and security policy (with focus on regional stability and international cooperation, non-proliferation of weapons of mass destruction, conflict prevention, and crisis management), and justice, freedom and security cooperation (covering data protection, migration, the fight against money laundering and terrorism, organized crime and corruption, tackling illicit drugs, as well as judicial cooperation and consular protection).

The EU–Central Asia Sustainable Connectivity Conference was held in November 2022 in Samarkand. The driving force was the search for a sustainable route from the EU to Central Asia, and on to China, that was not dependent on transiting Russia. Uzbek exporters responded quickly (see Section 7.5).

7.3.5 Regional cooperation

The most important forum for discussion of regional economic cooperation is Central Asian Regional Economic Cooperation. CAREC has existed for over two decades, going through a long slow process of confidence-building among members.[13] Today it is an active organization, supported particularly by the Asian Development Bank and the CAREC Institute as a provider of knowledge products and manager of the Corridor Performance Monitoring and Management (CPMM) project. Its focus has been primarily on trade facilitation, although CAREC also has a mandate to act on energy, transport. and trade policy.

Although in the past its meetings have had little economic content, summits of the Shanghai Cooperation Organization have provided an important forum to bring together Central Asian leaders as well as those of China, Russia, India, and Pakistan. The 2022 summit in Samarkand was attended by leaders of the eight SCO members, the three SCO observers – Belarus, Iran and Mongolia – and special guests Azerbaijan, Turkey and Turkmenistan; the represented countries constitute almost half of the world's population. Apart from the formal sessions, the conference provides many opportunities for bilateral discussion with regional and neighbouring leaders. Among the specific outcomes for Uzbekistan in 2022 was the final agreement on a long-discussed railway linking Kashi (Kashgar), the western-most point on the Chinese rail network with Andijon through the Kyrgyz Republic. The link will not only help Uzbek trade with China, but will also be part of a new China–EU rail link that avoids transiting Russia and repositions Tashkent as a transport hub.

7.3.6 Conclusions

From being an obstacle to almost every aspect of regional cooperation, Uzbekistan has become a positive agent of change in Central Asia. Considering Uzbekistan's central location, bordering all four other Central Asian countries as well as Afghanistan, a more open and trade-friendly Uzbekistan will benefit the whole region. As an indirect consequence of the opening and of accession to the WTO and other international institutions, exposure to international standards could encourage improved governance and decrease corruption.

7.4 Connectivity and logistics

Achieving the goal of diversifying Uzbekistan's economy through increased integration into the international economy, will depend critically on improving logistics and connectivity. From the standpoint of 2016, this required improving relations with neighbours and creating a more conducive environment for international trade by policy measures such as WTO accession, but it will also depend on reducing the costs of trading. By all measures, Uzbekistan had some of the highest costs in the world of conducting international trade. In part this could be explained by geography, one of only two double landlocked countries, and the legacy of rail, road, and pipeline connections that all went north to Russia, but it became increasingly clear that in addition to constraints of geography and hard infrastructure, the soft infrastructure for trade was poor.

The most commonly cited measures of the costs of crossing international borders have been in the World Bank's *Doing Business* reports. These reports indicate substantial improvement in the ease of doing business in Uzbekistan that started in Karimov's last years and was reinforced between 2016 and 2019 (the final *Doing Business* report); the 2019 ranking was ahead of EU members Malta and Greece. However, Uzbekistan has consistently ranked among the countries with the highest trade costs in both money and time (Table 7.8). The *Doing Business* 2017 report estimates that for both exports and imports a container took 285 hours to cross the Uzbekistan border and the cost was USD570.[14]

A more appropriate but less easy to summarize data source is the Corridor Performance Monitoring and Management (CPMM) programme coordinated by CAREC since 2010. The CPMM data are reported by people on the truck or train and record actual times and payments along major routes across Central Asia.[15] They reveal substantial variation in trade costs both from one border crossing point (BCP) to another and at the same BCP. Table 7.9 reports the time taken for trucks to exit and enter Uzbekistan in 2015

Table 7.8 Ease of Doing Business and Ease of Crossing Borders, Ranking

Date	*Ease of Doing Business*	*Ease of Trading Across Borders*
May 2006	151/175	169/175
May 2016	87/190	165/190
May 2019	69/190	152/190

Source: World Bank Doing Business legacy website at www.worldbank.org/en/programs/business-enabling-environment/doing-business-legacy

Notes: DB 2007, benchmarked to 1 May 2006, was the first to include crossing border rankings.

and 2019. Dautota (Karakalpakiya), the BCP between Uzbekistan and Kazakhstan on the E40 Tashkent-Berlin highway, is on the main road to Russia; for both outbound and inbound traffic it is one of the slowest border crossings in Central Asia – and the situation did not improve between 2015 and 2019.[16] In general, the BCP delays are long and, apart from outbound to the Kyrgyz Republic in 2019, all are above the Central Asian average.[17] Delays for outbound trucks tended to be longer than for inbound vehicles, and delays in both directions were somewhat longer in 2019 than in 2015.

The 2019 CPMM report describes (on pages 57–58) measures to simplify border procedures and modernize the truck fleet that could accelerate BCP clearance in the 2020s. Uzbek officials at the border are moving towards risk assessment rather than inspecting every piece of freight. The CAREC Customs Committee has been instrumental in improving coordination between customs services (e.g. in coordinating opening times so that trucks are not caught in no man's land after exiting a country while they wait to enter the neighbouring country). The COVID-19 pandemic accelerated the use of e-documents rather than paper. However, it is too early to assess the aggregate impact of such changes.

Hard infrastructure in Central Asia improved substantially in the decades after 1992. Rail links between Turkmenistan and Iran provide Uzbekistan with a connection to the Indian Ocean ports. Uzbekistan has access to the

Table 7.9 Time taken to Cross Uzbek Road Border Crossing Points, 2015 and 2019

	2015			*2019*		
	Average time (hours)	*Number of trips*	*Rank among Central Asian BCPs*	*Average time (hours)*	*Number of trips*	*Rank among Central Asian BCPs*
Inbound						
Dautota	5.9	104	21/22	7.6	214	10/18
Yallama	5.4	76	14/22			
Sariasiya				10.1	17	14/18
Alat				9.8	35	13/18
Outbound						
Dautota	6.8	88	17/18	9.6	124	20/24
Yallama	6.4	84	16/18	10.0	97	21/24
Alat	6.2	58	15/18	9.5	59	19/24
Sarasiya	5.6	51	12/18	4.6	123	16/24
Oibek	3.9	57	9/18			
Dustlik				0.9	19	6/24

Sources: CPMM Annual Reports 2015 and 2019 (Asian Development Bank, Manila).

Notes: omitting BCPs with < 5 observations. Rank, from fastest to slowest, is among BCPs of the five Central Asian countries.

pipeline from Turkmenistan to China that was completed in 2009, providing an alternative outlet for natural gas exports which had previously been limited to the Russian pipeline network. Uzbekistan's own investment in hard infrastructure was largely targeted at making the domestic road and rail network more secure, e.g. by reducing the need to transit Tajikistan when travelling between the Ferghana Valley and Tashkent or avoiding entering Kazakhstan when driving between Tashkent and Samarkand.

The most important development in improving Eurasian physical connectivity has been the establishment of regular rail services along the Eurasian Landbridge between the EU and China (Pomfret, 2021). After regular rail services were established in 2011 and became more frequent and regular, EU-China rail connections through Belarus, Russia and Kazakhstan have carried increasing amounts of freight from 46,000 containers in 2015 to 333,000 in 2019, and almost 700,000 in 2021 as ocean shipping was disrupted. Faster more reliable service than ocean transport was especially attractive to producers with Eurasian supply chains, e.g. in motor vehicles or electronic goods. Revenue from transit fees is commercially sensitive, but Kazakhstan has been reported to have earned 1 billion US dollars in 2015 and over 2 billion in 2020. Traffic through Russia was severely disrupted by the war in Ukraine and subsequent sanctions, which specifically included Russian Railways. Freight companies quickly established alternative routes crossing the Caspian Sea, and Uzbekistan can benefit from such routes, especially after the connection through the Kyrgyz Republic to the Chinese rail network is constructed.

Other connectivity developments include lifting in 2020 of restrictions on the use of regional airports, reduction in fees at all Uzbek airports, and simplification of border controls and other procedures which have been streamlined by the use of new technology. Samarkand airport was upgraded for $150 million by a public–private partnership. Cargo shipped for export by Uzbekistan Airways (UzAir) increased from 3,300 tonnes in 2019, to 5.5 in 2020 and 7.9 in 2021. The majority of cargo shipped internationally by UzAir was in its China–Europe transit plan (e.g. Tianjin–Athens, Hong Kong–Amsterdam) and, as of October 2022, UzAir was planning services to Lahore, Xian, Chengdu and Dhaka. Uzbekistan is also being used as a refuelling point by other Eurasian cargo carriers, e.g. Silk Way (Azerbaijan) flies Baku–Navoi–Hong Kong. The number of foreign airlines landing in Uzbekistan increased from 43 in 2019 to 63 in 2021.

Finally, digital connectivity is being improved. Until 2019, internet coverage, i.e. the percentage of the population with potential internet access, was 76% which was lower than in any other Central Asian country, and much lower than in neighbouring Kazakhstan or Kyrgyzstan (Table 7.10). Of the 76% of the population that had a physical connection to the internet in 2019, almost two-fifths did not use it, suggesting that the obstacle to increased internet connectivity was poor human capital rather than inadequate physical capital. Nevertheless, Uzbekistan increased its fibre-optic infrastructure

Table 7.10 Internet Coverage, Percentage of Population, 2019

	Connected	*Use Gap*	*Coverage Gap*
Kazakhstan	87	1	12
Kyrgyz Republic	80	9	11
Tajikistan	34	56	10
Turkmenistan	53	23	24
Uzbekistan	47	29	25

Source: Developing E-commerce in CAREC Countries: Current state and challenges in infrastructure development, *CAREC Institute Policy Brief*, May 2021.

from 36,600 km in 2019 to 68,600 km in 2020, and simplified permits for the construction and launch of cell towers.[18]

7.5 Conclusions

Until 2016 Uzbekistan's trade policy was inward-looking and, despite its history and geography as a regional centre, logistical and transit services were poor. The situation has changed greatly since then as trade barriers have fallen, logistics have improved, and Uzbekistan has re-engaged with neighbours and the global economy.

The full impact of these changes has been obscured by two unanticipated shocks. The COVID-19 pandemic with its associated lockdowns and closing of borders hampered both production and trade in 2020 and 2021. Then, as the world was recovering from the worst of the pandemic, the outbreak of war between Russia and Ukraine in February 2022 was a further disruption that remains unresolved at the time of writing and whose impact on Uzbekistan is unclear. An estimated 2 million Uzbeks work in Russia and, although there has been a war-driven increase in demand for their labour, the long-term prospects are unclear.[19] There is also reported to have been a much smaller migration of Russians to Tashkent in search of a bank account not subject to sanctions and perhaps a refuge to avoid being drafted for the war. A more permanent benefit for Uzbekistan is the search by the EU, China and others for new trans-Eurasian transport links that are not dependent on Russia. Uzbekistan is already part of the "Middle Corridor" routes that cross the Caspian Sea from Turkmenistan to Azerbaijan.[20] The country could eventually benefit from more attractive rail routes through Iran to the Indian Ocean or to the Middle East that do not require a boat connection.

Meanwhile, Uzbekistan has, by progressing its WTO application and other arrangements, been building institutional foundations for an internationalized economy that can benefit from trade and export-led growth. The use of protectionist measures to help import-competing producers is being reined in, as the government acknowledges the importance of low trade barriers in allowing producers to access the best inputs and to participate in global value chains – and not to forget benefits to consumers from lower prices and greater choice. Such "negative integration" into the global economy (i.e. reducing obstacles to trade) is being complemented by "positive integration" measures such as improved hard and soft infrastructure. The 2020s will show how well the economy can respond to the new opportunities.

Notes

1 In February 2021, Hutson and Olive (2021) observed that Kazakhstan's larger GDP, better connectivity with international markets and strong diplomatic relations with Russia and China "seemingly ensure that Kazakhstan remains the main driver of regional integration. Nevertheless, the reality is that the road to Central Asian stability and prosperity is increasingly running through Tashkent".

2 The March 2018 Almaty summit was followed by Tashkent (2019), Avaza, Turkmenistan (2021) and Cholpon-Ata, Kyrgyz Republic (2022). Examples of the 5+1 format include the December 2019 meeting in Delhi between the five Central Asian presidents and Prime Minister Modi, the three annual China-Central Asia foreign ministers' meetings since 2020, and the November 2022 EU-Central Asia Connectivity Conference in Samarkand attended by the EU High Representative for Foreign Affairs and the foreign ministers of the five Central Asian countries.

3 In his book *Uzbekistan: Its Own Model for Transition to a Market Economy*, Karimov (1993) outlined five principles of economic development: freeing the economy of ideology, the state as the main reformer, rule of law, strong social policy, and gradual reform to adapt to the market.

4 Popov (2013) sets out a more positive picture of "gradual economic reforms with the preservation of the capacity of state institutions, good macroeconomic policy and export oriented industrial policy". By contrast, Bogolov (2016) criticized official data and highlighted the 2 million Uzbeks working in Russia as evidence of failure to create jobs in Uzbekistan.

5 The high tariffs on car imports, which at times exceeded 100%, understated the level of protection as excise taxes, a road tax levied only on imported cars, and many technical barriers to trade (all of which would be illegal for a WTO member) ensured that few foreign cars could compete in Uzbekistan. Olma (2021) describes some of the costs of protecting the car industry by granting a domestic monopoly.

6 The *de jure* exchange rate is floating, but the IMF (2022, p. 39) classifies the *de facto* exchange rate as crawling given that the nominal exchange rate shows limited day-to-day volatility and the long-run path seems highly predictable.

7 Uzbekistan was a signatory of the Collective Security Treaty (also known as the Tashkent Treaty) which took effect in 1994 with nine CIS members. When the Treaty came up for renewal in 1999, Uzbekistan left the CSTO and joined the GUAM group, established in 1997 by Georgia, Ukraine, Azerbaijan, and Moldova. Uzbekistan withdrew from GUAM in 2005 and re-joined the CSTO in 2006. In June 2012, Uzbekistan suspended its membership in the CSTO.

8 Free trade agreements with Georgia and Azerbaijan, signed in 1995 and 1996, are also in force.

9 Uzbekistan can apply excise taxes on imports, which by far exceed taxes on similar locally produced goods. Uzbekistan does not provide national treatment according to Article III of GATT 1994 and can introduce non-tariff measures that do not comply with the WTO agreements. These exemptions are intended to be provisional until Uzbekistan became a member of the WTO, whichever came first.

10 In 2016, a Russian–Uzbek working group on the supply of fruit and vegetable products from Uzbekistan to Russia was established, in which Uzbekistan sought to establish an agreement on simplified procedures for customs and phytosanitary clearance to establish a "green corridor".

11 In their meeting at the Turkmen-–Uzbek border, Presidents Berdymuhamedov and Mirziyoyev opened rail and road bridges across the Amu Darya River, improving Uzbekistan's connectivity to Iran and the Middle East. Presidents Nazarbayev and Mirziyoyev announced the first scheduled high-speed passenger rail service between Tashkent and Almaty.

12 Following recognition at the end of 2016 of the eradication of the use of child labour in cotton harvesting in Uzbekistan, the European Parliament ratified the inclusion of a textile protocol in the PCA. The protocol reduces duties on the imports of textiles from Uzbekistan. The Senate of Uzbekistan ratified the inclusion of textile products in the bilateral trade agreement with the EU in May 2017 and the protocol came into force on 1 July of that year.

13 Kazakhstan, the Kyrgyz Republic, Tajikistan, and Uzbekistan are members together with Afghanistan, Azerbaijan, Georgia, Mongolia, Pakistan, and two regions of China and six development partners. Turkmenistan has observer status.

14 Until 2015 the Doing Business methodology was based on the costs of shipping a container, which was biased against countries like Uzbekistan most of whose trade was not containerized, but even after the change of methodology to counter that bias Uzbekistan continued to rank poorly. The *Doing Business* reports were discontinued after 2020.

15 Doing Business indicators were based on evidence from contributors who were mainly in capital cities., e.g. the 40 contributors from Uzbekistan in *Doing Business 2019* (page 300) were overwhelmingly at law firms. Such respondents are likely to report what should happen at the border given the country's rules and regulations rather than what actually happens at a BCP.

16 My (RP) personal recollection of the Karakalpakiya BCP from 2007, was of a bleak spot in the desert with a mountain of empty plastic water bottles testifying to the tedious and thirsty delays for truck drivers. Yallama is on the Tashkent-Shymkent road. Dustlik is on the Andijan-Osh road. Alat is the main BCP to Turkmenistan. Oybek and Sariasiya BCPs are on roads to Khujand and Dushanbe in Tajikistan.

17 After examining the CPMM data, Kalyuzhnova and Holzhacker (2021) conclude that transport times in Central Asia did not improve during the 2010s. Average speed along road corridors, including stops at borders and elsewhere, fell from 24.4 kph in 2010 to 22.6 kph in 2019. Sharafeyeva (2023) uses the CPMM data and a gravity model to show the economic costs of unpredictable border-crossing times.

18 Lilia Burunciuc, *How Central Asia can ensure it doesn't miss out on a digital future*, World Bank blog, 21 June 2021 at https://blogs.worldbank.org/europeandcentralasia/how-central-asia-can-ensure-it-doesnt-miss-out-digital-future

19 Joanna Lillis, Russia lures Uzbek migrants to fill war-related labor shortages, *Eurasianet*, 16 November 2022 at https://eurasianet.org/russia-lures-uzbek-migrants-to-fill-war-related-labor-shortages

20 The first Uzbekistan-EU train, as opposed to transit traffic, took 24 40-foot containers of fertilizers via Turkmenistan, Azerbaijan and Georgia to Constanta (Romania) in September 2022; see https://business.com.tm/post/9111/fertilizer-shipment-from-uzbekistan-transits-turkmenistans-turkmenbashi-port-to-europe.
In December 2022, a train with 46 containers of copper concentrate left Tashkent for Burgas (Bulgaria), a train of fertilizers went from Uzbekistan via Turkmenistan-Azerbaijan-Georgia to Lithuania, and a train from Izmir (Türkiye) brought household appliances to Tashkent.

References

Bogolov, P. (2016) An exodus amid tripled GDP: The mirage of Uzbekistan's economic miracle. Carnegie Moscow Center. Available at http://carnegie.ru/commentary/63771.

Hashimova, U. (2021) Uzbekistan takes further steps toward Eurasian Economic Union, *The Diplomat*, 25 January. Available at https://thediplomat.com/2021/01/uzbekistan-takes-further-steps-toward-eurasian-economic-union/.

Holzhacker, H. (2018) *Uzbekistan Diagnostic: Assessing Progress and Challenges in Unlocking the Private Sector's Potential and Developing a Sustainable Market Economy.* European Bank for Reconstruction and Development, London. Available at www.ebrd.com/documents/strategy-and-policy-coordination/uzbekistan-diagnostic-paper.pdf.

Hutson, N. and M. McGraw Olive (2021) Uzbekistan rising as Central Asian integration catalyst, *Eurasianet*, February 8. Available at https://eurasianet.org/perspectives-uzbekistan-rising-as-central-asian-integration-catalyst.

IMF (2022) Republic of Uzbekistan, *IMF Country Report* 22/189. International Monetary Fund, Washington, DC.

Kalyuzhnova, Y. and H. Holzhacker (2021) Enhancing Connectivity and Trade between Central Asia Regional Economic Cooperation Countries and the World: Benefits, risks and policy implications, *ADBI Working Paper* 1271. Asian Development Bank Institute, Tokyo.

Karimov, I. (1993) *Узбекистан–сёбственная мёдель перехёда на рынёчные ётнёшения (Building the Future: Uzbekistan – Its Own Model for Transition to a Market Economy)*. Uzbekistan Publishers, Tashkent.

Normatov, J. (2018) Uzbekistan's Long Way to the World Trade Organization, *L'Europe en Formation* 1 (385), 104–111.

Olma, N. (2021) Monotonous motorscapes: Uzbekistan's car industry and the consolidation of a post-socialist shortage economy, *Central Asian Survey* 40(2), 143–158.

Pomfret, R. (2000) The Uzbek model of economic development 1991–99, *Economics of Transition* 8 (3), 733–748.

Pomfret, R. (2019) *The Central Asian Economies in the Twenty-first Century: Paving a New Silk Road.* Princeton University Press, Princeton – Uzbek translation forthcoming with Yuridik Adabiyotlar Publish, Tashkent.

Pomfret, R. (2020) Uzbekistan and the World Trade Organization, *Silk Road: A Journal of Eurasian Development* 2(1), 54–61.

Pomfret, R. (2021) The Eurasian Landbridge: Implications of linking East Asia and Europe by rail, *Research in Globalization* 3. Available at https://doi.org/10.1016/j.resglo.2021.100046.

Pomfret, R. (2022) The European Union and Central Asia: Economic development and trade, *Australia and New Zealand Journal of European Studies* 14(2), 49–61.

Popov, V. (2013) Economic miracle of Post-Soviet Space: Why Uzbekistan managed to achieve what no other post-Soviet State achieved, *MPRA Paper 48723*. Available at: https://mpra.ub.uni-muenchen.de/48723/.

Ruziev, K. (2021) Uzbekistan's development experiment: An assessment of Karimov's economic legacy, *Europe-Asia Studies* 73(7), 1303–1329.

Sharafeyeva, A. (2023) Impact of high trade costs and uncertain time to trade on exports from Five Central Asian Countries, *ADB East Asia Working Paper Series* 59, Asian Development Bank, Manila.

8 Living standards, wellbeing and poverty

Akhtem Useinov and Kathryn Anderson

8.1 Introduction

Following independence in 1991, the Government of Uzbekistan took a gradual approach to economic reform (ILO, UNICEF, and World Bank, 2020). Similar to other Central Asian neighboring countries, in Uzbekistan, the 1990s were dominated by nation-building and the transition from central planning (Pomfret, 2021). High inflation rates and the loss of personal savings followed the initial transition from a planned to a market economy and negatively impacted the living standards (ILO, UNICEF, and World Bank, 2020). In the last two decades, many households experienced an improvement in living conditions. GDP per capita increased from 652.8 to 1,983.1 USD between 1991 and 2021 in Uzbekistan (Table 8.1). The low-income population share declined from 27.5 percent in 2000 to 11.5 percent in 2020.

A slow transition to a market economy followed the policy changes in the early 1990s; prices were liberalized, enterprises were provided with access to foreign currency, external trade was liberalized, and the exchange rate was unified (Izvorski et al., 2021). Enterprise restructuring, enterprise and bank privatization, restructuring of the financial sector, and the expansion of social protection took longer. Transition to a more effective and efficient delivery of education, health, and other social services to support human capital development progressed the least rapidly (Izvorski et al., 2021). Uzbekistan has almost universal literacy and high enrollment rates in primary and secondary education, but improvements in the quality and relevance of education to meet the needs of the labor market are needed (ILO, 2021). Enrollment in tertiary education increased during the recent ongoing reforms to 21.2 percent in 2021 (Table 8.1), mainly associated with establishing new local universities and branches of foreign universities. The infant mortality rate declined from 58 per 1,000 live births to 13 per 1,000 live births, and the under-5 mortality rate declined from 70.4 per 1,000 live births to 14 per 1,000 live births since 1991 (Table 8.1). However, the child mortality rates are still high compared to developed countries.

Services dominated Uzbekistan's production since independence contributing 42.5 percent of GDP in 2000 and 38.6 percent in 2021. Industry's

DOI: 10.4324/9781003473497-8

share (including construction) equaled 23.1 percent in 2000, and 34.5 percent in 2021 out of the total GDP. Agriculture, forestry and fishing equaled 34.4 percent in 2000, and 26.9 percent in 2021 out of the total GDP. The primary sectors of employment in Uzbekistan have been agriculture, forestry, and fisheries occupying about a quarter of employment, followed by industry and trade (ILO, 2020). Employment in agriculture decreased from 40.7 to 24.0 percent from 1991 to 2021, while employment in services increased from 33.5 to 51.0 percent out of total employment (Table 8.1); the structure of domestic employment gradually moved toward industry and services. Because agricultural employment is mainly in the informal economy, workers in this sector lack social protection and do not contribute to social insurance (ILO, 2020).

In the group of Central Asian countries, Uzbekistan has been dependent on natural resources (primary product) exports and remittances (Pomfret, 2021). Based on 2018–2019 data, Uzbekistan`s commodity dependence was equal to 71.9 percent (UNCTAD, 2021).[1]

Market-oriented reforms and economic uncertainties in the early 1990s caused internal and external migration to increase (Table 8.1). The lack of employment opportunities led to external labor migration and large remittance inflows (ILO, UNICEF, and World Bank, 2020). The dependence of Central Asian countries on remittances has grown over time, and remittances are a stable and important source of income for the countries in the Central Asian region (Poghosyan, 2020). Remittances are crucial for poverty reduction in many developing countries, particularly if they provide food, access to health services and quality education, and clean water and sanitation, and they facilitate small business development and entrepreneurship (Francois et al., 2022). Uzbekistan was sixth among the top Asian recipient countries by share of international remittances in their GDP in 2020 (International Organization for Migration, 2022). In 2021, the share of received personal remittances to GDP equaled 13.3 percent (Table 8.1). Russia is the main destination for Uzbekistan migrants (Kakhkharov et al., 2020), and Uzbekistan is among the largest recipients of remittances from Russia along with the Kyrgyz Republic and Tajikistan (Poghosyan, 2020). The majority of labor migrants from Uzbekistan are employed in low-skilled jobs; however, there are many migrants who have completed advanced education and are employed in high-skilled jobs around the world (Kakhkharov et al., 2020). Since 2017, Uzbekistan began to enhance its migration policies with the support of dedicated agencies, design programs, and initiate negotiations with destination countries to provide more protection for migrant workers (ILO, UNICEF, and World Bank, 2020).

Today, Uzbekistan stands at a window of demographic opportunity (UNICEF, 2018). The country's population, although still growing, has stabilized while remaining youthful. It is projected that Uzbekistan's working-age population would peak around the year 2048 at 27.7 million people, and then it would start to shrink. The working-age population (15–64) increased from 56 percent to 65 percent out of the total population from 1991 to 2021 (Table 8.1). Uzbekistan has a high youth-to-population ratio, creating a need for youth employment and active labor market policies (Honorati and Marguerie, 2021). Many young people, especially females, rural youth, and youth from economically disadvantaged households, face difficulties in the transition from education to employment. Around 16 percent of youth were unemployed in 2021 (Table 8.1). Most new jobs are in the informal sector (ILO, 2021), and many people are engaged in irregular employment (Dugarova, 2019). Around 40 percent of women have been in the labor force since 1991, and this rate remained around 40 percent in 2021 (Table 8.1). Males are more likely to be employed in high-paying occupations, while women are mostly employed in professional and service occupations (Shagazatova et al., 2020). Informal workers comprise more than half (54 percent) of the working-age population. The majority of these workers are young. The shortage of jobs in the formal sector is one of the main causes of informal employment (Shagazatova et al., 2020).

Since late 2016, Uzbekistan has initiated many significant and fast-moving reform programs, focusing on a market reform agenda to support international economic integration, increase competitiveness, and maintain a high economic growth rate (ILO, UNICEF and World Bank, 2020). With these reforms, Uzbekistan aimed to balance socio-economic development by increasing competitiveness, modernization, and diversification of industries and agriculture. At the same time, the government supported institutional and structural reforms to reduce government intervention in the economy and to stimulate business and private entrepreneurship (ILO, UNICEF and World Bank, 2020).

In this chapter we provide household-level evidence and analysis on living standards, wellbeing, and poverty using *Multiple Indicator Cluster Survey* (MICS) data for Uzbekistan for 2006 and 2021–2022. We analyze household wealth status measured by the wealth index and its determinants for 2006 and 2021–2022. We also review the Global Multidimensional Poverty Index (MPI), analyze its trends and compare the poverty indicators for Uzbekistan with other Central Asian countries. At the end of this chapter, we discuss our findings. The main goal of this chapter is to examine whether living standards increased over time following extensive policy reforms. We provide evidence that poverty, especially in the living standards, improved between 2006 and 2021–2022, which is consistent with the effectiveness of the policy reforms. We cannot estimate the policy impact itself with two waves of data, but our results suggest progress over time in economic development in Uzbekistan.

8.2 Household-level evidence on living standards, wellbeing and poverty

In this section we provide household-level evidence for living standards, wellbeing, and poverty using *Multiple Indicator Cluster Survey* data for

Table 8.1 Macroeconomic and Demographic Indicators

Economy and demography	*1991*	*1995*	*2000*	*2005*	*2010*	*2015*	*2021*
GDP per capita (current US$)	652.8	585.9	558.2	546.8	1,742.3	2,754.0	1,983.1
Share of low-income population – poverty rate (2,100 kcal a day)*	–	–	27.5	25.8	17.7	12.8	11.5
Population, total (million)	21.0	22.8	24.7	26.2	28.6	31.3	34.9
Population aged 0–14 (% of total population)	40	40	37	33	29	29	30
Population aged 15–64 (% of total population)	56	56	59	63	66	67	65
Population aged 65+ (% of total population)	4	4	5	5	5	4	5
Mortality rate, infant (per 1,000 live births)	58.0	57.3	50.8	37.4	25.4	17.3	13.0
Mortality rate, under 5 (per 1,000 live births)	70.4	69.5	60.7	43.4	28.7	19.3	14.0
Labor							
Labor force, total (million)	8.1	9.3	10.4	11.5	12.6	13.5	14.4
Female labor force (% out of total labor force)	42.4	43.1	42.8	42.1	41.0	40.2	39.4
Unemployment, female (% of the female labor force) (modeled ILO estimate)	2.2	8.9	14.2	8.3	6.4	5.0	7.0
Unemployment, male (% of the male labor force) (modeled ILO estimate)	1.7	6.9	10.8	6.2	4.7	5.3	7.2
Unemployment, youth total (% of total labor force ages 15–24)	3.9	15.8	24.4	14.5	12.0	12.4	15.9
Employment in agriculture (% of total employment) (modeled ILO estimate)	40.7	41.2	39.1	33.7	26.8	27.6	24.0

Economy and demography	*1991*	*1995*	*2000*	*2005*	*2010*	*2015*	*2021*
Employment in industry (% of total employment) (modeled ILO estimate)	25.8	23.9	21.5	21.3	22.7	22.9	25.0
Employment in services (% of total employment) (modeled ILO estimate)	33.5	34.9	39.4	45.0	50.5	49.5	51.0
Migration							
Net external migration	–41,584	–83,287	–57,127	–97,812	–39,755	–29,299	–18,265
Personal remittances, received (% of GDP)	–	–	–	7.2	6.9	5.6	13.3
Education							
School enrollment, primary (% gross)**	111.7	105.4	99.7	97.0	93.9	99.9	98.1
School enrollment, secondary (% gross)	99.5	92.9	88.1	88.9	89.9	91.8	92.2
School enrollment, tertiary (% gross)	17.5	–	13.1	10.1	9.4	8.2	21.2

Source: The World Bank Group, Agency of Statistics under the President of the Republic of Uzbekistan, TransMonEE.

Notes:
Some indicators have missing data – we mark them as "–"
Some indicators show considerable changes between 2015 and 2020/2021. The changes have been mainly associated with reforms since 2017.
*We report data for the share of the low-income population for 2020, while for 2021, the poverty rate was calculated based on a methodology of minimum consumer spending and was equal to 17%
**Gross enrollment ratio (GER) can exceed 100% due to the inclusion of over-aged and under-aged pupils/students because of early or late entrants, and grade repetition (https://uis.unesco.org/en/glossary-term/gross-enrolment-ratio)

Uzbekistan for two periods – 2006 and 2021–2022. MICS does not provide information on income or expenditure. The wealth index in the MICS datasets provides a crude measure of household living standards, particularly underlying long-term wealth. We also review the Global Multidimensional Poverty Index using MICS data for both periods calculated by UNDP and Oxford Poverty & Human Development Initiative (OPHI). Global MPI was previously calculated for Uzbekistan using MICS 2006 data.[2] It was also calculated using the most recent 2021–2022 MICS data for Uzbekistan (UNDP, 2023).

The *Multiple Indicator Cluster Survey for Uzbekistan* was collected in 2000, 2006 and 2021–2022. Data for 2006 were collected for 10,198 households, and data for 2021–2022 were collected for 10,879 households during the first round (2021) and for 4,180 households during the second round (November 2021–January 2022), in total of 15,059 households. Both datasets are representative at the national level. The sample selection methodology for both surveys was based on a stratified three-stage sample design (State Committee of the Republic of Uzbekistan on Statistics and UNICEF, 2022; UNICEF and State Statistical Committee of the Republic of Uzbekistan, 2007).

8.3 Wealth index as a substitute for income and consumption

The wealth index reported in the MICS is calculated through Principal Components Analysis (PCA), by using information on the ownership of consumer goods, dwelling characteristics, water and sanitation, and other characteristics that are related to the household's wealth, to generate weights (factor scores) for each of the items used. Although the assets used in the calculation of the wealth index follow a similar methodology, they are not identical in both periods.[3] The index is divided into five equal parts (quintiles) from lowest (poorest) to highest (richest).

Wealth indices are generally viewed as a measure of long-term wealth or socio-economic status (Poirier, Grépin, and Grignon, 2020), because household assets on which wealth indices are based are accumulated gradually over time. Shifts in income or consumption patterns do not affect wealth indicators immediately. The wealth index is far more stable than income and consumption over time which gives it an advantage over expenditures as a measure of household wellbeing. However, wealth indices can not fully identify improvements (or declines) in household living standards over the short and medium term (Poirier, Grépin, and Grignon, 2020).

Poirier, Grépin, and Grignon (2020) conducted a systematic review of previously published papers on the correlation between wealth indices and household consumption or income. The previously published papers in their study used data from household surveys for low- and middle-income countries collected between 1988 and 2008. Their aggregation of all published associations of wealth indices with consumption or income indicates a

Spearman rank correlation wealth indices of 0.55 for consumption and 0.42 for income (Poirier, Grépin, and Grignon, 2020).

We classify households in the MICS into two categories based on the wealth index: *wealthy* and *not wealthy.* Households in the richest and fourth quantile categories from the wealth index are the *wealthy*, while households in the lower three quantiles are the *not wealthy.* We use the constructed binary wealth index as the dependent variable in our multivariate analysis. We control for a set of demographic variables of the household head and household-level characteristics to explain living standards; our model is similar to models found in previous studies (Shaukat, Javed, and Imran, 2020; Gondwe et al., 2021).

Characteristics of the household head include education, age, gender, and mother tongue. We also control for the number of people in the household by age and household size and for the location of a household. Table 8.2 below provides summary statistics of the variables of interest for both periods of data. The table shows very similar wealth distributions in both periods of interest. Almost half of the households are *wealthy:* 46 percent in 2006 and 43 percent in 2021–2022. However, these numbers should be interpreted with caution, since the assets used in the calculations of the wealth index naturally evolve over time. For example, mobile phones or computer technologies that are widely available today in the market were limited in the early 2000s.

There are also no changes over time in education, which could be explained by increases in education coverage parallel to the increasing population in the 2000s and early 2010s. Family sizes decreased, although not by a large amount. There are more elderly people in the households in 2021–2022 than in 2006, and most of the household heads are above age 50. There are 6 percent more female household heads in 2021–2022 compared to 2006. Most of the households (62 percent) lived in rural areas in 2006. In 2021–2022, about half of the population lived in rural areas in 2021–2022, a significant change in household location. There are more Uzbek language speakers (as the first language) in Uzbekistan in 2021–2022 compared to 2006.

We compare the wealthy and less wealthy groups of households in 2006 and 2021–2022, these comparisons are given in Table 8.3. Household heads with higher education on average come from wealthier households compared to the household heads with secondary and secondary special education for both periods. In 2006, most of the household heads had secondary special education and came from not wealthy households. In 2021–2022, most of the household heads have completed secondary education and come from not wealthy families.

Wealthier families on average have fewer children and working-age adults in both periods, while the number of elderly people is higher in wealthy families. Most of the wealthy households have family sizes from one to four people in both periods. The differences in family size by living standards were

Table 8.2 Summary Statistics: Full Samples for 2006 and 2021–2022

	MICS 2006					*MICS 2021–2022*				
Variables	*N*	*Mean*	*SD*	*Min*	*Max*	*N*	*Mean*	*SD*	*Min*	*Max*
Household wealth index (1 = Richest, Fourth quantile; 0 = Middle, Second, Poorest quantile) (1 = Wealthy; 0 = Not wealthy)	8,473	0.46	0.50	0	1	14,986	0.43	0.50	0	1
HH head has secondary education (1 = yes; 0 = otherwise)	8,473	0.33	0.47	0	1	14,986	0.37	0.48	0	1
HH head has secondary special education (1 = yes; 0 = otherwise)	8,473	0.45	0.50	0	1	14,986	0.44	0.50	0	1
HH head has higher education (1 = yes; 0 = otherwise)	8,473	0.22	0.42	0	1	14,986	0.20	0.40	0	1
Number of children (aged 0–15)	8,473	1.79	1.36	0	9	14,986	1.55	1.32	0	12
Number of working-age adults (aged 16–60)	8,473	3.20	1.71	0	13	14,986	2.85	1.44	0	11
Number of elderly (aged 60 and more)	8,473	0.23	0.53	0	3	14,986	0.39	0.67	0	3
Household has 1–4 people (1 = yes; 0 = no)	8,473	0.38	0.48	0	1	14,986	0.46	0.50	0	1
Household has 5–6 people (1 = yes; 0 = no)	8,473	0.40	0.49	0	1	14,986	0.37	0.48	0	1
Household has 7–8 people (1 = yes; 0 = no)	8,473	0.15	0.36	0	1	14,986	0.12	0.33	0	1
Household has 9 or more people (1 = yes; 0 = no)	8,473	0.07	0.26	0	1	14,986	0.05	0.22	0	1
HH head is less than age 40 (1 = yes; 0 = no)	8,473	0.33	0.47	0	1	14,986	0.20	0.40	0	1

	MICS 2006					*MICS 2021–2022*				
Variables	*N*	*Mean*	*SD*	*Min*	*Max*	*N*	*Mean*	*SD*	*Min*	*Max*
is aged 40–49 (1 = yes; 0 = no)	8,473	0.32	0.47	0	1	14,986	0.25	0.43	0	1
is aged 50–59 (1 = yes; 0 = no)	8,473	0.21	0.41	0	1	14,986	0.27	0.44	0	1
is aged 60 or older (1 = yes; 0 = no)	8,473	0.14	0.35	0	1	14,986	0.27	0.45	0	1
Gender of HH head (1 = male; 0 = female)	8,473	0.86	0.35	0	1	14,986	0.80	0.40	0	1
Location area of HH (1 = urban; 0 = rural)	8,473	0.38	0.49	0	1	14,986	0.50	0.50	0	1

Source: Authors' calculations.

Notes:
Mean values are the weighted averages.
N is the sample size.
SD is the standard deviation.

higher in 2006. This change in the age structure of households is consistent with the large outmigration of younger workers in the household.

There are more female-headed households in 2021–2022 than in 2006 in both the wealthy and less wealthy groups, but the largest increase in female household heads is among the less wealthy. Women headed 25 percent of wealthy families and 15 percent of not wealthy families in 2021–2022. In 2006 in comparison, 22 percent of wealthy households and 8 percent of non-wealthy households were headed by women. This large change in headship is also consistent with the large outmigration of male workers from the household.

We notice big disparities in living standards between urban and rural areas. Sixty-eight percent of wealthy households were based in urban areas in 2006, while only 13 percent of not wealthy families were in rural areas. In 2021–2022, 76 percent of wealthy households are from urban areas, and 30 percent of not wealthy families live in urban areas. We also notice that wealthy and non-wealthy households are more likely to report that Uzbek is their first language at home in both years; the use of the Uzbek language changed more among wealthy households over time. The primary non-Uzbek language is Russian.

8.4 Multivariate analysis – determinants of wealth

We estimate a probit model of household wealth with a set of demographic and household characteristics to explain the wealth level of households. The results of the probit models' marginal effects are presented in Table 8.4. The results show that higher education is positively and significantly associated with wealth and that the probability of being in a wealthy household is higher if the household head has higher education. Household heads with higher education are 13 percentage points and 22 percentage points more likely to live in a wealthy household in 2006 and 2021–2022. We find that household heads with secondary special education levels are 7 percentage points less likely to come from a wealthy household compared to their counterparts with secondary education in 2006.

Households having heads aged more than 40 are more likely to be wealthy (ranging from 3.9 percentage points to 11 percentage points higher probability) as compared to household heads aged less than 40 in 2006. This is not the case for 2021–2022. Higher age household heads in 2021–2022, are on average 2 percentage points less likely to be in a wealthy household.

Male household heads are less likely to live in a wealthy household (around 7 percentage points less). The results are similar in the two periods. This could be explained by the positive association between women empowerment and household wealth (Ali Khan, Khan and Bibi, 2018; Voronca, Walker and Egede, 2018); however further research on this topic is required to understand this question better.

Households situated in urban areas are more likely to have higher wealth in both years. There is a considerable difference in wealth between Tashkent

Table 8.3 Summary Statistics: Full Samples for 2006 and 2021–2022, by Wealth Index

	MICS 2006						*MICS 2021–2022*					
	Wealthy			*Not wealthy*			*Wealthy*			*Not wealthy*		
Variables	*N*	*Mean*	*SD*	*N*	*Mean*	*SD*	*N*	*Mean*	*SD*	*N*	*Mean*	*SD*
HH head has secondary education (1 = yes; 0 = otherwise)	4,718	0.34	0.47	3,755	0.32	0.47	6,928	0.26	0.44	8,058	0.44	0.50
HH head has secondary special education (1 = yes; 0 = otherwise)	4,718	0.33	0.47	3,755	0.55	0.50	6,928	0.44	0.50	8,058	0.44	0.50
HH head has higher education (1 = yes; 0 = otherwise)	4,718	0.34	0.47	3,755	0.12	0.33	6,928	0.30	0.46	8,058	0.12	0.33
Number of children (aged 0–15)	4,718	1.46	1.31	3,755	2.08	1.35	6,928	1.37	1.30	8,058	1.69	1.32
Number of working-age adults (aged 16–60)	4,718	2.98	1.67	3,755	3.38	1.73	6,928	2.66	1.49	8,058	3.00	1.38
Number of elderly (aged 60 and more)	4,718	0.26	0.56	3,755	0.21	0.50	6,928	0.40	0.66	8,058	0.38	0.67

	MICS 2006						*MICS 2021–2022*					
	Wealthy			*Not wealthy*			*Wealthy*			*Not wealthy*		
Variables	*N*	*Mean*	*SD*	*N*	*Mean*	*SD*	*N*	*Mean*	*SD*	*N*	*Mean*	*SD*
Household has 1–4 people (1 = yes; 0 = no)	4,718	0.49	0.50	3,755	0.28	0.45	6,928	0.54	0.50	8,058	0.40	0.49
Household has 5–6 people (1 = yes; 0 = no)	4,718	0.34	0.47	3,755	0.45	0.50	6,928	0.32	0.47	8,058	0.41	0.49
Household has 7–8 people (1 = yes; 0 = no)	4,718	0.11	0.32	3,755	0.18	0.38	6,928	0.10	0.30	8,058	0.13	0.34
Household has 9 or more people (1 = yes; 0 = no)	4,718	0.06	0.23	3,755	0.09	0.28	6,928	0.04	0.20	8,058	0.05	0.23
HH head is less than age 40 (1 = yes; 0 = no)	4,718	0.28	0.45	3,755	0.37	0.48	6,928	0.22	0.41	8,058	0.19	0.39
is aged 40–49 (1 = yes; 0 = no)	4,718	0.30	0.46	3,755	0.34	0.47	6,928	0.22	0.42	8,058	0.27	0.44
is aged 50–59 (1 = yes; 0 = no)	4,718	0.24	0.43	3,755	0.18	0.39	6,928	0.27	0.44	8,058	0.27	0.44
is aged 60 or older (1 = yes; 0 = no)	4,718	0.17	0.38	3,755	0.11	0.31	6,928	0.29	0.45	8,058	0.26	0.44

	MICS 2006						MICS 2021–2022					
	Wealthy			*Not wealthy*			*Wealthy*			*Not wealthy*		
Variables	*N*	*Mean*	*SD*	*N*	*Mean*	*SD*	*N*	*Mean*	*SD*	*N*	*Mean*	*SD*
Gender of HH head (1 = male; 0 = female)	4,718	0.78	0.41	3,755	0.92	0.27	6,928	0.75	0.44	8,058	0.85	0.36
Location area of HH (1 = urban; 0 = rural)	4,718	0.68	0.47	3,755	0.13	0.33	6,928	0.76	0.43	8,058	0.30	0.46

Source: Authors' calculations.

Notes:
Mean values are the weighted averages.
N is the sample size.
SD is the standard deviation.

Table 8.4 Results of Multivariate Analysis (Coefficients are the Marginal Effects for Probit Model), Dependent Variable is the Binary Wealth Index

		MICS 2006		*MICS 2021–2022*	
		(1)	*(2)*	*(1)*	*(2)*
Education of HH head *(Ref.: secondary)*	Secondary special	–0.072***	–0.072***	0.090***	0.091***
		(0.009)	(0.009)	(0.008)	(0.008)
	Higher	0.136***	0.136***	0.224***	0.227***
		(0.011)	(0.011)	(0.009)	(0.009)
Age of HH head *(Ref.: Less than 40)*	40–49	0.039***	0.061***	–0.039***	–0.018*
		(0.011)	(0.010)	(0.011)	(0.010)
	50–59	0.076***	0.103***	–0.018	0.008
		(0.014)	(0.012)	(0.012)	(0.010)
	60 and more	0.080***	0.110***	–0.028*	0.014
		(0.020)	(0.013)	(0.015)	(0.010)
HH head is male		–0.079***	–0.075***	–0.068***	–0.061***
		(0.012)	(0.012)	(0.009)	(0.009)
Household is located in urban area		0.392***	0.393***	0.365***	0.366***
		(0.005)	(0.005)	(0.004)	(0.004)
Number of children		–0.023***		–0.024***	
		(0.003)		(0.002)	
Number of working-age adults		–0.004		0.000	
		(0.002)		(0.003)	

		MICS 2006		*MICS 2021–2022*	
		(1)	*(2)*	*(1)*	*(2)*
Number of elderly		0.001		0.018**	
		(0.012)		(0.009)	
Household size (*Ref.: 1–4 people*)	5–6 people		–0.049***		–0.046***
			(0.00999)		(0.007)
	7–8 people		–0.080***		–0.028**
			(0.013)		(0.011)
	9 and more people		–0.064***		–0.059***
			(0.016)		(0.017)
	Pseudo R2 (Probit regression)	0.327	0.326	0.217	0.215
	Observations	8,473	8,473	14,986	14,986

Standard errors in parentheses

*** $p < 0.01$, ** $p < 0.05$, * $p < 0.1$

Source: Authors' calculations.

Note:
Ref. is the reference variable.

Table 8.5 Mean values of binary wealth index by rural, urban and Tashkent, MICS 2021–2022

	Mean of wealth	*SD*	*N*
Rural	0.21	0.41	7,125
Urban	0.58	0.49	6,350
Tashkent	1.00	0.03	1,511
Total	0.43		14,986

Source: Authors' calculations.

Notes:
Mean values are the weighted averages.
N is the sample size.
SD is the standard deviation.

(the capital of Uzbekistan) and other urban areas (regional centers). As shown in Table 8.5, all respondent households from Tashkent city have high wealth status (fifth and fourth quantiles).

We run the regressions for two models, first controlling for number of children, working-age adults and elderly, and second controlling for household size groups. For both periods, a higher number of children in the household is associated with less wealth. Similarly, the higher number of people in the household is associated with lower wealth status.

8.5 Global Multidimensional Poverty Index

As an alternative measure of living standards which could be developed using the available MICS data, we review the Global Multidimensional Poverty Index. MPI is a "*measure of acute poverty, understood as a person's inability to meet minimum international standards in indicators related to the Millennium Development Goals and to core functionings*" (Alkire and Santos, 2014, p. 251). MPI has proven to be a reliable framework for studying poverty and can complement traditional global income headcount poverty estimates.

MPI is based on ten indicators in three dimensions – *health, education* and *standard of living* (United Nations Development Programme and Oxford Poverty and Human Development Initiative, 2022). It follows the same dimensions and weights as the Human Development Index. MPI values are the product of the incidence of poverty and the intensity of poverty. The MPI ranges from 0 to 1. Higher values of the MPI imply higher poverty. Table 8.6 shows the methodological structure of the MPI.

Table 8.7 below shows estimates of the global MPI for Uzbekistan for 2006 and 2021–2022 by UNDP and Oxford Poverty & Human Development Initiative (OPHI, 2023). We have also provided comparison data for Kazakhstan, Kyrgyzstan, Tajikistan, and Turkmenistan for several years in order to better understand regional trends in poverty and wellbeing.

Table 8.6 Structure of the Multidimensional Poverty Index

Dimension	*Indicator*	*Weight*
Health	Nutrition	1/6
	Child mortality	1/6
Education	Years of schooling	1/6
	School attendance	1/6
Standard of living	Cooking fuel	1/18
	Sanitation	1/18
	Drinking water	1/18
	Electricity	1/18
	Housing	1/18
	Assets	1/18

Source: United Nations Development Programme and Oxford Poverty and Human Development Initiative, 2022.

Based on the numbers, in 2006, 4.38 percent of the population in Uzbekistan (1.2 million people in 2006) were multidimensionally poor. The intensity of deprivation in Uzbekistan in 2006, which is the average deprivation score among people living in multidimensional poverty, was 37.25 percent. The MPI value, which is the share of the population that is multidimensionally poor adjusted by the intensity of the deprivations, was 0.016[4].

The global MPI for Uzbekistan was recently calculated using 2021–2022 MICS data for Uzbekistan. Based on the estimates of OPHI, in 2021–2022, 1.73 percent of the population in Uzbekistan (610,194 people in 2022) are multidimensionally poor while an additional 0.24 percent are classified as vulnerable to multidimensional poverty (84,651 people in 2022). The intensity of deprivations in Uzbekistan in 2021–2022 is 35.29 percent. The MPI value is 0.006. In comparison, to the calculations in the neighboring countries using the most recent available data, MPI is equal to 0.002 in Kazakhstan (Data source: MICS, 2015), 0.001 in Kyrgyzstan (Data source: MICS, 2018), 0.029 in Tajikistan (Data source: DHS, 2017), and 0.001 in Turkmenistan (Data source: MICS, 2019).

We also report the incidence of deprivation in each of the MPI indicators for both 2006 and 2021–2022 data. We report the proportion of the population that is poor and deprived on each indicator. We do not include the deprivation of non-poor people. The highest incidence of deprivation in 2006 was for nutrition (3.29 percent) and child mortality (3.34 percent), followed by access to drinking water (1.61 percent) and cooking fuel (1.79 percent).

In 2021–2022, the calculated global MPI does not report incidence of deprivation for nutrition. However, the Central Asian region, along with Eastern Asia, experienced significant progress in stunting reduction and is expected to exceed the 2030 target if the current trends continue (WHO, 2023). Incidence of deprivation for school attendance and electricity are

Table 8.7 (Part 1) Global Multidimensional Poverty Index for Uzbekistan, 2006 and 2021–2022

Country	*MPI data source*		*Multidimensional poverty*		
	Survey	*Year*	*Multidimensional Poverty Index (MPI = H*A)*	*Headcount ratio: Population in multidimensional poverty (H)*	*Intensity of deprivation a mong the poor (A)*
			Range 0 to 1	*% Population*	*Average % of deprivations*
1. Uzbekistan*	MICS	2006	0.016	4.38	37.25
2. Uzbekistan*	MICS	2021–2022	0.006	1.73	35.29
3. Kazakhstan*	MICS	2006	0.002	0.60	36.90
4. Kazakhstan*	MICS	2015	0.002	0.45	35.56
5. Turkmenistan*	MICS	2006	0.025	6.65	37.35
6. Turkmenistan*	MICS	2019	0.001	0.25	34.05
7. Tajikistan*	MICS	2005	0.068	17.10	40.00
8. Tajikistan*	DHS	2017	0.029	7.44	38.96
9. Kyrgyzstan*	MICS	2005–2006	0.019	4.90	38.80
10. Kyrgyzstan*	MICS	2018	0.001	0.39	36.28

Source of the data of existing calculations (OPHI, 2023).

*Calculations from OPHI.

Table 8.7 (Part 2 continued) Global Multidimensional Poverty Index for Uzbekistan, 2006 and 2021–2022

Percentage of people who are poor and deprived in...										Indicators included in the MPI
Health		*Education*		*Living Standards*						*Total number of indicators included (out of ten)*
Nutrition	*Child Mortality*	*Years of Schooling*	*School Attendance*	*Cooking Fuel*	*Sanitation*	*Drinking Water*	*Electricity*	*Housing*	*Assets*	
% Population	*% Population*	*% Population*	*% Population*	*% Population*	*% Population*	*% Population*	*% Population*	*% Population*	*% Population*	
1. 3.29	3.34	0.00	1.16	1.79	0.15	1.61	0.09	1.15	1.17	10
2.	1.73	0.00	0.00	0.06	0.12	0.12	0.00	0.27	0.04	9
3. 0.20	0.50	0.00	0.20	0.50	0.10	0.30	0.00	0.00	0.30	10
4. 0.45	0.42	0.00	0.03	0.03	0.00	0.06	0.00			
5. 1.87	4.94	0.54	5.38	0.30	0.44	3.75	0.03	1.05	1.01	10
6. 0.24	0.18	0.00	0.08		0.00	0.00	0.00	0.03	0.00	9
7. 6.30	12.20	0.10	7.60	10.10	3.40	10.50	0.30	12.00	8.40	10
8. 6.22	2.09	0.12	4.48	3.46	0.32	3.59	0.10	5.68	0.31	10
9. 2.10		1.40	2.80	2.80	1.00	1.60	0.00	1.20	2.40	9
10. 0.39	0.16	0.04	0.11	0.26	0.05	0.10	0.00	0.04	0.00	10

Source of the data of existing calculations (OPHI, 2023).

*Calculations from OPHI.

equal to 0. Incidence of deprivation for other indicators declined considerably since 2006, but a small share of the population is poor including from deprivation associated with cooking fuel (0.06 percent), sanitation (0.12 percent), drinking water (0.12 percent), housing (0.27 percent) and assets (0.04 percent). Incidence of deprivation for child mortality declined since 2006 but remains high (1.73 percent) compared to other indicators. Similar declines over time in the MPI are observed in other Central Asian countries.

8.6 Discussion

The policy changes in Uzbekistan from a centrally planned economy in the early 1990s provided solid economic foundations for growth. Most of the growth was generated through increases in capital stock and the value of natural resource exports. Significant and fast-moving reform programs since 2016 focused more on market reforms supporting regional and global economic integration, diversification of industries and agriculture, institutional reforms, and expansion of social protection.

In this chapter we discuss our household-level analysis and review of wealth and poverty. The availability of MICS data for two points in time over a 15-year period (2006 and 2021–2022) enables us to evaluate these two dimensions of living standards descriptively and to isolate some of the more important determinants and dimensions of wellbeing and poverty.

In 2006, 4.38 percent of the population or 1.2 million people in Uzbekistan were multidimensionally poor. Today, based on the data for 2021–2022, 1.73 percent of the population or 610,194 people in Uzbekistan are considered multidimensionally poor. 0.24 percent of the population or 84,651 people in 2022 are classified as vulnerable to multidimensional poverty. The highest incidence of deprivation of poor population in 2021-2022 was for child mortality.

We find that higher education plays a crucial role in living standards. Our multivariate results suggest that wealth improves with higher education. We do not examine the labor market in this chapter, but higher education is likely associated with better jobs and higher income which is why durable expenditures increase with advanced schooling. Since 2006, household size structure has changed moderately to lower family sizes, which is positively associated with accumulated wealth. We also find a negative association between the number of children in the household and the wealth index. Migration to urban from rural areas could be an explanation for these changes in the demographic structure of the household and the relationship between these traits and our measure of wealth. Migration provides some household members with better jobs and income, and the household is better able to afford to own a home and purchase durable goods. Living in Tashkent and other cities is strongly linked to the ownership of durable wealth. Our findings confirm this for both periods.

The Government of Uzbekistan initiated multidimensional poverty measurement activities in 2021 (UzDaily, 2021). During the II International

Forum on Poverty Reduction organized by the Center for Economic Research and Reforms of Uzbekistan in May 2023 the agenda of the assessment of multidimensional poverty has been set as the priority development areas of Uzbekistan to reduce country-specific poverty (Review.uz, 2023). The reviewed global MPI in this study is an important contribution to the analysis of ongoing policies. To better evaluate how household wellbeing is changing over time, surveys that document income and expenditures are needed. Our measure of wellbeing captures only one component of the standard of living: durable consumption.

Notes

1 Commodity dependence is the share of exports that come from the commodity. In this case, it is the share of total exports from primary products.
2 https://ophi.org.uk/multidimensional-poverty-index/data-tables-do-files/
3 Please refer to the Multiple Indicator Cluster Survey 2006 and the 2021–2022 Multiple Indicator Cluster Survey in Uzbekistan Survey Findings Reports to review the assets used in the calculations of the wealth index. The surveys data and reports are available at https://mics.unicef.org/surveys.
4 We have also calculated (replicated) global MPI for Uzbekistan using 2006 MICS data. Our calculated indicator is equal to 0.017. The calculations are available upon request. Results for the 2021-2022 global MPI for Uzbekistan could be replicated using the do-file available at https://ophi.org.uk/multidimensional-poverty-index/data-tables-do-files/.

References

Ali Khan, R.E., Khan, T. and Bibi, S. (2018) Women Empowerment and Household Wealth: Implication for Child Health-Care, *Pakistan Journal of Applied Economics*, pp. 273–289.

Alkire, S. and Santos, M.E. (2014) Measuring Acute Poverty in the Developing World: Robustness and Scope of the Multidimensional Poverty Index, *World Development*, 59, pp. 251–274. Available at: https://doi.org/10.1016/j.worlddev.2014.01.026.

Dugarova, E. (2019) Poverty Reduction through Social Protection and Labor Policies in the Former Soviet Union, in *Social Policy, Poverty, and Inequality in Central and Eastern Europe and the Former Soviet Union*. Taylor & Francis, p. 45.

Francois, J.N.et al. (2022) Remittances Increase GDP with Potential Differential Impacts Across Countries. *World Bank Blogs*. Available at: https://blogs.worldbank.org/peoplemove/remittances-increase-gdp-potential-differential-impacts-across-countries.

Gondwe, K.W.*et al.* (2021) Predictors of Wealth Index in Malawi – Analysis of Malawi demographic Health Survey 2004–2015/16, *Public Health in Practice*, 2, p. 100059. Available at: https://doi.org/10.1016/j.puhip.2020.100059.

Honorati, M. and Marguerie, A. (2021) *Youth Employment in Uzbekistan: Opportunities and Challenges*. World Bank Group. Available at: https://documents.worldbank.org/pt/publication/documents-reports/documentdetail/666311634704762319/youth-employment-in-uzbekistan-opportunities-and-challenges.

ILO (2020) Women and the World of Work in Uzbekistan. Towards Gender Equality and Decent Work for All. Available at: www.ilo.org/moscow/information-resources/publications/WCMS_776476/lang–en/index.htm.

ILO (2021) Towards Full and Productive Employment in Uzbekistan: Achievements and Challenges. Available at: www.ilo.org/moscow/information-resources/publications/WCMS_782059/lang–en/index.htm.

ILO, UNICEF, and World Bank (2020) An assessment of the social protection system in Uzbekistan Based on the Core Diagnostic instrument (CODI). Available at: www.ilo.org/moscow/information-resources/publications/WCMS_760153/lang–en/index.htm.

International Organization for Migration (2022) World Migration Report 2022. Available at: https://publications.iom.int/books/world-migration-report-2022.

Izvorski, I.*et al.* (2021) *Assessing Uzbekistan's Transition. Country Economic Memorandum*. World Bank Group. Available at: https://documents.worldbank.org/en/publication/documents-reports/documentdetail/568911637235838877/overview.

Kakhkharov, J.*et al.* (2020) South-South Migration: Remittances of Labour Migrants and Household Expenditures in Uzbekistan, *International Migration* [Preprint]. Available at: https://doi.org/10.1111/imig.12792.

OPHI. (2023). Global MPI Data Tables 2023. Available at: https://ophi.org.uk/multidimensional-poverty-index/data-tables-do-files/.

Poghosyan, T. (2020) Remittances in Russia and Caucasus and Central Asia: The Gravity Model. *IMF Working Paper. Available at:* www.imf.org/en/Publications/WP/Issues/2020/07/17/Remittances-in-Russia-and-Caucasus-and-Central-Asia-the-Gravity-Model-49551.

Poirier, M.J.P., Grépin, K.A., and Grignon, M. (2020) Approaches and Alternatives to the Wealth Index to Measure Socioeconomic Status Using Survey Data: A Critical Interpretive Synthesis, *Social Indicators Research*, 148 (1), pp. 1–46. Available at: https://doi.org/10.1007/s11205-019-02187-9.

Pomfret, R. (2021) Central Asian Economies: Thirty Years After Dissolution of the Soviet Union, *Comparative Economic Studies*, 63 (4), pp. 537–556. Available at: https://doi.org/10.1057/s41294-021-00166-z.

Review.uz. (2023) Assessment of Multidimensional Poverty in Uzbekistan, *Review.uz*. Available at: https://review.uz/en/post/ocenka-mnogomernoy-bednosti-v-uzbekistane (Accessed: June 4, 2023).

State Committee of the Republic of Uzbekistan on Statistics, and UNICEF. (2022). 2021–2022 Uzbekistan Multiple Indicator Cluster Survey, Survey Findings Report. Available at: https://microdata.worldbank.org/index.php/catalog/5961.

Shagazatova, M.et al. (2020) Unlocking the Potential for Labor Productivity Growth, in *Uzbekistan: Quality Job Creation as a Cornerstone for Sustainable Economic Growth*. Asian Development Bank.

Shaukat, B., Javed, S.A. and Imran, W. (2020) Wealth Index as Substitute to Income and Consumption: Assessment of Household Poverty Determinants Using Demographic and Health Survey Data, *Journal of Poverty*, 24 (1), pp. 24–44. Available at: https://doi.org/10.1080/10875549.2019.1678550.

UNCTAD (2021) The State of Commodity Dependence 2021. Available at: https://unctad.org/publication/state-commodity-dependence-2021.

UNDP (2023). 2023 Global Multidimensional Poverty Index (MPI): Unstacking Global Poverty: Data for High Impact Action. Available at: https://hdr.undp.org/content/2023-global-multidimensional-poverty-index-mpi#/indicies/MPI.

UNICEF (2018) Generation 2030 Uzbekistan Investing in Children and Young People to Reap the Demographic Dividend. Available at: www.unicef.org/uzbekistan/en/reports/generation-2030-uzbekistan.

UNICEF and State Statistical Committee of the Republic of Uzbekistan. (2007). Uzbekistan Multiple Indicator Cluster Survey 2006, Final Report.

United Nations Development Programme and Oxford Poverty and Human Development Initiative (2022) 2022 Global Multidimensional Poverty Index (MPI). Available at: https://hdr.undp.org/content/2022-global-multidimensional-poverty-index-mpi#/indicies/MPI (Accessed: June 4, 2023).

UzDaily (2021) "Multidimensional Poverty" To Be Measured in Uzbekistan, *UzDaily*. Available at: www.uzdaily.uz/en/post/70071 (Accessed: June 4, 2023).

Voronca, D., Walker, R.J., and Egede, L.E. (2018) Relationship Between Empowerment and Wealth: Trends and Predictors in Kenya between 2003 and 2008–2009, *International Journal of Public Health*, 63 (5), pp. 641–649. Available at: https://doi.org/10.1007/s00038-017-1059-1.

WHO (2023) Levels and Trends in Child Malnutrition: UNICEF/WHO/World Bank Group Joint Child Malnutrition Estimates: Key Findings of the 2023 Edition. Available at: www.who.int/publications/i/item/9789240073791 (Accessed: June 4, 2023).

9 Institutions, gender, governance

Randall K. Filer, Nargiza Alimukhamedova and Ahliddin Malikov

9.1 Introduction

Uzbekistan is aiming to build a "New Uzbekistan" and has set ambitious goals toward socio-economic development and reforms. The role of institutions and governance is pivotal in these reforms, both in framing how they can be achieved and determining their ultimate success. Institutions are the basis on which reform may survive and grow or fail. As the founder of the Institutional School of Economics, Wesley Clair Mitchell put it: "Institutions" is merely a convenient term for the more important among the widely prevalent, standardized social habits (Mitchell, 1924). In this chapter, we focus on two subtypes of institutions. First, we review how formal institutions (such as the law or property rights) that are subject to a high degree of government influence have evolved in Uzbekistan in association with socio-economic transformations and different leadership styles. Second, we turn to more organic institutions that arise from among the population, primarily the family (encompassing areas such as marriage, gender roles, and child-bearing) religious communities, community organizations and NGOs, and the media. Throughout we try to hold in mind the insight of Powell and DiMaggio (1991) that institutions reflect both human design and evolution from a given historical and cultural context.

Obviously, institutions of this type existed during Soviet times. Some of these were harmful while others were merely seriously constrained. More than 30 years after the fall of the Berlin Wall and the breakup of the Soviet Union, economies in transition remain just that, in transition. We have attempted to portray institutions in Uzbekistan as accurately as possible at the time of writing this chapter in early 2023, but caution the reader that both formal and informal institutions, while influenced by their past, may well have evolved for better or worse by the time a reader views this work. Many of the sources we cite as authoritative will have published new analyses by the time our work is in print or read and the reader is advised to consult these regularly for more recent updates. One excellent summary of both the successes and challenges yet to be faced in Uzbekistan's institutional reforms was provided by the World Bank in April 2022 in a document entitled

DOI: 10.4324/9781003473497-9

"Toward a Prosperous and Inclusive Future, Uzbekistan: The Second Systematic Country Diagnostic."[1] We will refer to this in-depth analysis multiple times, but readers are encouraged to read the full document (and any subsequent updates) for themselves.

Even after declaring independence in August 1991, there have been structural breaks in Uzbekistan's institutions. According to Ruziev (2021), when most of the former Soviet Union member countries followed the reform package recommended by international financial institutions (IFIs), such as the World Bank and International Monetary Fund known as the "Washington Consensus" after the shared location of these two organizations, Uzbekistan followed its own path focusing on a more gradual transition, social protection, avoiding shock therapies, and a cautiousness around individual freedoms and open markets.[2] Given that the IFIs conditioned the level of financial and resource aid for transition on the adoption of certain reforms, Uzbekistan, by ignoring the recommendations of the international community and implementing its own reform agenda, lost access to recovery funds from IFIs. Over time, the government of Uzbekistan followed more and more isolationist and protectionist policies with respect to international relations. Domestic policies increasingly moved toward authoritarianism and centralization of power under President I. Karimov (Akimov, 2015).

Both the rhetoric and actual focus of the reforms have placed more emphasis on liberal, Western-oriented institutions after 2016 when Shavkat Mirziyoev replaced Islam Karimov as President. A further wave of reforms, some more liberalizing and others more restrictive, has taken place in recent years under the rubric of building a "New Uzbekistan." This strategy proposed prioritizing five areas of socio-economic development of the country, including (i) improvements in the state system and public construction; (ii) rule of law and further reforms of the judicial system; (iii) economic development and liberalization; (iv) the development of the social sphere; and (v) security, ethnic harmony, religious tolerance, and implementation of constructive foreign policy. As the World Bank has observed, however, Uzbekistan's transformation "progressed slowly for the first 30 years. Few institutions have changed from those prevailing at the time of the planned economy. A high share of the economy is still managed by centralized state institutions" (World Bank, 2022, p. 6).

9.2 The importance of institutions for socio-economic development

Institutions play a crucial role in shaping the behavior of individuals and organizations, thus creating a sense of predictability and stability in society. Formal and informal institutions are both essential for the proper functioning of society, as they provide the legal and social framework for interactions between the members of society and players of the economy (Acemoglu, 2012; North, 1990). The quality of institutions is an important prerequisite for sustainable economic growth and development. According to Robinson et al. (2005), countries with stronger economic institutions, such as favorable business climate, effective rule of law, secure property rights, and supportive social norms, are doing well in attracting foreign direct investment, utilizing capital and natural resources more effectively, and are more active in trade. These factors lead to better economic growth in the long run. Lehne, Mo, and Plekhanov (2014) identify determinants of the quality of economic institutions including openness to trade, investment and financial flows, lower natural resource endowments, as well as the country's history and geography. Scholars differ, however, on the extent to which institutions are the result of conscious decisions versus evolving organically out of the particularities of a given historical and cultural context (see Friel, 2017 for a discussion).

9.3 Uzbekistan's comparative success in reforms

Many international organizations attempt to summarize and evaluate the relative position of economic conditions across the world. These analyses often differ, reflecting different priorities and data used. Uzbekistan is no different and, indeed, in a rapidly changing environment ratings may be more inconsistent than elsewhere.

According to the World Bank's Worldwide Governance Indicators, Uzbekistan has made solid improvements.[3] This Index rates all countries in the world in six areas. Relative ranks are given in percentiles ranging from 1 (worst in the world) to 100 (best in the world). Uzbekistan's ranking has improved, sometimes dramatically, between 1998 and 2021 in all six areas (Table 9.1).[4]

Other sources, however, indicate much less progress. On the widely used Freedom House evaluation of Political Rights and Civil Liberties in 2023, Uzbekistan had a score of 12 on a scale of zero to 100 leading to a rating of "Not Free." Only 21 countries ranked lower out of the 210 evaluated. The report concluded that

Table 9.1 World Governance Ranking (Higher is Better)

Area	*1998 Ranking*	*2021 Ranking*
Voice and Accountability	3rd (from bottom)	13th
Political Stability	23rd	39th
Government Effect	7th	44th
Regulatory Quality	3rd	31st
Rule of Law	11th	20th
Control of Corruption	11th	23rd

Source: Authors' development based on World Governance Indicators, 1998–2021.

while reforms adopted since President Shavkat Mirziyoyev took office in 2016 have led to improvement on some issues, Uzbekistan remains an authoritarian state with few signs of democratization. No opposition parties operate legally. The legislature and judiciary effectively serve as instruments of the executive branch, which initiates reforms by decree, and the media are still tightly controlled by the authorities.[5]

Uzbekistan's performance on the IMF's indices of financial market institutions barely improved between first being reported in 1993 and 2020. The Financial Institutions Index rose from 0.46 to 0.49 (on a scale of 0 to 1 where most EU countries score 0.90 or above). On the Financial Development Index, Uzbekistan's rating rose from 0.24 to 0.28, while the Financial Institutions Efficiency Index fell from 0.91 to 0.60.[6]

Unfortunately, the EBRD's indices are not consistent over time, but in the last version from 2021 Uzbekistan scored 4.7 for governance quality on a scale from 1 to 10, where 10 corresponded to the "standards of a sustainable market economy."[7] By way of comparison, this ranking was about the same as in Kosovo, Moldova, and Mongolia and well below that of Kazakhstan or Armenia. Indeed, the country lagged behind Kazakhstan and Mongolia in almost all areas, although it did rank better than other Central Asian counties in most areas.

The World Justice Project's Rule of Law Index measures the legal framework and quality of justice in countries, including civil justice and the effectiveness of criminal justice. Uzbekistan ranked 81st, well below the world's best (The Netherlands) when the index was first created in 2015, and barely changed to 78th position in 2022.[8] Among specific components, Uzbekistan did especially poorly in "Constraints on Government Power," ranking 114 out of 140 countries, just below Sudan, and "Fundamental Rights" in 107th

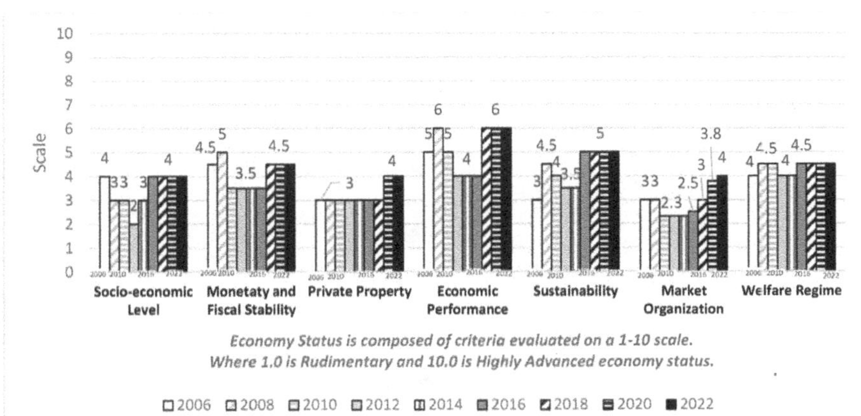

Figure 9.1 Economic status of Uzbekistan and its key components, 2006–2022
Source: Authors' development based on the data from Atlas BTI.

place. Not surprisingly, given much of what will be discussed below, Uzbekistan did particularly well on "Order and Security" ranking 16th among countries rated.

According to World Bank experts, Uzbekistan's economic reforms implemented between 2016 and 2021 have diversified the economy and increased the economic growth rate. These reforms have made Uzbekistan more attractive for foreign direct investments, creating a viable environment for entrepreneurship and private business. As a result, overall economic growth averaged 5.4% in 2016–2021, up from 4.8% in 2011–2015.[9]

The Bertelsmann Foundation in Germany has evaluated whether some 137 developing and transition countries are moving toward a strong social environment and a market economy. Sub-groups in each dimension are aggregated into four major categories. Figure 9.1 shows the extent to which the reforms initiated by the government of Uzbekistan during the period of 2006–2022 have improved specific areas of Uzbekistan's economy, although all still fall far below advanced economy scores of 10.0.[10]Figure 9.2 shows that, despite any reforms, Uzbekistan's economic structure still falls behind other countries in the region. This is not especially encouraging since the comparator group includes Belarus, Turkmenistan, and Tajikistan, which no one would hold up as paragons of reform.

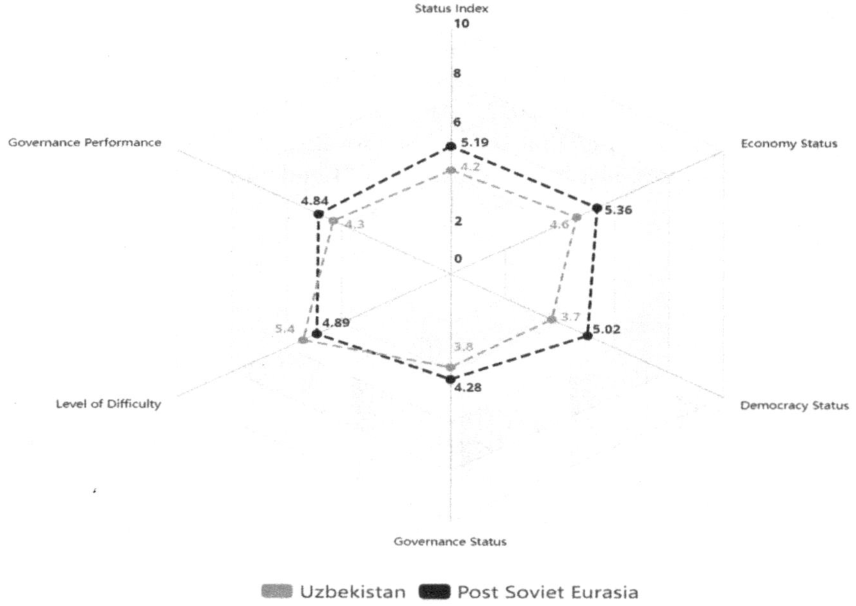

Figure 9.2 Ranking of Uzbekistan's economy, compared with regional peers, as of 2021

Source: Authors' development based on the data from Atlas BTI

9.3 Government and political institutions

Governance is defined as the processes of decision-making and the set of institutions and practices through which a common issue is decided upon and regulated. Good governance is the process whereby public institutions conduct public affairs, manage public resources, and guarantee the realization of human rights in a manner essentially free of abuse and corruption, and with due regard for the rule of law. According to the United Nations Office of the High Commissioner for Human Rights (OHCHR), key attributes of good governance include transparency, responsibility, accountability, participation, and responsiveness to the needs of the country's population. Governance and good governance best practices are fundamental for sustainable economic growth, political stability, and security in society.[11]

Uzbekistan has a presidential republic structure defined by a constitution.[12] The President of Uzbekistan is the head of the state, whereas the executive power is endorsed by the government led by the Prime Minister. The legislative power is nested in two chambers of the *Oliy Majlis*, the Senate, and the Legislative Chamber. The judicial power in the country is exercised by a supreme court, constitutional court, higher economic court, and various lower-level courts.

As in many areas, there is a stark difference between the narrow "form" of political institutions and the actual "reality" on the ground. This can be seen throughout the various reports of the OECD's Office for Democratic Institutions and Human Rights.[13] Examples of areas where Uzbekistan has room for improvement include:

- Fundamental human rights and freedoms are constitutionally guaranteed but continue to be restricted by subordinate legislation and not fully respected in practice.
- Recent reforms, although introducing welcome improvements, have not yet resulted in a genuinely pluralistic environment.
- Restrictions on fundamental freedoms and the right to stand for office continue to run counter to OSC commitments.
- The restrictive legal framework for media, cases of detention, intimidation, and harassment of journalists and bloggers … limited the scope of relevant political information available to the public.

For the three aspects of government other than economic reforms calculated by Bertlesmann, we report only the aggregate score, not the component subfactors. Over the period 2006 to 2021, Bertelsmann's evaluation shows both considerable progress and a long way yet to go in Uzbekistan's development. We examine three composite areas:

1 Democracy – Uzbekistan's score rose from 3.6 to 3.7 on a scale of 1 to 10, ranking it 102 out of 137 countries, placing it in the category "Hard Line Autocracy."
2 Governance – Here Uzbekistan performed better in absolute (but not relative) terms. Its score improved from 2.2 to 3.8, moving it from the category "Failed State" to "Weak State," although ranking 104 out of 137 countries.
3 Government Performance also improved in absolute terms, increasing from 2.4 to 4.3, moving from "Poor" to "Flawed." Although still ranked 102 out of 137, Uzbekistan showed the largest score improvement among post-Soviet countries.

9.4 Local governance

The mahalla is a traditional form of self-governance in Central Asia. The term "Mahalla" roughly translates to "neighborhood," and is the most pervasive traditional institution of local governance in Uzbekistan. It was formalized in the late 19th and early 20th centuries when mahalla councils were formed with representatives from ethnic, religious, and social collectives and made responsible for enforcing various local regulations. These were informal monthly gatherings of elders in a specific area where community members discussed local issues and problems, tried to peacefully resolve conflicts, and enforced local regulations. Given the absence of a formal legal or political system in Uzbekistan in the past, mahalla provided an opportunity for some citizen participation in governance and played a major role in the

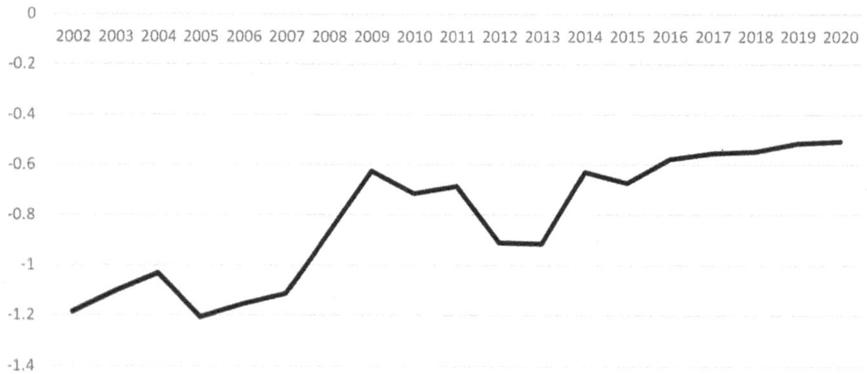

Figure 9.3 Aspects of government effectiveness in Uzbekistan, 2002–2020
Notes: This estimate reflects the evaluation of the quality of public service, the independence of services from political influence, the quality of policy implementation, and government commitment to chosen policy recommendations. Estimate gives the country's score on the aggregate indicator, in units of standard normal distribution, i. e., ranging from approximately –2.5 to 2.5.
Source: Authors using WGI data (Kaufmann, Kraay, & Mastruzzi, 2010).

maintenance of order and stability in the region. As such, the mahalla is deeply rooted in the social, political, and economic fabric of the country. Western readers might think of the traditional mahalla as a form of "homeowners' association." During Soviet times, the role of any self-governing institution was severely limited and mahallas became more of an organ of state policy, resembling the infamous juweihui (neighborhood committees) of communist China.

Post-independence, Uzbek mahallas have served in dual roles, both as an informal organization dealing with local concerns and as a representative agency enforcing the government's agenda. For a discussion of these conflicting roles, see Kandiyoti (2007), Dadabaev (2013), and, more recently Urinboyev and Eraliev (2022). Today, the mahalla system is formally recognized by the government of Uzbekistan as an officially sanctioned local governance institution. It is a part of the national civil society and is incorporated into the national legal framework, though it remains highly decentralized. Additionally, the government utilizes mahalla councils to enforce local regulations, coordinate sociocultural activities, solve intra- and intercommunity disputes, and provide a wide range of social services.

Although a formal leader (*rais*) is elected by the citizens' assembly (*fuqarolar yig'ini*) according to the Mahalla law, in reality there is a pre-determined outcome since the choice must be ratified by the local governor (Urinboyev & Eraliev, 2022). The *rais* is a state employee paid by the government. At the same time, there is a parallel leader, the *oqsoqol* (literally "white beard"), who works *pro bono* and represents the residents. Oqsoqols play a pivotal role in counseling, passing on values and traditions, and usually are recognized as wise persons from the community.

Central to Uzbekistan's budget reforms in 2021 and 2022 is the idea of public control and active public participation in budgeting. The reform has established new rules for how public spending is decided, giving citizens a direct role. It has also increased transparency in the budget process, allowing citizens to access up-to-date information on the budget. This is designed to reduce misappropriation, fraud, and embezzlement while increasing accountability.

This is intended to ensure that citizens' opinions and needs are considered, and a voice is given to traditionally marginalized groups, such as rural and impoverished people.[14]

The reforms are not without challenges. For example, some citizens are illiterate and do not understand the complexities of the budgeting process. Additionally, some may resist giving up power and control. Uzbekistan has, however, made strides in its budget reforms that could be a model for other countries looking to increase public participation in their budgeting process. Unfortunately, the World Bank reports that despite reforms, government institutions remain fragmented and the Mahalas often lack sufficient institutional knowledge, especially when confronted with civil defense issues (World Bank, 2022, pp. 82–83).

9.5 The rule of law

Citing the World Bank (2022, p. 10), "A competitive private sector needs the certainty that only the rule of law can provide … This means curtailing state discretion in favor of impartial, transparent, and rules-based governance." Economic actors (especially state-owned enterprises (SOEs)) should not be able to benefit from a targeted regulatory environment that creates an unbalanced and non-transparent playing field. Property rights must be protected by a fair legal system. A strong rule of law also ensures that individuals' rights are protected and that government actions are held accountable. Together these two institutions create a stable and predictable environment that encourages investment and economic growth (North, 1990).

Between 1991 to 2016, the Uzbek government's approach to property rights was often arbitrary and unpredictable, corruption was an obstacle to effective reforms and the government largely neglected the restitution of illegally seized assets. The judiciary was not independent. As a result, foreign investors and businesses often encounter difficulties in protecting their property rights in Uzbekistan (Ruziev, 2021; Abdullaev, 2020). In recent years, however, there have been significant efforts to improve the situation and Uzbekistan has seen a renewed commitment to the rule of law and property rights since 2016 (Ruziev, 2021).

The 1998 land code[15] was amended in 2022, paving the way toward a more transparent and predictable process of registering and transferring land in Uzbekistan. Uzbekistan has undertaken many other recent significant reforms to strengthen the rule of law and protect property rights. Five priority areas in the Strategy of the Development of Uzbekistan 2017–2021 included language designed to create a "judicial system based on human rights and the rule of law," indicating an intention of securing protection for citizens from arbitrary or unjustified interference by state agents and institutions, increasing public confidence in the state's legal systems, and providing better access to justice and expertise. Furthermore, the laws regarding human rights protection were amended to be more consistent with international treaties such as the European Convention on Human Rights (ECHR). Overall, five laws and more than 15 documents were adopted by the government thus developing "national mechanisms of securing property rights."[16]

With respect to the rule of law, Uzbekistan is still, however, lagging globally. According to the 2021 ranking of the Rule of Law Index from the Heritage Foundation, the country is ranked 108 out of 178 participant members.[17] In the World Justice Project's 2022 Rule of Law Index, Uzbekistan ranked 78 among 140 counties. Since this score was first calculated in 2015, Uzbekistan has increased its score on the scale from 46 to 50.[18] Not surprisingly, among the various components of this index, Uzbekistan scored by far the best on "Order and Security," where it ranked 16 out of 140 countries and lowest on "Constraints on Government Power" (114 out of 140), "Open Government" (122 out of 140) and "Fundamental Rights" (107 out of 140).

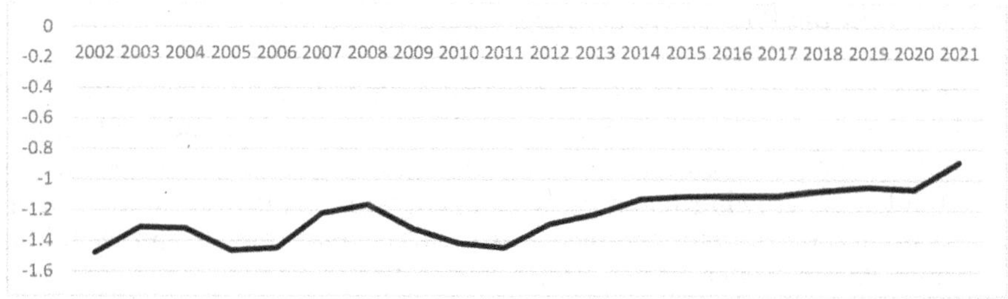

Figure 9.4 The rule of law in Uzbekistan, 2002–2021
Notes: The indicator captures the information about agents' trust in the rules of society and their ability to follow the contract's rules, property rights, police, and court recommendations. Estimate gives the country's score on the aggregate indicator, in units of standard normal distribution, i.e., ranging from approximately –2.5 to 2.5.
Source: Authors using WGI data (Kaufmann, Kraay, & Mastruzzi, 2010).

The World Bank (2022, p. 65) concluded that "the quality of the legal environment in business is behind peer group leaders." Reforms in the law have not yet been embedded in the consciousness of citizens, economic actors, and lower-level officials, resulting in only minor changes in the World Bank's Worldwide Governance Indicators.

9.6 Control of corruption

Uzbekistan has taken several steps to combat corruption in the public sector since 2017. New legislation was adopted to strengthen the legal framework regarding corruption. Independent bodies were set up to investigate bribery and fraudulent activities and ensure greater transparency and accountability of public policy in central and regional governments. The strategy was further reinforced by the law on the establishment of the State Anti-Corruption Agency which is specifically tasked with investigating and fighting corruption within the government (UNDP, 2020).

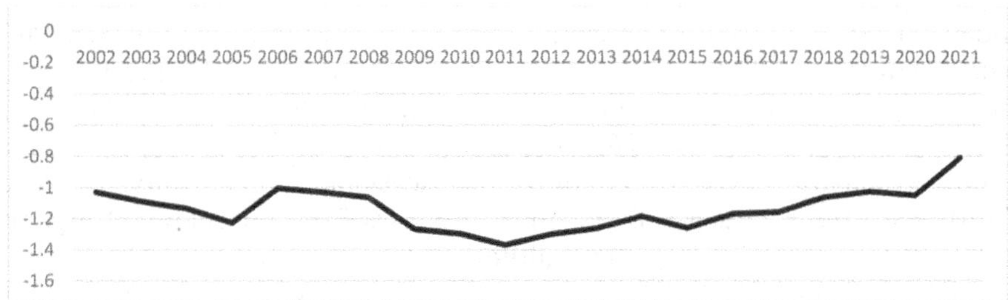

Figure 9.5 Control of corruption in Uzbekistan, 2002–2021
Notes: Estimate gives the country's score on the aggregate indicator, in units of standard normal distribution, i.e., ranging from approximately –2.5 to 2.5.
Source: Authors' development using WGI data (Kaufmann, Kraay & Mastruzzi, 2010).

The World Bank (2022, p. 79) reports that

> there was a strong consensus that corruption had declined in recent years but there was still a problem, especially in construction and land allocation … Private sector firms also commonly expressed strong concerns about their growing inability to compete with shadow economy operators who enjoyed close connections with law enforcement and were able to evade tax and customs payments.

9.7 Privatization

When the failed planned economies collapsed in the early 1990s, many naïve observers, both locally and internationally, assumed that "privatization" was the be-all and end-all of the "transition." While private ownership of the means of production is necessary for economic success, it is by no means sufficient. The success of a capitalist market as an institution depends on a complex, interlocking web of supporting sub-institutions. These include true independence, competition, openness, good corporate governance, and an open, consistent, and impartial legal system. Without all of these mutually reinforcing aspects, the institution of a market economy will fail to deliver its promise. Uzbekistan's efforts and successes have been mixed in each of these areas. As the World Bank (2022, p. 33) has noted

> Aside from a handful of oil-rich countries, the development trajectory of every high-income country in the world today has depended on the structural transformation process to reallocate land labor, and capital to the most productive uses. Markets are especially adept at efficiently supporting such continuous reallocations. In Uzbekistan, however, centralized decisions from the state, rather than market mechanisms, determine how these resources are allocated and used across sectors of the economy.

Uzbekistan, as with similar economies, started the transition with a highly state-centered economy. Privatization was slow during the first decades of independence but began to accelerate with the accession to the office of President Mirziyoyev. (Although this was slowed by the global pandemic and uncertainty introduced by the conflict in Ukraine.) On March 18, 2022, the President issued Decree PP-168 "On additional measures to further reduce state participation in the economy and accelerate privatization." These efforts have received generally positive responses from international organizations and market participants,[19] although the World Bank (2022, pp. 7–8) still observes that "Uzbekistan's areas of comparative advantage are dominated by state-owned enterprises that are shielded from private sector competition" and that "Uzbekistan's rate of new firm creation is among the lowest compared with regional and income-group peers."

In November of 2022, the IMF summarized the state of private sector development in a balanced manner, saying:

> Despite the headwinds, the authorities are continuing with market-oriented structural reforms, to enable a shift from public to stronger private sector-led growth. Building on the impressive progress already made in recent years, this will entail reducing the still large role of the state in the economy and further improving the business environment. Small and medium-sized enterprises – which will need to be the main source of new jobs for the rapidly growing labor force – will especially need to be able to grow and flourish. This will require:
>
> - **Continuing with the privatization of state-owned enterprises and state-owned banks.** The new privatization law will help to ensure that this will be done through transparent and competitive processes. Meanwhile, it is crucial to continue to improve corporate governance and transparency in state-owned enterprises and state-owned banks.
> - **Enhancing competition and creating a level playing field for businesses.** This requires further opening internal markets to entry by private firms and eliminating privileges for state-owned enterprises, as well as adopting the new competition law and ensuring the independence and adequate powers of the anti-monopoly committee.[20]

Along these lines, the consensus among economists is that a well-functioning private market requires several conditions:

- A leading share of economic activity in the private sector. To quote the World Bank (2022, p. 10) "Market institutions cannot effectively function if they are restricted to the margins of the economy. Reducing the state's dominant role in the production is a prerequisite …" In this context, Uzbekistan's decision in early 2023 to sell off at least 12 state-owned banks is encouraging although it would be far preferable if the purchasers were international banks from Europe or North America than Central Asian oligarchs.[21]
- Open disclosure of relevant information for investors. Here Uzbekistan has adopted and enforced International Financial Reporting Standards (IFRS) since early 2020.[22]
- Clear rules against "insider" links between supposedly private investors and the power structure. Links between the Uzbek government and insiders (including oligarchs under EU and US sanctions as a result of the invasion of Ukraine) remain controversial as of early 2023, although there are encouraging signs of a gradual response to international pressure.[23]
- The ability to compete on a "level playing field," without entrenched lack of access due to inability to get finance or regulatory and licensing designed to unable to start-up to get credit (or pay substantially more for

a suboptimal level of credit), hard-to-get permissions or other barriers to entry designed to protect current, typically state-owned, producers (World Bank, 2022, pp. 10, 15). The World Bank also notes that "the banking sector is highly concentrated, dominated by the state, and engages in directed lending to SOEs at below-market rates" (World Bank, 2022, p. 41).

- Compliance with international standards. In this context, it is encouraging that Uzbekistan seems to have recently increased its efforts to join the World Trade Organization although discouraging that this is occurring over two decades after the Kyrgyz Republic's WTO accession in 1998.
- One area of privatization remains of particular concern. As of late 2022, all agricultural land in Uzbekistan remains owned by the state and left to private operators for up to 50 years. Leased land cannot be bought or sold, mortgaged, gifted or exchanged, or subleased for longer than one year except in special cases. While long-term leases mitigate some of the problems associated with suboptimal use of the land, they clearly reduce the incentive for long-term productivity-enhancing investment or conservation, much less conversion to higher-value non-agricultural use.[24] Even long-term leases are rare. According to a study by the Uzbek Ministry of Agriculture, in 2019 the average tenure on agricultural plots was only 1.5 years.[25] Famers' ability to produce according to their own optimization calculations is further limited by the fact that the crops that can be produced on the vast majority of land in Uzbekistan are subject to state control (World Bank, 2022, p. 38) and must be devoted to wheat and cotton production by government decree (Khakimov et al., 2022).

9.8 Regulatory quality

The World Bank annually evaluates over 40 indices from multiple sources to provide an index of the quality of regulation across countries designed to capture the ability of the government to formulate and implement sound policies and regulations that permit and promote private sector development. In 2021 Uzbekistan was about half a standard deviation below the global average, ranking 132 out of 192 countries (just below Russia and well below Kazakhstan but above other Central Asian countries including Turkmenistan, which was ranked 190). With respect to women's role in society, Uzbekistan has made significant strides in the past decade to promote the participation of women in public life. As of 2019, Uzbekistan ranked the top 50 out of 190 countries in the world in terms of the share of women in parliament.[26] With this ranking, Uzbekistan was ahead of almost all peers in the former Soviet Union. Interestingly, Uzbekistan is one of the very few countries not evaluated in the World Economic Forum's Global Gender Gap Index in either 2021 or 2022. WEF did not provide any reason for its exclusion, but a lack of data access can be inferred.[27]

On the other hand, the World Bank observes that there is 28 percentage points difference between the genders in Labor Force Participation, much

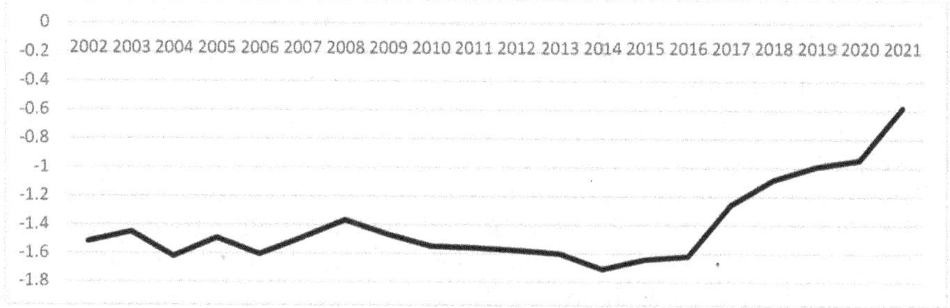

Figure 9.6 Regulatory quality in Uzbekistan, 2002–2021
Notes: Estimate gives the country's score on the aggregate indicator, in units of standard normal distribution, i.e., ranging from approximately –2.5 to 2.5.
Source: Authors using WGI data (Kaufmann, Kraay, & Mastruzzi, 2010).

higher in comparator countries such as Kazakhstan where it is only 12 percentage points. The World Bank concludes that

> The country is struggling with pervasive gender imbalances in employment arising at least in part because of norms and discrimination ... Gender norms in Uzbekistan often require women to assume responsibility for childcare and time-intensive household chores, such as fetching water, cooking, cleaning, working the garden, and caring for dependents.

It also reports that "gender discrimination in hiring decisions is prevalent and economically significant" and that vulnerable groups such as woman- headed households often have lower access to both formal and informal social support and that "Uzbekistan underperforms with respect to women's participation in business ownership and high-level business management positions."[28] The bank acknowledges that "recent laws to guarantee gender equality and reduce gender-based violence are an important first step toward addressing these imbalances."

Conclusions

To analyze a country in transition with any static evaluation is inherently dangerous. As we write this chapter, Uzbekistan is scheduled to vote on major revisions to its Constitution. By the time anyone reads this essay it is highly likely that the proposed revision will be in effect. It will take decades, however, to determine if any of the lofty goals set forth in the Constitution are, in fact, transformed into realities on the ground. It is concerning that the new Uzbek Constitution extends far beyond the role of specifying governmental organization and ensuring basic rights and freedoms, instead incorporating "access" to unspecified levels and quality of health care, employment, and tuition-free education thereby becoming what Feulner

(2013) has called "a laundry list of rights the government will 'give' to the citizen." Such detailed constitutions do not tend to survive long. Indeed, surveying all constitutions written since the US Constitution was adopted in 1789 Elkins, Ginsburg, and Melton (2009) found that the mean survival was 17 years with a median of eight years.

Thus, recent signs of institutional reform are encouraging but tentative. Uzbekistan must maintain an emphasis on implementing market-based principles led by the private sector. It must prioritize reforms that promote transparency and inclusivity in its political and economic systems, including anti-corruption measures, protection of property rights, and equal access to opportunities and resources. These reforms will create a more level playing field for businesses and individuals, reduce corruption, and promote economic growth. This includes promoting media freedom, establishing an independent judiciary, and allowing for greater civil society and political participation. It is important, however, to recognize that such reforms may face resistance from entrenched interests and powerful actors. It is essential, therefore, to build broad-based coalitions in support of these reforms and to have a sustained commitment to their implementation over the long term.

Acknowledgement

The author acknowledges the support from the Czech Science Foundation (GA CR), project no. 19-19158S.

Notes

1 https://documents1.worldbank.org/curated/en/933471650320792872/pdf/Toward-a-Prosperous-and-Inclusive-Future-The-Second-Systematic-Country-Diagnostic-for-Uzbekistan.pdf, retrieved February 27, 2023. In the future citations to this extensive report will simply be reported as WB, 2022.

2 Uzbekistan did accept some aspects of the Washington Consensus including monetary policies to stabilize economic activity and foreign exchange operations to increase export competitiveness.

3 https://info.worldbank.org/governance/wgi/, retrieved March 11, 2023.

4 It should be noted that these are relative rankings, so any countries improvement may reflect its better conditions or other countries' worse ones.

5 https://freedomhouse.org/countries/freedom-world/scores, retrieved March 11, 2023.

6 https://data.imf.org/?sk=F8032E80-B36C-43B1-AC26-493C5B1CD33B&sId=1485894037365&ref=mondato-insight, retrieved March 12, 2023.

7 www.ebrd.com/economic-research-and-data/transition-qualities-asses.html, retrieved March 12, 2023.

8 https://worldjusticeproject.org/rule-of-law-index/global/2022/, retrieved March 12, 2023.

9 https://data.worldbank.org/indicator/NY.GDP.MKTP.KD.ZG?locations=UZ retrieved March 12, 2023.

10 https://bti-project.org/en/atlas, retrieved February 27, 2023.

11 www.ohchr.org/en/good-governance/about-good-governance#:~:text=In%20summary%2C%20good%20governance%20relates,economic%2C%20political%20and%20social%20rights. Retrieved February 2, 2023.

12 Source: Constitution of Uzbekistan. www.un.int/uzbekistan/uzbekistan/constitution-republic-uzbekistan.

13 We will refer extensively to the "Election Observation Mission Final Report" on the Uzbek Presidential Election of October 24, 2021 issued on April 22, 2022. www.osce.org/files/f/documents/9/e/516435_0.pdf, retrieved February 24, 2023.

14 www.bourseandbazaar.com/articles/2022/11/9/participatory-budgeting-opens-path-for-democratic-reform-in-uzbekistan.

15 The land code of the Republic of Uzbekistan. https://cis-legislation.com/document.fwx?rgn=845.

16 www.un.int/uzbekistan/news/national-mechanisms-securing-property-rights, retrieved February 26, 2023.

17 www.heritage.org/index/pdf/2021/book/regional, retrieved February 25, 2023.

18 worldjusticeproject.org/rule-of-law-index/country/2022/

19 See, for example, www.dentons.com/en/insights/articles/2022/april/27/uzbekistan-accelerating-the-privatization-of-state-assets, retrieved February 26, 2023.

20 www.imf.org/en/News/Articles/2022/11/15/pr22385-imf-staff-concludes-visit-to-uzbekistan, retrieved February 26, 2023.

21 https://eurasianet.org/uzbekistan-kickstarts-banking-privatization-with-sale-of-ailing-lender, retrieved March 15, 2023. As of January 2023, the largest international bank operating in Uzbekistan was ABN-Amro, the country's 18th largest,

22 See www.ifrs.org/use-around-the-world/use-of-ifrs-standards-by-jurisdiction/view-jurisdiction/uzbekistan/, retrieved February 26, 2023.

23 See www.rferl.org/a/uzbekistan-investigation-insiders-energy-projects/32262127.html, retrieved February 26, 2023.

24 See www.state.gov/reports/2022-investment-climate-statements/uzbekistan/, retrieved March 12, 2023, and Akhmadiyeva and Herzfeld (2021).

25 www.gazeta.uz/ru/2019/09/18/agiculture/

26 https://data.ipu.org/women-ranking?month=1&year=2023, retrieved March 7, 2023.

27 www.weforum.org/reports/global-gender-gap-report-2022, retrieved March 23, 2023.

28 The quotations in. this paragraph are from pp. 98, 103, 105, and 106 of World Bank (2022).

References

Abdullaev, U. (2020). State-owned enterprises in Uzbekistan: Taking stock and some reform properties, *Asian Development Bank Working Paper* 1068.

Acemoglu, D. (2012). Introduction to economic growth. *Journal of Economic Theory*, 147 (2), 545–550.

Akimov, A. (2015). The Political Economy of Financial Reforms in Authoritarian Transition Economies: A Comparative Study of Kazakhstan and Uzbekistan, in K. Ruziev & N. Perdikis (Eds.), *Development and Financial Reform in Emerging Economies*. Pickering & Chatto.

Akhmadiyeva, Z., & Herzfeld, T. (2021). How does practice match land laws in Central Asia? *Land Use Policy*, 109, 105726.

McCleary, R., & Barro, R. (2006). Religion and economy. *Journal of Economic Perspectives*, 20 (2): 49–72.

Dadabaev, T. (2013) Community life, memory and a changing nature of Mahalla identity in Uzbekistan, *Journal of Eurasian Studies*, 4, 181–196.

El Harmouzi N. & L. Whetstone, Eds. (2016). *Islamic Foundations of a Free Society*. Institute of Economic Affairs.

Elkins, Z., Ginsburg, T. & Melton, J. (2009) *The Endurance of National Constitutions.* Cambridge University Press.

Feulner, E. (2013) The key to a long-lasting constitution, *The Washington Times*, February 17, 2013.

Friel, D. (2017). Understanding institutions: Different paradigms, different conclusions, *Revista de Administração (São Paulo)* 52, 212–214.

International Labour Organization (2021). *Third-Party Monitoring of Child Labour and Forced Labour During the 2020 Cotton Harvest in Uzbekistan.* International Labour Organization.

Kandiyoti, D. (2007) Post-Soviet institutional design and the paradoxes of the Uzbek path. *Central Asian Survey*, 26 (1), 31–48.

Kaufmann, D., Kraay, A., & Mastruzzi, M. (2010). The worldwide governance indicators: Methodology and analytical issues. *Policy Research Working Paper* WPS 5430. Retrieved from www.undp.org/uzbekistan/stories/uzbekistan%E2%80%99s-path-overcoming-corruption.

Khakimov, R., Sarsengaliy, B., Rozikov, J., Mamatkulov, M., Ismailov, K. & Durmanov, A. (2022). *Current State of Agriculture in the Republic of Uzbekistan and the Need for Improving the Efficiency of Agro-Clusters in the Fruit and Vegetable Industry.* IOP Conference Series: Earth and Environmental Science.

Lehne, J., Mo, J., & Plekhanov, A. (2014). What determines the quality of economic institutions? Cross-country evidence, *EBRD Working Paper No.* 171, European Bank for Reconstruction and Development.

Mitchell, W.C. (1924) The Prospects of Economics. *The Trend of Economics.* Crofts.

Ministry of Higher Education, Science, and Innovation (2023). Content and essence of the constitutional reforms: Why should the constitution be updated? [Konstitutsiyaviy islohotlar mazmun-mohiyati: Konstitutsiya yangilanishiga qanday zarurat bor?]

North, D. (1990). *Institutions, Institutional Change and Economic Performance.* Cambridge University Press.

Powell, W., & DiMaggio, P. (1991). Introduction, in W. Powell, & P. DiMaggio (Eds.), *The New Institutionalism in Organizational Analysis* (pp. 1–40). University of Chicago Press.

Robinson, J., Acemoglu, D., & Johnson, S. (2005). Institutions as a fundamental cause of long-run growth, *Handbook of Economic Growth, Vol. 1A*, 386–472.

Ruziev, K. (2021). Uzbekistan's development experiment: An assessment of Karimov's economic legacy. *Europe-Asia Studies*, 73 (7), 1303–1329.

UNDP. (2020, September 30). Uzbekistan's path in overcoming corruption. Retrieved from www.undp.org/uzbekistan/stories/uzbekistan%E2%80%99s-path-overcoming-corruption.

Urinboyev, R. & Eraliev (2022) Informal civil societ initiatives in non-Western societies: Mahallas in Uzbekistan, *Central Asian Survey*, 41 (3), pp. 477–497.

World Bank (2022). *Toward a Prosperous and Inclusive Future. The Second Systematic Country Diagnostic for Uzbekistan.* The World Bank Group, April 2022. Retrieved from https://documents1.worldbank.org/curated/en/933471650320792872/pdf/Toward-a-Prosperous-and-Inclusive-Future-The-Second-Systematic-Country-Diagnostic-for-Uzbekistan.pdf.

10 Sustainable development goals, COVID-19 and the government's response

Etenesh B. Asfaw, Obid Khakimov and Zohid Askarov

10.1 Introduction

Uzbekistan declared its commitment to implementing the United Nations Sustainable Development Goals (SDGs) in 2015. With the election of Shavkat Mirziyoyev as the new President of Uzbekistan in December 2016, the country entered a new era of rapid and ambitious socio-economic reforms in all spheres of the economy and society. The state adopted a strategy of action to guide the reforms in 2017–2021.[1] In line with the strategy, in 2018, the government adopted 16 national SDGs and 125 targets for 2030.[2] The national SDGs, like the global ones, seek to eradicate poverty and food insecurity, fight social inequalities, protect the planet, and promote prosperity and partnerships.

Evidence shows that the COVID-19 pandemic has distracted global commitments to the SDGs, posing risks to realizing the 2030 targets (Santos-Carrillo et al., 2020; Odey et al., 2021). This chapter reviews the revealed effect of the pandemic on Uzbekistan's national SDGs and analyzes the government's response to the pandemic-induced crisis. The chapter has three main objectives:

1 to discuss the multiple effects of the pandemic on the achievements of Uzbekistan's national SDGs, and the country's goal to become an upper-middle-income country by 2030.
2 to assess the government's policy response to mitigate the effects of the COVID-19 crisis on the SDGs and;
3 to draw lessons for a similar crisis.

The chapter is structured into five sections. The next section discusses the research methods and data used to meet the study's objectives. The study findings are presented in Section 10.3, which shows the trends in the performance and the pandemic's revealed effects across the SDGs. The section also analyzes the wide range of policy measures taken by the government of Uzbekistan to prevent the adverse effects of the pandemic. Additionally, the section discusses the potential effects of the announced public measures on

DOI: 10.4324/9781003473497-10

SDGs. The fourth section concludes and discusses lessons learned for future crises. The chapter benefits from other studies the authors conducted on the impact of the COVID-19 pandemic.

10.2 Materials and methods

This study uses quantitative and qualitative data analysis methods and presents the study findings using narratives, tables, and figures.

10.2.1 Data sources

The main data sources are described in Table 10.1.

10.2.2 Methods

We use open-access data to assess and visualize the evolving trends in selected national SDG indicators since 2016. We focus our analysis on what happened during the COVID-19 pick period.

We conduct a content analysis of legislative documents to capture the government's announced responses to the pandemic. We first searched for

Table 10.1 Sources of Data Used in the Chapter

Type of data	*Source*	*Open databases: Link*
SDG performance data	SSC of Uzbekistan-SDG database	https://nsdg.stat.uz/en
	World Bank-WDI and WGI databases OECD.stat database, Fao.stat database	https://databank.worldbank.org/source/world-development-indicators https://databank.worldbank.org/reports.aspx?Report_Name=WGI-Table&Id=ceea4d8b https://stats.oecd.org/Index.aspx?DataSetCode=GREEN_GROWTH www.fao.org/faostat/en/
COVID-19-related legislation/policies and COVID-19 response measures	legal documents	from the official legislation database of Uzbekistan https://lex.uz/docs/
Impact of the COVID-19 pandemic on achieving SDGs	studies conducted in 2020–2022,	Example: the World Bank-Listening to Citizens of Uzbekistan(L2CU)
Financial commitments and expenditures on the COVID-19 pandemic	Uzbekistan Ministry of Finance reports	www.mf.uz/

Source: Authors analysis.

legal documents from the Lex.uz database to identify measures announced during 2020–2021. We then selected only those legal documents whose content is relevant to the SDGs' themes. Out of the 34 legislative documents we gathered, we selected 16 relevant legislative documents for further content analysis. We did not include containment and closure announcements or actions to stop the spread of the pandemic in the short run.[3] The 16 selected legislative documents are listed in Section 10.3.

Next, we identified 169 independent COVID-19 policy measures in the 16 legislative documents reviewed. We then mapped the 169 policy measures to the national SDGs. The qualitative content analysis method enabled us to see how many legislative documents each SDG theme appears in, the policy texts related to each SDG, and what main changes the SDGs are expected to experience due to the government's response. The detailed mapping of the 169 policy measures across the SDGs was performed using Excel software.

For convenience, we adopted the five SDGs sub-groups known as the "5Ps" to categorize the 169 government policy measures toward the pandemic systematically.[4] These are:

- i People: includes SDG 1 to 5 measures to mitigate poverty, food insecurity, health, and education crisis, and gender inequality.
- ii Prosperity: includes SDG 7 to 11 interventions to protect the economy, income equality, access to energy, decent work, smart cities, social inclusion, and protection.
- iii Planet: includes SDG 6, 12, 13, and 15 interventions to ensure freshwater access and use, sustainable consumption, climate change mitigation, and land and forest protection.
- iv Peace: includes SDG 16 policy initiatives to promote national and community security, peace, community support, and generosity during the crisis.
- v Partnership: includes SDG 17 measures related to providing foreign aid and direct investment to fight against and recover from the pandemic.

10.3 Results and discussion

10.3.1 Statistical trends in selected SDG performance indicators and challenges posed by the COVID-19 pandemic

People *(SDG1–5)*: Before the 2020 pandemic, the economy of Uzbekistan grew on average by 5.4% annually and was stable in the SDG years (Figure 10.1). The GDP growth rate decelerated during the 2020 pandemic crisis to 1.9% from 5.7% in 2019. According to the State Statistics Committee of Uzbekistan, in 2020, like in previous years, the highest share of the economy was contributed by the service sector (36.6%), followed by the industry sector (35.5%), and then the agriculture sector (28.2%). Except for the agriculture

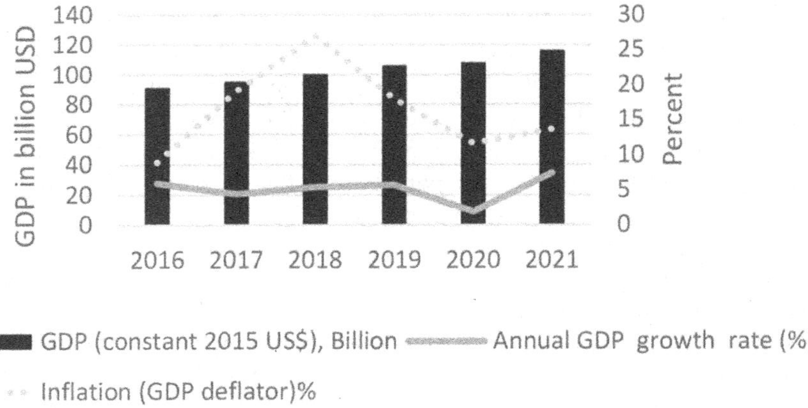

Figure 10.1 GDP (left), GDP growth rate, and inflation (right) in Uzbekistan
Source: Authors, using World Bank (WDI) data.

sector, the growth rate of all other sectors of the economy slowed down in 2020. Agriculture GDP grew by 3%, while the industry and service sectors grew by 0.7% and 0.1%, respectively. Transportation services decelerated by –2.2% (State Statistics Committee of Uzbekistan, 2021).[5]

The overall inflation for 2020 was 11.6%, compared to 17.9% in 2019 (Figure 10.1). The highest monthly inflations were experienced in the first half of 2020, compared to 2018 and 2019, with a peak in April (State Statistics Committee of Uzbekistan, 2021). The 2020 inflation index dropped in June and July and relatively stabilized in the last quarter of the year.

According to the Central Bank of Uzbekistan, the average monthly foreign exchange rate in 2020 was 10,081 Uzbekistan soums (UZS) to 1 US dollar (USD). This was 13% higher than the 2019 monthly exchange rate of 8,878 UZS. The highest monthly exchange rate in 2020 was registered in April (10,124 UZS). This relates to when Uzbekistan devaluated its currency (by 4.4% against the USD and 5% against the Euro) on April 15. The currency devaluation in 2020 came soon after the 2019 currency depreciation by 14% against the USD.[6] The currency depreciation resulted from the abrupt financial drops in remittance inflow and from trade turnover.

Uzbekistan had an economic contraction expressed by a budget deficit of 9% of the GDP equivalent by July 2020 (World Bank, 2020a). Half of the country's economic activity was suspended by April 2020, while travel restrictions eroded the trade and tourism economy. Weaker remittance flows and export declines intensified the economic contraction. The budget deficit, however, fell to 4% of the GDP by the end of 2020.[7]

10.3.2 Food and nutrition security

On average, the proportion of food insecure population was 23.5% for the three years between 2019 and 2021, compared to 14.9% between 2016 and

2018, showing that food insecurity was on the rise during the SDG years (Table 10.2). Nevertheless, Uzbekistan was among the countries with a low level of hunger in 2020, ranking 30 place out of 107 countries in the Global Hunger Index and 83 among 113 countries in the Global Food Security Index for 2020.[8]

Despite claims that Uzbekistan is food self-sufficient as of early 2000 (Spoor, 2000; Musaev, et al., 2010); there is no publicly available data on the country's food stock, balance, and reserve pre-COVID-19 nor during the pandemic in 2020. Thus, it is difficult to back the claim for food self-sufficiency amid the COVID-19 crisis with official statistics. At the same time, there is evidence that shows that Uzbekistan ensured a secure food supply to the population in 2020, as before the crisis. People also had access to a wide range of food products during the pandemic.

Before the pandemic, domestic food production in 2019 grew by 2.7% throughout 2018, with the highest (10%) growth rate in grain crops (Table 10.3). More so, food production in 2020 did not drop, compared to 2019. Available food per capita for 2020 for major food groups, except eggs, is above the recommended adult equivalent dietary nutrition norms set by the Uzbekistan Ministry of Health (Resolution No. 251, 2015).[9] Total domestic food production continued to increase in 2021.

An online survey conducted in July 2020 in major cities of Uzbekistan amidst the lockdown revealed that consumers (60% of survey respondents) were satisfied with the variety and quality of food products available in the market at the time of the survey (Rudenko et al., 2020).

Despite its availability, food became inaccessible during the pandemic lockdown. Food became especially unaffordable to families whose purchasing ability dropped with the sharp declines in employment and remittance incomes. Consumers' food purchasing power was eroded as early as April, as many households were temporarily out of a job or had lost their jobs during the first months of the strict lockdown regulation.[10] According to the FAO, per capita GDP at purchasing power parity declined in 2020, but recovered in 2021 (Table 10.4).

Table 10.2 Prevalence of Food Insecurity in Uzbekistan

	Food Insecurity	
Three years average	*Proportion of the population (%)*	*Number of people (in millions)*
2015–2017	12.6	4.2
2016–2018	14.9	4.8
2017–2019	17.2	5.6
2018–2020	19.7	6.5
2019–2021	23.5	7.9

Source: FAO.stat, 2022.

Table 10.3 Food Production in Uzbekistan

Type of food	*Production volume in thousand tons*					
	2016	*2017*	*2018*	*2019*	*2020*	*2021*
Cereals & legumes	8,261	7,289	6,536	7,438	7,636	7,635
Potato	2,790	2,794	2,912	3,090	3,144	3,286
Vegetables	10,184	10,220	9,760	10,215	10,431	10,850
Melons	2,045	2,031	1,837	2,069	2,134	2,285
Fruits & berries	2,613	2,615	2,706	2,753	2,813	2,853
Grapes	1,613	1,626	1,590	1,603	1,607	1,695
Livestock live weight	2,173	2,287	2,431	2,474	2,520	2,635
Milk	9,703	10,048	10,466	10,714	10,977	11,274
Eggs (in a million pieces)	6,153	6,333	7,459	7,771	7,781	7,788

Source: State Statistics Committee, 2022.

Table 10.4 Purchasing Power Parity (2016–2021) in Uzbekistan

Year	*GDP per capita USD (PPP) (constant 2017)*
2016	6,663.9
2017	6,840.7
2018	7,082.9
2019	7,348.1
2020	7,344.2
2021	7,734.8

Source: FAO.stat, 2022.

A study finding from a survey conducted in July 2020 in 3 cities in Uzbekistan shows that most (40% of respondents out of 652) adjusted their food purchase volume downward compared to prior to the pandemic in June and July 2020 (Asfaw et al., 2021). Consumers' dietary preferences also shifted from expensive protein meat products to less costly but indispensable bread, cereals, oil and fats, and some vegetables. The country's food supply chain did not experience long periods of food shortages during lockdowns in 2020, except for some logistics delays. The World Bank (2020b) reveals that the number of citizens reporting on local food out-of-stock shortages was reduced (to 1%) in June, compared to in April (16%).

Despite the availability of diversified food, the Uzbek population has a deficiency in micronutrients, such as iodine, iron, and vitamins. Malnutrition among the population was 2.5% in 2020, compared to 6.3% in 2016 (FAO). Over 1.8% of children under 5 years were wasted in 2017, and 24.8% of women aged 15–49 had anemia in 2019.[11] Adult obesity is on the rise among Uzbeks, with 28% of the population obese in 2020, compared to 16.6% in

2016 (Shodmonov, 2020). Malnutrition indicators are expected to have been exacerbated during the pandemic lockdown, given households' decreased food budgets, rising and fluctuating prices for healthy diets, unstable dietary consumption, and reduced physical mobility.

10.3.3 Health

The average life expectancy in Uzbekistan was 74 years in 2020. It increased by 5.2 years between 1990 and 2020. Life expectancy is higher than the average age of 71 years for lower-middle-income countries (World Bank).

Uzbekistan currently registers a maternal mortality rate (MMR) of 15 women dying out of every 100,000 live births due to complications from pregnancy or childbirth. This rate is less than the global SDG target of 140. Uzbekistan's MMR dropped to 19% in 2020 (Figure 10.2), with a 67% decline from 1991. The high drop in MMR resulted from expanding public maternal health programs (UNICEF, 2021). Under-5 mortality rates have also declined during the SDG years. The statistics show no difference in maternal and under-5 mortality rates during the pandemic year.

Despite positive trends, the SSC reports show that Uzbekistan's health system exhibits limitations in meeting the population's needs. Before the pandemic, the number of medical doctors per 10,000 people was only 27, and the number of hospital beds per 10,000 population was 45 (SSC, 2022). The limitation of the health system was exacerbated during the pandemic. According to the World Bank L2CU study, the rate of regular health checks by the elderly, pregnant women, and children went down in rural areas. Many families postponed the vaccination of their children. Also, healthcare facilities in remote rural areas had limitations in serving COVID-19 patients. According to the World Bank's survey, the country's healthcare system was under strain when COVID-19 cases increased in the summer of 2020 (World Bank, 2020b).

By the end of December 2020, Uzbekistan recorded a total of 77,060 COVID-19 cases and 614 deaths. On average, 8,000 people were infected per month with the peak in August, and 60 died from COVID-19 per month after the first death in March 2020. Uzbekistan registered over 175,000 all-cause deaths and had an average of 14,636 deaths per month in 2020. The number of deaths increased by 13.6% in 2020 compared to that of the 2019 number. The proportion of official COVID-19-related deaths out of the total deaths in 2020 was only 0.35%. Such official statistics indicate that the pandemic did not hugely impact Uzbekistan's mortality statistics. However, reports suggest that Uzbekistan's official COVID-19 infections and death counts are inaccurate, and affected by limited testing capacity, reporting policy, and underreporting.[12]

10.3.4 Education

The number of students attending school increased during the SDG years, including 2020 (Figure 10.3). However, reports show that the quality of

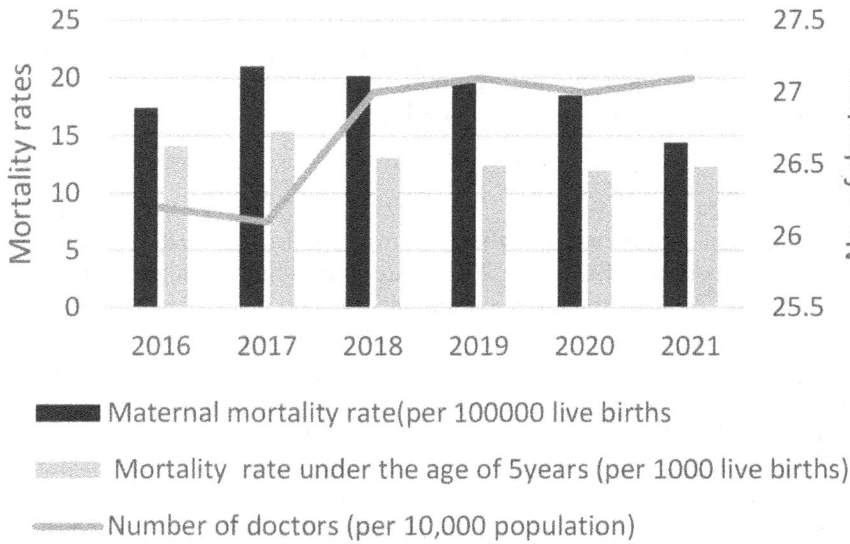

Figure 10.2 Maternal and under-5 mortality rates (left) and number of doctors (right), Uzbekistan
Source: Authors, using SSC data.

education was severely affected during the 2020 pandemic-related closures. During the lockdown, school and university students had limited access to tele-education due to unstable electric supply in remote rural areas, and rural students had fewer gadgets needed for online education (World Bank, 2020b). Digitalization (internet access) for education increased in 2021 after the worst pandemic crisis in 2020 (Figure 10.4).

Though the education system in 2020 mostly went online (or tele-) during the pandemic, Uzbekistan had limited experience in online teaching before the COVID-19 pandemic, and the educational institutions were not ready to adjust to new systems. Accordingly, the quality and accessibility of education were affected, given the limited internet coverage and computer and digital literacy of school children. According to the SSC, connectivity was a problem where only 71% of the population used the internet. Also, only 40% and 37% of schoolchildren had a computer and digital literacy, respectively (UNICEF, 2020).

10.3.5 Gender equality

The share of women's employment per active population is lower than that of men. The share dropped during the SDG years, and was 41% in 2020 (Figure 10.5). In 2020, only 86% of the active female population was employed, compared to 92% of the male active labor population employed, showing that men had better employment opportunities during the pandemic.

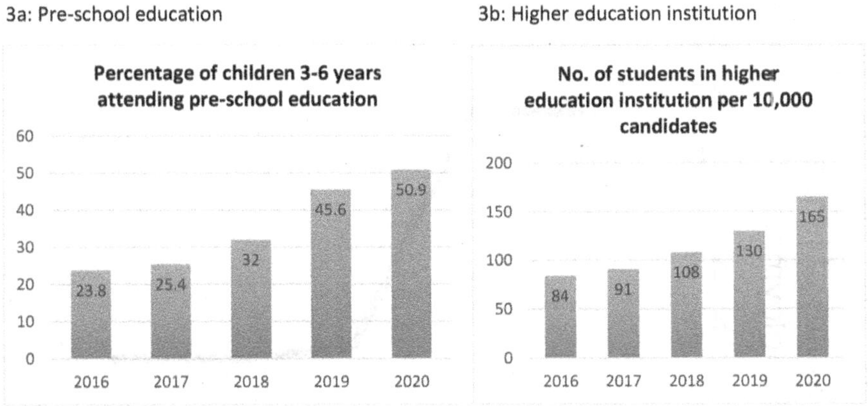

Figure 10.3 Number of Students attending Schools in Uzbekistan. 3a: Pre-school education. 3b: Higher education institution

Source: Authors, using SSC data, 2022.

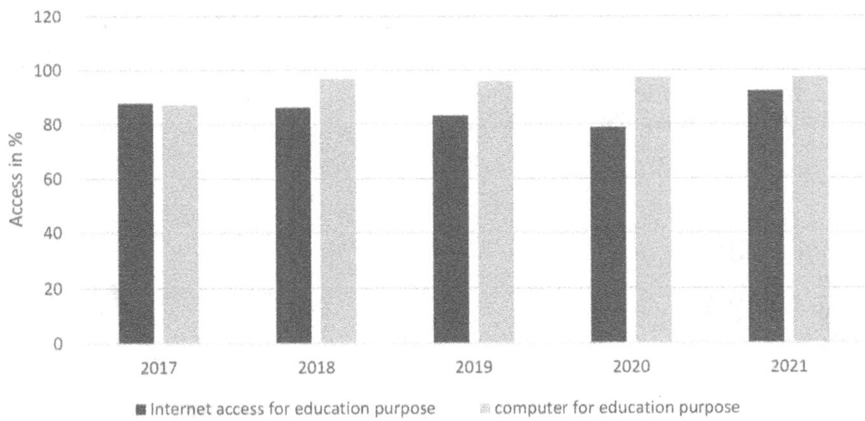

Figure 10.4 Access to the internet and computers for education purposes in Uzbekistan

Source: Authors, using SSC data, 2022.

The proportion of women in political participation (parliament) stagnated at 16% during the SDG years prior to the 2020 pandemic. The share of female parliamentarians, however, increased to 32% in 2020 (Figure 10.6).

Uzbekistan has gender inequality in the labor market. On average, women earned 36% less than the monthly wages of men between 2016 and 2019.[13] Moreover, over 50% of women were employed in the informal sector by the end of 2019. Existing vulnerabilities in the informal labor market are believed to have made women less equipped to cope with the COVID-19 crisis (World Bank, 2020c). More so, women are said to have been squeezed out of the rural labor market in 2020 due to competition from returned male migrants (United Nations, 2020).

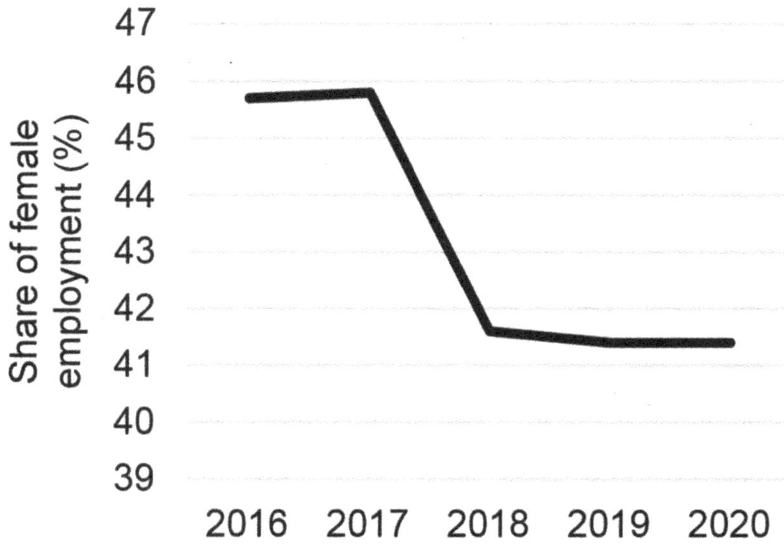

Figure 10.5 Share of female employment (%)
Source: Authors, using SSC data, 2021.

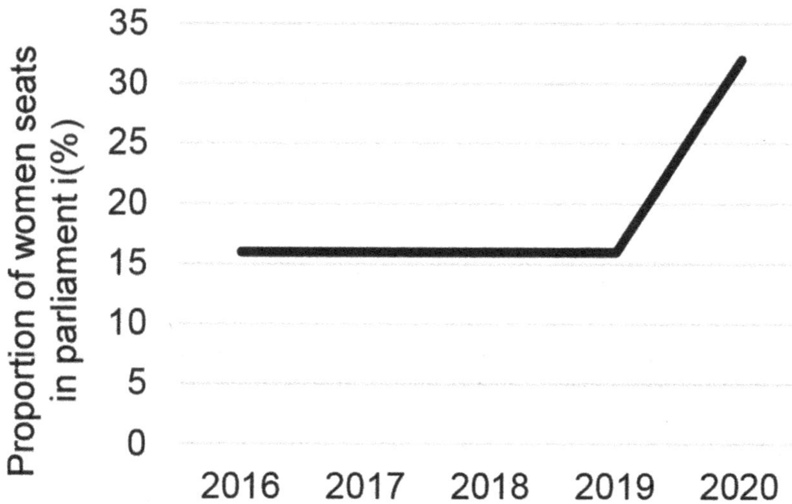

Figure 10.6 Proportion of seats held by women in the parliament
Source: Authors using SSC data, 2021.

10.3.6 Prosperity

The economic growth in Uzbekistan was accompanied by the steadily increasing prosperity of citizens before the pandemic. Income per capita, however, dropped in 2020, as in Figure 10.7. The GDP per capita (in constant 2015 dollars) amounted to 3,160 USD in 2020, compared to 3,161 in 2019, with a contraction in the annual growth rate by 0.1 percentage points compared to the 2019 rate of 3.7%. In 2021, per capita GDP bounced back, increasing by 5%.

According to the findings of the World Bank L2CU survey, per capita income in 2020 fell sharply by 38% in April, compared to March. Income declines were more prominent in urban areas – falling 46%, while they fell by 37% in rural and semi-urban areas (World Bank, 2020b). Employment income declined sharply, especially among self-employed people and labor migrants.

Uzbekistan was on a trend of reducing the low-income population before the pandemic.[14] However, in 2020, the proportion of low-income people in Uzbekistan increased by 0.5%, as in Figure 10.8. The proportion of low-income households is higher in rural compared to urban areas. The poverty rate rose to 10% of the population following the pandemic outbreak, compared to the pre-COVID-19 7% rate. An additional half a million people (over 1.3% of the population) are said to have fallen into poverty by June (World Bank, 2020b; UN-VNR, 2020).

The amount of income from remittance inflow that was upward and higher than in 2019 in the first two months of 2020 started to decline as of March

Figure 10.7 GDP per capita (left) and growth rate (right) in Uzbekistan
Source: Authors, using World Bank, WDI data, 2022

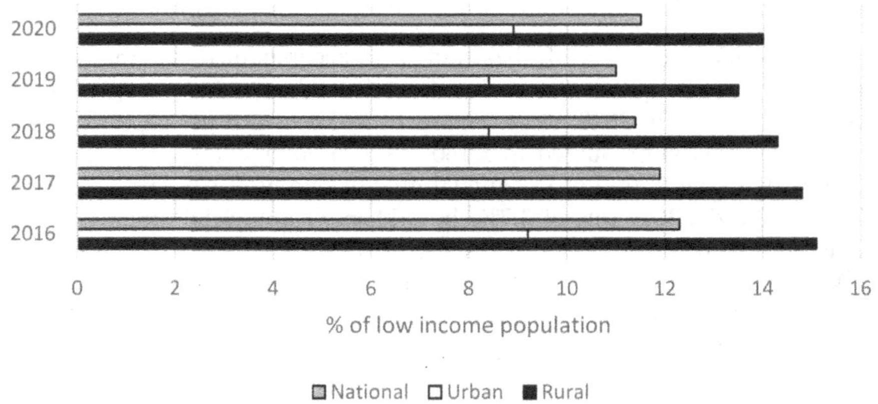

Figure 10.8 Proportion of low-income population in Uzbekistan
Source: Authors, using SSC data, 2022.

2020, and it was lower than it was in 2019 until September 2020. The central bank of Uzbekistan indicated that several factors negatively affected remittance during the pandemic: suspension of international flights, border closing, devaluation of national currencies of Russia and Kazakhstan in March related to oil prices, and partial suspension of production and construction works in some countries (Kun.Uz, 2020)

10.3.7 Social safety net and unemployment

The proportion of the total population receiving pension (social protection) increased over the SDG years, and in 2020 it reached 8.2%, compared to the 7.4% level in 2016 (Figure 10.9).

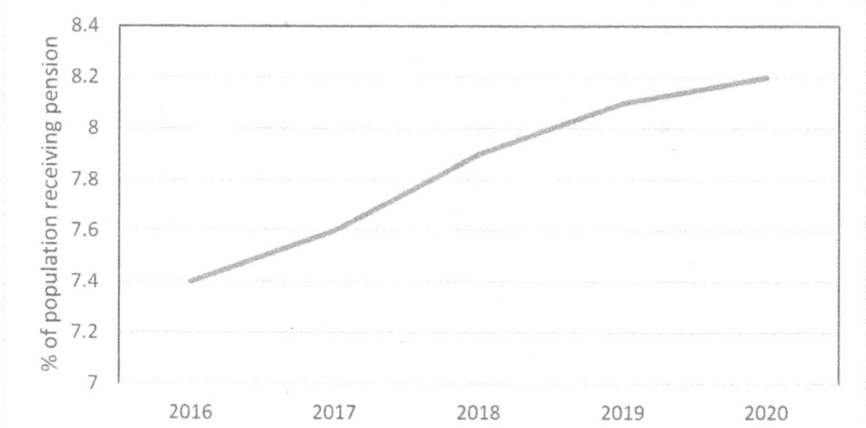

Figure 10.9 Proportion of the population receiving a pension in Uzbekistan
Source: Authors, using SSC data, 2022.

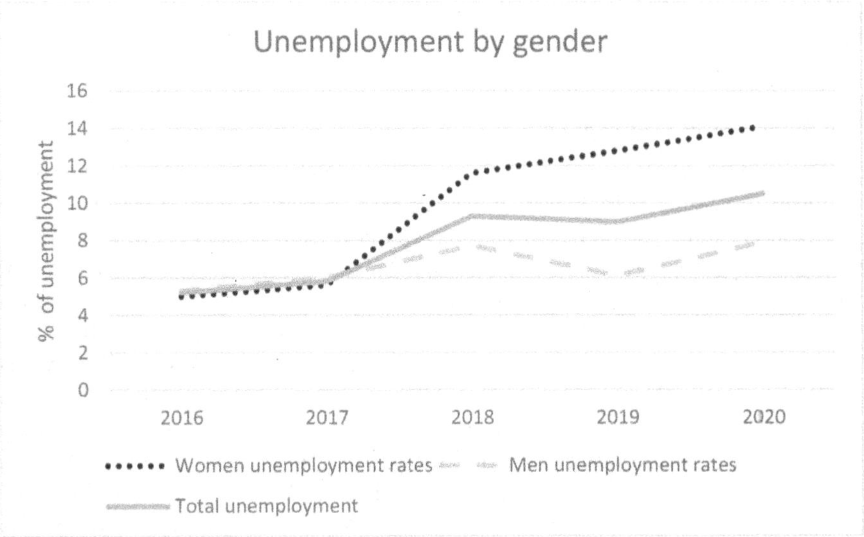

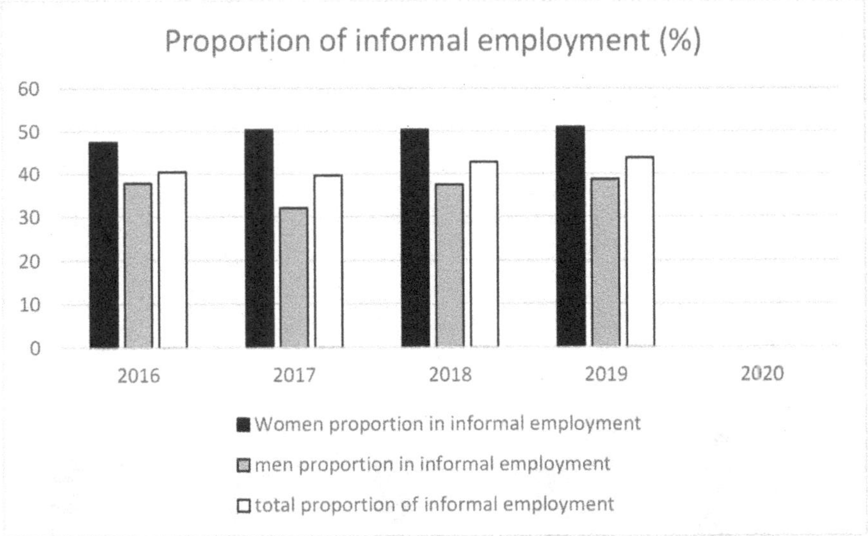

Figure 10.10 Unemployment by gender in Uzbekistan. a. Unemployment by gender. b. Unemployment rates

Source: a. Authors, using SSC data. b. Authors, using World Bank, WDI data.

Though Uzbekistan has made much effort to reduce unemployment, the rate has increased in the SDG years women's unemployment (% of the female labor force) increased steadily after 2017 and was 14% in 2020 (Figure 10.10a). On the contrary, the unemployment rate for men declined in 2019 by over 1% compared to 2018. However, in 2020 the male unemployment rate was higher than the female rate. The International Labor Organization (ILO) estimates lower unemployment rates than the national data but still rises in the SDG years, as in Figure 10.10b. Total unemployment spiked from 5.2% in 2016 to 7.2% in 2021.

10.3.8 Access to clean energy

Uzbekistan's primary energy sources are natural gas, oil, and hydropower. All households in Uzbekistan have access to electricity (Figure 10.11) primarily generated from natural gas. On the contrary, only 55% of households have access to natural gas for cooking. The proportion of households with access to natural gas decreased from 67% in 2016 to 55% in 2020. Access to energy amidst the COVID-19 pandemic crisis of 2020 remained as before.

The total energy supply from diverse sources increased in the SDG years, as in Figure 10.12. The International Energy Agency (IEA, 2022) indicates that Uzbekistan has one of the most energy-intensive economies in the world (35% higher than Kazakhstan and three times more than Germany). Total energy used per GDP slightly decreased during 2020 (Figure 10.12). However, energy used per capita data is unavailable for the pandemic years. The share of renewable energy sources in the energy mix is low (Figure 10.13). The development of electric power from renewable energy sources is also low. The proportion of renewable electricity to total generated electric power dropped to 7.5% in 2020, compared to 10.2% in 2019.

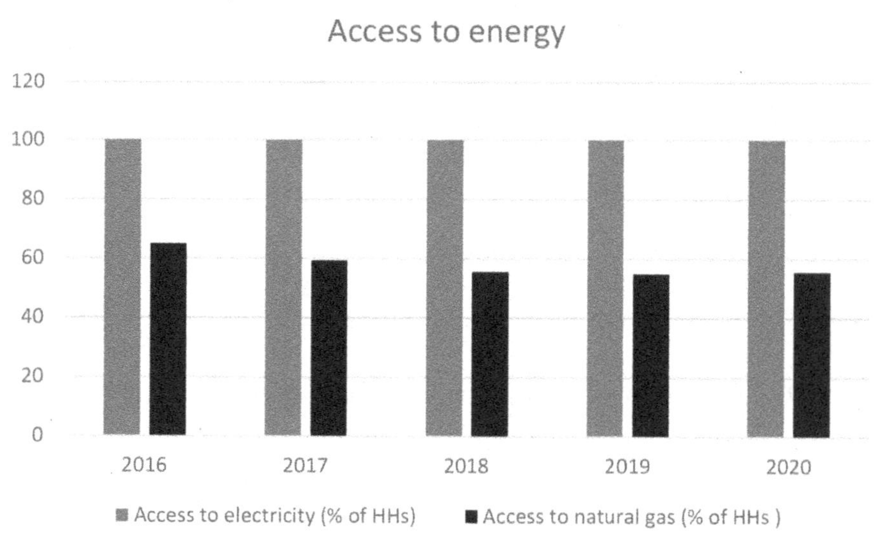

Figure 10.11 Households' access to energy in Uzbekistan
Source: Authors, using SSC data

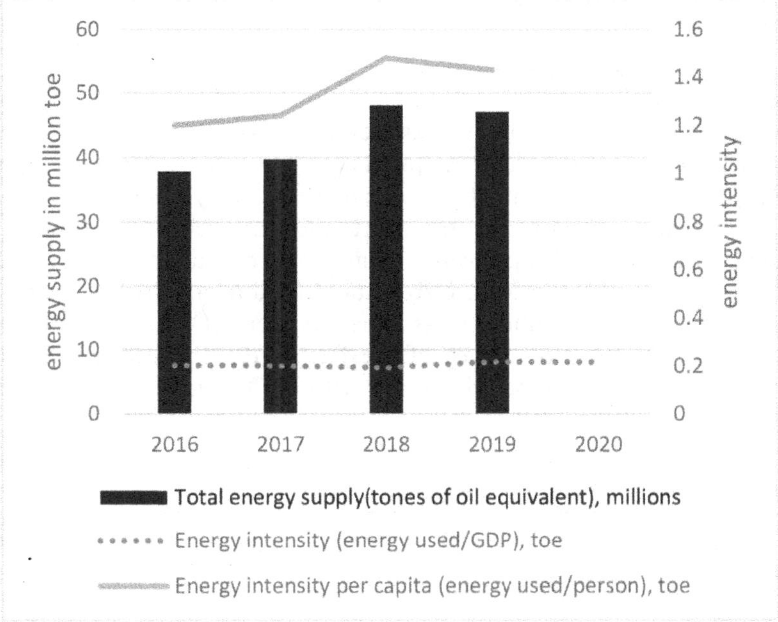

Figure 10.12 Energy supply, in million tons oil equivalent (left) and energy intensity (right)

Source: Authors, using SSC and Organization for Economic Cooperation and Development (OECD) data, 2023.

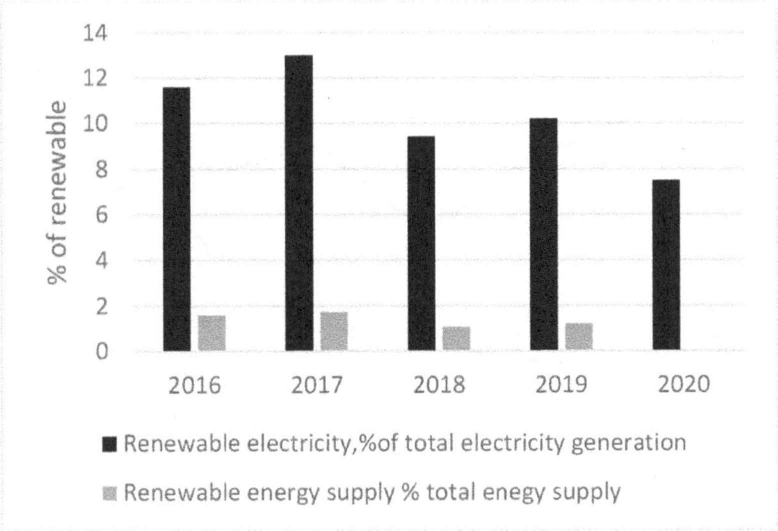

Figure 10.13 Proportion of renewables as % of total energy and % of total electricity generation in Uzbekistan

Source: Authors, using the OECD and SSC data, 2022.

10.3.9 Planet

Almost 98% of the Uzbek population had access to drinking water services during the pandemic year. Uzbekistan is one of the most water-stressed countries in the world, with a stress level of 68%. The agriculture sector consumes 90% of all the water supply. The volume of freshwater withdrawn for various uses decreased in 2020 compared to prior years (Table 10.5).

Carbon emissions from air transport and surface temperature change declined during 2020, but per capita emissions from air transport increased in 2021 (Figure 10.14). In 2021, Uzbekistan raised its ambitions and pledged a 35% reduction of greenhouse gas emissions per GDP by 2030 (from the level of 2010) at the Conference of the Parties (COP 26) event. This is a substantial increase compared to the 10% CO_2 reduction commitment initially announced in 2019.

Table 10.5 Freshwater Withdrawal in Uzbekistan

Indicators	*2016*	*2017*	*2018*	*2019*	*2020*
Annual freshwater withdrawal, total (billion m^3)	4,943	5,374	4,570	4,856	4,593
Withdrawals, agriculture (% of freshwater withdrawal)	90.60	91.22	89.60	89.97	89.68
Level of water stress: (withdrawal/available freshwater)	156.4	168.9	168.9	168.9	169

Source: Authors, using SSC data.

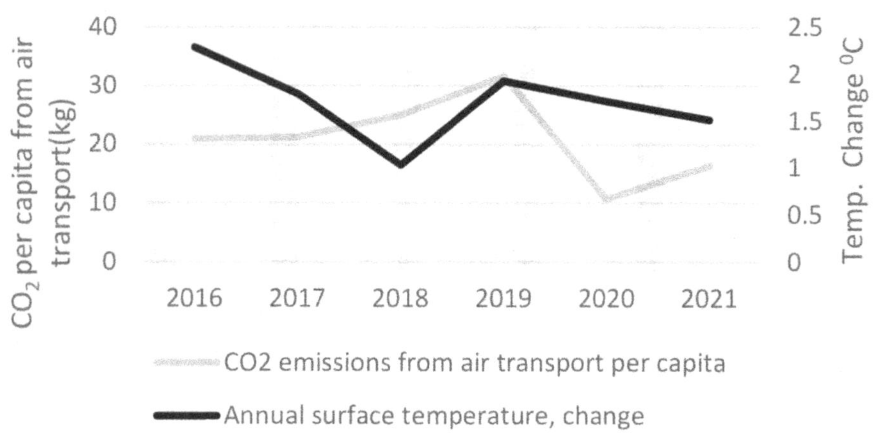

Figure 10.14 Carbon emissions(left) and annual temp. change(right) in Uzbekistan
Source: Authors, using OECD data, 2022.

10.3.10 Urbanization

Over 50% of the total population of Uzbekistan is urban. On average, the annual urban population growth rate between 2016 and 2021 was 1.72%, increasing from 1.5% in 2016 to 2% in 2021. However, the Asian Development Bank (ADB, 2021) indicates that urbanization in Uzbekistan is unsustainable, calling for reforms in urban planning. The forest cover in the country slightly increased from 8.1% to 8.4% of total land area during the SDG years.

10.3.11 Peace and good governance

Uzbekistan has improved its global rank in all five dimensions of the World Bank governance indicators in the SDG years, as in Figure 10.16. However, the ranks for the indicators are below 50 (on a scale of 0–100) and the estimates are below zero on a scale of –2.5 to 2.5, showing room for improvement. During COVID-19 recovery, in 2021, all governance indicators showed an increase, compared to pre-covid times.[15]

10.3.12 Partnerships

Uzbekistan enjoys an open and increasing international and public–private partnership in ensuring all areas of the SDGs. Accordingly, the country has been able to mobilize financial and technical resources to ensure the implementation of the SDGs. Foreign direct investment (FDI) net inflow (both in USD and as % of GDP) was on the rise in 2018/2019 (Figure 10.17). The net FDI inflow, however, declined in 2020.

Figure 10.15 Urbanization rate (annual %), Uzbekistan
Source: Authors, using World Bank (WDI) data, 2022.

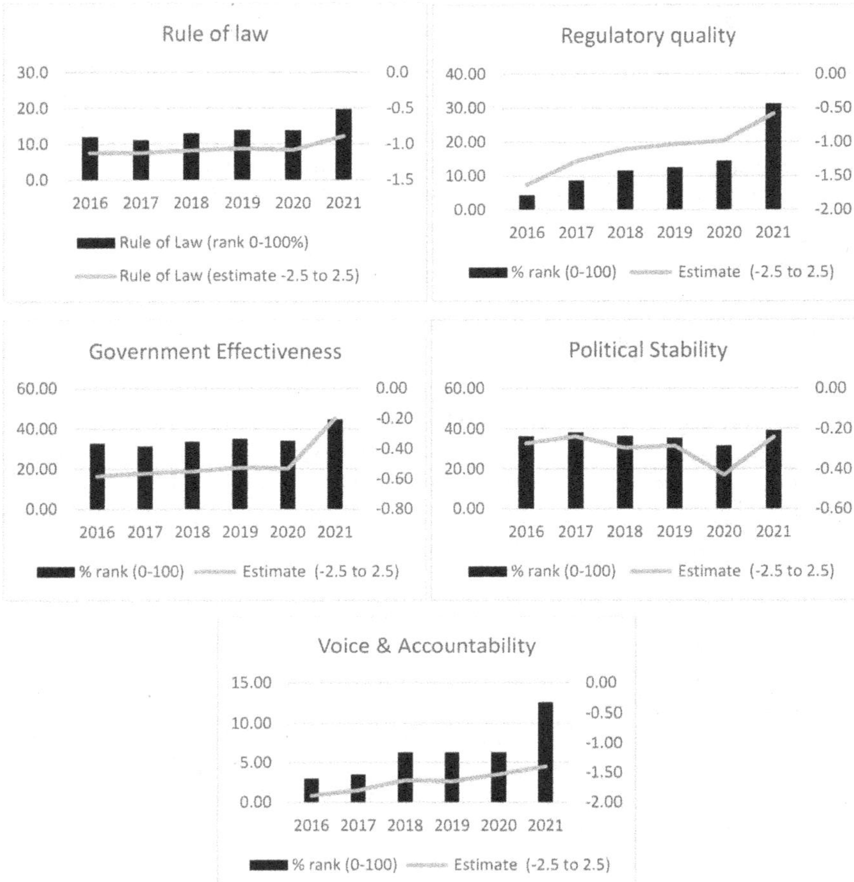

Figure 10.16 Governance indicators in Uzbekistan
Source: Authors, using WB, Worldwide Governance Indicators (WGI), 2022.

In 2020, 17 UN agencies and six international financial institutions (IFIs) worked together to address the COVID-19 impact on vulnerable people and the economy in multiple sectors. The partnership with IFIs was guided by a joint multilateral socio-economic response and recovery offer developed by the United Nations and multilateral agencies under the technical lead of the United Nations Development Programme.

10.4 Government's response to the COVID-19 pandemic

Uzbekistan responded to the COVID-19 pandemic as early as January 29, 2020, when the government launched a special commission to manage the pandemic crisis. The state announced a lockdown and closure of national and international borders on March 18, 2022, after the first COVID-19 case.

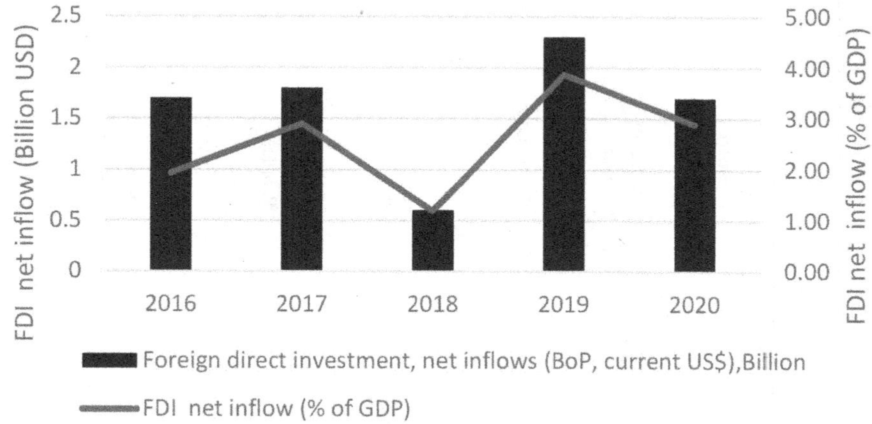

Figure 10.17 Foreign direct investment net inflow (% of GDP) in Uzbekistan
Source: Authors, using World Bank, WDI data.

Until June 2020, the government banned all public events, including international events and sports competitions, theater, movie and concert programs, weddings, and other family celebrations. The only social gathering allowed was for funerals with no more than 10–15 people. Later, between May–July 2020 and September 2020 onwards, family celebrations with no more than 30 people were allowed.[16]

All citizens were forced to stay and work from home during the lockdown. Isolation was recommended for people older than 65 years. The first wave of stay-home restrictions was announced from March 24 to May 1, 2020; the second wave was between July 1 and August 15, 2020.

Together with the containment measures to minimize the pandemic spread, the government took policy responses and designed financial and monetary packages to counter the negative impacts of the pandemic on the longer-term national SDG priorities. Table 10.6 summarizes the selected 16 legislative documents announced throughout the pandemic years 2020–2021 by SDG categories. Most measures had a transitory character, were rescue type and were only valid for a short period (mainly until the end of 2020).

10.4.1 Assessment of the government's response measures

Uzbekistan made timely efforts, backed by finance, to contain the pandemic and keep people and businesses alive during the crisis. Table 10.7 synthesizes the main findings from the content analysis of the diverse government response announced in the 16 legislative documents (listed above). The Table 10.7 shows how many pieces of legislation (measures) are related to each of the five SDG categories, how many legislative documents and measures each SDG category appeared in, and what the main interventions focus on by

Table 10.6 Legislative Documents Announced in 2020–2021 to Counter the Impacts of the COVID-19 Crisis on SDGs in Uzbekistan

#	*Reviewed Policy type and title*	*Date when the response was announced*	*Source*	*SDG group it contributed to*
1	#5969: Presidential Decree on priority measures to mitigate the adverse effects of the coronavirus pandemic and the global crisis on the economic sector.	March 19, 2020	https://lex.uz/docs/4770761	People Prosperity
2	#5978: Presidential Decree on additional measures to support the population, economic sectors, and business entities during the coronavirus pandemic.	April 3, 2020	https://lex.uz/docs/4780477	Prosperity People
3	#4691: Presidential Resolution on measures to attract external funds to support the population, budget, basic infrastructure, and businesses during the coronavirus pandemic.	April 22, 2020	https://lex.uz/docs/4797084	Partnership
4	#247: Decision of the Cabinet of Ministers on temporary restrictions on the export of raw materials for the production of medical products during the coronavirus pandemic.	April 23, 2020	https://lex.uz/docs/4796929	Prosperity
5	#4695: Presidential Resolution of the President of Uzbekistan on measures for further stimulation of sanitation and epidemiological services during the pandemic.	April 24, 2020	https://lex.uz/docs/4798007	People
6	#5986: Presidential Decree on additional measures to support the population and businesses during the coronavirus pandemic.	April 27, 2020	https://lex.uz/docs/4800007	People Prosperity

#	*Reviewed Policy type and title*	*Date when the response was announced*	*Source*	*SDG group it contributed to*
7	#4700: Presidential Decree on additional measures to ensure food security, rational use of available resources, and state support of agriculture during the coronavirus pandemic.	May 1, 2020	https://lex.uz/docs/4803523	People Prosperity
8	#5996: Presidential Decree on subsequent measures to support the population and businesses During the coronavirus pandemic.	May 18, 2020	https://lex.uz/docs/4815482	People Prosperity
9	#6002: Presidential Decree on urgent measures to support the sphere of tourism and to reduce the negative impact of the coronavirus pandemic.	May 28, 2020	https://lex.uz/docs/4831122	Prosperity
10	#6029: Presidential Resolution on additional support measures for the population, businesses, public food, trade and services to reduce the negative impact of the coronavirus pandemic.	July 20, 2020	https://lex.uz/docs/4903382	People Prosperity
11	#449: Resolution of the Cabinet of Ministers on measures to improve the turnover of drugs, medical devices, and equipment during the coronavirus pandemic.	July 22, 2020	https://lex.uz/docs/4908750	People
12	#6035: Resolution of the President on measures to mitigate the coronavirus pandemic, cardinal improvement of the system of sanitary and epidemiological wellbeing and protection of public health.	July 25, 2020	https://lex.uz/docs/4914688	People

#	*Reviewed Policy type and title*	*Date when the response was announced*	*Source*	*SDG group it contributed to*
13	#6038: Resolution of the President on additional measures for material support of the population in need of help and social protection during the coronavirus pandemic.	July 30, 2020	https://lex.uz/docs/4922155	People
14	#602: Resolution of the Cabinet of Ministers on support and development of tourism infrastructure and facilities amidst the economic situation caused by the COVID-19 pandemic.	October 6, 2020	https://lex.uz/docs/5031869	Prosperity
15	#665: Resolution of the Cabinet of Ministers on additional measures to support foreign economic activity, tourism, and construction during the pandemic.	October 29, 2020	https://lex.uz/docs/5073158	Prosperity
16	#763-Iv: Resolution of the Legislative Chamber of the Supreme Assembly on measures to ensure peace, including the planning work on coronavirus vaccination for the population.	February 22, 2021	https://lex.uz/docs/-5329280	Planet People Peace

Source: Authors, using data from Lex.uz, 2022.

SDG category. Further, Table 10.8 summarizes the government's response by type and focus area.

Responses to protect people: A range of rescue, recovery, and social protection measures expanded throughout the pandemic to protect and maintain people's livelihoods. Responses on people primarily aimed to better the livelihoods of the low-income and vulnerable groups of the society, e.g., female-headed households, families with children, unemployed, youth, returned migrants, and owners of informal and small business enterprises.

Healthcare service: Support to the health sector, including support to health workers, was the most announced, with 45 out of the 169 measures. To reduce the spread of the virus, all vehicles, goods, and cargo entering Uzbekistan's territory from foreign countries and Tashkent from other provinces and markets were regularly disinfected. Wearing masks and keeping distance was mandatory throughout 2020.

Education institutions: Schools were closed to reduce contamination. Uzbekistan announced the closure of all educational institutions on March 18, 2020, earlier than the scheduled spring break, following the first COVID-19 case. The school closure was prolonged until the end of 2020. The Ministry of Education indicates that 9,700 secondary schools, 1,500 specialized schools, and 98 higher education institutions were closed. The education system shifted to an online learning format and tele-schools on TV channels from March 30 until May 25, 2020, to ensure continuity of education during the school closure.[17]

Online teaching in schools and universities continued until the end of the 2020 academic year. However, schools and universities resumed conventional teaching formats in January 2021. Still, an online teaching–learning system, or a hybrid of the online and offline system, was practiced at universities in 2021. Parents were granted additional annual leave due to the closure of schools during the lockdown. Moreover, internet packages were promoted and continued for two months, even when payments were not made.

Food security: Food security interventions, including price stabilization and food import support, featured in 19 of the 169 measures. The government considered the agriculture and food sector essential and took several measures to facilitate production, market price, trade, and supply measures to ensure availability. The state monitored market prices of staple food products and ensured a stable food supply by controlling artificial price increases. The state released the public and private strategic food reserves/stocks to avoid food shortages and stabilize market prices during the lockdown. The state also expanded pre-existing food security interventions where public entities in every dehqan (green) market traded food produce like meat, oil, and potato at a state-fixed (low) price.

Income: The third most important response area during the pandemic was support for household income, which featured in 20 of the response measures out of 169. The government established an "Iron book" with a list of low-income and vulnerable families that needed a social safety net. Those enlisted

Table 10.7 SDG Measures Announced in COVID-19 Related Legislative Documents (in Decreasing Frequency Order) in Uzbekistan

SDG category	*Number of legislation documents dedicated to the SDG out of 16*	*Frequency of measures/texts dedicated to the SDGs, out of 169*	*Proportion (%) of the SDG measures out of 169 measures*	*Envisaged Effect of the measure*
People	11	75	44%	• healthcare services support (vaccine, healthy lifestyle) • food security support • agriculture land improvement • targeted cash transfers • job creation • reduced prices for products and services
Prosperity	10	73	43%	• support for businesses • tourism and leisure industry incentives • trade support • income tax cuts • support for start-ups and SMEs • waiver of interest/tax payments for businesses, business tax and VAT cuts; business tax deferrals, • investment in energy infrastructure
Partnership	1	19	11%	• IFIs support to SDG, Anti-Crisis Fund • Neighbor countries support
Peace	1	1	0.006%	Promotion of kindness, peace and security, Social and cultural investment (non-infrastructure)
Planet	1	1	0.006%	Clean/green transport and energy infrastructure investment
Total		**169**	**100**	

Source: Authors' analysis.

Table 10.8 COVID-19 Response Measures by Frequency and Type

Specific sector	*Frequency of measures*	*Proportion (%)*	*Type of support*
Health care support	45	27	rescue
Tax cuts and deferral	31	18	rescue
Business support	26	15	rescue
Household Income support	20	12	rescue
Agriculture, land, and food security support	19	11	rescue/recovery
Infrastructure (energy, building, maintenance)	12	7	recovery
Tourism support	9	5	rescue
Diverse sectors	5	3	rescue
Peace	1	0.5	rescue
Clean transport	1	0.5	recovery
Total	**169**	100%	

Source: Authors' analysis.

in the Iron book were supported with 0.01 ha of a greenhouse for growing vegetables (Presidential Decree No. 4700). The district authority leased land plots of up to 1 ha, primarily for low-income families and the rural youth with agricultural knowledge and skills. The measure also supported vulnerable returning migrants. Also, each low-income family participating in agricultural cooperatives received an additional 500,000 UZS.

The state took measures to re-count the number of vulnerable families with children under 14 years of age to provide support with childcare. Families with children were paid childcare allowances and financial assistance for six months ending in June 2020. Parents (guardians, trustees) who have been quarantined due to the coronavirus infection or suspected infection or else were taking care of children up to 14 years old were also provided with a pension. The government also increased financial assistance to families with children under 2 years of age by 10% compared to the pre-pandemic amount.

Gender equality: The "Women's book" (Uzb.: "Ayollar daftari") is a state measure to support female-headed households and women. During the pandemic, the women listed in the Women's book received a one-time financial payment.[18] In 2020, the government initiated a state program that promoted women's equal participation and benefits in socio-economic activities. The program established separate grants for increased female student participation in higher education. The state program also endorsed actions to increase women's participation in civil services and supported young and unemployed women's entrepreneurial skills through vocational training. The program invested in soft loans for 5,500 female-managed small businesses in the regions and provided affordable houses to 1,576 vulnerable women.

Response to protect business and preserve prosperity: The government invested in the economic recovery of essential sectors, primarily in service and tourism, energy, and trade. Out of the 169 measures reviewed, 31 (18% of all the measures reviewed) were directed to income tax cuts or suspension, 26 (15%) to liquidity support for businesses, and nine (5%) to tourism and leisure industry incentives. Moreover, the government announced critical infrastructure maintenance/establishment like energy and irrigation in 12 out of the total 169 measures. The state-supported small businesses, shopping malls, cinemas, public catering establishments, public transport enterprises, sports and health facilities, and other legal entities by exempting property tax, decreasing social tax, and canceling penalties. Tax audits of business entities were suspended. Local state authorities provided a six-month delay (or payment in installments) to business entities without charging interest on property tax, land tax, and water use tax. The state also mandated public and other services to be "online" as much as possible.

Entities in tourism and Uzbekistan Airways were exempted from land and property taxes, and they paid 1% social tax instead of 12%. The state also freed traders (entrepreneurs) from paying 50% of the established social tax. Local authorities were recommended to reduce the income tax of entrepreneurs whose activity is directly or indirectly related to tourism by 30%. To compensate for the entrepreneurs' costs in the hotel–recreation–catering sectors, the state set a lowered social tax (from 12% to 1%). Measures were also taken to support public catering entrepreneurs to ensure the extension of several tax benefits.

Uzbekistan's central bank facilitated liquidation, and the commercial banks delayed (till October 2020) all loan repayments for individuals and businesses, including individual traders.[19] The state introduced additional measures to support entrepreneurship in the form of compensation for interest expenses; the government compensated for interest rate payments (10% points) up to 500 million UZS on credit for businesses with a good credit history.[20]

Trade: The government suspended the export of raw materials used for medical devices from May 1 to December 31, 2020. Business entities were permitted to export goods without collateral for 12 months before the date of customs clearance.[21] Entrepreneurs could also import technological equipment and raw materials if they repaid on foreign trade operations in 2020.

The state introduced an expedited mechanism of customs clearance for imported food products through the issuance of permits.[22] The state also established zero tariffs on the import of certain food items, hygienic goods, building materials necessary for the construction of medical and quarantine establishments, and goods essential for express tests for the detection of coronavirus infection.[23] The state covered up to 50% of the road transportation costs of fruits and vegetable exporters.[24] Procedures for refunding value-added tax for textile exports were also simplified.[25]

The government suspended penalties on business entities for foreign trade operations, forced commercial banks to extend the delay in loan repayment for entities in the tourism sector, and revolved loans to replenish the consumer market with the most necessary goods. It extended the deadline for conducting audits of business entities and postponed the collection of rent for the use of state property by business entities that were forced to suspend their activities during the quarantine period.

The local government established strict control over preventing artificial price increases for cement and raw materials used to produce medical products. The state also obligated the purchase of textile garments, shoes, and office uniforms from local enterprises in 2020. It called for the optimization of expenditures by state-owned enterprises and entities with a state share of 50% or more, and the transfer of full dividends from 2019 to the state budget.

Responses to protect the planet: COVID-19 response measures did not have explicit green elements. Besides, the promotion of a few "green" response measures on renewable energy, response measures were not vigilant against environmental impacts. The planet was not a priority during the crisis as interventions focused on people, social, and business economic goals. The announced interventions were not emission-neutral. Poor attention to the environmental impact of measures was not unique to Uzbekistan. For instance, the OECD (2021a, 2021b) highlights that COVID-19 response investments by OECD member countries had negative and mixed impacts on the environment. On the other hand, new/revised legislations were initiated with certain green initiatives as of 2020. Green elements introduced in 2020 and 2021 include measures on waste management, biodiversity, sustainable forest land use, ecosystem payments, and the introduction of agriculture water-saving technologies and water metering.

The first year of implementation of the long-term (2020–2030) green economy transition strategy was 2020. The country, however, only developed the program action plan/roadmap for the green growth economic transition in 2022. The roadmap, designed by the Ministry of Economy and Poverty Reduction together with national and international partners, has six priority pillars: sustainable natural resource use, climate change response, low carbon emission, sustainable urbanization, green public investment, and inclusive transition. The strategy also has identified three cross-cutting areas: capacity building, enabling policy environment/institutions, and good governance.

Response to ensure peace: The state was consulting with religious and cultural institutions to promote peace, community support, and security amidst the pandemic.

Response to promote partnership: Uzbekistan received more than 1.4 billion USD of foreign and private aid to mitigate the severe effect of the pandemic and protect the economy, as shown in Figure 10.18.

The government approached international financial institutions like the World Bank, Asian Development Bank, Islamic Development Bank, and

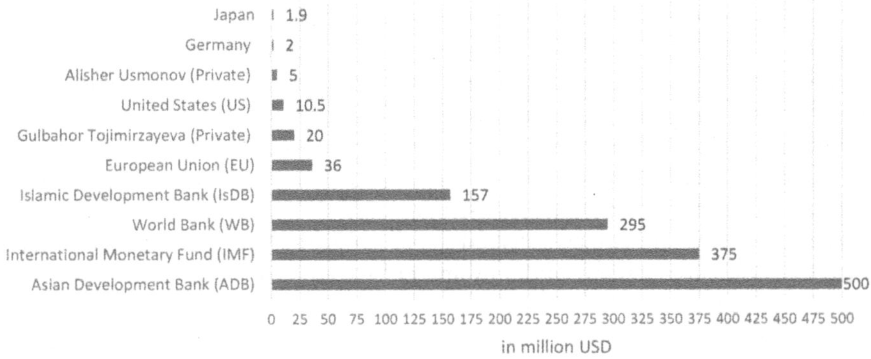

Figure 10.18 Amount of foreign and private aid committed in 2020 to address the COVID-19 Crisis in Uzbekistan
Source: Authors, using FPRI data, 2021.

Asian Infrastructure Investment Bank to attract long-term soft loans and grants totaling more than 3 billion USD.[26] On the other hand, in 2020, Uzbekistan delivered 4,000 and 8,000 tons of aid including medical supplies, medicines, and food to Tajikistan and Kyrgyzstan, respectively.[27] Green corridors established earlier between Uzbekistan and Russia and the Baltic states, Belarus, Kyrgyzstan, and Kazakhstan, facilitated the trade of perishable agricultural and food products with neighboring countries.[28]

10.5 Government spending for COVID-19 measures

The President of Uzbekistan established an Anti-Crisis Fund to operationalize the COVID-19 pandemic response measures, support entrepreneurship and employment, expand social support, and ensure sustainable operation of the economic sectors during the pandemic. The Anti-Crisis Fund was established by the Decree of the President of Uzbekistan No. UP-5969, dated March 19, 2020. The state budget included funds saved from cost optimization by state-owned enterprises.

According to the Uzbek Ministry of Finance (MoF, 2021), the actual public spending for the COVID-19 measures (from the Anti-Crisis Fund) in 2020 amounted to 12.8 trillion UZS (or 1.2 billion USD). Table 10.9 shows how the fund was used. The Anti-Crisis Fund was abolished on January 1, 2021, and the unused funds at the end of 2020 were transferred to the national budget. Since 2021, measures to combat the COVID-19 pandemic and the purchase of vaccines have been funded within the national budget framework.

Source of the Fund	Billion UZS	Proportion % of Fund
ADB	5,872	43.8
IMF	3,826	28.6
IBRD	2,024	15.1
State budget	1,678	12.5
Total	13,400	100

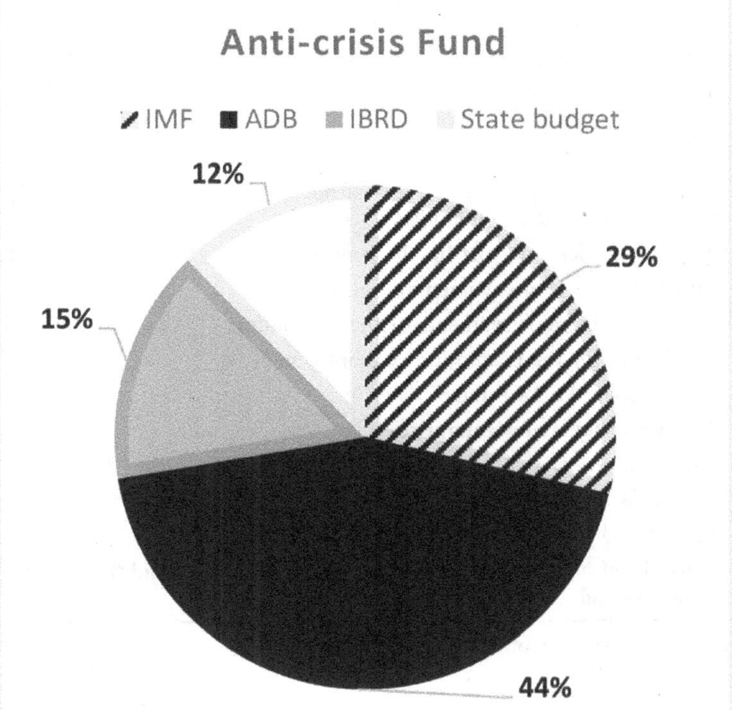

Figure 10.19 The structure of the Anti-Crisis Fund
Source: Uzbekistan Ministry of Finance, 2021.

Table 10.9 Expenditure of the Anti-Crisis Fund in 2020, Billion UZS.

No.	*Indicators*	*Billion UZS*
	Total expenses	**12,827**
1	**Funding for measures to combat COVID-19**	**4,985**
1.1	protective and testing equipment, medicines, and medical supplies, as well as to strengthen the logistic bases of medical institutions, maintenance, and treatment	1,534
1.2	incentives for medical workers and protective measures of the sanitary and epidemiological service	2,428
1.3	construction, equipping, and creation of infrastructure for quarantine zones and healthcare facilities for the treatment of COVID-19	1,022
2	**Construction, reconstruction, and overhaul of social facilities infrastructure**	**3,423**
2.1	Drinking water and sewerage	455
2.2	Irrigation	410
2.3	Development of public roads	1,004
2.4	Educational institutions and other social facilities	742
2.5	Physical culture and sports facilities	75
2.6	Infrastructure facilities of small industrial zones	236
2.7	Loans to the local budget of the city of Tashkent for the construction of three overpasses	168
2.8	Development of empty/marginal lands for agriculture	194
2.9	Funds for the Support Fund for Farmers, “dekhqan” Farms and Owners, household lands	82
3	**Expanding social support for the population**	**1,339**
3.1	Support low-income women and girls	100
3.2	Support vulnerable segments of the population	653
3.3	State fund for the promotion of employment	224
3.4	State Public Works Fund	300
4	**Financial support for enterprises**	**2,485**
4.1	Budget loans	1,464
4.2	Subsidies	921
4.3	State Fund for Entrepreneurial Development Support	100
5	**Cover local budget losses due to tax-related measures and the Pension Fund**	**595**

Source: Uzbekistan Ministry of Finance, 2021.

10.6 Beyond the pandemic: conclusion, policy implications, and prospects for sustainable development and growth by 2030

Uzbekistan aspires to be reclassified as an upper-middle-income country by 2030. To be an upper-middle-income country according to the World Bank classification, the GNI per capita should reach USD 4,256. Since the launch of the SDGs in 2016, Uzbekistan has made tangible progress toward achieving all goals. Nevertheless, our study reveals that the COVID-19 pandemic has backpedaled the trajectory and the positive efforts experienced some setbacks, with attention shifting to curbing the spread of the novel coronavirus.

The uncertainty generated by the COVID-19 crisis has significantly increased the already existing concerns about the potential of the 2030 Agenda to be an effective instrument of development worldwide. Given continuing uncertainties and the lingering impacts of the COVID-19 crisis globally, Uzbekistan needs to build the resiliency of the SDG-implementing sectors.

In December 2021, President Mirziyoyev declared the second stage of reforms in the country and adopted the "Strategy of New Uzbekistan for 2022–2026".[29] The long-term strategy is focused on the development of the economy along seven main directions,[30] which aim to bring the country to a dramatic leap from a lower- to upper-middle-income country by 2030 and the goal of building "New Uzbekistan". GDP per capita is expected to increase 1.6 times over the five years and is expected to reach 4,000 USD by 2030.[31] Also, the government recalibrated its commitment to the SDGs in 2022, taking account of the backpedal performance that the COVID-19 pandemic might have induced.[32] In connection with this, it would be helpful to carry out an ex-post impact assessment of the COVID-19 response interventions in the short and long run.

It is normal for Uzbekistan to prioritize rescue measures that focus on containing the pandemic during the COVID-19 crisis. Nevertheless, as a way forward, Uzbekistan's policies can be cautious to "do no harm" while recovering from the crisis. Meeting this includes:

i) ensuring that any scale-back or suspension of SDG activities that have resulted from the COVID-19 response measures are temporary; ii) being vigilant against any rollback of SDG standards and goals; and iii) using fiscal stimulus for fastening the SDGs achievement by 2030.

For Uzbekistan to achieve sustainable development and graduate to an upper middle-income country status beyond COVID-19 recovery, strategic actions which involve innovations, evaluations, and strong political will toward implementations must be taken by the relevant stakeholders. In the context of governance, the institutional nature of the SDG agenda would require further strengthening and more precise and binding rules for the cooperation of all entities to make the 2030 commitments more credible.

Notes

1 On the Action Strategy for the further Development of Uzbekistan for 2017–2021. 2017. "PD N4947: On the Action Strategy for the Further Development of Uzbekistan for 2017–2021". Accessed April 14, 2021. https://lex.uz/ru/docs/3107042#3109624
2 The national SDGs are available in the resolution of the Cabinet of Ministers No. 841. https://lex.uz/docs/4013358
3 Containment measures include school closures, restrictions in movement, closings of workplaces, canceling public events, limits on gatherings, the closing of public transport, confinement to the home, restrictions on internal movement between cities/regions and restrictions on international travel.
4 See the 5 SDG subgroups "5P" on: https://whatcanyoudo.earth/selecting-the-sdg-for-your-action/the-5-ps/
5 The GDP deflator, relative to 2019, used by the State Statistics Committee is 11.9%.
6 News of the devaluation on April 15, 2020. www.rferl.org/a/uzbek-central-bank-devalues-currency-for-second-time-in-three-days/30557460.html
7 News on the economic situation during 2020: Kun.uz, May 1, 2020. https://kun.uz/en/news/2020/05/01/central-bank-of-uzbekistan-assessed-impact-of-pandemic-on-economy
8 See Global Hunger Index ranking, 2020.
9 This food norm is what the SSC uses to calculate minimum income by basket of healthy food items for the population of Uzbekistan .
10 See https://unsdg.un.org/sites/default/files/2020-10/UZB_Socioeconomic-Response-Plan_2020.pdf; and http://pubdocs.worldbank.org/en/197351492011115514/mpo-uzb.pdf
11 See SSC report on SDG Goal 2. https://nsdg.stat.uz/en
12 Uzbekistan was reluctant to produce accurate death counts and had one of the highest COVID-19 death undercounts globally: see David Trilling, "Statistics show Central Asia underreporting COVID deaths: New calculations suggest Uzbekistan is the world leader in misleading COVID mortality statistics", *Eurasianet*, February 18, 2021. https://eurasianet.org/statistics-show-central-asia-underreporting-covid-deaths, and Gazeta.uz, January 18, 2021. www.gazeta.uz/ru/2021/01/18/deaths-stat/
13 According to the State Statistics Committee, around 20% of households in Uzbekistan are female-headed households.
14 Based on the national definition of "low income", from September 1, 2021, low income was if the average monthly total family income does not exceed 440,000 soums for each family member. From 2022, low income is if the average monthly total income for each family member does not exceed the amount of minimum consumer spending.
15 See https://info.worldbank.org/governance/wgi/Home/Documents for the methodology on how the governance indicator ranks and estimates are calculated. Higher values correspond to better outcomes.
16 Key COVID-19 related events by time can also be found in detail in: COVID-19 pandemic in Uzbekistan – Wikipedia.
17 Ministry of Education of Uzbekistan, 2020. www.uzedu.uz/oz/sarisob-online-maktab-lojiasining-1-boskici-muvaffakiatli-akunlandi and Gazeta.uz, June 5, 2020. Available at: www.gazeta.uz/oz/2020/06/05/online-maktab/
18 https://review.uz/uz/post/ayollar-daftariga-kiritilgan-xotin-qizlarga-33-mln-450-ming-UZS-miqdorda-kreditlar-ajratiladi (accessed February 17, 2021).
19 Presidential Decree No. 5978. Available at: https://lex.uz/docs/4780475
20 Presidential decree No. 5996. Available at: https://lex.uz/docs/4815474
21 Presidential Decree No. 5969. Available at: https://lex.uz/docs/4770761

22 Presidential Decree No. 5969. Available at: https://lex.uz/docs/4770761
23 Presidential Decree No. 5989. Available at: https://lex.uz/docs/4805518
24 Presidential Decree No. 4700. Available at: https://lex.uz/docs/4803523
25 Presidential Decree No. 5989. Available at: https://lex.uz/docs/4805518
26 Presidential Decree 4691. Available at: https://lex.uz/ru/docs/-4797083
27 Kun.uz, July 4, 2020. https://kun.uz/47607598
28 Azernews, January 10, 2018. www.azernews.az/region/125284.html
29 www.euronews.com/2021/12/20/uzbekistan-set-for-second-stage-of-reforms
30 https://invest.gov.uz/mediacenter/news/development-strategy-of-the-new-uzbekistan/
31 https://review.uz/en/post/strategiya-novy-uzbekistan-2022-2026-makroekonomicheskaya-stabilnost
32 On additional measures to accelerate the implementation of national goals and objectives in the field of sustainable development until 2030. https://lex.uz/docs/5870397

References

Asfaw, E., Li, M., Rudenko I., and Saydullaeva F. (2021). Urban Food Security and the COVID-19 Crisis: The Case of Uzbekistan Cities. In: *Food Security in Eurasia 2020: Case Studies by Eurasian Center for Food Security*. Available at: https://ecfs.msu.ru/images/ECFS_case_studies_2020_ENG.pdf.

Asian Development Bank (ADB) (2021). *Harnessing Uzbekistan's Potential of Urbanization: National Urban Assessment*. Asian Development Bank. Available at: www.adb.org/sites/default/files/institutional-document/735126/uzbekistan-national-urban-assessment.pdf.

International Food Policy Research Institute (IFPRI) (2021). Foreign Aid. *COVID-19 Policy Response (CPR) Portal*. Available at: www.ifpri.org/project/covid-19-policy-response-cpr-portal.

International Energy Agency (IEA) (2022). Uzbekistan 2022: Energy Policy Review. Available at: www.iea.org/reports/uzbekistan-2022/.

Kun.Uz (2020). Central Bank of Uzbekistan Assessed Impact of Pandemic on Economy. Available at: https://kun.uz/en/news/2020/05/01/central-bank-of-uzbekistan-assessed-impact-of-pandemic-on-economy.

Ministry of Finance of Uzbekistan Government (MoF) (2021). Citizens state budget: execution in 2020 (БЮДЖЕТ ДЛЯ ГРАЖДАН ГОСУДАРСТВЕННЫЙ БЮДЖЕТ: ИСПОЛНЕНИЕ В 2020 ГОДУ). Available at: www.mf.uz/media/file/state-budget/2020/budget2020/bfc2020_ru.pdf.

Musaev, D., Yakhshilikov, Y., and Yusupov, K. (2010). *Food Security in Uzbekistan*. UNDP, Tashkent, Uzbekistan.

Odey, G, A. Alawad, O. Atieno, E. Carew-Bayoh, E. Fatuma, I. Ogunkola, and D. Lucero-Prisno III (2021). COVID-19 Pandemic: Impacts on the Achievements of Sustainable Development Goals in Africa. *The Pan African Medical Journal*, 38.

Organization for Economic Cooperation and Development (OECD) (2021a). The OECD Green Recovery Database: Examining the Environmental Implications of COVID-19 Recovery Policies. Available at: www.oecd.org/coronavirus/policy-responses/the-oecd-green-recovery-database-47ae0f0d/.

OECD (2021b). Key findings from the Update of the OECD Green Recovery Database. Available at: www.oecd.org/coronavirus/policy-responses/key-findings-from-the-update-of-the-oecd-green-recovery-database-55b8abba/.

Resolution No. 251 (2015). Cabinet of Ministers (August 29, 2015). About approval of the Concept and the Package of Measures for Providing Healthy Food to the Population of the Republic of Uzbekistan in 2015–2020. Available at: https://cis-legislation.com/document. fwx?rgn=78612.

Rudenko, I., E. Asfaw, M. Li, and F. Saydullaeva (2020). *Food Consumption In Uzbekistan Cities During COVID-19 Lockdown,* Proceedings of TSUE International Online Conference' Sustainable Agricultural Development and Regional Cooperation for Inclusive Growth in Central Asia, October 20–22, 2020. Available at: http://iqtisodiyot.tsue.uz/sites/default/files/1.%20Food%20security%20amid%20COVID-19%20pandemic_removed.pdf.

Santos-Carrillo, F., L. Fernández-Portillo, and A. Sianes (2020). Rethinking the Governance of the 2030 Agenda for Sustainable Development in the COVID-19 Era. *Sustainability*, 12 (18), 7680.

Shodmonov, A. (2020). 51% of the Population of Uzbekistan is Overweight. Available at: https://kun.uz/uz/news/2020/03/20/alisher-shodmonov-ozbekiston-aholisining-51-foizi-ortiqcha-vaznga-ega.

Spoor, M. (2000). "White Gold" Versus "Food Self-Sufficiency" in Former Soviet Central Asia. In: A. van Tilburg, H. Moll, and A. Kuyvenhoven (eds.), *Agricultural Markets Beyond Liberalization*. Springer, Boston, MA. Available at: https://doi.org/10.1007/978-1-4615-4523-1_3.

State Statistics Committee of Uzbekistan (SSC) (2021). Gross Domestic Product (GDP) of Uzbekistan for 2020. Available at: https://stat.uz/images/uploads/docs/vvp_dek_2020_en.pdf.

SSC (2022). SDG Goal 3. Good Health and Well-Being. Available at: https://nsdg.stat.uz/en/goal/6.

United Nations Children Fund, (UNICEF) (2021). Maternal and Child Health. Available at: https://www.unicef.org/uzbekistan/en/maternal-and-child-health.

UNICEF (2020). Education Continuity in COVID-19 Pandemic Times: Impressions on Introducing Distance Learning in Basic Education in Uzbekistan. Available at: https://www.unicef.org/uzbekistan/media/3606/file/DL%20Rapid%20Assessment%20report%20Oct%206%202020%20eng.pdf.

United Nations (2020). Uzbekistan: Consolidated Multilateral COVID-19 Socio-Economic Response & Recovery Offer. Available at https://unsdg.un.org/sites/default/files/2020-10/UZB_Socioeconomic-Response-Plan_2020.

UN-VNR (2020). Implementation of National Sustainable Development Goals and Voluntary National Review of The Republic of Uzbekistan. Available at: https://sdgs.un.org/sites/default/files/documents/26423VNR_2020_Uzbekistan_Report_English.pdf.

World Bank (2020a). Uzbekistan Macro Poverty Outlook. Available at: https://www.worldbank.org/en/publication/macro-poverty-outlook#sec1.

World Bank (2020b) Economic and Social Impacts of COVID-19. Listening to Citizens of Uzbekistan (L2CU) survey. Available at: http://pubdocs.worldbank.org/en/834051595427687698/L2CU-COVID19-impacts-June2020-en.pdf.

World Bank (2020c). As Winter Approaches, Female-Headed Households in Uzbekistan often Struggle to Pay for Utilities and Basic Needs. Available at: https://www.worldbank.org/en/news/infographic/2020/12/23/energy-vulnerability-of-female-headed-households-in-uzbekistan.

Sources for databases used in tables and figures

FAOSTAT, 2022. Food Insecurity. www.fao.org/faostat/en/#data/FS.

FAOSTAT, 2022. GDP PPP (2017). https://www.fao.org/faostat/en/#data/FS.

International Food Policy Research Institute (IFPRI). 2021. www.ifpri.org/project/covid-19-policy-response-cpr-portal.

Lex.Uz, 2022. https://lex.uz/docs/.

Ministry of Finance.Uz, 2021. www.mf.uz/.

Ministry of Finance.Uz, 2021. www.mf.uz/.

OECD. Stat, 2022. https://stats.oecd.org/Index.aspx?DataSetCode=GREEN_GROWTH.

Stat.Uz, 2022. Agriculture Production. https://stat.uz/en/official-statistics/agriculture.

Stat.Uz, 2022. Demography & Social Protection. https://stat.uz/en/official-statistics/demography; https://stat.uz/en/official-statistics/social-protection.

Stat.Uz, 2022. Education Outcomes. https://stat.uz/en/official-statistics/social-protection.

Stat.Uz, 2022. Internet Access. https://stat.uz/images/uploads/docs/104__Number_of_subscribers_with_Internet__en.pdf.

Stat.uz. 2022. Social Protection. https://gender.stat.uz/en/additional-indicators/social-protection.

Stat.Uz, 2022. Income Distribution. https://stat.uz/en/official-statistics/living-standards.

Stat.Uz. 2022. Social Protection. http://stat.uz/en/official-statistics/social-protection.

Stat.uz, 2022. Labor Market. https://stat.uz/en/official-statistics/labor-market.

Stat.Uz2022. Industry-Energy. https://stat.uz/en/official-statistics/industry.

Stat.Uz2022. Environment. https://stat.uz/en/official-statistics/environment.

Stat.Uz, 2022. Clean Energy in SDG. ЦУР (stat.uz).

Stat.uz2022. Water in SDG. Water Stress ЦУР (stat.uz).

World Bank, WDI2022. Gross Domestic Product, GDP Growth Rate and Inflation. https://data.worldbank.org/indicator/NY.GDP.DEFL.KD.ZG?locations=UZ; https://data.worldbank.org/indicator/NY.GDP.MKTP.KD.ZG?locations=UZ.

World Bank, WDI2022. Employment to Population Ratio, 15+, Female (%) (Modeled ILO Estimate) – Uzbekistan | Data (worldbank.org).

World Bank, WDI, 2022. GDP Per Capita. https://data.worldbank.org/indicator/NY.GDP.PCAP.CD?locations=UZ; https://data.worldbank.org/indicator/NY.GDP.MKTP.KD.ZG?locations=UZ.

World Bank, WDI, 2022. Urban Development. https://data.worldbank.org/topic/urban-development?locations=UZ.

World Bank, WGI, 2020. Governance Indicators. https://databank.worldbank.org/reports.aspx?Report_Name=WGI-Table&Id=ceea4d8b.

World Bank, WDI, 2022. Foreign Direct Investment (FDI). https://data.worldbank.org/indicator/BX.KLT.DINV.WD.GD.ZS?locations=UZ.

Index

Note: *Italic* and **Bold** page numbers refer to *figures* and **tables**. Page numbers followed by 'n' denote endnotes.